UPON THE ALTAR
OF WORK

THE WORKING CLASS IN AMERICAN HISTORY

Editorial Advisors
James R. Barrett, Julie Greene, William P. Jones,
Alice Kessler-Harris, and Nelson Lichtenstein

A list of books in the series appears at the end of this book.

UPON THE ALTAR OF WORK

CHILD LABOR AND THE RISE OF A NEW AMERICAN SECTIONALISM

BETSY WOOD

UNIVERSITY OF ILLINOIS PRESS
Urbana, Chicago, and Springfield

© 2020 by the Board of Trustees
of the University of Illinois
All rights reserved
1 2 3 4 5 C P 5 4 3 2 1
⊗ This book is printed on acid-free paper.

Library of Congress Cataloging-in-Publication Data
Names: Wood, Betsy, author.
Title: Upon the altar of work : child labor and the rise of a new
    American sectionalism / Betsy Wood.
Description: Urbana : University of Illinois Press, [2020] |
    Series: The working class in American history | Includes
    bibliographical references and index.
Identifiers: LCCN 2020006470 (print) | LCCN 2020006471
    (ebook) | ISBN 9780252043444 (cloth ; alk. paper) |
    ISBN 9780252085345 (paperback ; alk. paper) | ISBN
    9780252052323 (ebook)
Subjects: LCSH: Child labor—Political aspects—United States—
    History. | Sectionalism (United States)—History.
Classification: LCC HD6250.U3 W66 2020 (print) | LCC HD6250.
    U3 (ebook) | DDC 331.3/10973—dc23
LC record available at https://lccn.loc.gov/2020006470
LC ebook record available at https://lccn.loc.gov/2020006471

For Andrew and Julian

Contents

Acknowledgments   ix

Introduction   1

1   Fields of Free Labor: Child Rescue and Sectional Crisis   7

2   Testing Ground of Freedom: Child Labor in the Age
of Emancipation   25

3   Seeds of a New Sectionalism: Southern Origins
of Child Labor Reform   51

4   Child Labor Abolitionists: A Northern Progressive Vision   85

5   Cultural Warriors: A Southern Capitalist Vision   113

Conclusion   149

Notes   153

Bibliography   213

Index   235

Acknowledgments

For their wisdom, insights, and support over the years, I am deeply grateful to my teachers at the University of Chicago. Thomas C. Holt took me under his wing and gently guided me as a budding historian and a young person finding her way in the world. As he taught me how to view the past through the eyes of those who lived it, he imparted an approach to history that shaped my understanding of the world. For the knowledge I gained through study with him, I am grateful. For the wisdom he imparted, which continues to guide me, I am equally grateful.

I count myself blessed to have worked with other University of Chicago historians whose guidance proved no less crucial. Julie Saville knew that holding me to high standards was key to unlocking the very best within me. Her bold, incisive questions pushed this book into the best iteration of itself. Catherine Brekus had a rare ability to transform the faint outlines of my thoughts into a lucid vision that would prompt a spring in my step as I rushed back to the library with renewed faith. Tara Zahra has set such a high bar as a historian that I am unable to keep track of her awards and accomplishments, yet she somehow always found time to provide me with meticulous feedback. The exceptionally gifted Amy Dru Stanley and her lifelong pursuit of the history of moral problems within capitalist society have so deeply marked my work that every page bears her influence. I am grateful to her for inspiring my pursuit of these questions and deeply thankful that our paths again crossed in Washington, DC, several years ago.

For offering me feedback, encouragement, or simply gainful employment as a historian over the years, I am grateful to Antonio Acevedo, John Cavanaugh, David L. Chappell, Jefferson Cowie, Ileen DeVault, Jan Golinski,

Matthew Hild, Louis Hyman, Monica Mercado, Keri Leigh Merritt, Aaron Shkuda, and Marilyn Sneiderman. A heartfelt thanks to my local independent bookshop, WORD Bookstores, for being a refuge for readers, artists, and authors in Jersey City. I am forever grateful to my WORD friends for inspiring me to complete this book. For sharpening and honing this project into a book, I am grateful to the editors and anonymous scholars at the University of Illinois Press, especially my editor, James Engelhardt, who expertly shepherded me throughout the entire publishing process. For the opportunity to teach American history within a vibrant and dynamic community, I am grateful to my colleagues in Jersey City, especially Antonio Acevedo and the entire faculty in the Social Sciences Division at Hudson County Community College. A special thanks to my students at HCCC, who inspire me every single day.

I am deeply grateful to the librarians and archivists who graciously assisted me throughout this project at the Library of Congress, the New York Public Library, the Regenstein Library at the University of Chicago, the University of Chicago Special Collections, the Gabert Library at HCCC, the Center for Research Libraries, the Kheel Center for Labor-Management Documentation and Archives at Cornell University, the Brian Sutton-Smith Library and Archives at the National Museum of Play, and the Southern Historical Collection at the University of North Carolina–Chapel Hill. A special thank-you to my old neighbor Bronwen Bledsoe for letting me stay with her when I was doing research at Cornell. For generous financial support throughout my studies, I thank the University of Chicago for awarding me a five-year Century Fellowship to pursue my Ph.D. in History, the University of Chicago Department of History and Social Sciences Division for awarding me multiple research and travel grants, and the Andrew W. Mellon Foundation for funding my final year of dissertation writing.

This book would not exist without the support and nurture of family, especially my devoted and loving parents, Danny and Becky Wood. Their deep commitment to my development at a young age and strong faith that I was born to do great things led them to selflessly support me throughout this journey even though they knew it might take me far away. They have read my work, engaged my questions, and shaped my moral convictions for as long as I can remember. For their love and sacrifices and, most of all, the example they have set as remarkable human beings, I thank them. I have been blessed with a host of other supportive family members, including my two intrepid brothers, Matt and Tim, who have cared for and loved me their entire lives; my saintly Uncle Mike who has supported me for as long as I can remember; my history-loving Aunt Ginger and her wonderful

Acknowledgments

family, especially my cousin Camille, who has believed in this endeavor for many years; my cousin Libby, who has endlessly listened to and nurtured my dreams; and many other aunts, uncles, and cousins who are too plentiful to name. For their ceaseless support of me, I am grateful to my parents-in-law, Don and Jacqueline Erwin; Suzanne Alford-Hodges; Micah and Michelle Erwin; and Susanna and Rick Aich. For their hard work and sacrifice, I am forever indebted to my grandparents Carlos and Eula Wood and my grandpa Mike Spades, who cultivated my love of learning when I was a little girl and planted the seeds that became this book.

Since meeting Andrew Erwin more than twenty years ago, I knew the greatest blessing of my life would be our love for each other. For reading every word of everything I've written, driving with me to archives, picking up extra household tasks, and reminding me to drink water, I am deeply grateful. Through our wild journey of graduate school, cross-country moves, and finally settling in the New York City area, no one has kept me more grounded or loved me more. For helping me think through the nuances of every single argument of this book, caring about my well-being, and nurturing my dreams as if they were his own, I thank him. For our son, Julian, who has filled my life with a renewed sense of joy and wonder, I am equally grateful. Since you were born, I have measured time by your birthday, your height on the wall, and your growing sense of self. My love for you is deep and wide and knows no end. This book, which will remain as time passes by, is my gift to you.

UPON THE ALTAR
OF WORK

Introduction

A deep and abiding antagonism between the North and South shaped fundamental values on both sides of the Mason-Dixon Line. Reaching a fever pitch in the 1850s, the sectional crisis evinced a nation torn apart by slavery. At stake in this epic battle were questions about labor, morality, political economy, family, and religion. The sectionalism that resulted from the slavery conflict was woven into the fabric of thought and morality in both societies, rearing its head in every corner. Southerners defending slavery in the 1850s, for instance, pointed to the rise of industrial child labor in the North as evidence of the inferiority of a free capitalist society. Southern slavery, they claimed, was a bulwark against the tide of free market capitalism that subjected everyone, including children, to its whims. In their view, Northern capitalism had broken down ties of benevolence and affection that Southern slave society had supposedly left intact. Northern antislavery reformers, on the other hand, condemned enslaved children's labor in the South as devoid of the moral values inherent in free labor. Free labor was a kind of salvation for impoverished Northern children that was denied to all Southern children because their society denigrated labor. Northern reformers believed that poor children in the North could rise out of the economic class into which they were born through free labor, eventually learning the superior values of free society. For decades after slavery's downfall, debates about children and their labor bore the traces of this sectionalist conflict.

This book examines the evolution of ideas about child labor and the on-the-ground politics of the issue from the 1850s through the 1930s. During this period, the ideological and political struggle over child labor shaped how Northerners and Southerners renegotiated and acted on fundamental concepts of American life such as work, freedom, the market, and the state. Reformers, who eventually came to see child labor as the worst evil of the nation since slavery, mobilized politically in a national movement to abolish child labor with the power of the progressive state, liberating children to develop their potential in a burgeoning consumer market society. To defeat this movement, the opponents of reform also mobilized politically, asserting an opposing vision of American freedom that drew on traditional understandings of familial authority and the moral value of free labor. Tracing the ideological origins and the politics of the battle over child labor over the course of eighty years, this book tells the story of how child labor debates bequeathed an enduring legacy of sectionalist conflict to post-emancipation American society.

At least fifty years' worth of scholarship has tried to explain the consequences of slavery in American society not only for emancipated persons and their descendants but also for modern American capitalism, morality, ideology, and politics.[1] Historians of slave emancipation have long argued that the meaning of freedom in capitalist societies has never been self-evident but instead was continually struggled over and debated.[2] My goal in writing this book was to extend our scholarly perspective on the historical reach of the moral and social questions broached by antislavery and slave emancipation into the twentieth century. I was seeking to understand how some of the particularities of modern American capitalist society developed out of nineteenth-century ideological and political disputes over slavery and freedom. In doing so, I have endeavored to use the lens of the battle over child labor to draw new connections between nineteenth- and twentieth-century moral and social reform.

Although the history of child labor in America can be traced back to colonial child apprenticeship, the Poor Law of England, and the Puritan ethic of virtuous work, my book begins in the 1850s in order to show how the pivotal battles over child labor in the early twentieth century had roots in the sectional crisis over slavery.[3] In writing this book, I was less interested in the factors that led to child labor's ultimate decline in the modern era and more interested in what debates about child labor over time would reveal about the legacy of sectionalist conflict within an emerging capitalist society. To date, most studies of child labor reform have not been connected to historiography on slavery and freedom or post-emancipation societies.[4] Foundational studies have probed the reasons for child labor's decline, arguing that both mechanization of labor and the sentimentalization of childhood—made possible by falling birth rates—can explain the removal of children from the labor market.[5] I contribute to this literature by situating child labor reform

Introduction   3

in a new historiographical context and reinterpreting its significance for understanding modern American capitalist society.

In the broader landscape of Progressive reform, child labor reform was distinct in both its impact and legacy. No other reform effort displayed the same level of sectional hostility that so deeply marked the child labor battle. Of three major Progressive amendments to the Constitution that reflected iconic reform struggles—Prohibition, women's suffrage, and child labor—the Child Labor Amendment is the only one that was soundly defeated despite having the backing of the entire political establishment. Explaining how and why this happened is one of the goals of this book. As historian William A. Link has said, "The child labor crusade yielded the most meager results among all the southern social reform crusades."[6] Unlike other Progressive reforms, such as Prohibition, women's suffrage, public hygiene, and sanitation, child labor reform never achieved a truly intersectional character.[7] Targeting Southern textile mills as the worst perpetrators, child labor reformers adopted a strategy of shaming the South for harboring the nation's new slavery. Not only did Southern manufacturers mobilize against child labor reform, but rural farm families in the South also rejected the reformers' agenda and formed a collective resistance of their own, wielding opposing cultural values as a weapon against reformers.[8] While Link noted the sectional tensions of child labor reform to distinguish it among other Progressive reform efforts in the South, my book examines a deeper and longer history of sectional tensions in child labor debates over time and what these debates reveal about the legacy of sectionalism within modern American capitalist society.

Gender and race played crucial roles in debates about child labor. The North, governed by the idea of free labor, applied the notion specifically to males and the families they constructed. Men, who were expected to make their way in the world, required appropriate training as youth. Free labor principles in the North became a cornerstone of male identity and development that incorporated females only insofar as these principles helped train them to become good wives and mothers, not to achieve independence on their own. In the South, where white leaders believed that African Americans, male and female, should continue to serve as wage laborers, the idea that boys or girls should be exempt from labor was anathema. Instead, child labor in the South was initially defined as wrong because of the textile industry's overreliance upon poor white children, which reformers deemed a crisis of white racial deterioration.[9] As reformers sought the protection of women and children as a central aim of the modern bureaucratic state in the Progressive Era, the gender and racial dimensions of the child labor issue shifted in a new market context. Farm families in the rural South defended the use of their children's labor, especially sons, against reformers' criticism by resurrecting free labor principles that emphasized the values boys learned from farm labor. Meanwhile, Northern reformers focused on freeing both boys and girls to fulfill their potential in a consumer-oriented culture that valorized self-fulfillment and the gender-specific skills to be gained through play and leisure. As both regions adapted to an emerging modern capitalist society, the child labor battle became the fulcrum of an effort to preserve differing value systems based in competing understandings of labor, freedom, morality, and the market.[10]

The chapters that follow are chronological and trace both the ideological debates and political struggles over child labor in the North and South from the antebellum period through the era of the New Deal. The first chapter establishes the centrality of free labor ideology to Northern reform activity regarding children and their labor before the Civil War. It reveals that moral opposition to Southern slave society and its disrespect for free labor principles formed the ideological framework within which Northern reformers sought to "rescue" impoverished children in the 1850s. Debates about child labor in this period were not only shaped by the sectional crisis, but they also helped Northerners and Southerners articulate distinctions between free and slave society.

In the aftermath of slave emancipation, disputes over children and their labor hinged on determining the boundary between free and unfree labor. Juxtaposing post–Civil War battles over formerly enslaved children in the South with simultaneous battles occurring over child laborers in the North, the second chapter reveals that free labor principles were the primary means of resolving such disputes. As the market expanded nationally, postwar debates about children and their labor helped to clarify the distinction between free and unfree labor while simultaneously reinforcing free labor principles in both the North and South.

As industrialization swept over both regions in the late nineteenth century, free labor ideology broke down as the measure for when and how children ought to labor. The third chapter reveals that in the late nineteenth century, when the region's textile mill industry increasingly employed poor white children, the child labor issue was remade into a symbol of the breakdown of the prevailing racial order in the South. Reformers in both regions redefined the child labor issue as a crisis of white racial deterioration, launching the issue onto a national stage. Dubbing child labor in Southern mills the nation's "new white slavery," Northern reformers justified expanded federal authority in the market on the basis of saving the South's white children—girls as well as boys. Southern reformers rejected such expanded federal authority, calling instead for local control of the issue. A split in the movement left in its wake a growing opposition to national child labor reform in the South.

With the purging of Southern regionalists from its ranks, the national movement to abolish child labor entered its peak political and cultural phase in the first two decades of the twentieth century. The fourth chapter reveals that the movement's embrace of federal authority became increasingly religious in nature as it joined forces with the Social Gospel movement of the same era. Pointedly, this turn paid particular attention to girls, whose paid work was thought to threaten their future roles as wives and mothers. As debates about child labor heated up with religious fervor on both sides, cultural animosity between North and South intensified. A more unified Southern opposition emerged as Northern reformers shamed Southern industrialists as sinful and defined federal intervention as a Christian duty. This chapter argues that the spiritual underpinnings of the movement diminished during World War I as reformers' faith in the modern bureaucratic state grew, setting the stage for the rise of a consumerist ethos and a secular Northern bureaucratic vision of child welfare.

The fifth chapter reveals why the battle over a proposed child labor amendment to the US Constitution in the 1920s came to embody the new sectionalism of the modern industrial age. This battle shaped opposing visions of labor, freedom, morality, and the market within an emerging capitalist society. The campaign for expanded federal authority over child labor through an amendment enabled Southern manufacturers to spur a collective grassroots protest against modern secular bureaucracy. Defining the amendment as a spiritual threat to an agrarian way of life, opponents resurrected free labor principles—especially for boys—and traditional moral values as weapons against the encroachment of the modern bureaucratic state.

Although Southern manufacturers' endgame was market deregulation, the battle to defeat the amendment was a spiritual one for the grassroots warriors who fought it. Ironically, as the North became the heart of a new market orientation toward consumerist values of personal growth and self-fulfillment guaranteed by a modern progressive state, free labor ideology was reborn in the rural South as a weapon against the encroachment of such values. When Southern manufacturers learned how to arm the cultural warriors, the amendment was defeated by an emboldened opposition. From a weakened position, Northern reformers secured the federal child labor provisions of the Fair Labor Standards Act in 1938, but these provisions were limited and reflected the legacy of a new imaginary Mason-Dixon Line within capitalist society.

Upon the Altar of Work argues that debates about children and their labor brought to the fore opposing visions of labor, freedom, morality, and the market in the modern industrial age. On the one hand, reformers conjured up images of children upon altars, sacrificed to the gods of capitalism. The "altar of work" was a symbol of capitalism's excesses, as child laborers were sacrificed in the name of profit. On the other hand, opponents of reform conjured up images of children, especially boys, engaged in healthy farm labor as a sacred ideal that was being eclipsed by secular, market-oriented society. For them, the "altar of work" was a shrine to the spiritual value of labor in an agrarian way of life that was under threat by emerging consumerist values. In the midst of the struggle over child labor, both sides were attempting to negotiate, materially and spiritually, the changes wrought by capitalism.

1 Fields of Free Labor

Child Rescue and Sectional Crisis

Let him that stole steal no more:
but rather let him labour,
working with his hands
the thing which is good.
—Ephesians 4:28

On the eve of the American Civil War, a white, orphaned fourteen-year-old boy named John showed up at the Children's Aid Society in New York City. Years earlier, John had been picked up by police officers and taken to the House of Refuge, an institution for poor children that "bound out" John and another white, orphaned boy named Henry to a slaveholder in Delaware in an effort to reform them.[1] When the staff of the Children's Aid Society (CAS) greeted John, he told them about his experiences on the Delaware plantation. John and Henry had tried to be "honest" and "to work as well as we could," but it was challenging since they were "not treated right." The CAS staffer who recorded the story wrote that the boys "never had a chance . . . to improve"—though the slaveholder pretended the boys were doing well when a superintendent from the House of Refuge visited to inquire about them. When John decided he would rather quit than be "bound to such a man," Henry was afraid that John would "be killed by the savage man, our master." The two boys, along with "one of the colored boys" from the plantation named Robert Wilson, "who had been nearly killed with lickings," decided to run away together.

The Delaware slaveholder found the boys and beat them as punishment for running away. "Five times after this I ran away, and four times I was catched [*sic*] and brought back," John said. After he had been on the plantation for four years, John made up his mind "to run off again, to escape another flaying."

Running and hopping trains, he arrived in Philadelphia where he landed a job as a mess boy on a steamship. After "doing the slush work for some time," John was promoted to storekeeper. He came to the Children's Aid Society because his job was ending and he needed a place to stay. The staff decided to send John with a company leaving two days later for the West. As part of the CAS's 1850s plan to populate newly acquired territories in the West with "vagrant" boys from the North, John would be placed with a farm family where he was supposed to learn the values of hard work and upward mobility that made Northern free society superior to Southern slavery. As John boarded the train headed for the West, a CAS staffer wrote that he "was the merriest of the party—all smiles and good humor. . . . We anticipate good news from him soon."[2]

In the 1850s, at the height of sectional tension over slavery in the South and its spread into territories in the West, debates about how to "rescue" poor children in the capitalist North shaped the way antebellum Americans articulated distinctions between free and slave society. Through the "rescue" of poor urban children in the North—especially boys, who were expected to become independent laborers and heads of household within free society—child reformers praised the virtues of Northern free society while condemning the evils of Southern slavery. When the Children's Aid Society designed a plan to send poor, orphaned Northern boys like John to work on farms in the West, they were joining a national debate about the fate of the West as either slave or free. Unlike juvenile asylums and other penal institutions that aided poor children, the Children's Aid Society developed an approach to child rescue in response to the sectional conflict over slavery.[3] As antislavery sentiment gathered steam in the northern United States, free labor ideals were popularized by antislavery Republicans, who mounted a defense of Northern free society, arguing that it was superior to Southern slavery.[4] These free labor ideals shaped the work of the Children's Aid Society. In turn, the CAS shaped free labor ideals by applying them to Northern child rescue and promoting their tangible effects upon poor Northern children.

Children's Aid Society reformers thought they could end Northern child poverty by sending poor orphaned boys to farms in the West where they would become free laborers. The prospect of settling the West with boys who had been "rescued" from what reformers called a "life of vagrancy" in the city became one of the CAS's primary goals in the 1850s. In their view, this plan would not only help to rid the city of a labor surplus while supplying Western farms with laborers, but it would also demonstrate the superiority of Northern free society. The expectation was that through free labor, boys like John could learn values of free society such as discipline, honesty, and

Fields of Free Labor　　9

frugality that were thought to produce socially mobile, independent male citizens. This expectation was in contrast to enslaved labor, which was supposed to produce fixed hierarchies rather than social mobility and was believed to promote idleness, dishonesty, and wastefulness. On the Delaware plantation, according to the CAS's retelling, John was subjected to a system of enslaved labor in which he did not benefit or learn from his labor. In a nation on the verge of civil war, child rescue in the North helped to shape the meaning of free labor as chattel slavery's opposite. Through debates about poor Northern children, the CAS inveighed against the evils of chattel slavery while lauding the virtues of free society. In comparison to adults, children's malleability made them a powerful tool for sharpening and testing free labor ideals in a nation torn apart by the slavery dispute.

Shaping the work of the Children's Aid Society was a commitment to a producer ethic grounded in free labor Republicanism. This ethic valorized the independence of property-owning male producers as the objective of dignified labor. According to this ethic, both permanent wage status and permanent pauperism signaled dependency, which was thought to be the antithesis of free labor.[5] For adherents of this worldview, labor was a moral activity at its core, instilling values such as discipline and frugality that would produce independent male citizens able to advance the overall populace. The belief that labor was the basis of virtuous citizenship underlay the principle of male social mobility. If the objective of dignified labor was to escape wage dependency and obtain independence through accumulating property, then there could be no permanent classes in free society. Slavery, in this view, was a violation of the producer ethic.[6] "Enslave a man," said free labor Republican Horace Greeley, "and you destroy his ambition, his enterprise, his capacity." "In the constitution of human nature," he explained, "the desire of bettering one's condition is the mainspring of effort."[7] Free labor Republican Cassius Clay wrote that for Southerners, "labor is not connected" with their "ideas of freedom."[8]

In the 1850s the Southern way of life emerged as a violation of free labor's most cherished principles. Not only was labor unfree in the South, the argument went, but it was also disparaged as the fate of enslaved persons. For free labor Republicans, contempt for labor had produced Southern values of indolence and disorder, leading to the region's stagnation.[9] In Southern slave society, both social mobility and virtuous citizenship were inaccessible to the vast majority of laborers. As free labor proponents increasingly condemned the evils of chattel slavery, proslavery Southerners mounted an articulate defense of slave society.[10] As Virginian George Fitzhugh wrote in 1857, free laborers were "already slaves without masters."[11] Free society had turned men, women, and children into "isolated, selfish, and antagonistic positions—in which each man was compelled to wrong others, in order to be just to himself." Unlike free society, slave society did not exalt the sovereignty of the individual but rather "parental, fraternal, and associative relations" in recognition that "man's nature is social, not selfish."[12] Proslavery Southerners argued that all laborers were worse off in free society because the market would ensure no benevolence or affection from employers, unlike masters, who purportedly had a social responsibility toward their slaves, women, and children. This increasingly polarized clash of ideas led to sharp sectional antagonism, paving the way toward civil war.[13]

The Children's Aid Society's approach to "rescuing" poor Northern children turned on deeply held views about the purpose of labor. "Honest work," the CAS argued, had the ability to teach Northern urban boys how to be independent and free. In its *First Annual Report*, the Children's Aid Society discussed in some detail the unhealthy relationship to labor that poor Northern children had developed. The CAS sought to engineer social mobility in the lives of boys for whom mobility was difficult, since their circumstances prevented them from learning industrious values or benefiting from their labor. In this inaugural report laying the groundwork for their agenda, the organization articulated a pro–free labor program emphasizing Northern urban boys' proper relationship to healthy and honest labor. This free labor ideology relied on the presence of slavery in the South for coherence and was intended to strengthen the moral legitimacy of industrial capitalism and superiority of Northern free society.

The founder of the Children's Aid Society, Charles Loring Brace, explained his purpose in its founding in 1853: "This Association—The Children's Aid Society—has sprung from the increasing sense among our citizens of the evils of the city." Brace's understanding of the "evils of the city" is instructive. For him, a thriving capitalist city did not inevitably lead to social problems. Under the "natural" conditions of a healthy city, equality and enterprise would be the rule rather than exception. Poverty would, on its own, "float off through the thousand channels of livelihood over the whole country." However, the early 1850s witnessed a new challenge: an unprecedented influx of immigrants, mostly from Germany and Ireland, arriving in New York at the rate of "one thousand a day, for every week day." If this wave of immigration had "spread over our land, to be influenced by the *new circumstances*, the effect would not have been so bad."[14] Immigrant families, he wrote, could have found "honest labor"—perhaps out west—and the opportunity for self-improvement would have advanced free labor principles. Brace's diagnosis was that urban overcrowding had disrupted the natural conditions of free labor, producing a surplus of labor in an overcrowded market.[15] A mass of potential laborers without work was "settled and stagnated in the city."[16] This surplus of people without opportunity for free labor, and the values supposedly learned from it, left in its wake a concentration of poverty and vice.[17] But the surplus did not constitute a permanent proletariat or a genetically diseased "dangerous class"—a term Brace himself would famously coin years later. For the Children's Aid Society of the 1850s, the antidote to poverty was to change circumstances by providing ample opportunity for free labor. The CAS's mission was to be an instrument for ensuring new conditions, especially for poor boys in the North. Thought to be more malleable than adults, children were the gateway for preventing a lower class from becoming a permanent feature of Northern free society.[18]

The CAS's work was shaped by assumptions about the causes of pauperization. Because poor Northern boys in the city did not engage in honest labor, the argument went, they were subject to a life of dependency. Without free labor, poor Northern boys would never learn the values of a free society that were meant to prepare them for a life of independence. The organization compared the boys' dependency to slavery, reinforcing distinctions between free and slave society. Earlier approaches to child rescue were inadequate, the CAS argued, because they did not target the scourge of dependency. The CAS's frequent diatribes against asylums, poorhouses, and almsgiving—early nineteenth-century institutions and methods of giving aid to the poor—reveal that reformers' apprehension about dependency shaped how they approached child rescue.[19] Asylums, Brace wrote, "breed a species of character which is monastic, indolent, unused to struggle; subordinate . . . with little independence and manly vigor."[20] When the CAS launched its first boys' lodging houses in the 1850s,[21] it emphasized their distinctiveness from asylums and poorhouses: "The first thing to be aimed at in the plan was to treat the lads as *independent little dealers*, and give them nothing without payment."[22] The lodging house did not "merely confer alms"; it "buil[t] up character" and "render[ed] its subjects superior to the aid it gives." Most importantly, the lodging house was meant to prevent "the growth of a future dependent class."[23] Almsgiving could never accomplish the same because it was not accompanied by "influences to lead the recipients to take care of themselves." The "worst evil in the world," Brace wrote, was not poverty or hunger but "the want of manhood or character which alms-giving directly occasions." The Children's Aid Society, on the other hand, was "only to give assistance where it bears directly on character, to discourage pauperism, to cherish independence."[24]

When Brace and other CAS reformers spoke of the dangers of "dependency," they did not mean that young boys should be without parents, without care, or without support. Instead, they associated dependency with a set of values that threatened Northern free society. Dependency was encouraged not only by almsgiving and asylums but also by the unaided poor life in which poor children turned to "dishonest" means of labor and did not have an opportunity for social mobility. Like slavery in the South, this static condition supposedly encouraged menacing values such as ignorance and debauchery. If the growth of these values went unchecked among a class of people for too long, Northern free society would be threatened. Like free labor Republicans, the Children's Aid Society embraced as its patriotic duty upholding Northern free society and the values it rested upon. Their sense of this duty was enhanced by the political and ideological climate of the 1850s, which associated dependency in its most appalling form with the Southern system of slavery. By eliminating the scourge of dependency and building up the foundations of independence in the North, the CAS believed it was not only helping to "rescue" children from poverty but was also preserving Northern free society. As Brace explained in the *Second Annual Report*, "We owe a solemn duty to our country that the children of the miserable population . . . do not form a class of degraded and ignorant men and women, who shall hereafter *endanger her liberties.*"[25]

Brace had many antislavery influences that shaped his approach to the Children's Aid Society.[26] He had been raised at the center of the revivalist fervor and reform activity in the new nation.[27] While in seminary, Brace was exposed to the free labor Republican wing of the antislavery movement.[28] Free labor Republicans such as Horace Greeley and Cassius Clay delivered antislavery speeches at the Union Theological Seminary in New York City during Brace's tenure. Years later, Brace would recall the impact these speeches had on him.[29] Horace Bushnell, who openly espoused free labor ideals, was a mentor figure to Brace.[30] Frederick Law Olmsted, who befriended Brace after they met at Yale, was an influential voice shaping Northern views about "the Slave Power" conspiracy, which held that Southern slaveholders planned to expand slavery into newly acquired territories in the West, thereby controlling the nation.[31] And Brace's wife, Letitia Neill, was from an abolitionist family that regularly hosted famous abolitionists, including Frederick Douglass and William Lloyd Garrison.[32]

When Brace decided to focus his reform efforts on children, it was in part because of newly popularized understandings of the "child,"[33] which suggested children were malleable and more capable of changing than adults.[34] Brace's experiences working with impoverished adults in New York had reinforced this view. The first of Brace's child rescue efforts was organizing "Boys' meetings" every Sunday evening for the "roughest class of loafers" in the city. Through these meetings, Brace concluded that a "thorough reformation of character" could be brought about for these boys by "changed conditions." This experience led to Brace's founding of the Children's Aid Society, which was intended to be a "more comprehensive effort" than had yet been attempted to rescue poor Northern boys.[35]

Apprehension about dependency also shaped the Children's Aid Society's approach to its lodging houses. By requiring payment from the boys who lodged, the CAS aimed to ensure the boys would not become "charity pensioners." For lodging, the CAS required six cents for a bed and three cents for supper. With few exceptions, the lodging houses would "not take them in unless they can pay," since "the best thing for these boys is to teach them to take care of themselves." Of the lodging houses' total expenses, which equaled $2,133 in one year, the boys paid about $1,000.[36] Other than taking care of their own livelihood, spending among the boys was discouraged. Because these boys lived "from hand to mouth," reformers concluded that the boys spent their money carelessly, leaving them "little capital to do business with." C. C. Tracy, head of a lodging house for newsboys, developed a "Savings Bank" plan for his lodgers. Each lodger received a money box where his earnings could be deposited. This was called the "Bank," and it would be closed for at least two months. The Bank would then be opened and the boys would be "astonished with the amount of deposits accumulated." Tracy taught the boys to save for a future business investment or to spend the money on necessities, such as warm clothing for the winter.[37] The CAS endorsed the plan as encouraging values of self-reliance, self-control, and patience. Brace reported that the Savings Bank plan was working. Lodgers, he wrote, had "saved to such a degree, that within the last sixteen months, an average of sixteen boys per month have saved . . . *six hundred and forty-five dollars and fifty-two cents!*"[38] For the Children's Aid Society, this was a step toward eliminating the threat of dependency in Northern free society.

The best way to encourage independence in poor Northern boys was the introduction of free labor. Brace wrote that the young boys of the city had, regrettably, been driven to "dishonest means of making a living."[39] According to a report filed by the chief of police in 1848, there were approximately 10,000 "vagrant children" in New York. In eleven wards of the city, 2,995 of these children were engaged in various forms of thieving. "Pick-pocketing," Brace wrote, "is now a profession among a certain class of boys."[40] Though pick-pocketing was the most widespread "dishonest" labor, other types existed as well. "Cotton-picking on the wharves," "iron stealing in the dry-docks," "'smashing' of baggage," and "book-bluffing" were some of the "means of livelihood for the dishonest poor boys of New York." Of the young girls in the city, Brace's primary concern was prostitution, a form of "debasement" for females in "the pure and sunny years of childhood." However, the CAS's work in the 1850s focused primarily on boys as future free laborers and heads of household in Northern free society. When girls were a focus of reform, it was to prevent female sexual immorality rather than to promote their independence through free labor. Child rescue of the 1850s, particularly the free labor agenda, was primarily aimed at boys. In the district east of the Bowery were "thousands of children, whose sole occupation [was] picking rags and bones in the street to sell." These children were German, mostly Bavarian boys, and like the city's child street sweepers, match sellers, candy sellers, and newsboys, they were engaged in "honest little trades" that were "infinitely better than begging" but still "dangerous to the morals."[41] For CAS reformers, child labor such as street sweeping, candy selling, or rag picking threatened Northern free society because such activities were not accompanied by social mobility or independence.[42]

In an 1856 letter to an English friend, Brace summarized the CAS's success with regard to "our enterprises among the poor children." While the lodging houses, reading rooms, and other experiments were useful, it was the schools and "*our field of free labor*" that were "vastly better curatives for our evils than all these expedients."[43] In the 1850s, "field of free labor" was a term that invoked the national debate about territorial expansion. In an 1854 speech, William H. Seward, an outspoken enemy of "the Slave Power," referred to the expansion of slavery into the Kansas and Nebraska territories as extending the "fields of slave labor" into the West instead of the "fields of free labor."[44] Brace revealed in the same letter his own preoccupation with territorial expansion regarding slavery: "There are some very alarming features just now, and we apprehend a bloody collision in Kansas next spring. There is something to a statesman ominous and sad in these first collisions which are to go on for centuries perhaps, and which may utterly shatter our Republic. But it is right. Justice avenges itself, and our fall may be one step in the progress of mankind."[45] The dispute over Kansas—set in motion by the Kansas-Nebraska Act of 1854, which granted popular sovereignty to the inhabitants of the Kansas Territory to decide themselves whether to be free or slave—lay bare the conflict between Northern free society and Southern slavery. As one historian has put it, the Kansas-Nebraska Act "may have been the most important single event pushing the nation towards civil war."[46] Though antislavery began as a moral crusade, it became more political in the 1840s and '50s.[47] The passage of the Kansas-Nebraska Act of 1854 enhanced Northern fears of a Slave Power conspiracy. Effectively a repeal of the Missouri Compromise of 1820, the Kansas-Nebraska Act impelled many Northerners to "finally accept as fact the existence of an aggressive

Slave Power."[48] The bloody guerilla warfare that occurred in Kansas in 1855 and continued through 1859 bore out this fear.[49] Many free labor Republicans thought the Slave Power aimed to nationalize slavery. An Ohio Republican wrote that proslavery Southerners were working for slavery's "legalization and extension into every region protected by the American flag."[50] Prominent Republicans such as William Seward and Abraham Lincoln stated publicly on many occasions that the nation must eventually become either all-free or all-slave. Fear of slavery's expansion into Northern free society became especially pronounced after the Dred Scott decision.[51] One Republican asked, "Does the Constitution make slaves property? If so, slavery exists in Ohio today, for the Constitution extends over Ohio, doesn't it?"[52] The Slave Power conspiracy prompted many Northerners to conclude that Southerners were not content with confining slavery to the South.

In antebellum America the West loomed large geographically, politically, and ideologically for both Northerners and Southerners. Beginning with the Northwest Ordinance of 1787, which disallowed the expansion of slavery northwest of the Ohio River, the fate of Western territories was central to maintaining the balance of slave and free states in the new nation.[53] The Louisiana Purchase of 1803 reopened the question of balance, which received an eventual answer in the Missouri Compromise of 1820. Crafted by statesman Henry Clay, the compromise consisted of three parts: (1) Missouri would be admitted as a slave state, (2) Maine would separate from Massachusetts and be admitted as a free state, and (3) the remaining territory of the Louisiana Purchase north of the 36°30' parallel would be closed off to slavery.[54] New Western territories acquired as a result of the Mexican-American War (1846–1848) would upset the balance once again, leading to the fierce sectionalism of the 1850s.[55] Although the Compromise of 1850—a five-part solution that included the highly controversial Fugitive Slave Act—did much to quell the fury between pro- and antislavery factions, the peace was broken just four years later when the Kansas-Nebraska Act escalated sectional antagonism.[56]

The West was important not only for the maintenance of a national balance between slave and free but also because it was thought to be a "safety valve" regulating the relations of labor and capital.[57] Encouraging the westward movement of Eastern workingmen would reduce the surplus labor population of the East while giving many working men a chance to be socially mobile and economically independent. Horace Greeley was a leading proponent of a homestead act that would provide free land to settlers who wanted to develop land west of the original thirteen colonies. As the editor of the *New York Tribune*, Greeley frequently publicized the opportunities for labor that existed in the West and encouraged young men to "Go West."[58] The homestead issue became increasingly sectionalist in the 1850s. Free labor Northerners began to cast homesteading as an effective barrier against the spread of slavery in Western territories, while proslavery Southerners increasingly opposed homesteading for the same reason.[59]

The Children's Aid Society developed its emigration plan in response to the sectional conflict over slavery's fate in the West. At the founding of the CAS in 1853, Brace outlined a plan whereby poor Northern boys would be transported to Western states such as Indiana, Michigan, Ohio, and Illinois and occasionally as far as Kansas, Minnesota, and Missouri. The plan's main purpose was to introduce poor Northern boys to free labor by putting them to work on farms in the West. In a political climate in which Northerners feared the expansion of slavery in the West and nation, this approach to the "rescue" of poor Northern boys was well received. The CAS's first circular, distributed in March of 1853, stated:

> "Boys' Sunday Meetings" have already been formed, which we hope to see extended. . . . With these we hope to connect "Industrial Schools," where the greatest temptations to this class arising from want of work may be removed, and where they can learn an honest trade. Arrangements have been made with manufacturers by which . . . boys in different localities can be supplied with paying work. We hope, too, especially to be the means of draining the city of these children, by communicating with farmers, manufacturers, or families in the country, who may have need of such for employment.[60]

The belief that free labor could lift poor Northern boys out of poverty and preserve free society in the process was evident in the CAS's first year. Early in 1853 the CAS experimented with opening a workshop on Wooster Street that would teach boys the trade of pegging shoes. The boys who gathered there would learn the trade and be "paid according to their labor." Other workshops followed a similar plan. But the plan that received the most enthusiasm in the 1850s was the emigration plan. After sending out circulars across the country, the CAS received "over 300 applications for our poor boys and girls. . . . A number of these applications are from the West."[61] The emigration plan was particularly appealing to reformers because it embodied their core belief that changing the child's conditions could transform the child.[62] With this plan, Brace wrote, "we have attempted . . . *to change the whole social condition* of the outcast child."[63]

The plan also offered a tenable solution to a labor market problem: a labor surplus in the city and a labor shortage in the West. Like proponents of homesteading, the CAS perceived its efforts as following "the natural laws of economy." The CAS noted that it had "attempted to work through natural laws, especially such as were in play in this country." It was a "most fortunate fact" that there was a "complement existing between the vast supply of youthful labor in our cities, and the immense demand for it in our rural communities."[64] Not only did the emigration plan address the "great economic problem of poverty in our cities," but the West was thought to be fertile soil for the cultivation of free labor and independence.[65] The "*warm-heartedness* of the Western people" and the "equality of all classes" there gave them a "special adaptation to this work, and account for their success."[66] In 1856 the CAS wrote that the emigration plan was "destined to be the most permanent and useful of our enterprises."[67] To grow the plan, they needed "a more comprehensive and systematic arrangement for carrying these children to the West, which can only be made under considerable expense."[68] With increasing public support and funding—including from ship and railroad companies who agreed to transport the CAS's children at little or no cost—the number of children "transplanted" into Western families grew or remained steady every year. Between 1855 and 1865, anywhere between eight hundred and twelve hundred children per year were transported either to the West or to the nearby countryside.[69]

One company of boys headed west made a lasting impression on people who came into contact with them after they left New York in November 1856—first by steamer, then by train—to reach Michigan and Illinois. One reformer wrote, "Such general sympathy and such cordial cooperation in the efforts and views of the society; such open-handed and open-hearted reception . . . as I have witnessed and experienced during this trip, I have never known in the whole history of the Society." The man who directed the steamer's passage to Albany had "refused any payment whatever for the passage of the entire company." The same courtesy was then extended by the president of the New York Central Railroad Company, who "passed" them all from Albany to Niagara Falls, as well as by the director of the Great Western Railroad Company, who "ticketed" them from Niagara Falls to Detroit. Finally came the president of the Michigan Central Railroad, who conferred upon them a free "passage order from Detroit to Chicago." The children in this company, a group of "fifty little ones," were clever, a reformer wrote, at garnering the attention of passengers and eliciting support and donations for the Children's Aid Society. Having been given an American flag by a supporter of the CAS before the company left New York, "a clever little black boy" in the company led the group of children, holding the flag and waving it as though he were the company's standard-bearer, which "everywhere attracted attention." The children would frequently deliver a statement to surrounding adults explaining who and what they were, which induced spontaneous

18 CHAPTER 1

donations from passengers and passersby.[70] The mission to promote free labor and independence in the West had a strong resonance for observers in 1856 as donations were likened to supporting the cause of Northern free society.

In claiming the benefits of free labor, reformers tended not to emphasize racial or ethnic distinctions among children.[71] At the height of sectional crisis, they were more concerned about establishing an ethic of salvation through free labor than promoting hierarchies of race or ethnic origin. The CAS sent more than three thousand children of varying backgrounds to engage in free labor in the West and uniformly praised the outcomes, claiming that "very few" of them had "turned out badly or come back to a vagrant life." The vast majority of the children had become "engaged in an honest calling."[72] The CAS touted the hundreds of letters they received from formerly "vagrant" children and farm families in the West to underscore free labor's promise of uplift. One farmer wrote, "It gives me much pleasure to be able to state that Johnny S——continues to grow in favor with us all. Having been reclaimed from his vagrant habits, which at first clung pretty close to him, he may now be said to be a steady and industrious boy."[73] Another farmer wrote, "Albert H——is now a very good boy; he does his work very well, and does much better than anyone could expect. . . . He is painting blinds for us, and does nearly as much as a man. He earns one dollar a day much of the time. . . . He talks of saving all his money, and we think he will do so."[74] In discussions of free labor, reformers were more likely to note gender rather than racial differences. Reformers believed that different virtues would result for girls engaged in free labor. Though boys far outnumbered girls in the CAS's work, girls were also sent to the West. When reformers discussed free labor for girls, they did not emphasize independence and social mobility as they did for boys. Poor Northern girls could improve themselves through honing their domestic skills and thereby become "useful members of society" as future wives and mothers.[75] One family wrote of a young girl: "Sarah G——has been with us nine months, and we think she is a different girl, in all respects, from what she was when she first came. It has been her chief business to look after our 'little one,' . . . and we have no reason to complain. . . . It is our intention . . . to bring her up in such a way as to be useful to herself, and also to be a useful member of society."[76]

In the years preceding the Civil War, the CAS's emigration plan helped to reinforce support for Northern free labor principles by applying them to poor children, especially boys. On the one hand a "rich blessing to the city,"[77] the emigration plan was meant to preserve Northern free society by confronting a threat that existed within it. A great "advantage to the West," on the other hand, the plan extended free labor by planting the seeds for "useful and good men" to grow up in the "land of the West."[78] In these years, the Children's Aid Society became more intractable toward the asylum system—or, as they had termed it, "the Asylum-Interest."[79] Like Southern slavery, the Asylum-Interest became a foil for the Children's Aid Society in the late 1850s as reformers began claiming that asylums promoted an "unfree" system of labor. Like John and Henry, who were bound out to the Delaware plantation, youth in the care of asylums were routinely being indentured, or "bound out," to work for persons under a "legal restraint."[80] This practice, reformers argued, would "enervate and unfit them" for the "strains of life" they would experience as adults in free society. The CAS's emigration plan, on the other hand, was "free" and had "no power of indenture," "no legal restraint over the children," and was completely "voluntary" for both the children and the families who received them "solely on condition of their good behavior."[81] As a result of the "free" nature of the labor, the CAS's children would be transformed unlike those bound out through the asylums. As one reformer wrote, "Once [our children] were ragged, hungry, and idle. Now, their condition is so much improved. . . . They are comfortably clad, sheltered, cared for; and of the greatest blessings to the young, *healthily worked*."[82] The CAS's ongoing dispute with the Asylum-Interest—and their disagreements about the best way to rescue poor Northern boys—helped the organization articulate in clear terms the distinction between free and slave society.[83]

The CAS set into motion what was essentially a public relations battle between it and the asylum system over the best way to reform poor Northern boys.[84] Judging by the surge in annual donations the CAS was receiving by 1865, as well as the asylums' increasingly defensive posture, the Children's Aid Society emerged as the victor, surpassing other child rescue organizations in size, scope, and influence by the time of the Civil War.[85] One explanation for the CAS's growth in popular support is that its approach to child rescue reflected changing views of childhood. The growth of a less Calvinistic and more optimistic view of human nature had consequences for religious, cultural, and social beliefs about children that departed from Puritan understandings of infant damnation and child depravity.[86] This more optimistic view of human nature conflicted with juvenile asylums and other penal institutions that had rigid, disciplinary practices based on pessimistic views of human nature and the causes of poverty.[87] Another explanation is that an increasing emphasis on the domestic sphere made the emigration plan of transporting children into Western families a more appealing option than the long-standing practice of child institutionalization.[88] While both changing views of childhood and an emphasis on the domestic sphere played a role, Northern child rescue was profoundly shaped by the sectional crisis over slavery. Debates about Northern child rescue openly engaged national disagreements about slavery, and the emigration plan shaped and reinforced free labor ideals by applying them to poor Northern boys. In the 1850s the CAS's approach to child rescue resonated with a Northern audience anxious about the fate of Southern slavery. When reformers spoke about Northern child rescue, they articulated in clear terms the distinctions between free and slave society. By applying free labor principles to poor Northern children in the West, reformers reassured a Northern audience of free labor's superiority.

The Children's Aid Society gained support not only from Northern donors and enthusiasts but also from the children themselves. One boy, J. K., a former newsboy from New York, wrote, "All the newsboys of New York have a bad name; but we should show . . . that we can become as respectable as any of their countrymen." He was "getting along well" and was "satisfied with [his] place." J. K. sent a message to the other boys in the lodging house: "Now, boys, you know I have tried everything. I have been a newsboy. . . . I have smashed baggage. . . . I have sold nuts, I have peddled. . . . I was a boot-black; and you know when I sold my papers I was at the top of our profession. . . . But I found that all that would not do." Now that he was in the West, he was "going ahead." Receiving board plus ten dollars a month, J. K. felt he was on a path toward social mobility: "We are all on an equality, my boys, out here, so long as we keep ourselves respectable."[89] Many others' letters thanked the CAS for rescuing them from a life of poverty.[90] One boy delivered a lively speech at the lodging house in 1860, just before the departure of a company to the West:

> Boys, gentlemen, chummies: Perhaps you'd like to hear something about the West, the great West, you know, where so many of our old friends are settled down and growin' up to be great men, maybe the greatest men in the Republic. Boys, that's the place for growing Congressmen, and Governors, and Presidents. Do you want to be newsboys always, and shoe-blacks, and timber merchants in a small way by sellin' matches? . . . Do you want to be gentlemen and independent citizens? You do—then make tracks for the West, from the Children's Aid Society. . . . If you are honest, and good, and industrious, you may get so much up in the ranks that you won't call a general or a judge your boss. . . . I want to be somebody, and somebody don't live here, no how. You'll find him on a farm in the West.[91]

A close reading of the speech reveals an embrace of free labor principles: "Do you want to be newsboys *always*?" The boy showed an understanding of social mobility. Free labor in the West held not only the promise of mobility but also the chance to become a "gentleman" who was "honest," "good," and "industrious." The newsboy linked his understanding of free labor and mobility with notions of citizenship. The purpose of going west was not just

Fields of Free Labor

to become industrious but to be "the greatest men in the Republic." The West was the land where lodging house boys would grow into "Congressmen, Governors, and Presidents." Regardless of whether the boy was repeating what reformers had told him or reflecting his own desires, the speech reveals how central free labor was to the Children's Aid Society's message and how thoroughly they had communicated this message to children.

The firing on Fort Sumter on April 12, 1861, and the subsequent outbreak of war recast the Children's Aid Society's work even more so than the controversial legislation that pitted free society against the "slave interest" in the 1850s. "In the hour of our peril," Brace wrote, "at the first shot of our flag, we find the foreign-born rising, if possible, with more enthusiasm and patriotic self-devotion to defend the Republic than our own citizens."[92] These "foreign-born" were in many cases the former boys of the Children's Aid Society, now young men no older than eighteen serving as Union soldiers. The CAS would begin referring to them as the "children of the Republic." More than sixty boys who had once resided at the Newsboys' Lodging House joined the Union Army in the war's first year, and at least four hundred boys who had been sent to the West had volunteered to fight for the Union.[93] Reformers seized on this fact to reinforce to their Northern supporters that the CAS's efforts had been successful.

For CAS reformers, there was no better measure of their success than the phenomenon of CAS boys volunteering to fight for freedom. In the organization's first annual report published after the outbreak of war, Brace wrote that "a large number of our boys, in every part of the country, have entered the army and are doing manly service for the Republic." Even more noteworthy was the soldier boys' "devoted patriotism" and "love for the Union." For the Children's Aid Society, there could be no more dramatic vindication of their organization's efforts than a vagrant boy turned Union soldier. Such a transformation helped legitimize free labor ideology, both in its claim that free labor encouraged independence and social mobility and that free labor was essential to the molding of loyal citizens. In their service as soldiers, these "brave fellows" were "offering their lives, if need be, to sustain a Government, [under] which many of them were not born, but to which and its institutions they owe allegiance and a debt of gratitude." In some cases the soldiers literally "repaid" the institutions that had helped them. Many boys were sending a "portion of their pay from the army" to be "deposited in the savings banks" at various Children's Aid Society institutions. Brace wanted his audience to remember the "poverty-stricken, crime-tempted street boys" they were years earlier and then to envision their transformation into "the advocates of good morals, the defenders of law and order, and the champions of the dearest rights of humanity." "It would be difficult," Brace wrote, "to find a more striking illustration of

22 CHAPTER 1

the elevating and Christianizing operations of our Republican Institutions, or a stronger guarantee of their perpetuity."[94] Throughout the war, the Children's Aid Society proclaimed the role played by former CAS boys as Union soldiers while touting their own role in preserving Northern free society.

During the war the CAS received letters from former CAS boys who were serving in the Union Army. The letters were from "almost every prominent military post in the country, from Fortress Monroe and the Potomac to New Orleans, Murfreesboro, and Memphis."[95] One soldier, E. T., who had been sent west on a train years earlier, wrote, "I am now in the army, in the Thirty-sixth Regiment, Indiana Volunteers. . . . I get $13 a month and my board and clothes. . . . I can whip a thousand 'Secesh,' and old Jeff Davis and all."[96] Another, W. J., wrote, "I thought I would write a few lines to let you know where I was. I enlisted in the army fourteen months ago, in the First Regiment Michigan Engineers. . . . We have had a great fight here lately, but you have heard of it, so won't write much about."[97] Former CAS boys would sometimes write to let the Children's Aid Society know why they had *not* joined the Union Army. One boy, S. W., wrote, "It is not my fault that I am not in the army. . . . My boss said that I had hired with him for a year, and I was bound by honor to stay with him. . . . O how often have I wished myself under that flag fighting for its defense! I would not be afraid of losing my own life; if I did, I would have the pleasure of dying for my country."[98] The CAS's reformers were pleased to receive such letters and commented that the CAS deserved credit. As one reformer wrote, "[These boys] are now fighting *for* their country, when, but for this Society, they would have grown up here in ignorance and sin, *to fight against it!*"[99]

The Children's Aid Society wrote about a former vagrant boy who had joined the Union Army in Tennessee that he was "first known to us as the neglected child of a poor widow; then as a petty thief; he was then confined in an asylum, and escaped, and afterwards was sent out by the Society to Indiana, where he earned good wages, and did well. . . . Now he has left . . . to aid in putting down the Rebellion."[100] This narrative suggested that becoming a Union soldier was possible because the boy had first learned free labor principles. A Western farmer echoed this sentiment, writing that "the most industrious boy for work that I ever saw" was also the quickest to "run off from home to enlist."[101] Another farmer wrote that "a German boy you sent me ten years ago has become a respectable citizen. . . . He is [now] a soldier in the Eighteenth Connecticut Volunteers. . . . The course he has pursued from his boyhood has been to me a source of great satisfaction."[102]

In the final year of the war, there were "a great number of individual instances of change of character and improvement," the Children's Aid Society reported. "Everywhere, we hear of boys whom we have sent [west] as having joined the army." A man from Pennsylvania claimed that in a neighborhood of "some one hundred and twenty children" from the CAS, "there is a not a single lad of those sent there who has not enlisted in the service of the country." By 1865 thousands of former CAS boys had joined either the Union Army or Navy and, according to the CAS, they made exceptionally good soldiers, as not a "single disgraceful act" had been committed. They "love[d] their country" and were willing to leap up at the "bugle-call of Freedom." One Union soldier wrote about a former CAS boy: "He did not hesitate to say to anyone, with a proud, manly self-reliance, 'I am one of the Children's Aid boys.' A person in his company . . . came to us the next day to ascertain if it was really so."[103]

The CAS's wartime rhetoric reflected its stake in the slavery debate. CAS reformers believed their work had helped preserve the Union and that they were crucial in laying the foundations of a "democratic form of society." "Even during the din of civil war, and the heroic efforts of the nation to maintain the Government and execute the laws, we feel it right to call the public attention to those quiet and simple methods of charity which are slowly laying the solid foundations of the structure [now] so rudely assailed," wrote Brace. During the war the Children's Aid Society was emboldened in its claims to public financial assistance. Its usual practice of relying upon private donations shifted. In 1862 the CAS's treasurer, John E. Williams, wrote, "This year we confidently appeal to the State for aid . . . in view of the widespread usefulness of this Society." Williams claimed the state was receiving "great advantages, directly and indirectly" from the Children's Aid Society's operations of the past nine years and that the organization was "entitled to an appropriation from the public treasury."[104] In the CAS's estimation, each boy saved from the fate of an impoverished life was equal to *two men*—"the man who would have required another man to guard or prosecute him is now converted into a defender of the laws, instead of being an offender thereof."[105] The public took note of this claim. On February 25, 1862, the *Cleveland Herald* reported, "The Children's Aid Society is doing great and good work in providing homes in the West. . . . Many boys who have gone West are now in the army. . . . [One] youth is now in the grand army, and writes: 'This has been a good country to me, and it is my duty to do something to defend its institutions.'" The writer concluded, "An army of such men are invincible!"[106] This attitude contributed to a surge in private donations toward the end of the war. In 1864 the CAS had "been even more liberally supported by the public than in years of peace." "Our work during the past year," Brace wrote, "has been more extended than in any one year since the formation of the Society." Brace attributed this support to the "pressing call" that "good citizens" felt during wartime to support effective reform institutions.[107]

Just months after Brace founded the Children's Aid Society in January 1853, the Kansas and Nebraska territories were organized, the debate over slavery intensified, and the Republican Party was formed. While Brace was organizing the first companies of boys to be sent west in 1854, the newspaper on his desk, likely the *New York Tribune* or *New York Daily Times*, was filled with reports about "Bleeding Kansas"; editorials about the Slave Power conspiracy; and letters written by his friend Frederick Law Olmsted, who contributed to both newspapers a series of highly unfavorable descriptions of the South. Later in 1857, while Brace was expanding the emigration plan and opening more industrial schools in the city, he likely read Horace Greeley's articles about the West and spoke with fellow Northerners about the Dred Scott decision and how it confirmed their suspicions about the South. The free labor ideology that had been growing was now the cornerstone of the Republican Party and had more supporters than ever. On November 6, 1860, that party would officially come into power by electing the most eloquent free labor Republican in the country, Abraham Lincoln—an election that presaged the conflict that was to begin just over a month later, determining whether the nation was to be free or slave.

The Children's Aid Society developed its approach to Northern child rescue in light of the sectional conflict over slavery. Through debates about how to rescue poor Northern boys, the CAS articulated in clear terms what it meant by a free or slave society. At the heart of this distinction was a commitment to free labor principles that prioritized the outcomes of independence and social mobility in Northern child rescue efforts. When appraising Northern child rescue approaches such as the asylum system, the CAS censured the outcomes of dependency and immobility as resembling Southern slavery. The CAS's emigration plan emerged not only as a rescue effort to remove poor Northern boys from the city and place them in farm families in the West but also as an antislavery effort to preserve and extend Northern free society in a moment of sectional crisis. This aspect of the CAS's work became more pronounced once war broke out in 1861. The emancipation of four million slaves and the adoption of the Reconstruction amendments answered the question of whether the nation would be free or slave. But the momentous occasion of slave emancipation along with unparalleled industrial growth ushered in by the Civil War created new uncertainties about the distinction between free and unfree labor. Debates about children and their labor would help Northerners and Southerners distinguish between free and unfree labor and would shape how they understood the market's expansion in both regions.

2 Testing Ground of Freedom

Child Labor in the Age of Emancipation

This is the word that
came unto Jeremiah
from the LORD . . .
to proclaim liberty unto them.
—Jeremiah 34:8

In October 1865, news of the Louisiana Freedmen's Bureau commissioner's decision to order the closing of two black orphanages in New Orleans traveled through the informal channels that black men, women, and children relied on to stay informed about public affairs.[1] Established by Northern relief societies during the Civil War, these orphanages cared for the children of deceased Louisiana freed people. The commissioner, General James S. Fullerton, decided to close the orphanages to bind out the children as apprentices to former slave owners. Arriving in the wake of Fullerton's address the previous year when freed people were informed that they would not receive lands promised them, news about the orphanages was troubling. "The news fell upon the community like the land order, giving . . . sadness to all the colored people in the city," according to a newspaper account.[2] Former owners showed up at the orphanages requesting children who were "fit to black boots" or who could do "dirty work" for them. "The orphans themselves, learning that General Fullerton had ordered that they be apprenticed . . . *ran away from the asylums.*" The next morning, the staff found "about one-half" of the children missing. A newspaper noted that "*even the children of the freedmen would rather die than be bound again by any chains.*" Fullerton reconsidered his decision.[3] This incident was not unique to New Orleans. Across the South, debates about formerly enslaved children and their labor shaped the way formerly enslaved people, former owners, and Northern officials defined the distinction between free and unfree labor. These debates also provided a testing ground for assessing the legitimacy of different kinds of authority over formerly enslaved children in the post-emancipation South.

After Fullerton caused a firestorm over the fate of black orphans in New Orleans, A. E. Cerqua, a Children's Aid Society reformer, was preoccupied with a different child labor issue in the post–Civil War North. In New York, Cerqua had encountered a seven-year-old Italian boy musician soliciting money from passersby. Cerqua tried to find out as much as he could about the boy, but the boy had been trained to protect his *padrone*, or master, from authorities. Cerqua learned that the boy hailed from Naples, did not remember his mother or father, and lived in the city with a padrone who had multiple children in his employment. The boy soon grew nervous and refused to reveal his padrone's location.[4] Cerqua was concerned that the padrone system was a new type of child slavery on Northern soil. An effort to end the padrone system over the next several years helped Northern reformers define the distinction between free and unfree labor in the post–Civil War North. The battle also helped reformers assess the legitimacy of different kinds of authority over child laborers in the North.

As the market expanded after the war, child labor in Northern factories and mills increased as well. In 1872 a night-school teacher from the Children's Aid Society expressed alarm at the number of students who were exhausted from overwork in factories and mills. The organization sent agents to the factories and mills of New York, Brooklyn, and nearby towns to investigate. They found a staggering number of children working excessively long hours. Many of them did not have "the rudiments of even common school education."[5] Reformers, educators, journalists, and others began warning that factory labor harmed children, but the reasons for this were not always clear. Factory child labor had grown out of Northern industrialization, which was supposed to represent progress and freedom. Capitalists argued that factory child labor benefited children in most cases. Poor parents who required their children to work excessively were the real threat, capitalists contended. Whereas the forced apprenticeship of formerly enslaved children and the padrone trade in Italian children were often likened to slavery, factory child labor prompted a more complicated debate. Northern capitalists could not be vilified in the same way as former slaveholders or Italian padrones. Capitalists embraced free labor principles, and factory labor could teach children industrious values. However, excessive factory labor might harm children, especially when they were not educated. The rise of factory child labor in the industrial North complicated the distinction between free and unfree labor and prompted a debate about capitalist authority over children in the free labor market.

Debates about children and their labor shaped how post–Civil War Americans understood the market and its expansion in both the North and South. Northern officials in the South argued that in order to have legitimate authority over formerly enslaved children, former owners had to conduct themselves like capitalists promoting free labor principles. They could not establish legitimate authority by wielding their former control as the children's owners. Northern officials might support apprenticing black children under former owners as long as the apprenticeships operated according to free labor principles that encouraged habits of industry. In the North, reformers argued that Italian padrones were not legitimate authorities in capitalist society, since they operated like Southern slaveholders. An effort to "emancipate" padrone children led to the conviction of Italian padrones under newly secured laws designed to protect formerly enslaved persons in the South. In both North and South, reformers relied on free labor justifications for their actions regarding children. Child labor in factories in the North raised new questions about free labor. Northern capitalists were legitimately employing children as long as the factory labor was not excessive, conditions were safe, and social mobility was possible. Northern factories emerged as a new testing ground for determining the boundaries of capitalist authority over children. Child labor there also helped reformers determine the limits, if any, of free labor as a beneficial activity for children.

Although emancipation and the Thirteenth Amendment ended slavery,[6] the post–Civil War South was fraught with conflict over the labor system that would replace slavery.[7] As historians have shown, the conflict involved not only formerly enslaved people and former owners but also Freedmen's Bureau agents, who frequently settled disputes between these groups.[8] While former owners attempted to retain the old system, formerly enslaved people pushed for their own aspirations in freedom. Emerging in the midst of these struggles was a battle over freed children. In the months following the Civil War, former owners seized upon antebellum child apprenticeship statutes—which had formerly been used to secure support for orphans—in an attempt to wrest formerly enslaved children from their parents.[9] Under the guise of providing protection for freed children who had been orphaned or whose parents were unable to care for them, former owners availed themselves of apprenticeship statutes to bind out freed children whose parents were fully capable of caring for them.[10] The final months of 1865 witnessed a spate of apprenticeships that were highly contentious as former owners convinced state legislatures and judges to grant them legal status of mastery over freed children.

After the war the Freedmen's Bureau received numerous complaints on behalf of freed persons regarding the forced apprenticeships of their children.

Derinda Smothers, a freedwoman from Maryland, testified that shortly after emancipation she had hired out her fourteen-year-old son to a Mr. Frederick Grayson to work for wages. Without warning, the boy's former owner, Ira Young, "took possession of the boy" from his mother, falsely claiming that the boy was legally bound to him. After months of brutal treatment, the boy ran away but was "caught and taken back."[11] A justice of the peace decided in favor of Young, notwithstanding that it had been "proved on trial that the boy was hired out by his mother" and had been receiving wages from Grayson.[12] A formerly enslaved man named Daniel Chase returned after the war was over to his former owner's house in Prince Frederick, Maryland, asking for the five children he had left behind. Daniel wished to bring them to Washington, DC, to live there with him and his wife, Mina, the mother of his children. But Daniel's former owner, Virgil Gant, "refused [him] possession" of his children, informing Daniel that he had already had them "bound" to himself through the Orphans Court of Calvert County and was the children's legal master.[13] Lucy Lee, a freedwoman from Maryland, sought assistance for her apprenticed daughter, whom she described as a "prisoner" in a "free land." "We were delighted when we heard that the Constitution set us all free . . ., but God help us, our condition is bettered but little; free ourselves, but deprived of our children. . . . It was on their account we desired to be free."[14]

As former owners attempted to reinstitute slavery through the apprenticing of freed children, formerly enslaved parents—alongside grandparents, aunts, uncles, and other extended kin—asserted their rights to their own children as a nonnegotiable part of freedom. Jane Kamper from Talbot County, Maryland, testified that her former owner, William Townsend, went along with her decision to leave for Baltimore after emancipation but that he believed her "children should be bound to him." Even though Townsend took pains to hide her children from her, Jane was able to get possession of them "by stealth" and take them with her. When he discovered the children missing, Townsend pursued her all the way to the boat where this time she had hidden her children from him.[15] Like parents, extended kin went to great lengths to reclaim freed children who had no immediate parents. A Freedmen's Bureau agent in Louisiana wrote that "the binding out of children Seems to the freedmen like putting them back into Slavery—In every case where I have bound out children thus far Some Grandmother or fortieth cousin has come to have them released."[16] A bureau agent from Tennessee wrote to the regional Freedmen's Bureau assistant commissioner about his experiences dealing with the apprenticing of formerly enslaved children who had been orphaned. The Tennessee agent supported the binding out of children whose parents were not "known to be living." The problem was that every time an orphan was bound out, "an Uncle, Aunt—brother or sister-in-law comes up & claim[s] they will support and care for their relatives."[17] In a few cases, formerly enslaved children made their own statements to the Freedmen's Bureau. Carter Holmes, a twelve-year-old Maryland boy, told an agent, "I was indentured . . . to James Suit living in Prince George County Md. . . . I have been whipped by Mr. Suit without justification. . . . I have been so tired of not receiving any compensation for my services." Carter made a final plea to the bureau: "Please don't let Mr. Suit take me back for I have a mother and father (named *Sylva* and *Abraham* Holmes) who would care for me if they knew where I was. I think they are in this city."[18]

Freedmen's Bureau agents and other Union officials were called upon to solve disputes between formerly enslaved persons and former owners, which often meant clarifying the distinction between free and unfree labor. Like free labor proponents before the war, Northern officials relied on free labor justifications for their actions regarding formerly enslaved children. Davis Tillson, a Georgia Freedmen's Bureau commissioner, deliberated over what advice he should give to John Walker, a former owner who had retained several formerly enslaved children and elderly on his plantation in Morgan County. "I dislike to see them starve," Walker wrote, "yet it is utterly impossible to feed them, for I have not Fifty Dollars in money. . . . Will you allow me to Send [them] to the Bureau. . . . Can I send them to Atlanta? Please Give me an order [what] to do." Commissioner Tillson replied, "I am unable to tell you what to do with your former slaves—I can only say they must work for their support. The husband must take care of his wife and children. If a woman has more children than she can support, they can be bound out *with* her consent, as shown by the enclosed order." Thus, fatherless children could be bound out, according to the order, but only if the consent of the children's mother had been secured. However, if the mother was judged to be a pauper and therefore incapable of supporting her children—a judgment formerly enslaved people most often protested and believed was unfair—then an agent of the bureau would decide whether or not to allow her children to be bound out.[19]

Tillson lectured the former slaveholder about free labor. The bureau's aid was only "temporary" relief for Southern whites and blacks, Tillson wrote. The bureau would not under any circumstances relieve them "of the necessity of exerting themselves."[20] The "material salvation" of both whites and blacks in the South "depend[ed] upon the success of the free labor system." But Tillson was ambivalent about the role of freed children. He suggested, on the one hand, that freed children should be supported as dependents in a household with an adult provider. On the other hand, he argued that binding out freed children as apprentices could serve a positive social function in a newly free society. It was the abuses of apprenticeship laws by former owners—not apprenticeship or child labor per se—that Tillson and other agents found objectionable.

Eliphalet Whittlesey, North Carolina Freedmen's Bureau assistant commissioner, wrote in a circular distributed in November 1865 to bureau officers, agents, and teachers of freedmen that he believed child apprenticeship could be an appropriate institution for a free society, provided it was practiced according to state laws and that no distinction was made between white and black children.[21] Apprenticing orphans and children of parents who had no "honest calling" or "means of support" could serve to prevent the children from becoming "vagrants & paupers." Such children might learn "some good trade or occupation" that could prevent them from becoming "dependent upon the government."[22] One month earlier, the federal Freedmen's Bureau commissioner, Major General O. O. Howard, had released a similarly worded circular from Washington, DC, indicating that the bureau would recognize state laws regarding apprenticeship "provided that they make *no distinction of color*, or, in case they do so, the said laws applying to white children will be extended to the colored."[23] Like Howard, Whittlesey was supportive of child apprenticeship to the extent that it encouraged children to become independent free laborers. However, if the institution encouraged "the old ideas of compulsory labor and dependence," he was "very suspicious" of it.[24] Former owners' abuse of child apprenticeship made this labor system resemble slavery. Many Northern officials would compare the abuses of child apprenticeship with the old system of Southern slavery.

Before war's end, Union officials came to define former owners' use of child apprenticeship not only as a reinstatement of slavery but also as an act of rebellion. On November 1, 1864, Maryland became the first border state to adopt a new constitution abolishing slavery.[25] Three days later, Andrew Stafford, provost marshal of the first district of Maryland, pleaded with Brigadier General Henry Lockwood for assistance on how to deal with the "Rebels here" who were "showing an evident determination to still hold this people in bondage." After the governor of Maryland adopted the new constitution, "a rush was made to the Orphan's Court of this County, for the purpose of having all children . . . bound to their former owners." Stafford reported that at least two prominent members of this court were "disloyal parties" who did "not regard the rights" of former slaves. As such, these men refused to consider any testimony that might prove "the capability of the parents to support their children." Stafford's request was that he be given the authority necessary to "lay an injunction on the court." On November 23, 1864, George W. Curry, provost marshal in Annapolis, Maryland, described the judges of the orphans court as "sympathizers with (and to some extent) aiders of the rebels." Curry complained that these rebel sympathizers had been "binding out colored children to whoever might apply for them (but giving their former owners the preference) against the express wish of their parents." He then requested wartime authority to "annul indentures" that had been made since the adoption of Maryland's new constitution.[26] Two weeks after Curry's request, General Lockwood issued a circular warning that Union officials had "orders to break up the practice now prevalent of Apprenticing Negroes." In the instance of both Lockwood and Curry, they interpreted the apprenticing of formerly enslaved children as a wartime act of rebellion that was in violation of the constitutional mandate providing for emancipation.

The judges of the orphans court of Anne Arundel County justified their actions using free labor principles. In response to a warning they had received from Provost Marshal Curry, they explained that there was a large number of children whose "previous owners [were] known to the court to be proper persons to care for & bring them up to habits of industry."[27] The judges claimed to have been "misrepresented by some mothers" who were, according to the opinion of the court, utterly unable to "properly provide & teach habits of industry" to their children. Selecting "proper employers" for such children was "an act of humanity," these judges maintained.[28] Moreover, the judges insisted they were not doing anything against the law. Citing article 6 of the *Maryland Code of Public General Laws*, they suggested there was nothing wrong or unusual about the apprenticeships they were approving.[29] In a similar vein, the orphans court of Talbot County routinely declared formerly enslaved persons to be "vagrants" before they had "enjoy[ed] liberty a single week—in many instances before they have ever been permitted to leave their masters."[30] In declaring these parents "vagrants," the court believed it was entitled to bind out their children to supposedly more "industrious" masters. Like the judges of the Anne Arundel County orphans court, the Talbot County judges invested their apprenticeship rulings with free labor principles. They argued that the apprenticing of formerly enslaved children would serve a dual purpose of punishing vagrant parents while teaching their children habits of industry.

Many officials continued to regard former owners' apprenticing of formerly enslaved children as a misuse of an institution that was otherwise benign. General Lockwood argued that the problem was that the "spirit of the apprenticeship law" was disregarded by former slaveholders. For Lockwood, these apprenticeships were working "advantageously only for the rich slave holder." He argued that if the apprenticeships were executed in their "proper spirit," the outcome was generally "good." The problem was the "gross abuses" of former owners who were not behaving like free labor capitalists. These former owners were treating child apprenticeship the same as slavery, in which case the children would learn nothing about free labor and its values. Like Lockwood, Nelson G. Gill, a Mississippi Freedmen's Bureau agent, argued that apprenticeship laws "were being used here to the injury of the Freedmen." A formerly enslaved woman had complained to Gill that her twelve-year-old daughter had been bound to her former owner until she turned eighteen. The judge who ordered the binding determined that the mother "had not the means to support" the young daughter.[31] However, Gill noted that the former slaveholder had offered the mother "*good wages* if she would go and work for him." Gill sent a letter to the judge "protesting against the binding on the ground that the mother was not proven unable to support her child."[32] In these cases, Northern officials argued that employing formerly enslaved children was legitimate when free labor principles were applied. According to officials, these arrangements were also not legitimate unless the children's parents were proven incapable of providing for their children and thus of teaching them "habits of industry."[33]

Formerly enslaved parents wanted authority not only over caring for their own children but also over the benefits of any labor performed by their children.[34] Recognition of their families' integrity both as a legal and economic unit was a privilege they had been denied under slavery.[35] As with most farming families in the post–Civil War South, their economic survival depended on the labor of children. One Union official wrote that formerly enslaved people "would do very well" if they could "get their children unbound or restored to them and have the privilege of hiring them or working them themselves."[36] The same Unionist spoke "on behalf of the colored people," claiming that they wanted "to know if they can't have justice done them in order that they may have the hiring of their children themselves and to draw the wages for them or take them home to help them work if they choose."[37] For formerly enslaved people, the struggle for authority over their own children meant not only legal recognition of their families' integrity but also the right to their children's labor as part of securing their own economic survival.

Under pressure from formerly enslaved people, most Freedmen's Bureau agents by 1867 had concluded that the apprenticing of formerly enslaved children to former owners was not consistent with free labor principles and took measures to restore the children to their parents. During that year, Congress mandated that every Southern state rewrite its constitution to ratify the Fourteenth Amendment, which, in principle, extended the "privileges and immunities" of citizenship, due process, and equal protection to all United States citizens.[38] This mandate effectively nullified the Black Codes, though child apprenticeship technically remained legal as an avenue of child welfare as long as it did not distinguish between black and white children.[39] Several state and circuit court rulings around the same time declared the forced apprenticeships of formerly enslaved children to be unconstitutional.[40] But even though the tide was turning against the apprenticing of formerly enslaved children, some agents resisted nullifying existing apprenticeships. Such officials rigidly adhered to the principle of enforcing contracts, "even those made on false premises." In these cases, Bureau agents' preconceptions about the "fitness" of formerly enslaved parents prejudiced them in favor of former owners.[41] By 1867, however, the Freedmen's Bureau had cleared the way for formerly enslaved parents to challenge apprenticeship in order to retrieve their children. With the institutional backing of the bureau, formerly enslaved people's position relative to their former owners had been strengthened.[42]

In the North, new child labor debates reflected the ideological and legal consequences of emancipation. The emergence of Italian padrone children in the North soon became a national symbol of a new form of child slavery. In 1873 twelve-year-old Joseph—or "Giuseppe" as he had been called back in Italy—was found frightened and hungry in Central Park. He had been wandering alone for two days. For the previous three years, Joseph had lived at 45 Crosby Street in New York City with his padrone, far from his family farm in the southern Italian region of Basilicata. Joseph could no longer endure the beatings he received from his padrone, so he ran away to hide out in Central Park. A park keeper took Joseph to a nearby cottage to eat and rest. Joseph told the park keeper of the night three years ago in 1870 when an unknown man had come into his parents' home and taken him from his bed. Along with eight other children from the same neighborhood, Joseph found himself aboard a ship with another man they were instructed to call "padrone." The padrone told the children he possessed "great powers" and that they should obey him. After arriving in New York, the padrone took the children to Crosby Street, where he lodged them in a cellar with straw to sleep on. The next day, Joseph was sent out to ask passersby for money while playing a triangle on the streets of Manhattan. When he returned to the Crosby Street house that evening, he was beaten because he had not collected enough money. After several weeks of the same outcome, Joseph was taught to play violin. The padrone instructed Joseph not to return to Crosby Street until he had at least one dollar. Frequently working past midnight to meet this quota, Joseph was fearful of his padrone's vengeance. One time the padrone had pinched Joseph's ear so hard that it removed a small piece of flesh. Another time the padrone tied Joseph up by his wrists so tightly that it left gash marks on his skin. Joseph was reluctant to run away, because he believed his padrone had the backing of the king of Italy, the president of the United States, and the pope and would be tracked down and killed if he attempted to leave.[43]

Though dramatically rendered, Joseph's story is an example of the experiences of thousands of Italian youth who left their rural homes in the nineteenth century to labor under a padrone in American cities.[44] Part of a larger movement of peoples in the nineteenth century from Europe to the United States[45]—a migration that included Germans, Irish, British, and, increasingly toward the latter half of the century, Italians, Hungarians, Russians, Poles, Norwegians, Swedes, and others—the padrone system constituted part of the first wave of Italian immigration to the United States.[46] Parents often signed a contract with a padrone, agreeing to a three-year apprenticeship, during which their child would learn to play a musical instrument—usually a harp, violin, triangle, or bagpipes—for payment in exchange for food, clothing, and shelter from a padrone entitled to the child's remuneration. At the end of the apprenticeship, the child's parents would sometimes receive a predetermined amount of money.[47] In other instances, children were purchased from their parents or, as in the case of Joseph, kidnapped without their parents' knowledge.[48] Sometimes parents accompanied children to the United States and worked for a padrone themselves alongside their children.[49] Padrone children played their instruments on the streets daily. Like Joseph, most children were required to meet quotas and received punishment when they did not.[50] In the 1870s Italian padrone children became an obsession of journalists, reformers, and others who fashioned them into a symbol of child slavery in the North.

Until the 1870s New York newspapers did not pay much attention to Italian padrone children despite the fact that the sight of a young Italian child playing a musical instrument and begging for money on the streets of Manhattan had been common since at least the 1850s.[51] Reformers had also not paid much attention. In 1856 the Children's Aid Society had opened an industrial school in the Five Points district of New York, an Italian residential area, to serve poor Italian children, including child street musicians. But the purpose of the industrial school was to teach the children "useful" trades whereby they could become industrious, honest citizens.[52] Although the CAS was suspicious of the child musician trade—as they were of all street trades that were "vagrant" and not likely to lead to mobility—they did not place the child musician trade under any unusual scrutiny. After the Civil War the CAS began receiving tips from concerned New Yorkers that Italian child street musicians had abusive slave masters holding them captive in "child dens" and taking all of the children's earnings. These concerned New Yorkers demanded to know what the Children's Aid Society planned to do about it. Charles Brace addressed their concerns in an 1869 letter to the editor in which he noted that CAS officers had recently "been questioned about these unhappy little musicians" and insisted they were trying "to break up the business, as it is now carried on; but it is extremely difficult to find the employers of these children."[53] After 1872 the padrone system became a regular topic in CAS annual reports.[54]

Public dialogue about padrones grew louder. An 1872 *New York Times* article, "The Italian Slave-Trade," sounded a warning bell, insisting the public must understand that this "traffic in children" was "as absolutely a slave trade as ever existed down South."[55] In an editorial headlined "Slavery of the Street Minstrels," the authors remarked on the overwhelming response they had received to Joseph's story: "The facts which we published, yesterday, in regard to the Italian children employed in this city as street musicians [have] come . . . to the general public, with all the force of a new revelation."[56] It was shocking for readers to learn that "the world had given up stealing men from the African coast, only to kidnap children from Italy, and that the auction-block for negroes had been overturned in the Southern States, only to be set up again for white infants in New York."[57] Because of its reception, Joseph's story launched a three-month stint of investigative journalism in the summer of 1873.

Begging, scavenging, bootblacking, flower making, candy selling, street sweeping, soap peddling, rag picking—these were street trades and activities of poor children that had been part of the everyday fabric of life in New York for several decades. Yet, child street musicians were singled out as the foremost "child slavery" of the day. The padrone system became a focal point of moral outrage that helped reformers and others define the distinction between free and unfree labor in the post–Civil War North. It also helped them assess the legitimacy of different kinds of capitalist authority over children in the North. Like former slave child apprenticeship in the South, the padrone system in the North was defined as a menacing presence that breached the rules of normally functioning free market society.

The threat that the padrone system posed was multifaceted. On the one hand, it was perceived as the result of a dangerous "foreign" influence, a reflection of strange values that originated outside of America's borders. The Children's Aid Society described the trafficking of Italian children as having begun in far-off "villages, the inhabitants of which [were] half savages in habits, with misery and starvation steadily staring at them from the beginning to the end of the year."[58] On the other hand, the padrone system presented a threat to free society because it operated with trickery and deception. Like former slave masters who abused child apprenticeship laws to gain control

Figure 2.1. "The Italian Boys in New York--Tortures of the Training Room." Printed in *Harper's Weekly*, September 13, 1873, p. 801. By permission © HarpWeek.

over formerly enslaved children, Italian padrone masters signed deceptive contracts with parents to inveigle Italian children from their homes. Even if parents had agreed to the arrangement, the children were being held against their will. In public discourse it was the padrone who emerged as the ultimate object of scorn. He was depicted as a ruthless slave master who abused children to live off their labor. The corporal punishment thought to be meted out regularly by the padrone earned particular contempt. As *Harper's Weekly* wrote, "Numerous proofs have recently appeared of the shocking cruelties practiced by the Italian slave-dealers upon the poor little boys. . . . The lash is freely used if they fail to satisfy the demands of their inhuman task-masters."[59] Moreover, the "heartless padrone" was "growing rich upon the misery of these little waifs." An illustration that appeared in the same issue portrayed an Italian child, instrument still in hand, being whipped mercilessly by his padrone while other children looked on.[60]

In the investigative journalism of 1873, reporters extracted as much information as they could from padrone children. The same week Joseph's story appeared, a *New York Times* journalist fluent in Italian joined the effort. The reporter went into the upper part of the city in the morning hours to locate padrone children as they played their instruments. He tried earning their trust by speaking to them in Italian, but the children had been "instructed, through fear, to refuse to answer any questions." He then tried connecting with "new arrivals," who were "young and docile."[61] When he found three very young Italian boys with instruments, eating scraps from a garbage can on Fifth Avenue, he asked, "Why do you eat such stuff?" "Because I am hungry," one of the boys replied. Promising them a hot breakfast, the reporter persuaded the boys to follow him to a private house for an interview. A boy with a triangle said his name was Franceschito and that he was six years old. He had been sold by his mother for "60 ducats" and brought to this country by his present master, whose name was revealed but not printed to "save the boy from a beating." The second boy, Rocco, had a similar story, though he had been sold from one padrone to another since arriving in New York. The third boy, Pietrocito, lived with five other boys who were "all cruelly treated" by their padrone. Pietrocito had arrived in New York only six days earlier. The reporter gathered all the data he could, as his goal was "to obtain evidence to convict those who are guilty of trading in human flesh."[62]

Placing advertisements in newspapers for runaway children and offering a monetary reward for their return was a fairly common practice for padrones. Even the return of the public's beloved runaway Joseph was requested in such an advertisement: "$10 Reward—Runaway, an Italian boy, eleven years of age, named Joseph Golone; plays violin; had on striped pants and check vest, and cap without peak; missing since June 21. Any person returning him to Luie Carlile, No. 45 Crosby Street, New York City, will receive the above reward, and all expenses paid."[63] This advertisement did not appear in the *New York Times*. Reporters there had been notified of its appearance in several smaller local papers in the area: Long Island, New Jersey, and Westchester County. Noting that the padrone had used a false name, the *Times* reporters revealed his actual name, Luigi Careli. Careli was considered a catch by authorities, since he had in his charge "over 100" children, with more arriving daily. In the meantime, Joseph was like a "fugitive slave of antebellum times, who would lay close all day, and travel stealthily at night." In addition to the fugitive advertisement, the padrone circulated a flier among the various park keepers and workers in Central Park, which offered a thirty-dollar reward for information leading to Joseph's capture. Newspaper reports stressed the "unfree" nature of Joseph's condition. Fugitive slave laws had been "abolished by a long and bloody war," yet Joseph was "not free," as he was "liable to be captured by his enemies at any moment." For Northerners, padrones were like Southern slave masters, and padrone children were slaves who needed to be emancipated. The padrone system was not new, but opposition to it coalesced when slavery in the South was eradicated and new laws protecting freed persons were established.

The July 21, 1873, arrest and subsequent trial of Giovanni Glione, a padrone who once lived at Crosby Street in New York but moved to New Haven, at least partly satiated the public's appetite. "At last," the *New York Times* reported, "the American public has awakened to the fact that slaves are held in their very midst. . . . Under the pressure of the late articles in The Times relative to the slavery and traffic in Italian children, the citizens of neighboring cities have become aware of the evil . . . only to discover it at their very door-steps." Giovanni Glione was arrested by the district attorney in New Haven and was being held on a one-thousand-dollar bail. The charge issued by the district attorney was the unlawful "holding [of] four Italian children as slaves."[64] Citing the Personal Liberty Bill of 1854, a statute that was part of a series of Connecticut laws designed to protect fugitive slaves, the district attorney argued that Glione was holding "free persons in servitude," which was "in violation of the provisions" of the bill.[65] Thrilled by the prospect of a padrone on trial for slavery in New Haven, the reporters lamented that New York City wasn't doing more to emancipate padrone children: "Glione was arrested for having four children in a den, but in this city the same man might have held twenty children in the same manner . . . and no one would have troubled themselves sufficiently to discover the fact." The padrone children of New York were "slaves, awaiting emancipation."[66]

At issue in the hearing was whether or not the children in Glione's charge were slaves. Glione's attorney argued that the children were apprentices who should be returned to their master in accordance with Connecticut apprenticeship law.[67] This argument did not persuade the judge, since the children had not signed a contract and were not learning a trade.[68] At the hearing the boys testified that Glione had brought them to New Haven from New York City seven weeks earlier. They were physically abused for not reaching quotas, and they were told to steal if they could not earn the money.[69] Glione told them they would be arrested if they attempted to run away and that he had a "legal right to hold them." When asked if they wanted to be free, "they all said they would be glad to be free, if the law would give them freedom and protect them from Glione."[70] The judge ruled that Glione was "guilty of imprisoning free persons with intent to keep them in a state of servitude against their will." Bail was set at four thousand dollars, and the children were placed in custody of the state reform school until Glione's trial in October.[71]

In the week following Glione's arrest, two boys, Vito Nicola Saraceno and Giuseppe Gallicano, approached the Italian consul in New York and complained that they were being mistreated by their padrone, Michele Carcone. The boys had come to the consul to request protection.[72] This action reflected a growing confidence among padrone children.[73] The public atmosphere of moral opposition to padrones likely emboldened the children. Vito and Giuseppe sought out an official authority to secure their freedom. Using information obtained from the boys, police officers set out to find and arrest Carcone, but he had escaped to Philadelphia. Vito and Giuseppe were placed in custody of the sheriff and appeared before a judge, who "ordered that the boys be discharged from all claim, control, and custody of Michele Carcone."[74] The Children's Aid Society assumed guardianship of the boys "until suitable callings should be found for them."[75]

For Northern reformers, free labor was still the best route for poor children. The threat to Vito and Giuseppe was a padrone who stood between them and the rewards of free society. In fact, the Children's Aid Society believed the padrone system could be dismantled by introducing free labor principles in schools where padrone children would be required to attend. Before the breakup of the padrone system, the organization introduced a "Half-Time School Act" that would require all children engaged in street trades, scavenging, or begging to carry a certificate from a teacher proving they had attended a half-time school at least one day out of the week: "A few months of such training would transform these street children into industrious and orderly workers. The *padroni* would be obliged to educate their little apprentices; and these, as soon as they learned English, would understand their rights, and would set themselves free, or be freed by others."[76] The freedom that awaited emancipated padrone children was the opportunity to be free laborers in the capitalist North.

Post–Civil War laws designed to protect emancipated persons were deployed to protect padrone children in the North. After the *New York Times* hired attorney John Lewis to assist in finding the runaway Joseph's padrone, Lewis proposed that laws for emancipated persons would be most effective in breaking up the padrone system. As he explained, the fact that "the whole nefarious traffic" had not yet been broken up "was not owing to a lack of interest, but rather that there was no law under which to proceed."[77] Instead of looking to antebellum fugitive slave laws as the New Haven authorities had, Lewis used the Civil Rights Act of 1866, which was designed to protect emancipated persons in the South, and issued a formal complaint with the US commissioner.[78] The commissioner agreed that Joseph's circumstances were an "unlawful" deprivation of the "rights of citizenship," which, according to the Civil Rights Act, included the right "to full and equal benefit of all laws and proceedings for the security of person and property."[79] A warrant for the padrone's arrest was issued. Lewis was pleased, stating that "if the [padrone] could be held upon the charges made, it will open an avenue to destroy the entire traffic."[80] An arrest was made, but it turned out to be a possible case of mistaken identity. A well-publicized trial followed, including the long-awaited testimony of Joseph.[81] After listening to testimony on both sides, the US commissioner declared that "even though he had not the slightest doubt" that a "state of slavery existed" for the boy Joseph, "a case of mistaken identity had clearly been proven, and he would therefore honorably discharge the prisoner."[82] Joseph and several other Italian children who had been called as witnesses were placed under the temporary care of the Commissioners of Public Charities and Corrections.[83]

As public sentiment grew in favor of ending the padrone system, some onlookers argued for new legislation specific to the padrone trade. An Italian statesman living in New York, Celso Caesar Moreno, had become deeply involved in the effort to end the trade. In November 1873 Moreno decided an effective way to get new legislation passed would be enlisting the support of a famous abolitionist. Moreno set his sights on Charles Sumner, an abolitionist turned US senator, and wrote him a letter saying:

> DEAR SIR: You, the Moses of the late slaves in the Southern States, why do you not raise your powerful voice in behalf of oppressed and defenseless infantile humanity? Seven-thousand of Italian children of both sexes are in the principal cities of the United States kept by heartless padroni (slaveholders) in the most abject slavery, and subjected to the most cruel treatment, after having been kidnapped or torn away from their parents in the southern provinces of Italy, under some subterfuge. . . . I have done all in my power to bring before the public this infamous traffic in Italian children. . . . Now, respectfully, I request you, Mr. Sumner, to introduce a bill in the Senate this session, for the abolishment of this great wrong. . . . Mr. Sumner, these wrongs are not only an undeserved dishonor upon the proud Italian name, but are also a direct violation of the American laws, and an insult to this age of freedom and progress.[84]

Sumner responded that he would "be glad to do something for [the children]."[85] Sumner's bill, "An Act to protect persons against inveigling from abroad, kidnapping, forcible constraint, or involuntary service," would make any of the above a felony, subject to imprisonment and fines.[86] Popularly known as the "Padrone Act," the Senate passed the measure on June 23, 1874.[87] Other laws were passed the same year, including bills in both the New York and Pennsylvania state legislatures prohibiting child street performers less than sixteen years old.[88] By that year the Italian parliament had also passed legislation with the intent to suppress the padrone traffic in Italian children.[89] The Society for the Prevention of Cruelty to Children (SPCC), founded in 1875, dealt the final blow to the padrone trade in children in New York. Introducing "An Act to Prevent and Punish Wrongs to Children" in the New

Testing Ground of Freedom 41

York Senate in 1876, the SPCC assumed the lead in finding and arresting any padroni still operating in American cities.[90] By the late 1870s, most of the frenzy surrounding Italian padrone children had faded. A final federal trial, *Ancarola v. United States*, was widely publicized and ended in the conviction of a padrone, Antonio Giovanni Ancarola, under Senator Sumner's 1874 "Padrone Act." The *New York Times* could finally print its long-awaited headline "Padrone Convicted."[91] By the 1880s padroni continued to operate in the United States but shifted their focus to importing adult immigrants.[92]

In the 1860s and '70s, both former slave child apprenticeship and the padrone system emerged as testing grounds for assessing the legitimacy of capitalist authority over children in free society. In both cases, reformers relied on free labor justifications for their actions regarding children. Among reformers and in popular literature, free labor was the salvation awaiting bonded children in post-emancipation America. An 1872 novel by Horatio Alger, *Phil, the Fiddler; or, the Story of a Young Street Musician*, depicted the plight of padrone children in the city, drawing on journalistic articles and Children's Aid Society reports. The original frontispiece was a sad-faced boy with a fiddle in hand. Alger wrote in the preface that he wanted to "reveal to the American public the hardships and ill-treatment of these wandering musicians" in order to "excite an active sympathy in their behalf." Alger's hero, Filippo (or Phil), dramatically escapes from a cruel padrone to the neighboring city of Newark, where he begins a new life as a free child. Detailing the moment of Phil's emancipation is a chapter titled "Phil Finds a Capitalist." The capitalist encourages Phil to run away from his padrone and explains to him that his arrangement with the padrone is neither legal nor free. He explains the concept of saving and lends Phil money to buy a new fiddle so that he can begin earning money. After meeting the capitalist, Phil "was elated with the thought of his coming freedom, and for the first time since he landed in America the future looked bright to him."[93] The padrone was caricatured as a fraudulent slave master within capitalist society. Alger's novel argued that free labor was the salvation that awaited bonded children in America. However, the rise of factory child labor in the North belied Alger's simplistic rendering.

On Saturday, September 19, 1874, ten-year-old Margaret Healy arrived at daybreak to begin work at Granite Mill, a large, six-story cotton mill in Fall River, Massachusetts. Making her way to the fifth story, Margaret began work alongside the other youngest girls employed at the mill in the spooling and warping of cotton. Margaret's task as a warper, along with some thirty other girls, would have been tending to a rotary warping machine that wound warped yarn onto spools for use in thin or strand fabrics.[94] She likely had not yet finished her first spool by the time pandemonium broke out in the mill. Shortly before 7:00 A.M., Margaret was startled by cries of "fire" as smoke escaped into the warping room from the fourth story. On that floor a fire caused by friction in a mule-head had started on the north end and was spreading rapidly through oil-doused machinery and floorboards. Heavy smoke and flames obstructed the shoddily constructed fire escapes, of which there were two on both the north and south ends of the mill.

Margaret's options were few. The tower in the center of the mill that connected by stairway every story of the building was ablaze and thick with smoke. Some girls fashioned makeshift ropes out of cotton and attempted to climb down from windows. A similar movement of child workers was occurring from the fourth story. Many children clustered around open windows to breathe. Others leaped out of windows to the ground, some sixty feet below. Along with forty other child workers who perished, Margaret did not survive the fire. Eighty other workers, mostly children, suffered serious wounds and injuries.[95]

Dramatic fires such as this one dotted the American landscape in the 1870s—fires that injured and killed workers in mills, factories, and mines; fires that powered the refineries, steamboats, and locomotives of the age; fires that engulfed cities like Chicago in the Great Fire of 1871; and fires of protest set by labor strikers and convicts.[96] In an age that was accustomed to fires, the Granite Mill fire was especially tragic because the vast majority of the fatalities were children under fourteen, some as young as five. "Nothing could be more sad," wrote the editors of the *New York Times*, "than the story of the terrible calamity in Fall River yesterday."[97] Remarkably, at least forty persons, "most of them girls, many of them very young," were "either burned or suffocated, or killed in leaping to the ground."[98] The *Boston Daily Globe* remarked on the particularly tragic nature of the Fall River incident: "The picture of the agony and distress of the poor girls who saw themselves at the mercy of the flames that enveloped the great mill is almost too terrible to dwell upon."[99] While most public commentary focused on the necessity of improving safety regulations, some observers asked why there had been so many children in the mill. One Massachusetts resident wondered why "the fourth and fifth stories of a cotton mill [were] full of children." The "lesson of the terrible Fall River disaster," he wrote, was simple: "Take the children out of the mills."[100] An editorialist for the *Chicago Daily Tribune* wrote, "This was not only a holocaust of working people . . . but mostly little children with whom labor was a necessity, who were compelled to wear out their young lives in toil . . . little children who heard no sounds but the whir and hum of machinery in the great mill, who saw no sights but the loom or the spool at which they worked." But this editorialist focused on the importance of making mills and factories where children were present "as secure as possible." If these "little companions" were to be "doomed to ceaseless and wearing toil," then the "pockets they enrich [should] see to it that their lives are protected."[101]

Margaret Healy was one of an estimated 750,000 children under the age of fifteen employed in factory labor in the United States in the 1870s.[102] Since the late eighteenth century, the employment of children in mills, factories, tenement houses, and the street trades had risen. By the outbreak of the Granite Mill fire, there were few legal restrictions on child labor not only in Massachusetts but throughout the rest of the country as well.[103] In the early 1870s, Charles Brace and the Children's Aid Society opened night schools to teach young children who worked long hours in factories or mills during the day. Brace found it admirable that these children were eager "to pick up a morsel of knowledge," but he worried they might be suffering from "overwork." Many of these children were working more than sixty hours per week. These "children of tender years," Brace wrote, were likely to grow up "weak in body and ignorant or untrained in mind."[104] For Brace, "children of tender years" meant under the age of ten. For children over the age of ten, factory labor was beneficial for them as long as they attended night school. In an act drawn up by the Children's Aid Society, children would be allowed to work only nine months out of the year, with three months reserved for formal schooling, and children's working hours would be restricted to no more than sixty per week.[105] The organization also supported a "gang system" plan in which gangs of children would switch out—one gang in the factory while another was in school and vice versa.[106] In New England certain states had in place antebellum laws that stated no child could be required to work in a factory or mill more than ten hours per day, but these provisions were regularly bypassed by employers who claimed that the long hours were voluntary and not required.[107]

In a nation that had recently eradicated slavery, there was enhanced anxiety over making clear the distinction between free and unfree labor.[108] Reflecting this anxiety was the urgency with which Americans reacted to labor arrangements for children that resembled slavery, such as former slave child apprenticeship and the Italian padrone system. In the 1870s the padrone system became a symbol of Northern slavery that needed rooting out. In some ways, factory child labor resembled the padrone system. Long working hours, greed, ignorance, deception, and cruelty were features of factory child labor that were surfacing at the same time the public worried about the padrone system. When factory child labor first emerged as a topic of public interest in the 1870s, complaints were similar to those of the padrone system.

Factory children were working excessively long hours, and capitalists and parents were willing to exploit the labor of defenseless youth. Many factory children were uneducated, as their work hours allowed no time for formal education, and employers often lied about how many child workers they had or defended their use of child labor as within the bounds of free society. Corporal punishment of factory children was not unheard of. The Massachusetts Bureau of Labor Statistics issued reports of corporal punishment of children in the factories and mills of New England. One bureau agent wrote, "A witness described to us an instrument for whipping children at a factory in Rhode Island, consisting of a leather strap, eighteen inches long, with tacks driven through the striking end."[109] To keep factory children working efficiently, some employers hired overseers to "corporally chastise" children when necessary.[110] Even more common than corporal punishment was the physical danger that faced children like Margaret Healy who were working in unsafe mills and factories, which was depicted as a form of cruelty.

Despite these similarities, most Americans did not condemn factory child labor as they had the padrone system. It was regrettable that thousands of factory children were working long hours, lacking education, and physically endangered, but factory children were not enslaved in the same way padrone children were. Their condition was not born from an attempt to reintroduce slavery on American soil. In the aftermath of the Granite Mill fire, it is not difficult to imagine a public backlash against the mill owner, who depended upon hundreds of children to keep his cotton mill running seven days a week. But when trying to make sense of the kind of oppression faced by factory children, most public commentators and reformers made a distinction between the capitalist and the padrone. The figure of the "greedy parent" often helped them make this distinction.

A New York reporter wrote, "There are trades in this city where from eight to ten thousand children under the age of thirteen years are employed ten hours a day; that infants as young as four and eight years are kept steadily at work by the greed of their parents."[111] A writer for *Scribner's Monthly* lamented, "So many children are born into the world without competent protectors." Instead, parents sent their children out to "begin the terrible struggle of life for food, shelter, and clothing" when the children were "scarcely out of their cradles."[112] Writing in support of a half-time education requirement for all school-age children, a *New York Times* editorialist made an explicit connection between cruel Italian padroni and the supposedly selfish parents of factory children. Child workers with "selfish parents" were just "like the little Italians . . . the apprentices of cruel masters."[113] Though the circumstance of factory children was being described in terms of slavery, the capitalist was not the slave master. Reinforcing this ideological distinction, a reporter wrote, "In the tenderest years, they are sent forth to workshops and factories, to earn their little quota each week for their parents."[114] Like the padrone who waited for his little street musicians to return each day with their quotas for him to pocket, greedy parents were imagined to be in the background, waiting for their children to return home from the factory with their wages.

Though parents were often the object of public censure, the capitalist did turn up in some condemnations of factory child labor. But the capitalist was often shielded from moral responsibility. For instance, a *New York Times* journalist pointed out that just as the majority of parents "show[ed] no conscience" with regard to the "overwork" of their children in factories, "capitalists and employers" did not "show much more conscience in regard to the kind of labor they accept." But there was a notable difference between the feeble moral consciences of parents versus capitalists. Unlike parents, capitalists "must execute their orders; they have their capital and machinery prepared; they offer work, which is bread to the laboring people, and they must take the cheapest labor which presents itself." More a disinterested player following the rules of the market than a moral actor, the capitalist could "not be expected to be more considerate of the little ones than are the parents." It was merely a rule of the market that "if one manufacturer refused to employ children in his work, another would use them, would produce more cheaply, and soon undersell his competitors."[115] In this world the capitalist could not be blamed for exploiting child labor. The Children's Aid Society echoed this premise in their annual report of 1871 when they declared that factory children needed to be protected from "the greed of their parents" and from "the indifference of employers."[116] Brace wrote, "The parent or relative wants [the child worker's] wages, and insists on his laboring in a factory when he ought to be in an infant-school." But less censoriously, he described the capitalist as being "in the habit of getting labor where he can find it."[117] Capitalists shielded themselves using similar logic. In an interview with *Scribner's Monthly*, a tobacco manufacturer who depended on child workers defended his use of their labor on the grounds that another capitalist would hire them if he did not: "The children will go elsewhere and get work; their parents are in want and need their labor, and so it seems impossible to avoid hiring them."[118]

Some observers began grappling with the limits of capitalist authority over children. In some corners, factory child labor was described as a type of oppression, but there were different ways of understanding this oppression. One was through an emphasis on the overworked child's body. Brace worried that factory children's bodies might be "stunted in growth" and "enfeebled in health" due to overwork.[119] A journalist commented that an overworked factory child was likely to "carry in his body the seeds of weakness and disease."[120] Long hours that an adult laborer could handle were more likely to physically debilitate a child, some observers noted.[121] Equally salient were concerns about the mind of the child laborer. Overworked factory children were feared to be "ignorant or untrained in mind."[122] The demand for compulsory education for elementary age children intensified in this period. Slave emancipation, foreign immigration, and native poverty had led to racially charged fears among the reform-minded elite that American democracy would suffer without some form of compulsory education, especially for children.[123] "Owing to foreign immigration and to unequal distribution of wealth, large numbers of people have grown up without the rudiments even of common-school education," one commentator warned.[124] In 1871 the National Commissioners of Education reported that the number of minors between the ages of ten and twenty-one in New York City that could be classified as "illiterate" was 42,405.[125] For that year the commission produced statistics on illiteracy in every state of the Union. These figures included both children and adults, native-born and immigrant.[126] The Children's Aid Society had been concerned about illiteracy among poor and working children since the 1850s, citing their belief that it was linked to crime. In the city prisons, Brace pointed out, more than one-third of the prisoners were functionally illiterate.[127] The organization began agitating in 1871 for half-time schools for street children, focusing particularly on Italian padrone children but also drawing attention to factory children in their efforts to secure a minimum amount of education for overworked children.[128]

In 1871 Brace asked Charles E. Whitehead, who was the legal counsel for the Children's Aid Society, to draft a bill requiring that New York's factory children receive at least some education throughout the year.[129] Whitehead's bill, "An Act for the Protection of Factory Children," would have eliminated children under the age of ten from industrial labor, required factory children to attend school three months out of the year, prove that they could "read intelligibly" before accepting employment, and work no more than sixty hours per week.[130] The bill contained numerous loopholes that should have comforted New York's manufacturers. If a family's dependence on a child's earnings was shown to be necessary for survival (based on the judgment of a "Poor Commissioner"), the bill's provisions would be null and void. The education requirements were vague, and determining a child's age was often impossible. Despite these loopholes, the manufacturing interest in the New York state legislature strongly resisted the measure. Unlike the legislature's swift passage of legislation to break up the padrone system, the "Act for the

Protection of Factory Children" was defeated by the same legislature four consecutive times.[131] The defiance of state legislators, many of whom were manufacturers employing children, frustrated the bill's supporters. "Our efforts to obtain the passage by the legislature of a 'Bill to Protect Factory Children' have failed now during two years," the Children's Aid Society reported. The bill had been "uniformly defeated," they believed, "through the selfish maneuvers" of a few legislators who "supposed their interests to be endangered by the law."[132] The *New York Times* ran a series of articles lamenting the "manufacturing interest" in the state legislature: "We regret to see that one or two Senators . . . have expressed themselves in opposition to one of the most humane and useful bills which have ever been before the legislature." The bill had been "framed carefully," they wrote, "not to hamper or annoy manufacturers."[133] But several key legislators still could not bring themselves to support Whitehead's bill.

In 1874, the peak year of legislation condemning the Italian padrone system, the bill was again strongly resisted. Days before the bill would be up for a vote in the House, Brace and Whitehead made a final plea. Addressing the Committees on Manufacture in the House and Senate, they offered rebuttals to the various objections of the legislators.[134] A House member, George West of Saratoga, objected to the ten-hour-per-day restriction on the grounds that "he had two boys who labored twelve hours, and for whom men would have to be substituted if the law passed."[135] Senator John W. Lowery, a manufacturer and chair of the Senate committee, objected that "the public had no right to interfere with his labor" and that "he had picked up his own schooling as he could, at night."[136] Lowery, the ring leader in opposition to the child labor law, voted the same year in favor of a bill to prohibit child street performance, which targeted the Italian padroni. As a state senator, Lowery exercised his power to condemn the Italian padrone system while sanctioning his own right to employ children as factory workers. In arguments on the Senate floor, Brace tried to convince Lowery that it was only his access to a night school that had "enabled him to be where he is now." But Lowery would not budge.[137] The strong resistance of the child-employing capitalists to such meager protection for factory children was not helpful for their public image. An editorial lambasted the handful of "men with votes or money or influence" who were defeating the interests of "ten thousand of these unfortunate children . . . bound to labor." Reflecting a growing exasperation among social reformers and public supporters who initially believed the bill would pass, public discourse about the "manufacturing interest" in the state legislature became harsher in tone: "It is not right for any employer of labor to keep little children in a close[d] factory all day long, without opportunity for relaxation or education. It is wrong to the child's body and mind. It is a species of slavery."[138] Whereas the "greedy parent" had previously shielded the capitalist from public censure, the defiant resistance of New York capitalist legislators to a law providing only meager protection to factory children opened them up to harsher scrutiny. The *New York Times* thought it ironic that both Lowery and West had been "poor factory boys themselves, who, by their industry and ability, had raised themselves to their present positions of wealth and honor."[139] It seemed uncharitable, even cruel, that they would not use their high positions to ensure that thousands of other New York factory children had the same opportunities.

To garner the votes of the "manufacturing interest," the Senate gutted the bill. According to an Albany reporter, the Senate removed "the really vital portions of the bill for the protection of factory children."[140] What remained was the exclusion of children under the age of ten and a restriction that no child under the age of fourteen (rather than sixteen) could work more than sixty-six hours (rather than sixty) per week. But the provisions of the bill that had called for half-time compulsory education were omitted.[141] Various safety regulations that called for a clean work environment and reduction of hazards were struck from the final bill as well.[142] "This is not the law which the community called for," the *New York Times* declared.[143] For New York's factory children, it was a pyrrhic victory. But the unexpected difficulties that reformers encountered when trying to achieve such meager reform foreshadowed a subtle shift in the debate. The protracted battle in the legislature had belied the notion of a blameless class of indifferent manufacturers playing by the rules of the market. These capitalists were willing to block any legislation that might interfere, however slightly, with the advantages they were accruing from their unfettered employment of children. Still, the New York capitalist was not the equivalent of a slave master, and the free labor market was not anathema to children. New England's manufacturers had argued that capitalists could be "enlightened" and that the excesses of capitalism could be mitigated to accommodate children. New England capitalists were exalted in the New York press for having "opened night schools for their young operatives." In contrast, New York's manufacturers, due to their display of defiance in the state legislature, were described as having a "selfish and unenlightened character."[144]

In the age of emancipation, the threat posed to factory children was not necessarily capitalists or the free labor market. With certain restrictions on the number of hours they worked, provisions for minimal education, and safety regulations, factory labor was a form of free labor that could benefit children. But without these remedies, the capitalist who employed child labor might be harming children. As Charles Brace pointed out to the state legislators who had been "factory boys" as children, social mobility was possible for factory children if they were given an opportunity for formal education. In this regard, compulsory half-time education was a surrogate for the educative function normally present in socially mobile labor. But the absence of an educative function was not the only aspect of factory child labor that became suspect. The damaging effects of excessively long work hours on a factory child's mind and body could be, and occasionally were, likened to slavery. The hazardous conditions that placed factory children in physical danger were seen by many as a form of cruelty. Capitalists' resistance to even meager protections for factory children called into question their authority over children in the free labor market. At the same time that reformers were able to clearly define the padrone system as a form of child slavery, their response to factory child labor was more ambiguous. In the age of emancipation, the stability of meaning implied by the crusade to end the padrone system was belied by the ambiguities inherent in factory child labor.

3 Seeds of a New Sectionalism
Southern Origins of Child Labor Reform

Masters, give unto your servants
that which is just and equal;
knowing that ye also have
a Master in heaven.
—Colossians 4:1

In 1898 Edgar Gardner Murphy, a pastor in Montgomery, Alabama, toured the cotton mills of Montgomery's West End. Shocked by the number of poor white children working at the mills, Murphy investigated the status of child labor laws in his state. He learned that Alabama's state legislature had repealed its only child labor protections a few years earlier under the influence of cotton mill manufacturers, clearing the way for employment of children in the Alabama textile industry. In 1887 Alabama had been the first Southern state to enact a child labor law, but it was not a very strict measure, and the effort to pass it had not received much attention.[1] The legislature repealed the law just as unceremoniously in 1894.[2] With new sanction from the state, Alabama cotton mill owners dramatically increased their employment of children in the coming years. From 1890 to 1900 there was a 386 percent increase in the employment of children under sixteen in Alabama mills. By 1900 one-fourth of the workers employed in the Alabama textile industry were under the age of sixteen.[3] Similar conditions existed in Georgia and the Carolinas. Though the US census typically did not include a breakdown of child workers' ages, one historian has estimated that there were at least thirty-two thousand children under the age of fourteen and ten thousand to twelve thousand under twelve in Southern mills by the turn of the century.[4]

The cotton mill industry took hold in the Piedmont section of the South in the 1880s and 1890s, with North Carolina, South Carolina, Georgia, and

Alabama leading the way in terms of both textile production and industrial employment of poor white children.[5] No longer just a Northern issue, factory child labor had arrived in the South. In the age of emancipation, Northern factory child labor complicated the distinction between free and unfree labor. Though factory labor could teach children industrious values, excessive factory labor might harm them. Still, the excesses of capitalism could be mitigated to accommodate children's needs, and capitalist employers could be enlightened. But in the late nineteenth and early twentieth centuries, the labor of poor white children in Southern textile mills sounded the death knell of child labor reformers' free labor ideology. In the age of American imperialism and racial segregation in the South, fears of white racial degeneracy became the basis for saving the South's white children, boys and girls. By 1900 the image of pale, shrunken-faced, debilitated poor white boys and girls in Southern textile mills was sensationalized in the North as "white child slavery" and the issue became a national obsession.

As the leading spokesperson for Southern child labor reform, Edgar Gardner Murphy used the child labor problem to articulate a vision of Southern market society that emphasized local control, racial order, and regional identity. Murphy's vision was shaped by his belief that Reconstruction had been a disastrous experiment in Northern interference that should not be repeated.[6] The so-called best men of the South, the former planter class, should be restored to power in a New South social order built on white racial unity.[7] For Murphy, Southern mill child labor was threatening to this racial order because poor white boys and girls were physically debilitated and uneducated. Poor whites could be raised up to their rightful position in the New South's racial order, Murphy thought, by ensuring they were in schools, not factories. Though Murphy welcomed the sympathy and cooperation of Northern reformers in this effort, he advocated for local control of the issue. Southern market society, he believed, should enforce a racial order that was regionally distinctive, locally controlled, and absent of Northern interference. Despite his emphasis on preventing Northern interference, Murphy was a strong ally for Northern child labor reformers. He helped them grow their movement by launching the child labor issue onto the national stage. Murphy's vision of Anglo-Saxon superiority as the basis of a strong civilization resonated with a broader national discourse about white racial unity in an age of American imperialism when the United States fought the Spanish-American War.[8] But ultimately, Northern reformers did not embrace Murphy's local control agenda, opting instead for federal regulation of child labor. This decision drew regional battle lines around child labor reform, echoing the sectionalist conflict over slavery. It also created an opening for Southern capitalists to gain public support for anti–child labor reform within a familiar paradigm of Northern coercion.

At the turn of the century, debates about Southern white child labor among Northern and Southern reformers facilitated a redefinition of factory child labor as "unfree," eclipsing reformers' earlier emphasis on free labor ideology. Southern white child factory workers were unfree because their labor physically and mentally debilitated them. For both Northern and Southern reformers, this reality posed a threat at a time when white racial supremacy was taking on new significance in the United States.[9] This way of framing the Southern white child labor problem resonated with national political leaders in the age of American imperialism and helped unite Northern and Southern reformers in a national movement to abolish factory child labor, especially in the South. However, debates about Southern white child labor also planted the seeds for the rise of new sectionalist conflict over child labor reform. Because of the potential for white racial degeneracy, Northern reformers latched onto the Southern white child labor problem as the most egregious form of "child slavery" in the nation. Presenting themselves as the nation's new abolitionists, they called Southern white child labor the South's "new slavery," judging it even worse than slavery in the Old South. When Northern reformers embraced expanded federal authority in the market, it caused a split with Southern reformers who insisted on local control. It also fueled the flames of Southern opposition to child labor reform, now recast in familiar terms of sectionalist conflict. Ironically, the redefinition of unfree labor in racialized terms initially united Northern and Southern reformers while eventually dividing them into sectionalist camps. Murphy's plan to garner national support for ending Southern white child labor ultimately backfired, as the very people whose support he needed to be successful, especially Southern manufacturers, resented Northern reformers' sensationalizing of Southern white child labor, especially their embrace of expanded federal authority. Southern manufacturers were then able to gain widespread support for anti–child labor reform in the South.

The development of a significant textile industry in the South did not get under way until after the end of Reconstruction.[10] As cotton prices fell, yeoman families in the rural South experienced economic decline and, increasingly, were dispossessed of their land. Motivated by an expanding white labor force of dispossessed yeoman families and an adequate water supply in the Piedmont, textile manufacturers spread over this region.[11] While mills sprouted up around rivers and streams in the upcountry, yeoman families were both actively recruited and drawn toward the new opportunity for wage labor. The Southern cotton mill industry grew steadily, and it seemed

54   CHAPTER 3

to portend the arrival of a "New South" that would be industrialized and modernized. While the iron and steel industries in the South were faltering, the textile industry flourished. In part, this was because the textile industry required less capital than did the metals industry and could be built anywhere there was water to provide power to run the machinery. But the industry's prosperity also relied on a labor force that included workers of all ages who could be paid low wages. Unlike the metals industry, the textile industry did not require a labor force with much physical strength or previous work experience. Entire families were often offered employment at the same mill, which encouraged them to relocate their households to burgeoning mill villages.[12]

An unusually high percentage of the labor force in Southern textile mills consisted of child laborers under the age of fifteen. According to the US Census, in 1880 there were 12,913 total cotton mill operatives in the states of Alabama, Georgia, South Carolina, and North Carolina, 3,170 of whom were under the age of fifteen. In 1880 around 25 percent of all mill operatives in the South were classified as children. In that same year, New England states still employed more children in industry overall than did Southern states, but the percentage was lower, at 14 percent of the total.[13] In both regions mill children as young as six or seven were engaged in "doffing," spinning, and other forms of casual labor.[14] To compensate for their shorter height, child doffers would stand on top of electric looms to reach the top shelf where spindles were located. The first contact children usually had with mill labor was while accompanying older siblings or parents as they worked. Typically, very young children would begin an informal training whereby they would "help" their relatives, but this regular assistance would soon seamlessly transition into full-time labor, since most children knew as much as their parents about the ins and outs of the mill. A mill child's tenure sometimes began as an infant when the child's mother would bring her baby to the mill, where it would remain all day with her while she worked. Many mill children enjoyed working and described it as "the only time we got [together] with other children."[15] Other former mill workers recalled that mill children were proud of their ability to do their jobs well, despite their young age.[16]

Child labor in Southern textile mills emerged after the end of Reconstruction when self-proclaimed "Redeemer" Democrats took control of the South after the Compromise of 1877.[17] Southern Redeemers shared "a commitment to dismantling the Reconstruction state, reducing the political power of African Americans, and reshaping the South's legal system in the interests of labor control and racial subordination."[18] Redeemer constitutions slashed public spending and aid, reducing state governments to mere skeletons of what they

Figure 3.1. Helpers in a Georgia cotton mill. Photograph by Lewis Hine, January 19, 1909. The National Child Labor Committee Collection, Library of Congress Prints and Photographs Division, Washington, DC. Courtesy of the Library of Congress, LC-DIG-nclc-01581.

had been during Reconstruction. Gains made in public education during Reconstruction were rolled back, state-level attempts to weaken the significance of the Fourteenth and Fifteenth amendments were commonplace, and election fraud in black majority counties was routine.[19] In addition, new credit and property laws were passed that tilted the scales in favor of planters, and separate schooling requirements for black and white children were written into Southern constitutions. It was in this post-Reconstruction context that the Southern textile industry emerged and grew. The new Southern ruling coalition included not only planters but also merchants and industrialists who advocated a New South creed of modernization, industry, and progress.[20] In 1879 a New Orleans editor pronounced that that year marked a Southern "commercial revolution unparalleled in the annals of American progress."[21] But industrial progress in the post-Reconstruction South was not a neutral development. The policies of Redeemer governments ensured a Southern economy in which the majority of Southerners—black and white—would remain impoverished while economic investors in the region sought the South's cheap labor. Other than the Upper South, where mines, iron furnaces, and tobacco factories employed black workers, most of the South's industrial jobs in the late nineteenth century were reserved for white workers.[22] In the Southeastern cotton states, the industrial workforce in the textile mills was entirely white because of an agreement between planters and manufacturers that industrial growth should not encumber planter control of rural black labor. In many areas of the Deep South, planters were able to block industrial development altogether.[23]

Some Southern white elites became concerned about the textile industry's reliance upon poor white children's labor. The most outspoken was Murphy, whose journey to child labor reform began years earlier when he was a student of theology and Southern history.[24] Educated at the University of the South–Sewanee, Murphy was taught by former Confederate generals and former slaveholders who instilled in him a belief in the virtues of a paternalistic white supremacy in which the prosperity of the New South must rest on the leadership of its best men.[25] At Sewanee, Murphy's mentor was William Porcher Dubose, a former Confederate soldier from a wealthy South Carolinian slaveholding family. Murphy's mentors taught him that as a result of Reconstruction, Southern civilization had broken down and the New South was headed toward instability and chaos. In this view, formerly enslaved people had been raised up into political leadership, poor whites were descending into violence, and former owners had been stripped of power. For Murphy, the specter of poor white children in Southern factories became a symbol of what was wrong with the New South. Poor whites were becoming violent, Murphy feared, because they were uneducated and ignorant about racial paternalism. Their ignorance made them susceptible to unthinking "race hatreds."[26] For instance, Murphy believed the violent lynch mobs of the era were due to the ignorance of poor whites.[27] The lynching of Henry Smith, an African American, in Paris, Texas, in 1893 made a particularly strong impression on Murphy. This "barbarous" affair in which men, women, and children had created "an orgy of torture" and "a festival of agony" as they publicly burned Smith alive for the alleged murder of a police officer's daughter proved that the social order of the New South's civilization was under threat.[28] To restore racial order, the South must focus on the racial advancement of its poor white people. To this end, Murphy resigned from ministry and in 1901 founded the Alabama Child Labor Committee, the first such committee in the nation.[29]

Murphy's understanding of civilization reflected, among other things, the social Darwinism that was influential at the turn of the century. According to social Darwinist thinking, "civilization" was an advanced stage of human evolution that was explicitly racial.[30] Along the spectrum of human evolution, the races were assumed to evolve from "simple savagery," to "violent barbarism," to "advanced and valuable civilization."[31] Popularized under-standings of social Darwinism reflected the belief that only white races had advanced to the "civilized" stage, whereas nonwhite races could also evolve, but their potential would be limited, since they supposedly had not inherited the most evolved traits from their ancestors.[32] In Murphy's framework, social Darwinism was combined with Southern mythology. His education had persuaded him that the most "civilized" men of the South were the heirs of the former slaveholding class. This Southern white aristocracy with roots in the Old South was "the true basis of an enduring peace between the sections and between the races."[33] In the Old South, Murphy reasoned, the institution of slavery was the basis of advanced Southern civilization. The slaveholding class had been able to "stand alone" in leadership while "non-participants," which included slaves and non-slaveholding whites, enabled and reinforced the supposed benevolent power of the white Southern aristocracy. When emancipation occurred, the basis of an entire civilization crumbled. Be-cause the old aristocracy "could no longer stand alone," it would now need cooperation from "the two great classes of non-participants."[34] However, the policies of Reconstruction had destroyed the old bonds between masters and slaves, leading "the negro to distrust the South" and "the South [to] distrust the negro."[35] The result of this alienation of the races was "to draw together the separate classes of *the stronger race* and to fuse them—men of ignorance with men of culture—into a racial unity far more powerful, far more effective, than the South had known before."[36]

Murphy was an active Southern reformer, joining the Ministers' Union, the Southern Society (a group of twenty-four prominent white Montgom-ery men devoted to writing and speaking on the "race problem"), and the Southern Education Board (SEB) before founding the Alabama Child Labor Committee.[37] Like Murphy's child labor group, these other groups also had a "whites first" mentality that guided their various efforts to improve Southern society. As the rich literature on Southern Progressivism has shown, the South developed its own brand of Progressive reform in the late nineteenth and early twentieth century.[38] Attentive to achieving progress and uplift but also maintaining hierarchies of race and culture, Southern Progressivism was characterized by paradox.[39] Murphy's interest in Alabama's child labor situation merged with his previous work on the SEB, which had reinforced his view that white illiteracy was at the core of disorder in the New South. Education was the key to developing the God-given potential of the South's poor white people, the SEB maintained. Murphy and other SEB members did not see their prioritizing of white education as neglecting black education. Rather, they justified their work on the grounds that racial discord hindered the advancement of the black race and could be ended only by attacking its supposed foundation: the ignorance of poor whites. If poor whites were educated, the race problem would presumably solve itself.[40] Murphy understood Alabama's child labor problem in similar terms. While Northern reformers after the Civil War had begun to point out the deleterious effects of industrial labor on the bodies and minds of children in Northern factories, this aspect of child labor—its physically and mentally degenerative effects—assumed a new and distinctive meaning at the turn of the century.

As a proponent of the New South creed (a post–Civil War ideology that linked white supremacy to the New South's economic progress while embracing a mythology about the Old South's innocence and beauty[41]), Murphy was very much in favor of the textile industry and its promise of modernization and economic progress. However, the industry's reliance on poor white children's labor threatened white supremacy. Although the textile industry was bringing economic development to the South, its success rested on the backs of poor white children, debilitating and preventing them from developing their supposed God-given potential as members of a superior Anglo-Saxon race. Thus, even as one facet of the New South creed was fulfilled, another was undermined. While Southern mill owners tended to emphasize the former, reformers like Murphy emphasized the latter.[42] Regardless of the economic benefits, the South should not build its progress "over the heart-springs of the childhood of the South." Protecting poor white children in cotton mills became a crusade for Murphy that represented for him "one of the holiest interests of civilization." "The sacrifice of the childhood of our poorer people, the exhaustion of their best skill and of their fullest vigor and intelligence" could result in "the degradation and extinction of the race." It was in the interest of not only the South but the whole country as well that the South's mill children be granted "emancipation," or "the freeing of [their] capacity," as Murphy put it.[43]

Labor unions in the North took an early interest in Southern child labor. The same year Murphy toured the mills of Montgomery's West End, Samuel Gompers of the American Federation of Labor (AFL) offered one of the first public reactions to Alabama's 1894 repeal of its child labor law. Gompers published an editorial in the *American Federationist* referring to the repeal as the "Crime of '94–5."[44] He heard about the repeal while trying to organize garment workers in the South.[45] Like most labor union activists, Gompers was opposed to child labor because it "depressed wages" and "threatened to enslave working men."[46] As labor unions in America grew throughout the 1880s and '90s, organizations such as the AFL began including condemnations against child labor in their political platforms.[47] But the AFL's specific interest in the child labor of Southern textile mills reflected the impact it was having on the wages of unionized textile workers in New England.[48] Textile workers in New Bedford, Massachusetts, for instance, went on strike in the 1890s because of a 10 percent reduction in their wages. The workers on strike blamed "cheap southern labor."[49] When Gompers heard about Alabama's repeal of the child labor law, he saw it as an opportunity to expose the mill industry's exploitation of cheap child labor. Gompers hired a woman named Irene Ashby to travel to Alabama on behalf of the AFL to investigate the extent of child labor in the mills.[50] Until that point there had been no systematic investigations of child labor in the South.

Ashby was an Englishwoman who had been educated at Westfield College in London, where she had been a labor organizer and social reformer. She moved comfortably in Southern white elite society, befriending the society page editor of the *Montgomery Advertiser*, the leaders of white middle-class volunteer societies in the state, several local Alabama clergymen, and Murphy himself. Ashby's task in 1900 was to investigate twenty-four of the forty-three cotton mills in Alabama to obtain information about the extent of child labor, the ages of the children, and firsthand narrative accounts in order to publicly shame the mill industry. The plan was for her to use this information to push for new child labor legislation in the state. Ashby's reports estimated that there were twelve hundred children under the age of twelve in the mills and predicted that the number would continue to rise.[51] During that year, Ashby spoke to volunteer societies, churches, and other groups across the state, urging support for the passage of legislation then pending at the state level. Early in this process she sought out Murphy for help.[52] Together, they secured signatures on petitions favoring new child labor laws and oversaw the crafting of the bill that would go before the state legislature in 1901. Known as the Reilly-Morrow Bill, it was the first of its kind to receive any public attention in the South.[53] This bill provided an age limit of twelve for child workers with an exception for the children of widows or disabled fathers. For children over the age of twelve but under sixteen, a sixty-hour workweek would be enforced, with a limit of eleven hours in one day. Employers would also be required to prove that mill children could read and write. Measures for the appointment of a state factory inspector along with hefty fines and up to three months' imprisonment for violations were included in the bill.[54]

A hearing for the Alabama Child Labor Bill was set for February 5, 1901. The first speaker before the congressional committees to which the bill had been referred was Murphy. "I am here not to arraign men or to abuse individuals," he began, "but to arraign a system and to advocate a public measure."[55] The system of child labor was, Murphy argued, a "policy of compulsory

60   CHAPTER 3

ignorance." But Murphy's main argument to the committees hinged on the racial order of the New South:

> We have in the South one of the greatest race problems of history. I feel that the welfare of the negroes themselves is dependent on the leadership and control of our white population; but how are we to maintain that wise and conservative and just control if the white children of this State are kept by the operation of our factory conditions, from the schooling which our negroes are eagerly seeking? I do not oppose the educational facilities of the black man, but this is not a time to embarrass the educational opportunities of the white man.[56]

Murphy suggested that a potential consequence of white child labor in Alabama's mills was not just racial degeneracy but a reversal of the racial order. At a moment when the South was working out one of the "greatest race problems of history," it could not afford the type of social risk that white child labor posed. Murphy closed by arguing that the legislators must "act now" while "we can still bear the hardships of the change." Regardless of the outcome, local agitation on this issue would not cease, because "the Christian heart of the state [was] now aroused."[57]

Southern cotton manufacturers were put on the defensive. They appealed to sectionalist sentiment in their arguments justifying the employment of poor white boys and girls in Southern mills. Led by an Alabama City mill owner, a railroad attorney, and a corporation clergyman, the bill's opponents accused Ashby of being a "foreigner" who was being paid by Northern mill interests to "make trouble in the South" in order to "reduce [the South's] competitive power."[58] They accused Murphy of being influenced by Northern capitalists who were funding his efforts.[59] The people of Alabama—not foreigners or Northern capitalists—should decide what was appropriate for Alabama's children, they argued. A majority of Alabama legislators were convinced that the measure was not indigenous but was a scheme of Northern capitalists to reduce the South's competitive advantage. The argument was convincing at a time when many white Southerners put their hope in cotton manufacturing as the route to restoring prosperity in the South.[60] While the vote was split, both committees voted against recommending the bill for debate (House committee, 9–4; Senate committee, 5–2). The bill's proponents requested that it be presented before the legislature without recommendation, but the committees denied this request as well. The Alabama Child Labor Bill had been defeated.[61]

This brief foray into the state-level politics of child labor reform convinced Murphy that much more effort and organization would be necessary to achieve child labor legislation in Alabama. Too few Alabamans or

Southerners understood what was at stake in the region's child labor problem, he believed. Shortly after the Alabama legislative battle of 1901, Murphy founded the Alabama Child Labor Committee (ACLC), the first organization of its kind in the nation. Recruiting members from the other organizations in which he was involved, Murphy enlisted additional prominent Southern white men who understood the problem of child labor as he did within a broader context of issues facing Southern social order, progress, and civilization.[62] But by the time Murphy founded the ACLC, there had been a subtle shift in his discourse about the South's social problems. Since moving to Montgomery in 1898, Murphy had developed a more expansive, bolder rhetoric that emphasized the responsibility of the entire nation in solving the South's social problems. While never abandoning the principle that the South should lead the way in solving its own problems, he complicated this idea at the turn of the century to include what was at stake in terms of American civilization as a whole, not just Southern civilization. Though the South's best men still bore the primary responsibility for leading the region, they needed the support of the nation to be successful. Moreover, there was a national stake in determining the future of the South, since the whole of American civilization was hanging in the balance.

Just months before Murphy moved to Montgomery, Alabama, the United States entered into war with Spain in April 1898. Initially the war was a military effort to help Cubans gain independence from Spain, but it soon evolved into a wider conflict fought in both the Caribbean and Pacific.[63] After a series of unequivocal victories within a ten-week period, it seemed that the United States was likely to strip Spain of its remaining empire. Near the end of 1898, the Treaty of Paris signaled the arrival of an American empire in Puerto Rico, Guam, and the Philippines and gave Americans temporary control of Cuba. But the historical consequences of the Spanish-American War reached far beyond military victory and colonial expansion. The conflict also helped to effect a patriotic reconciliation of North and South, which provided a new context for Murphy and his crusade against Southern white child labor. As historian David Blight has pointed out, "the furthering of sectional reconciliation" was one of President McKinley's explicit wartime aims.[64] But because the Spanish-American War also encouraged a national spirit of imperialism, the wartime reconciliation of North and South occurred on explicitly racialized grounds. As one historian has put it, the war "seemed to confirm the natural unity of southern and northern white people."[65] A major premise on which colonial expansion was based was late nineteenth-century racial assumptions similar to those held by Murphy about the benevolence of a superior Anglo-Saxon race to bring competent leadership, civilized values, and Christianity to "uncivilized" races.[66] In effect, the "race problem" that Murphy wrote and talked about so frequently became internationalized as a result of the Spanish-American War. White Southerners and Northerners could unite in their supposed natural dominance and spread "civilization" benevolently under the supposition that nonwhite races around the world were "savage" and "uncivilized."[67]

The consequences of linking white racial supremacy with the nation's imperial ambitions during the height of racial lynching, Jim Crow, and white child labor in the South were profound. As the United States waged a war that intensified rhetoric about the uncivilized nature of darker races, Southern "best men" arguments like Murphy's took on a heightened resonance with international events. The irony that approximately ten-thousand African Americans enlisted and fought in the Spanish-American War was not lost on black contemporaries.[68] Hundreds of black lynchings in the South continued to go unpunished even as Southern white men were hailed as the new civilizers of the world. In 1899 the Colored National League of Boston sent a letter to President William McKinley declaring that Southern lynchers had "out barbarized barbarism" and implored the president to give the "colored people of the United States . . . equal consideration with the Cuban people."[69] Like many Americans, Murphy followed the conflict closely and commented on its significance while it was happening. In June 1898 he described the war as "the trial of the nation, a trial that will bring its strain not only to our military . . . but to the moral resources of the country."[70] Murphy supported the war and a benevolent imperial expansion but cautioned against the high sentiments of wartime degenerating into savage-like "lust for mastery" and "passions of spoil." It was the duty of American clergymen, Murphy wrote, to "dignify the military passions of the moment" by seizing upon the crisis from their pulpits to "develop the national character."[71] This new "national character" underscored white racial unity and superiority as a dominant principle of the United States as a nation and burgeoning imperial power in the world. In the post-Reconstruction South, Murphy had suggested that white racial unity should be the basis of the New South civilization. In the new imperialist age, such unity was now being touted as the basis of American civilization.

The ideological and patriotic ferment that resulted from a new imperial age heightened the significance of Murphy's rhetoric and aims regarding child labor. During a speech he gave to a Northern audience in 1900, Murphy stressed the importance of a "broader patriotism" that he believed undergirded a new "national responsibility" for the South's problems. He explicitly attributed this shift to the national unity that had been brought about by the Spanish-American War:[72] "Since the close of our war with Spain and through the growing identity of our commercial interests, the North and the South have been so closely drawn together, that it is now possible, perhaps for the first time, for Northern and Southern men to discuss [the South's problems] apart from the past prejudices of either section."[73] Reiterating one of his usual arguments about the enmity between the races, Murphy told his Northern audience that it was "the poorer classes of the white population" that were the "most violent" toward blacks in the South. Suggesting that Northern philanthropists had "provided for the Negro" more than for the "poor white population," Murphy implied that they had inadvertently worsened racial antipathies in the South by engendering jealousy among the "thousands of white boys for whom no Booker Washington has arisen."[74] It is not difficult to imagine, he told them, "how within the heart of the mother of the poor white boy of the South there might arise a question as she looks upon the educational facilities of Tuskegee: 'How can I gain such things for my son? Must he become a Negro?'"[75]

While Murphy supported "appropriate industrial education" for blacks, he feared an overemphasis of the advancement of blacks at the expense of poor whites. In reality the argument was a canard. The Jim Crow system of education taking shape in the South could hardly be considered to give black children an upper hand.[76] But the racial paranoia provoked at the suggestion was powerful. In effect, Murphy was taking his Southern rhetoric about white racial unity to a national stage and benefiting from the ideological ferment of the moment. In the age of American imperialism, he encouraged Northern whites to consider a cross-regional sense of racial unity not only with the best men of the South but with poor whites as well. Reminding them that they shared "Anglo-Saxon blood" with the South's poor white population, Murphy closed his speech on a note of reunification: "The [race] problem has now come for solution into the hands of the New South and into the hands of the New North; a South with its boundaries at the Lakes and at the St. Lawrence, a North with its boundaries—through the fields and the pines of a reunited country—at the waters of the Southern Gulf."[77]

Murphy's deep engagement with Southern Progressivism prompted him to pursue reform work on a full-time basis. In 1901 he accepted a position as executive secretary of the Southern Education Board, determining that he could achieve God's work more effectively outside the church walls than within them.[78] Stepping down from his former position in full-time ministry, Murphy declared his commitment to "the education of the poorer classes of our white people."[79] In a resignation speech published in the *Montgomery Advertiser*, Murphy said that the time had come to approach the problems of the South by appealing to "national patriotism." Northerners and Southerners

64   CHAPTER 3

must come together in the presence of "the deepest problems of our national civilization."[80] Just as sectionalism had receded from view in the midst of the national emergency of the Spanish-American War, so too must the sections unite "in the presence of the great human need" of the education of the poor white population in the South. Americans were "bound to educate [Southern poor whites] as a measure of self protection to the State," but they were bound upon "far broader and higher" grounds as well:

> The blood of our own manhood and womanhood is in their veins. They belong to us, and our abilities and capacities belong to them. Their presence among us in such large numbers makes the task of their education one of formidable magnitude, but the best life of the South has never been frightened or enfeebled by the presence of difficulties. Difficulties have always brought out the best in us. The work before us is of stupendous importance, and now that there are men from the country at large who are ready, with us, to put a hand to the plow, I think we may take heart indeed.[81]

Murphy's belief in cultivating "racial potential" had taken on new significance. In the age of imperialism, the figure of the white, degenerate mill child became a symbolic blemish on the national character and a stain on American civilization. Emerging at the turn of the century as a national crisis, the child labor problem became a means by which white Southerners and Northerners could perform a kind of moral reunification.[82] They performed this moral reunification by symbolically cloaking themselves in a righteous cause that reflected high-mindedness and a mutual commitment to preserving white racial supremacy. The rescue of the South's poor white children from the mills and their advancement through education was no longer the sole responsibility of the South. White Northerners had a sacred obligation and duty to protect "their own."[83] Efforts to combat child labor in the North would also benefit from the fervor of the moment as a national child labor movement came into existence.

This newfound national unity was temporary and, ironically, planted the seeds for an even stronger sectionalist discourse around child labor in the North and South. As interest in the Southern child labor problem went national, the Northern press sensationalized Southern child labor as a new national "white slavery." A genre of anti–Southern white child labor journalism arose in the North, which bore out Southern manufacturers' warnings that child labor reform was a surreptitious type of Northern interference. Southern mill children captured the Northern public imagination and became a national obsession.[84] Sensational books about Southern mill children, which presented the facts of child labor as Harriet Beecher Stowe's

Uncle Tom's Cabin had presented the facts of slavery, also began to appear.[85] Southern mill children were depicted as little slaves chained to machines, while Southern manufacturers were brutal slave masters accumulating wealth from the lifeblood of children. Elbert Hubbard, who had toured the cotton mills of South Carolina, wrote, "I know the sweat-shops of Hester Street, New York, . . . I know the lot of the coal miners of Pennsylvania, . . . but for misery, woe, and hopeless suffering, I have never seen anything to equal the cotton-mill slavery of South Carolina."[86] Along with Hubbard's piece, Irene Ashby's articles about Southern mill children were highly sensational and provided a blueprint for Northern journalists.[87] A prominent South Carolina manufacturer called Hubbard's piece "a second Uncle Tom's Cabin."[88] Other manufacturers responded similarly to the growing genre of anti–Southern child labor journalism.[89]

The battle over child labor legislation in Alabama had created an uproar in the national press, giving a wide platform to both Murphy and Irene Ashby, who were frequently solicited by Northern journalists. *The World's Work*— a popular monthly magazine devoted to supporting America's expanded imperialistic stance in the world—took a special interest in Southern white child labor. *World's Work* published a series of Irene Ashby's investigative reports about child labor in Alabama along with other commentary and articles about child labor in the South.[90] The visual image of Southern mill children that Ashby painted in her investigations—"pale, shrunken, and bowed" with "hypnotized brains" and "paralyzed souls"—would become a standard trope in national child labor discourse. In the coming years, this image of physically and mentally degenerate child workers would recur in photographs, illustrations, pamphlets, and descriptions of the child labor problem. *Gunton's Magazine, The Outlook, Harper's Monthly*, and *Charities Review* were other national periodicals that took up an interest in Southern white child labor at the turn of the century.[91]

Sometimes the Northern press would highlight its support for Southern reformers. In 1903, *The Outlook*, a New York–based magazine, remarked that child labor had grown into a "national evil" and praised the efforts of reformers everywhere to abolish it. However, the authors reserved their highest praise not for reformers in the North but for Edgar Gardner Murphy and the Alabama Child Labor Committee: "The Alabama committee [has] lighted a fire which is [now] burning brightly all over the Nation for the extirpation of this crying industrial abuse."[92] The North had its own child labor problem, which had begun receiving public criticism after the Civil War. But it was "sympathy with the child victims of premature toil at the South" that had made Northern reformers "more sensitive to kindred evils at home."[93] This narrative—that the national campaign began in earnest at the inspiration of the Alabama committee—became among reformers and commentators alike the standard way of explaining the origins of the rise of child labor as a national problem.

Southern mill owners grew angrier about child labor reform in these years, accusing Murphy and other members of the newly formed Alabama Child Labor Committee of being controlled by Northern agitators bent on disrupting Southern progress. In October 1901 the ACLC fought back with an investigation that found that mill interests in the North had actually been behind the defeat of the Alabama Child Labor Bill instead of endorsing its passage as the Southern mill lobbyists had suggested. In a series of pamphlets titled "An Appeal to the People and Press of New England," the ACLC accused Massachusetts capitalists who owned mills in Alabama of being behind the effort to defeat the Alabama Child Labor Bill.[94] Many Northern capitalists had an interest in the continuation of cheap child labor in the mills, the Alabama committee asserted. Alluding to child labor statutes in Massachusetts that limited the working hours of children to ten hours per day and required at least three months of schooling out of the year, the ACLC suggested that capitalists in that state were deliberately exploiting the children of the South: "We believe that Massachusetts, having defended her own children from a cruel . . . system will question the heartless policy with which her capital is striving to perpetuate the defenselessness of the children of the South."[95] In their efforts to defeat meager legislative protection for Alabama's mill children, Massachusetts' capitalists were "doing here what it dare not do at home."[96]

These pamphlets set off a firestorm of controversy. Howard Nichols, treasurer of the Alabama City cotton mill and a Boston native, published a reply in the *Boston Evening Transcript* immediately after publication of the ACLC's "Appeal" in a Boston newspaper. While conceding that child labor in the mills—especially regarding those under age twelve—was not preferable, Nichols defended himself and other Northern capitalists from the ACLC's charges of a "heartless policy" toward the "defenseless children of the South." Echoing an argument used often by factory owners in the North, Nichols blamed the parents: "The trouble comes largely from the parents, who make every effort to get their children into the mill, and often because of refusal, take their families . . . where no objection is made to the employment of children."[97] Pointing out that the mill town he operated in Alabama City provided "comfortable housing" and many other resources for "uplift," Nichols drew on free labor principles to suggest that mill life was itself a civilizing force. In Alabama City the mill company ran its own school and had built a church and a library for mill families. Rather than causing the "degeneration" of the South's common white people as the ACLC feared, Northern mill men were actually civilizing them.

Horace Sears, treasurer of the West Point Manufacturing Company in Langdale, Alabama, published an even more scathing reply to the ACLC, which was reprinted in several newspapers. Referring to Edgar Gardner Murphy as "a well-meaning but ill-advised humanitarian," Sears argued that mill children "were better off in the mill than running wild in the streets and fields, exposed to the danger of growing up into an ignorant, idle, and vicious citizenship." Like Nichols, Sears intoned free labor principles to argue that mill towns were civilizing forces. Unlike poor white children's previously isolated lives in upcountry regions where they had no contact with church, school, or the state, their lives in mill villages were "surrounded with Christianizing, educational, and civilizing influences." Painting a very different picture from that of Murphy and the ACLC, Sears asked the public to imagine "a happy mill settlement at Langdale, with its pretty church filled to the doors on Sundays with an attentive, God-fearing congregation" that also had a library and school and "streets lighted by electricity." This type of mill settlement was "typical of many in the South, especially of those under Northern management."

Murphy published rejoinders to both Nichols and Sears, prompting much national debate. Regarding Nichols's argument that parents were to blame for taking their families elsewhere if a mill refused to hire their children, Murphy wrote that if child labor "were prohibited everywhere," then "there could be no pressure to withdraw the children and to enter them in other mills." The question remained, why would a "paid and delegated agent" of Nichols's mill in Alabama City plan and organize "for weeks to thwart a simple legislative remedy for the abuses he [supposedly] deplores?" Murphy strongly disputed the benevolent child labor argument. No child labor could ever be "good," he wrote, despite the opportunities that may exist in a mill town. The issue was analogous to slavery: "The presence of the good plantation could not offset the perils and evils of the system itself, any more than the 'good factory' can justify the system of child labor." Murphy's most biting remarks invoked the race of the South's mill children. Intoning arguments he made in Philadelphia, Murphy accused the Massachusetts capitalists of caring more about black children than poor white children. The racially sensitive hypocrites from Massachusetts were "always solicitous for the negro" but "largely indifferent to the fate of our white children." Murphy invited any New Englanders following the debate to consider how they might respond differently "if the mills of Southern men were full of negro children."[98]

68 CHAPTER 3

The "national turn" in the child labor problem was dramatically rendered when Murphy was invited to speak in Atlanta on May 6, 1903, at the National Conference of Charities and Corrections, an organization that brought together different charity and reform groups to discuss mutual concerns.[99] The president of the conference, Robert W. DeForest, signaled a new tone: "The time has passed when the men of the South and the men of the North hold such relations to each other that they need hesitate to speak their minds with absolute freedom."[100] In the preface to the volume on the conference proceedings, the secretary noted that members had been asked to limit their presentations in the interest of space but that the members interested in child labor did not abide by the restrictions. These men and women "did not know how to lay down their pens when that important subject was under discussion and as this was the first time a chapter had been devoted to that topic, it seemed only gracious to yield all the space desired."[101]

By nearly all accounts, Murphy delivered the most riveting address in Atlanta. His speech, "Child Labor as a National Problem," captivated audience members. One attendee referred to it as "the greatest speech against child labor ever delivered in America."[102] Murphy declared the scope of the child labor problem to be national. "North and South, it belongs to all of us," he said. If the proportionate number of child workers was "greatest at the South," the actual number was "greater in the one state of Pennsylvania." The moral problem of child labor that had accompanied industrialization in late nineteenth-century Alabama was but a sampling of a larger problem that already existed in the North. Anywhere industry arose, children were drawn into factories, mills, and mines. As an "instrument of progress," the factory brought far-reaching blessings to society. However, it also brought evils that must be acknowledged and remedied "in the name of our children [and] our country." The realization of this national curse had revealed "the essential soundness of the national heart." That men and women across the country had discovered the problem of child labor in their respective towns, cities, and regions and had separately attempted to secure a modicum of legislative reform for child workers was "the most conspicuous evidence of the inherent right-mindedness of American life." Defining child labor as the worst national evil of the day, Murphy framed America's response to this evil as the ultimate test of the "common conscience of the land." Under threat were "the most defenseless elements of an industrial society" and the "potential citizenship" of America's child laborers.[103]

Recognizing that child labor was a national problem did not mean indicting capitalism. "We are all agreed [upon] the advantages and blessings of the factory," said Murphy. The question now before the nation was not whether capitalism was a blessing but whether the progress and prosperity bequeathed by capitalism should be "based upon the labor of our children." High-minded Americans must recognize this distinction and not be deceived by capitalist arguments that conflate economic progress with the "monotonous and confining labor of our little children." The capitalist is "my friend," said Murphy, but the capitalist was in danger of waging a war against civilization if he refused to recognize the fundamental and important issues that were at stake in the industrial labor of children. As in his past speeches, Murphy wanted Northern reformers to understand that the problem of mill children in the South was linked to the future of American civilization. "The children of these humbler people of our southern soil . . . of our own race and blood" were "rich in capacities and aptitudes." They were "the heirs with us of a deeper and more compelling patriotism," Murphy told his mostly Northern audience. Murphy also acknowledged the North's child labor problem. "The children of the northern mills . . . are largely the children of the foreigner," he said.[104] Like the white mill children of the South, the foreign mill children of the North should be protected through legislation and provided with a decent education. But Murphy admitted that he was no expert on the Northern child labor problem and that its specificities would have to be taken up by other speakers. The main purpose of Murphy's address was to praise the moral reunification of the two sections in terms of the child labor problem. As he put it, in "all cases" where child labor was being opposed—whether through the enactment of legislation, the investigation of child labor conditions, or the writing of child labor narratives—"the heart of our country, North and South, has shown itself to be a sound heart, and the soul of the Republic has kept watch above its children."[105] In this sense Murphy was endowing previously disjointed efforts around the country with a singular meaning. To a rapt audience, he defined the national child labor cause as the essence of the nation's moral conscience.

The nationalizing of the child labor problem was twofold. On the one hand, it was a kind of racial compact between white Northern and Southern reformers—as well as among a broader white public—that was nurtured by a heightened anxiety over the vitality of the Anglo-Saxon race in a new age of imperialism. The problem of Southern mill children was, in effect, nationalized through white Northerners' agreement that the future of the South's white mill children was linked to the strength of American civilization. On the other hand, the national turn in child labor reform was part of a symbolic reunification of Northern and Southern moral sentiment, bringing together disparate local and regional instances of child labor through the articulation of a discourse about the "national child labor problem." An outgrowth of Murphy's crusade for Southern white children, this national discourse found favorable conditions for ideological ascendancy at the turn of the century when other moral atrocities such as lynching, Jim Crow, and imperialistic warmongering belied a straightforward tale of national decency. The "essential soundness of the national heart" could be displayed through a nationwide effort to combat the moral evil of child labor. Laboring children were in bondage to the shackles of a capitalist labor market that sacrificed their vigor, physical well-being, and mental aptitude on the altar of immediate economic gain. But the abiding power and strength of the American nation would have to rest on a firmer foundation. Child labor could not be the basis of a vibrant capitalism, strong civilization, or lasting and influential empire in the world. At issue in the emancipation of child laborers—which Murphy defined as the "freeing of [the child's] capacity"—was the abiding strength of the nation and its empire abroad. "The child must be worth something to the country" so that his country could be "worth something to the world."[106]

After the conference in Atlanta, Murphy published an article in *Charities Review*, a journal for New York reformers, praising the work of Northern reformers to combat the problem of child labor in their own geographic section. "The subject was, of course, no new one" in the North, wrote Murphy. "The long and earnest work of Mrs. Florence Kelley, of Miss Adams and of many other workers . . . had been attended by marked and permanent gains." But it was the particular problem of cotton mill children in the South that had garnered the most public attention at the turn of the century. As Murphy saw it, the factory evils in the South had prompted the question, "How are matters at home?" for Northerners. "In answer to that question, the Northern public gained a clearer and more vivid perception of the fate of child workers [in] the North." A "new interest" in the subject was generated, and thus the national problem of child labor was pushed to the forefront of national discussion as "one of the conspicuous general interests of all sections of our country."[107]

In addition to increased public attention, new legislation was sought. From 1902 to 1903, twelve states passed new child labor laws.[108] In seven of these states, the new laws represented the first acceptance of such legislation. Separately organized forces across the country had been "laboring toward a common aim, yet without the advantages of a common understanding."[109] Even before Murphy's 1903 Atlanta speech, other developments were trending toward a centralized campaign against child labor. In the spring of 1902, Florence Kelley and Lillian Wald, leading reformers in New York City, appointed a temporary committee on child labor to investigate the problem in New York. By November this temporary committee became a formal organization, the

New York Child Labor Committee, the second of its kind in the nation, and modeled itself after Murphy's Alabama Child Labor Committee.[110] Its charter members were Florence Kelley, New York settlement house leader Robert Hunter, Columbia University professor of ethics Felix Adler, and several other prominent reformers.[111]

Meanwhile, Murphy's resignation from his ministerial post in Alabama had brought him to New York on a fairly regular basis, since the Southern Education Board was headquartered there. Murphy heard about the newly founded New York Child Labor Committee in 1902 and was eager to meet the New York reformers. He became acquainted with Adler, Hunter, Kelley, and others in the New York reform scene. Almost immediately, these reformers began discussing the possibility of a national Child Labor Committee.[112] After Murphy's Atlanta speech in 1903—which had all but announced plans for founding a national organization—Murphy met again with the New York reformers, and together they decided a national organization was necessary. In October 1903, five months after the Atlanta speech, the reformers appointed Kelley, Adler, and William Baldwin (a member of the New York Child Labor Committee and president of Long Island Railroad Company) to a committee that would draft a plan for a national organization.[113] The committee called for a national committee to be composed of members throughout the country that would be run by an executive committee of nine people.[114] Announcements were sent out to reform-minded persons, philanthropists, businessmen, and religious and community leaders across the country, explaining the purpose of the new organization and urging them to both contribute money and attend the committee's opening meeting at Carnegie Hall on April 15, 1904, when the National Child Labor Committee (NCLC) officially came into existence.

The 1904 gathering at Carnegie Hall was historic not only because it officially ushered in the national movement against child labor but also because it marked the coming together of the descendants of both antislavery and proslavery Americans at a meeting that declared America's "new slavery" to be the national problem of child labor. Neal Anderson, N. B. Feagin, and Judge J. B. Gaston, all of whom were members of Murphy's Alabama Child Labor Committee, were present at the meeting along with other well-known Southerners, such as Georgia state representative Clark Howell and soon-to-be governor of Georgia Hoke Smith (later US senator); former governor and US senator Benjamin Tillman of South Carolina; and James Kirkland, the chancellor of Vanderbilt University. Alongside these Southerners were Florence Kelley and Jane Addams, both daughters of prominent antislavery fathers who had been founders of the Republican Party. Northern reformers

72   CHAPTER 3

such as Felix Adler; William H. Baldwin of New York; settlement house worker Lillian Wald of New York; secretary of the Missionary Society (Protestant Episcopal Church) John W. Wood; and Robert W. DeForest, president of the Charity Organizations Society, were also in attendance.[115]

At the meeting, Professor Felix Adler of Columbia University was elected chair of the NCLC, and Edgar Murphy was elected its secretary. After Murphy read the official membership list of the newly formed NCLC, Adler made a statement about the committee's purpose: "[We] shall be a great moral force . . . to combat the danger in which childhood is placed by greed and rapacity." A pattern of economic dependence upon child labor had emerged across the entire industrializing nation: "Whenever any state passes over into the industrial or commercial stage, it is subjected to a great temptation to underbid the older industrial states by offering cheap labor for the mills and factories. [And] *cheap labor means child labor.*" The purpose of the NCLC would be to "create a national sentiment" against child labor in order to halt and prevent the "needless sacrifice of child life."[116] The committee boldly outlined its initial goals: "Whatever happens in the sacrifice of adult workers, the public conscience demands that children *under twelve years of age* shall not be touched; that childhood shall be sacred; that industrialism and commercialism shall not be allowed beyond this point to degrade humanity."[117]

Murphy, the "founder and father" of the NCLC, was insistent that "national" did not mean "federal."[118] An NCLC leaflet distributed in 1904 addressed the question directly. The national committee was "not to act as a substitute for State committees nor to cross the lines of local initiative; but to serve in relation to existing committees as a clearing house of information and suggestion; to call committees into existence at points where they are wanting; and to aid in coordinating the efforts of local committees."[119] The committee's purpose, then, as Adler had also suggested at Carnegie Hall, was "not to advance federal legislation" but "to aid in creating and interpreting a national sentiment upon the subject of child labor" that could become "operative under local conditions and through the specific laws of each of our several States."[120] This initial agreement among the executive members would be tenuous. But in the meantime, the NCLC began a public relations campaign in national magazines and newspapers; established its own library, which included books, articles, and reports on child labor; and developed plans for child labor investigations and outreach strategies to areas of the country that did not yet have local campaigns against child labor.

Murphy's insistence that "national" should not be interpreted as "federal" reverberated with other Southern reform efforts he was pursuing simultaneously. The work of the Southern Education Board, for instance, boasted of several prominent Northern members but carefully crafted its strategy and rhetoric to reflect a Southern-led effort that eschewed "Northern interference" in the South's problems.[121] Often referencing the "trauma" of Reconstruction and its supposed disaster as a federal experiment, Murphy believed it was necessary to reassure fellow white Southerners that his reform activities did not open a back door for Northern agitators to "interfere" once again in the South's problems through federal legislation. But since the Spanish-American War, Murphy had promoted the idea of applying a broader patriotism to moral issues in the service of a new "national responsibility" for the South's problems. This new patriotism did not signify federal action, however. Rather, it was to be the basis of a national reunification of moral sentiment between North and South. The most practical and sympathetic Northerners knew how to "help without hindering" and how to "cooperate without interfering," argued Murphy.[122] The new "Americanism" was "non-political and non-sectional" and revealed a North and South of "common sense and fraternal kindliness."[123] In Murphy's schema, political or legislative action at the federal level would actually serve to undermine the fraternal unity of Northern and Southern moral sentiment. The national child labor problem symbolized this fraternal unity in an age when much was at stake in the question of federal intervention. Indeed, the celebratory founding of the NCLC in 1904 occurred just as a new political and social regime of racial segregation—which rested on the absence of federal intervention—was being consolidated in the New South. Murphy spoke and wrote about the necessity for Jim Crow even as he forged alliances with the most prominent "Progressive" reformers from the North over the issue of child labor.[124] Eight years earlier the Supreme Court of the United States had upheld the constitutionality of state laws requiring racial segregation in what became known as the "separate but equal" doctrine.[125] But the strong moral alliance forged at the turn of the century in the national child labor movement did additional work at a cultural level to ensure that the new "Southern way of life" would be left alone.

Initially, the executive members of the NCLC held to their pact. As the founder and executive secretary of the NCLC, Murphy largely set the tone for the committee's operations. But increasing bouts of fever and influenza forced him to step down from his salaried position while remaining on the board. Samuel McCune Lindsay, a sociology professor at the University of Pennsylvania and commissioner of education in the newly acquired colony of Puerto Rico, was offered Murphy's salaried position.[126] The board thought Lindsay's sociological expertise and experience as commissioner would be advantageous to the NCLC's goals. He was also well connected to prominent officials, including President Theodore Roosevelt. Murphy insisted that a Southerner be appointed assistant secretary to direct the committee's work on Southern child labor. Alexander McKelway, a Presbyterian minister from Charlotte, North Carolina, and editor of the *Presbyterian Standard*, was Murphy's first choice. McKelway had been following Murphy's reform efforts in Alabama since before the founding of the ACLC in 1901 and had written a series of editorials that made use of Murphy's arguments from the widely publicized Murphy-Nichols-Sears debates.[127] With these appointments in place, the NCLC launched its first year of operations, coordinating local child labor efforts with the support of the national committee and boasting of several early successes. Of the thirty-nine state legislatures that met in 1904, twelve passed some kind of child labor legislation, including Delaware, which had no previous child labor laws.[128] During the same year, Lindsay traveled to twenty states and helped to organize local or state child labor committees in seventeen of them. By the end of the year, the national committee had a mailing list of 2,500 and had distributed 48,500 child labor pamphlets. They had also accumulated a war chest from annual dues and contributions.[129]

Lindsay spoke at the second annual meeting on the threat that child labor posed to American civilization. As Murphy had suggested in his Atlanta speech, Lindsay defined child labor as a fundamental contradiction of civilization. The demand for child labor increased "with the growth of competition for markets and the consequent desire to sell goods more cheaply."[130] The more societies made "progress of inventions and mechanical devices," the more children would be drawn into the industrial labor market. Advanced civilization was thus accompanied by an undesirable consequence that interfered with the "natural" development and growth of the nation's children. On the one hand, America's advancing civilization—including its empire abroad—was a reflection of the supposed superiority of American values, the Christian faith, and the Anglo-Saxon race. On the other hand, advancing civilization produced anxieties such as the fear that what was "natural" would be sacrificed on the altar of commercial progress.[131] Lindsay's reports from England reinforced this fear. In certain areas of London, he reported, "industrial processes" had taken over "natural processes," weeding out "the unfit and incompetent workers and segregating them into slums." "Thousands of men, women and children are segregated in East London, living in dire poverty and distress, because they do not possess the physical vitality or intellectual capacity to perform the kind of labor demanded in modern society." This class of English laborers had been described by one journalist as "a race distinct . . . with strongly marked characteristics, . . . a race stunted in size, sallow complexioned, dark haired. Its moral sense is blunted. It has even evolved a speech of its own." Lindsay urged his audience to imagine this as "a picture of what the neglect and non-development of children in the past means for the British people today."[132]

McKelway warned that what had happened to England was "beginning already in the South." There had developed in the South a "factory type, easily recognizable—the children distinguished by their pallor and a certain sallowness of complexion." What would happen when America needed them to defend its empire abroad? Even Jefferson Davis, the president of the Confederate States, had understood this principle, McKelway noted. When asked to lower the age limit for Confederate soldiers, Davis allegedly replied, "We must not grind the seed corn." On that note, McKelway reminded his audience that "the little children of the South, with their heritage of heroic blood, untainted and pure, are the hope of the South and . . . the hope of the nation."[133] In his talk Lindsay did not specifically reference Southern mill children but spoke in more general terms about the future of the empire. Since "the one great contributory cause" of the physical deterioration in England was "the system of child labor," the same fate awaited America in the not so distant future "if we fail to grapple with the great problem of child labor in our own country."[134]

To "create a national sentiment" against child labor, the NCLC developed a press outreach strategy. The NCLC's press committee—Murphy, Felix Adler, Florence Kelley, and Edward T. Devine—was responsible for outreach to national magazines, newspapers, and other publications.[135] In addition to issuing hundreds of pamphlets, the press committee persuaded the editors of the *Annals of the American Academy of Political and Social Science* to devote one volume each year to publishing papers presented at the NCLC annual meetings.[136] Other than print media, the NCLC's main public outreach was to churches. This outreach was reflected in the NCLC's decision to have Rev. William N. McVickar, an Episcopalian bishop from Rhode Island, speak on the topic of "Child Labor and the Church" at the first annual meeting.[137] McVickar believed that the Church should be "in the very front rank of the defense of childhood." As followers of "Him who once called a little child unto Him," Christians should remember that "'whoso should offend one of these little ones, it were better for him that a millstone were hanged about his neck and that he were drowned in the depth of the sea'" (Matthew 18:6).[138] Child labor was responsible not only for the physical and mental degeneration of more than two million children in America, but it was also responsible for their spiritual degeneration. As McVickar noted, these children's souls could not be easily reached, since their minds and bodies were "haggard, stunted, and deformed."[139]

76   CHAPTER 3

McVickar had been introduced to the child labor problem when he visited a mill village in Rhode Island and was stunned by how "small and puny" the children were. During the year before his NCLC address, McVickar had lobbied the Rhode Island state legislature for child labor protective measures. He noted that the Church must be the "great moral force" that "awakens the feeling" of the nation. Drawing on the discourse of empire prevalent at these meetings, McVickar explicitly linked the role of the Church in the child labor campaign to missionary ventures abroad. The Church was currently "sending into the world men and women, well equipped and inspired with the highest ideals, to do her work in every department of life." The Church could "be depended upon" to spread the ideals of "Christian citizenship" abroad. "Those from other lands, under different rules, must be enlightened." McVickar pledged that the Church could be counted on not only to spread "Christian citizenship" to other parts of the world but also to "assimilate that vast tide of immigration which is inundating our shores" through the Christian rescue of the foreigner's laboring children.[140] McVickar's ideas about the importance of the Church made an impression on the NCLC leadership. At their second annual meeting, they aggressively reached out to churches, asking local ministers in Washington to observe Sunday, December 10, 1905, as Children's Day. The committee requested that ministers make "at least one reference" in their sermons "to the work being done to free children from premature toil and its evil effects."[141]

A wave of national interest in the child labor issue bolstered the committee's work. A national discourse about child labor that linked the physical, mental, and spiritual degeneration of child laborers with the fate of American civilization and empire abroad had spread into the cultural sphere of American life. Edwin Markham, a poet and teacher from California with no formal ties to the national movement, created a sensation in 1906 with a piece on child labor that he contributed to the widely read *Cosmopolitan* magazine.[142] Markham began his piece with a story of mythic proportions about an "old Indian chieftain" who visited New York City. The Indian gazed in wonder at "the cathedrals, the skyscrapers, the bleak tenements, the blaring mansions, the crowded circus, and the airy span of Brooklyn Bridge." A group of "Christian gentlemen" asked the "benighted pagan, whose worship was bowing down to sticks and stones," what had surprised him the most about the city. The "savage" answered the men in three words: "Little children working." Civilization had "given the world an abominable custom which shock[ed] the social ethics of even an unregenerate savage," lamented Markham. Perhaps "our savage friends" should send their "medicine men as missionaries" to American cities to shed "the light of barbarism" upon our

"Christian civilization." Like other popular child labor narratives of the day, Markham's story placed the discourse of national child labor reformers in a popular idiom: "One million seven hundred thousand children are at work in our land of the free." Was this the Christianity that self-congratulatory Americans "parade[d] in Madagascar and unsaved Malabar?" Was this what orators meant "when they jubilate[d] over civilization and the progress of the species?" Markham had not attended child labor reform meetings nor organized for child labor legislation, but he learned about it from newspapers and magazines. In the Northern public imagination, the child labor problem was assumed to be worse in the South. Echoing the discourse of NCLC reformers, Markham wrote, "These are not the children of recent immigrants, . . . nor are they negro children who have shifted their shackles from field to mill. They are white children of old and pure colonial stock . . . a people that must now fling their children into the clutches of capital." As these children were being "starved, stunted, and stunned," the future strength of the nation was under threat. As a result, North and South had "banded [together]" to "save the children of the nation."[143]

Markham's piece created a stir among *Cosmopolitan* readership. One of the most widely read magazines in America, it had a readership of over one million shortly after the turn of the century.[144] In 1905 the magazine had been taken over by William Randolph Hearst, the newspaper magnate from New York and a member of the US House of Representatives.[145] After Markham's piece appeared in the September 1906 issue, thousands of letters from readers poured into the magazine's headquarters in New York, asking how they might join or help the cause.[146] This response to the Markham piece prompted the staff at *Cosmopolitan* to contact the National Child Labor Committee. Felix Adler told them that "in addition to good laws, there is need of a vigorous and imperative public sentiment in favor of the enforcement of the laws, for without the pressure of public sentiment the best laws remain dead letters." To this end, *Cosmopolitan* announced the formation of a national club to be called the Child Labor Federation, which would "help create this deep public sentiment." The magazine invited its readers to join the club free of charge.[147] The November issue boasted that "the widespread indignation aroused by Edwin Markham's portrayal of child labor conditions and the responses that keep pouring in to the new Child Labor Federation, show the detestation with which the exploitation of children is viewed."[148] *Cosmopolitan* reader T. W. Shank of Texas wrote, "Edwin Markham's articles have caused the scales to drop off my eyes." Mrs. William Pollock of New Jersey wrote that she was "pained by the article on child labor, and while I haven't the means to be of much assistance financially, still I am deeply interested in these poor children as I have three lovely children of my own." M. B. Kreeger of New Orleans said, "I have little time to devote to such things, yet Mr. Markham's vivid picture is the kind that stirs men's souls." C. P. McCambridge of California wanted to know of "anything I can do in my humble sphere to assist in stopping this heathenish traffic in infants." A note of appreciation from NCLC secretary Samuel Lindsay was printed in the November issue: "The National Child Labor Committee welcomes the widest possible publicity . . . and rejoices that a periodical that reaches so many people as the COSMOPOLITAN MAGAZINE has seen fit to take up the serious discussion of this important matter."[149] Meanwhile, Edwin Markham was enlisted to write six more child labor articles for the magazine's upcoming issues.

As the national child labor problem regularly appeared in reformers' speeches and writings, popular magazines, newspapers, sermons on Sunday morning, and everyday discussions, prominent national leaders in the corridors of official power took note. The framing of the national child labor problem as an issue that had potentially dire consequences for America's burgeoning empire appealed especially to President Teddy Roosevelt. On December 9, 1905, during the NCLC's annual meeting in Washington, DC, President Roosevelt received the members of the national committee and their guests at the White House.[150] A few years later Roosevelt would be made an honorary member of the NCLC and would occasionally speak on the topic of child labor.[151] At this meeting he instructed his cabinet member and secretary of the navy, Charles Joseph Bonaparte, to speak to the group. Secretary Bonaparte opened the NCLC's annual meeting with "an earnest and sincere endorsement" of the movement to abolish child labor. He characterized the evils of child labor as one of "the most serious blemishes on our social and industrial life" and wished the national committee "God-speed" in the tasks it had set before itself.[152] But the member of the national governing elite who would take the greatest interest in the subject of child labor was US senator Albert Beveridge, a Republican from Indiana and one of the best known and most outspoken imperialists in the US Congress.

Senator Beveridge was an ambitious politician who made a name for himself as a passionate defender of American imperialism during his first term (1899–1905) in the US Senate.[153] His name was launched to national prominence in 1898 when he delivered a riveting speech at Tomlinson Hall in Indianapolis. Beveridge's address, "The March of the Flag," updated the older doctrine of Manifest Destiny by providing a religious and ideological justification for imperial expansion. The United States should acquire colonies and rule over them not only because it was profitable but also because it was the historic and divine duty of Americans to spread civilization, freedom, and Christianity to the rest of the world.[154] Just as Providence had "unfurled America's banner" from sea to shining sea, so was Providence now directing the "march of the flag" in Cuba, Puerto Rico, and the Philippines. The "impulse" for imperial expansion could not be explained purely by commercial or economic motives, for trade did not always "await us in [the] savage fastnesses."[155] White Christians in America were "God's chosen people," and it was "His power" that "directed the Spanish fleet into our hands."[156] "The March of the Flag" solidified Beveridge's growing reputation as an orator. Some three hundred thousand copies of the speech were distributed in pamphlet form during the congressional campaigns that were in progress. Beveridge hoped that the speech would help him get elected by the Indiana state legislature to the US Senate. His hopes were realized the next year when the legislature voted him into the Senate.[157]

Priding himself on his "instinctive knowledge" of the aspirations of the common man, Senator Beveridge supported several popular progressive reforms in his first Senate term, including the Pure Food and Drug Act, the Meat Inspection Law, and the Hepburn Railroad Rate Act.[158] When campaigning in the fall of 1906, he touched on the inheritance tax, the direct primary, stricter regulation of corporations, and a national child labor law. In a letter to President Roosevelt, Beveridge noted that he had received the greatest applause on the stump when he called for a national child labor law and was thus convinced that he had "struck a popular chord."[159] A US senator who openly harbored presidential ambitions, Beveridge seized the moment. "We cannot," he said on the stump, "permit any man or corporation to stunt the bodies, minds, and souls of American children [and] thus wreck the future of the American Republic."[160] Aware of *Cosmopolitan* magazine's series on child labor, Beveridge worried that William Randolph Hearst might beat him to the punch with a national child labor law. "We have got to beat them to the goal and score a touchdown before they begin to play," he wrote a fellow Republican.[161] But Senator Beveridge was drawn to the child labor problem for more complex reasons as well. The framing of the national child labor problem in popular discourse resonated with questions of race, empire, and civilization that Beveridge had been interested in for years. As a senator who had worked on other federal laws such as the Meat Inspection Act—which used the commerce clause of the Constitution to ban from interstate shipment meats that were uninspected—Beveridge saw no reason that the same logic could not be used to pass federal legislation banning the interstate shipment of products from factories and mills that employed children.[162]

Beveridge formally introduced the "Beveridge Bill" to the US Senate on December 5, 1906.[163] Representative Henry Parsons introduced an identical bill in the House. Seeking broad public support, Senator Beveridge turned to the National Child Labor Committee. The NCLC invited him to a meeting of the executive board in New York City, where heated discussion over the Beveridge Bill would ensue.[164] The committee's acceptance of a federal bill violated their initial agreement. Nonetheless, several key board members—including Samuel Lindsay, Felix Adler, and Florence Kelley—could not resist Beveridge's measure and believed the national committee should endorse it. Even McKelway decided to support it, since he had been repeatedly frustrated by state-level legislative efforts in the South.[165] DeForest was opposed on the grounds that "our influence in the South would be seriously impaired," since most Southerners would think the proposal was "of the Force Bill Variety."[166] As expected, Murphy was furious that the NCLC was even considering supporting the bill.[167] Though he was not in attendance, due to health reasons, he sent a letter expressing his disapproval. Despite Murphy's objections, the trustees voted to endorse the Beveridge Bill, maintaining that "it will establish a National standard to correct the evils of child labor in their important National aspects."[168]

When Murphy learned about the trustees' decision, he resigned. "I have no alternative but to ask that you will kindly present this letter to the Board as my resignation from the Board and from the National Child Labor Committee," he wrote. The committee had "departed from a compact" that Murphy regarded "as inviolable." He had faith that his colleagues had acted from a "high sense of personal and official obligation." But the "questions at issue" were "so vital" that remaining in his position on the committee would be "inconsistent and untenable."[169] NCLC board members did everything they could to convince him otherwise, but Murphy would not budge. Lindsay wrote to Murphy, "[Beveridge Bill] is not my chief thought in connection with your resignation. It is rather the sense of personal loss at your absence from our group. . . . You were a tower of strength to this work, and somehow it does not seem like the National Committee, which you organized and created, without your name." Lindsay noted that he "voiced the sentiment" of the rest of the committee: "Your work [has] given us all so much on which we are united."[170] But federal legislation was so far from Murphy's vision that he launched an "anti–Beveridge Bill" campaign, publishing pamphlets and articles explaining why he was against the bill.[171]

Meanwhile, Senator Beveridge was invited to be the featured speaker at the NCLC's third annual convention in Cincinnati, Ohio, on December 13–15, 1906. Over four thousand people attended the national convention, which was a record high.[172] The theme of the conference was "Child Labor and the Republic," and Adler's opening address to the attendees was "The Attitude of Society toward the Child as an Index of Civilization." Senator Beveridge delivered the keynote address, employing his well-known oratorical skills and enthralling the audience with "Child Labor and the Nation." Child labor, as he defined it, was a sin against God and America. As the bodies, minds, and souls of laboring children were "maimed" by industrial labor, this process over time would weaken the American nation and, thus, interfere with God's special plan for America. The time had come to "cast from our Nation the body of this death to which it is bound." Then and only then "shall our flag be unsullied; only so shall we indeed be a people whose God is the Lord; and only so shall this government . . . not perish from the earth."[173] The address was followed by Lindsay's announcement that the committee was endorsing the Beveridge Bill: "The National Child Labor Committee endorses cordially the principles of the Beveridge bill for a National Child Labor Law, believing that it will establish a national standard to correct the evils of child labor in their important national aspects, especially in the deterioration of our racial stock." On the Sunday after the convention, many of the churches of Cincinnati "gave over their pulpits to persons in attendance at this convention." Continuing its church outreach, the NCLC asked churches in Cincinnati and around the country to urge their congressmen to support the Beveridge Bill.[174]

On January 23, 1907, Senator Beveridge launched a three-day speech for his bill on the Senate floor. Armed with statistics and affidavits from the NCLC along with emotionally charged stories about Southern child labor from magazines and novels, Beveridge had a successful first day.[175] But on the second day, a growing opposition to federal child labor legislation led by Southern senators came prepared for battle. Though Beveridge attacked child labor everywhere it existed, saying that the "children of foreigners" could make "admirable American citizens" as long as "their bodies are not broken and their souls are not crushed and their minds are not stunted," he saved his deepest criticism for Southern child labor. As he put it, "[The South] is where the evil is greatest and most shameful and where it is practiced *upon the purest American strain that exists in this country*—the children in the southern cotton mills."[176] While Beveridge was reading aloud descriptions of emaciated, ignorant mill children who routinely "fell asleep" while working and had to be "doused with water" to remain awake, Senator Augustus Octavius Bacon of Georgia interrupted him to ask exactly where in Georgia these episodes had occurred.[177] Bacon continued to interrupt Beveridge on other points, asking detailed questions about Georgia and other Southern states that Beveridge would have trouble answering.

Other Southern senators—including Senator Edward W. Carmack of Tennessee, Senator Lee Slater Overman of North Carolina, and Senator Benjamin

Tillman of South Carolina—used similar tactics on the floor.[178] Even if the conditions of child labor were as appalling as Beveridge and other "agitators" implied, the necessity for federal legislation had not been sufficiently proven, they argued. Senator Beveridge did not give up easily. Citing the "racial deterioration" of the "English stock," Beveridge recounted the NCLC's reports on the Boer War and the long-term effects of child labor on the physical and mental stature of future citizens.[179] He also made an appeal to white racial solidarity: the white race could not "keep superior by *asserting* superiority. The truth of it is the South is face to face with the situation of their white children in the mills and their black children in the schools."[180] In conclusion, he said, "You are permitting a system to go on which is steadily weakening the white race for the future and steadily strengthening the black race."[181] The final phases of the debate focused on the bill's constitutionality.[182]

For months, the Senate refused to act on the Beveridge Bill. Murphy's warning that the "cause of the children" should not be mixed up with "the bitter issues of coercion" seemed to bear itself out as states' rights senators grew ever more intractable toward the idea of a national Child Labor Bill. In an ironic twist, Murphy had been working behind the scenes to defeat the measure. In February 1907 he sent a letter to President Roosevelt asking that "at least six months or a year's time be allowed to elapse before the Beveridge Child Labor Bill is pressed for passage." The country had "had almost no preparation for the consideration of this question as a Federal issue." Such a "brief season of delay may save the country from a serious departure involving questionable precedents."[183] Until then Roosevelt had not officially weighed in on the Beveridge Bill. While the NCLC, Beveridge, and other proponents of the bill assumed that the president supported them, the bill had not received his official endorsement. The president mulled over the question. He had long respected Murphy's opinions, believing him to be an enlightened Southerner. In a reply to Murphy's letter, he wrote that he had decided "not to advocate immediate action" but would eventually have to support federal action "if the several states do not do their duty." The issue of a national child labor law was "a very difficult question," but Roosevelt had a "high regard" for Murphy's opinion on such matters.[184] The Beveridge Bill seemed almost a dead letter. In November 1907 the NCLC Executive Board—citing continued disagreement in its ranks over the Beveridge Bill and increasingly grim prospects for passage—voted to withdraw its support.[185]

Murphy never returned to the National Child Labor Committee. At his untimely death six years later, his colleagues from the NCLC would gather at a memorial service in New York City to eulogize him as "the founder and father" of the national child labor movement, a "religious seer who opened

Seeds of a New Sectionalism 83

up a mighty outlook," a "soldier who laid his life on the altar of his country," and the mightiest "interpreter of the North to the South and the South to the North" that the nation had ever known.[186] By the time of his death, Murphy's crusade against child labor had resonated so deeply with larger national and international interests that it had taken on a life of its own, becoming much larger than Murphy and its Southern origins. Events did not unfold as he had planned and, in an ironic turn of events, Murphy was left toward the end of his life trying to contain the fire he had ignited. The membership numbers of the NCLC continued to climb, and public interest in the Southern child labor problem reached a national obsession. For the NCLC, future federal legislation of child labor seemed almost inevitable. But it was Murphy's particular framing of the Southern white child labor problem and his accurate appraisal of the historical moment that transformed child labor from a local issue into a national problem in the age of American empire.

4 Child Labor Abolitionists

A Northern Progressive Vision

Inasmuch as ye have done it
unto one of the least of these my brethren,
ye have done it unto me.
—Matthew 25:40

The menace of Southern white child labor was an entering wedge for reformers to justify expanded federal authority. Rejecting Edgar Murphy's regionally distinctive approach to reform, the national movement adopted a strategy that prioritized federal intervention. The laxity of the South's labor laws made the region a favorite target. Southern manufacturers were vilified as the worst capitalists, but Northern capitalists were also increasingly called out for their evil ways as they sought child labor in tenement houses, resisted meager reforms, and increasingly employed girls.[1] Reformers doubled down in these years on their abolitionist-style rhetoric and comparisons of child labor to slavery. Emancipating the child laborer became a rallying cry of the national movement, which became more religious in tone. Unfettered capitalism was sinful, and intervention was a Christian duty. Social Gospel principles infused the movement's rhetoric, and the national committee's new leader was a Social Gospel minister who injected a spiritual urgency into the cause. Likening the abolition of child labor to slave emancipation, the movement embarked on a religious crusade to shame capitalists and achieve federal intervention.

Bolstered by the 1914 publication of the book *Children in Bondage: A Complete and Careful Presentation of the Anxious Problem of Child Labor— Its Causes, Its Crimes, and Its Cure*, Progressive-era muckraking—which included the NCLC's own photographer, Lewis Hine—and a growing

86   CHAPTER 4

progressive state, reformers made passage of a federal child labor law their top priority.[2] The failed Beveridge Bill was never far from their minds. A shrewd opposition led by Southerners had taken them by surprise, and internal disagreement regarding the wisdom of federal legislation had weakened their resolve. Determined not to repeat their mistakes, the NCLC anticipated Southern opposition, producing an array of pamphlets, articles, and speeches explaining how their new bill—known as the Keating-Owen Child Labor Act, or Wick's Bill—was a legitimate use of federal power.[3] They were more united this time, securing permission from the NCLC's board to pursue a federal standard "even at the cost of the Committee's other work."[4] After the Beveridge defeat, they knew public support would be important. They sought and received the endorsement of multiple organizations, including the American Federation of Labor, the US Children's Bureau, the National Consumers' League, the American Medical Association, the International Child Welfare League, women's clubs, temperance groups, and thousands of churches.[5] Led by Social Gospel minister Owen Lovejoy, the national committee's new battle for a federal child labor law would focus on the spiritual awakening of America. Although reformers continued to define Southern white child labor as the worst instance of child slavery, they also expanded their descriptions of the national child labor problem in a religious crusade that shamed sinful capitalists in both the North and the South.

In the age of the Social Gospel, child labor debates deepened sectionalist divisions along religious and cultural lines. For Northern reformers, the desire for profit had pushed capitalists to a sinful exploitation of labor. Child laborers were slaves bound to sinful capitalists in a market without moral boundaries. Northern reformers embraced federal authority as the best way to restrain sinful capitalists and protect free society. As both religious shaming of capitalists and federal action were prioritized, the sectionalist tenor of the debates intensified. The argument that capitalists were sinful did not go over well with Southern manufacturers, who thought Northern reformers were trying to quash industrial progress in the region. In response to the Social Gospel rhetoric, Southern defenses of child labor included biblical arguments about labor as part of the original curse of man as well as the biblical injunction for children to obey their parents. Northern reformers became frustrated by resistance to meaningful reform in the South and embraced federal intervention as the only solution. Despite having state-level operations in several Southern states, the National Child Labor Committee "never achieved a true intersectional character" in contrast to other Progressive reform groups, according to William A. Link, a historian of Southern Progressivism.[6] More so than other signature Progressive reforms, such as

Child Labor Abolitionists

Prohibition, public hygiene, and suffrage, child labor reform exacerbated sectional tensions.[7] "Child labor crusaders were the most frustrated social reformers of the early twentieth-century South," wrote Link.[8]

Southern opposition to child labor reform grew more unified. One NCLC agent in North Carolina noted that reformers in the South faced a "determined opposition" similar to the Old South's reaction to abolitionism.[9] This growing opposition was partly due to the death of Murphy, who had pressured reformers to resist federal legislation in the first decade after the NCLC's founding. As the founder of the national movement, Murphy's opinion held sway with Northern reformers. After his death, reformers were less beholden to his vision and declared their intention to rescue the South's mill children through federal intervention.[10] Southern manufacturers were busy developing a new strategy for challenging reformers in court and awaiting an opportunity to strike. A more unified Southern opposition would eventually define freedom within market society as freedom from federal authority. Through national debates about child labor in the age of the Social Gospel, Northern reformers entrenched regional battle lines around child labor reform in religious and cultural terms. When the First World War broke out, reformers adapted their movement to wartime needs. A wartime campaign for modern child welfare unseated reformers' Social Gospel campaign, paving the way for a more secular, bureaucratic approach to child welfare. Reformers' faith in the modern bureaucratic state grew even as the spiritual underpinnings of that faith came unmoored. The encroachment of a consumerist ethos also shaped the wartime campaign as the American toy industry became an unexpected ally of reformers. By war's end, reformers had gained new allies in a modern child welfare movement that was firmly rooted in modern industrial society.

The gender and racial dimensions of the child labor debates also shifted in this period. As Progressive-era reformers sought the protection of women and children as a central aim of the modern bureaucratic state, child labor reformers adjusted their rhetoric with a focus on girls. Depicting female child laborers as capitalism's most pitiful victims, reformers were able to secure many victories. In the era of *Muller v. Oregon* (1908), in which the Supreme Court declared the state's special interest in protecting female workers because of their "maternal functions," reformers highlighted the tragic nature of girl workers whose future roles as wives and mothers were jeopardized by excessive labor. Southern opponents had difficulty mustering an effective argument against the protection of girls. Both free labor principles and biblical arguments about Adam's curse were more easily applied to boys. However, when World War I broke out, the discourse about child labor shifted back

88   CHAPTER 4

to boys when national leaders considered how and whether boys should contribute to the wartime effort. Joining forces with the American toy industry, Northern reformers launched a modern child welfare movement that focused on the patriotic values boys could learn through play and leisure. Boys, presumably white, could learn the skills to be America's future soldiers and empire builders by playing with toy guns and engineering sets, while patriotic white girls could learn the skills of future mothers and wives by playing with baby dolls. This wartime focus on play and leisure as the essence of modern child welfare would become the new cornerstone of the movement in the years following the war.

The national movement's embrace of federal authority had many causes. On the whole, industrial and agricultural child labor was getting worse. In 1912 at least one million children under the age of sixteen were employed in industry in the United States while another million were estimated to be working in agriculture, "only a part of whom [were] assisting their parents on the farm."[11] Though the numbers of child laborers remained high, some state-level regulation of child labor had been achieved by 1912. When the NCLC was founded in 1904, only fifteen states had age limits for children working in factories.[12] By 1912 thirty-four states and the District of Columbia had established age limits, most commonly at fourteen. Recent prohibitions of night work by children under the age of sixteen were another sign that the NCLC was making progress. In 1904 only eight states restricted night work whereas in 1912 thirty-two states and the District had night work prohibitions.[13] Street trades, tenement house work, and agricultural labor in a nonfamilial context—forms of child labor that were entirely unregulated in 1904—had begun to garner public attention as "harmful" occupations for children. Additionally, sixteen states had secured laws limiting the work day of children under age sixteen to an eight-hour day.[14] Southern cotton mills still had the highest percentage of child labor, and Southern states were the most resistant to passing meaningful child labor laws. By 1912 even some Southern states had minimal regulations, but they tended to be weak laws that went largely unenforced.[15]

Reformers had learned that state-level regulations were rife with loopholes and lacked enforcement mechanisms. Investigators regularly discovered that state laws were not enforced, children's ages were often fabricated, and literacy requirements were evaded. In twenty-three states there was no official way to determine children's ages, which made it easier for employers to claim ignorance of any violations.[16] The word "knowingly" was inserted into many state child labor laws, providing additional indemnity for employers. Other loopholes, such as exemptions for poor children who worked out of "necessity" and for the children of widows who were thought to depend on child labor for survival, were widespread in state-level regulation.[17] Because there was no national standard, industries that wanted to hire children could relocate to states with more lenient laws.[18] The spectrum of state laws was vast. At one end was Ohio, which prohibited the gainful employment of children under the age of fifteen, while at the other end was North Carolina, which had no age limit for children in mills.[19] Western states such as New Mexico had no child labor laws whatsoever. On the eve of the First World War, reformers had taken note that the passage of a rigorous child labor law in one state was followed by one or more factories in that state moving across state lines where such laws did not exist.[20]

Nearing its ten-year anniversary, the NCLC united around the goal of a federal standard. Reformers had become more aware of the limitations of a state-by-state approach and were emboldened by recent federal investigations. After the Beveridge defeat, Congress ordered an investigation into the condition of "woman and child wage-earners" in the United States.[21] The results, published in 1910 and 1911 in nineteen volumes, "Report on Condition of Woman and Child Wage-Earners in the United States," provided federal confirmation of the realities of child labor. On April 5, 1912, Congress approved a bill creating a federal children's bureau, which would be located in the Department of Commerce and Labor.[22] The bureau's purpose would be to "investigate and report upon all matters pertaining to the welfare of children and child life among all our classes of people."[23] Julia C. Lathrop of the Hull House in Chicago was chosen by President William Howard Taft (1909–1912) to lead the organization.[24] The bureau freed up the NCLC to focus less on investigation and more on securing legislation.[25]

The creation of the Progressive Party in 1912 also influenced reformers. Nine years after Murphy made his famous "Child Labor as a National Problem" speech at the 1903 National Conference of Charities and Corrections, Owen Lovejoy presented "Social Standards for Industry" at the same conference. Less than two months later, Lovejoy's statement was adopted as part of the platform of a new political party, the "Progressive" or "Bull Moose" party.[26] President Taft had been a disappointment to many progressive Republicans, including Teddy Roosevelt.[27] Sensing an opportunity, Roosevelt left the Republican Party and ran on another ticket, naming it the Progressive Party.[28] Seven weeks later, he and his supporters had established offices in every state and held a National Progressive Party Convention in Chicago.[29] NCLC reformers helped ensure that Lovejoy's "Social Standards for Industry" would be included in the party's new platform. The platform included minimum wage standards, an eight-hour workday, a maximum six-day workweek, the abolition of tenement homework (child labor in private homes; also called the "putting-out system"), and *the prohibition of child labor by means of a national child labor law.*[30]

Despite Roosevelt's popularity, the four-way race tipped in favor of Democrat Woodrow Wilson.[31] Regrouping after Roosevelt's defeat, reformers attended a meeting with President-elect Wilson. Lovejoy outlined the NCLC's vision for a federal child labor law. Though Wilson expressed sympathy, he made clear he could not support federal action. He believed government was "not so much an initiating agency as a responsive one, depending on the vigorous action of its citizens."[32] Wilson, a former academic with a PhD in political science, had written extensively about constitutional issues, including the constitutionality of federal child labor legislation. Four years before running for president, Wilson wrote a scathing piece about the unconstitutionality of the Beveridge Bill: "If the power to regulate commerce between the states can be stretched to include regulation of labor in mills and factories, it can be made to embrace every particular of the industrial organization and action of the country."[33]

When the Sixty-Third Congress convened in April 1913, Progressive politicians who had supported Roosevelt introduced several versions of a federal child labor bill in Congress, sending the message that they would continue pursuing the Progressive Party platform.[34] NCLC leaders reviewed the committee's official position on federal intervention. Long an advocate of a federal standard, Alexander McKelway believed "the only answer lay with 'Uncle Sam.'"[35] Felix Adler, still gun-shy from the Beveridge debacle of 1907, was more reluctant. But after "long deliberation," he came to "recognize the necessity and propriety of such action." Although states had the power to prevent child labor within their own borders, they did not have the power to prevent child-made goods from other states from being transported, marketed, and sold within those same borders, Adler reasoned. The child labor movement aimed for more than just abolishing child labor "in our own communities." It demanded that Americans not be "forced against our will . . . to encourage child labor by purchasing the products of child labor."[36] Since states had relinquished control over interstate commerce to the federal government, it was a national rather than state responsibility to abolish child labor, Adler concluded. The NCLC leadership agreed. Under Murphy's leadership, the NCLC had initially defined child labor as a national problem requiring a national sentiment but not a federal solution.[37] By 1913 the NCLC was in a new moment. Frustrated by state-level efforts and emboldened by the Children's Bureau and Progressive Party, the committee declared a federal standard its top priority.[38]

In December 1913 a special committee of the NCLC was formed to evaluate the child labor bills before Congress. Reformers decided to draft their own.[39] After months of consultations with attorneys, politicians, members of Wilson's cabinet, the US Children's Bureau, and child welfare experts, the committee drafted a new bill, "To Prevent Interstate Commerce in the Products of Child Labor and for Other Purposes." Like the Beveridge Bill, it used the commerce clause to prohibit from interstate commerce "goods in the production of which children under 14 have been employed in factories, mills, canneries, and workshops, or children under 16 in mines and quarries, and goods in the production of which children between 14 and 16 have been employed for more than 8 hours a day or at night."[40] An important distinction was that it targeted the employer of child labor as the perpetrator rather than the interstate carrier of child-made goods. The bill was also more extensive and detailed, reflecting the NCLC's expertise and experience. After securing its board's approval, the NCLC sought sponsors, selecting Mitchell Palmer from Pennsylvania in the US House and Robert Owen from Oklahoma in the Senate. The measure became known as the Palmer-Owen Bill.[41]

After Representative Palmer introduced the measure in the House on January 26, 1914, NCLC reformers decided to test the waters again with President Wilson.[42] Lovejoy, McKelway, and Adler visited the White House to meet with the president and plead for his support. President Wilson was still opposed. Though the Supreme Court had recently upheld the right of the federal government to use the interstate commerce clause to bar lottery tickets, impure food, obscene literature, and the transportation of prostitutes, President Wilson held fast to his view that a federal child labor law was unconstitutional.[43] But he did agree to maintain a neutral stance publicly.[44] Though reformers were uncertain whether the Supreme Court would uphold the law, they entered the congressional battle with optimism. With a guarantee of neutrality from President Wilson, the bill's supporters took their case to the public.

The NCLC's decision in 1913 to wage a full-time effort for a federal child labor law gave renewed focus and energy to the organization. Lovejoy, who had been executive secretary of the NCLC since 1907, came into his own as the movement's leader. Lovejoy had been active in Mount Vernon, New York, where he helped organize the Sociological Club, a group that discussed social and industrial problems from a spiritual perspective. Like the broader Social Gospel movement, Lovejoy's group sought to apply the teachings of Jesus to economic life and social institutions. For Social Gospel followers, industrial capitalism was inherently sinful and needed to be "Christianized." It was the responsibility of Christians to bring salvation not only to individuals but to society as a whole. According to this view, sin resided not just in individual hearts but in economic structures and social institutions as well.[45] Lovejoy first embraced the Social Gospel when he visited the anthracite coal district of Pennsylvania in 1902. The sight of child laborers in the coal mines made a lasting impression on him. "Sights like those cling to you. I dreamed about those boys," he later wrote.[46]

Through the NCLC's battle for a federal child labor law, Lovejoy found a new platform for his Social Gospel agenda. Setting the tone for the upcoming battle was the 1914 publication of the widely read *Children in Bondage*. The poet Edwin Markham, judge Benjamin Lindsey, and journalist George Creel wrote *Children in Bondage* in consultation with Lovejoy and the NCLC.[47] Markham and Creel had met in New York City, where they both had worked for William Randolph Hearst's *Cosmopolitan* magazine. Dubbed the "great spiritual writer of America," Markham became in these years a kind of ad hoc poet for the Social Gospel movement, frequently cited by clergymen, orators, and professors as a poetic voice for the spiritual transformation of American capitalism.[48] He made a name for himself with the publication of *The Man with the Hoe and Other Poems* (1899), a collection of poems about poverty and America's working class.[49] With a federal child labor law pending, Lovejoy, Markham, Creel, and Lindsey joined together to write a passionate denunciation of child labor. The book caused a stir among readers. A review in *Good Housekeeping* magazine said of *Children in Bondage*, "It fortifies you for any fight on child labor—and makes you want to fight."[50] *The Dial* predicted that the book would "appeal to many who have neither the industry nor the patience" to read sociological or technical reports. A few months after the book was published, its passions were "already taking effect."[51] The New York State Library declared it one of the "best books of 1914," calling it "a vehement outburst of holy anger over the shameful conditions" of child labor.[52]

The frontispiece depicted the new enemy of the child labor movement: PROFIT. "Childhood is sacrificed daily so that profit may flow from every turn of a mill-wheel," the caption read. A lifeless girl lay sacrificed on the altar of profit, reflecting reformers' new focus on girls in the Progressive era. On the heels of *Muller v. Oregon* (1908), in which the Supreme Court declared the state's special interest in protecting females due to their "maternal function," child labor reformers noted that as the nation's "future mothers," girls were especially vulnerable to capitalist greed.[53] The Triangle Shirtwaist Factory fire of 1911 also aroused new public concern about girls working in factories, since the majority of victims had been female.[54] *Children in Bondage* spoke to this tragedy by pointing out that not only were the girls "forced by necessity

CHILDHOOD IS SACRIFICED DAILY THAT PROFIT MAY FLOW FROM EVERY TURN OF A MILL-WHEEL

Figure 4.1. Frontispiece. In Edwin Markham, Benjamin B. Lindsey, and George Creel, *Children in Bondage* (New York: Hearst's International Library, 1914). Courtesy of the University of Chicago Regenstein Library.

to work," but the fire at the Triangle factory had also revealed that they were "locked in to their dreary tasks!" The authors argued that protecting girls added a new urgency to the effort for a federal standard. Because of girls' supposed passivity and helplessness, they were more vulnerable than boys to capitalist greed. Greedy capitalists preferred "small girls," they wrote, because little girls "are good: they ask for nothing, they object to nothing." As young girls, these "future mothers" were "timid" and did not "cry out against harsh conditions." These "good little girls" were the "profit-monger's ideal."[55] State protection of girls was therefore an urgent necessity, since girls were presumably less likely than boys to stand up for themselves.

Children in Bondage also reflected reformers' embrace of the Social Gospel. On the title page was one of Lovejoy's favorite verses: "Jesus called a little child unto him and said, Whoso shall offend one of these little ones . . . it were better for him that a millstone were hanged about his neck, and that he were drowned in the depth of the sea."[56] Lovejoy reminded readers that the NCLC had recently submitted to Congress a bill "to prohibit the interstate transportation of goods manufactured by children." However, the battle for a federal child labor standard was also a spiritual battle for America's soul. "Society must come to see this whole subject from a higher point of view," Lovejoy wrote. A spiritual call to arms, *Children in Bondage* was intended to be for the child labor movement what *Uncle Tom's Cabin* had been for antislavery. Its purpose was to move hearts and souls rather than to dispassionately relate the facts of child labor: "Calmness and dispassion are of no use in this crisis. It is possible to deal argumentatively . . . with sticks and stones, but blood and tears must be made to wrench at the heart-strings," the authors wrote.[57] Packed with biblical allusions and sensational accounts of child labor, *Children in Bondage* sought to define child labor as the slavery of the early twentieth century. The battle for a federal child labor law was "God's battle," they wrote.[58] The "bloods and bones of babies" were built into the rotting foundation of American capitalism. God would bring judgment on a nation that sacrificed its children to "Greed and Gain, the grim guardians of the great god Mammon."[59] Jesus had been a friend to children, the authors reminded their readers: "Suffer little children to come unto Me," Jesus had said, "and forbid them not: for such is the kingdom of God."[60] Every American should awaken to the child labor evil as a form of slavery. Two million small bodies were "mangled, mind, body, and soul" and "fed annually into the steel jaws of the modern industrial machine."[61] Their blood was on the hands of all Americans, and Judgment Day was coming. Americans had the power to cleanse capitalism of its sinfulness by supporting a federal child labor law, asking their pastors to preach on the child labor evil, and encouraging their neighbors to do the same.[62] Through supporting a federal child labor law, they could do Christ's work to bring about the Kingdom of God on earth.

Children in Bondage reserved special criticism for the Southern textile industry. In a chapter titled "The Crimson in Our Cotton," the authors dubbed the textile industry a "Herod among industries" and held nothing back in their disparagement of the South's leading industry. "New England has its evils," they wrote, "but it is in the South, the real center of the cotton industry, that the essence of this social infamy is found."[63] After describing in gruesome detail the conditions of Southern mill children, the authors reiterated Murphy's white racial degeneracy argument: "These are not the children of recent immigrants. . . . Nor are they negro children who have shifted their shackles from field to mill. They are white children of old and pure colonial stock. . . . Here is a people that has outlived the bondage of England, that has seen the rise and fall of slavery—a people that must now fling their children into the clutches of capital."[64] The authors' descriptions were sensational and hyperbolic. In the world of *Children in Bondage*, Southern mill children were "spectres—shapes, doomed to silence and done with life," and "choked and blinded by clouds of lint." When Southern mill children returned home after working, they ate "cheerless meals" and "fell asleep with the food unswallowed in the mouth."[65] The authors even suggested the mills were grinding down the lives of Southern mill children to such an extent that it would be "less cruel for a state to have children painlessly put to death than it is to permit them to be ground to death by this awful process."[66]

The authors claimed that the South's new "white child slavery" was worse than the South's old slavery. Intoning Murphy's "lost cause" mythology, the authors described the "negro of the old days" as "well fed and sure of shelter," "singing as he toiled," and "finding time to weave . . . a poetic folklore," whereas the new white slavery "suck[ed] life dry of all vigor and joy." Like Murphy, the authors defined mill children's slavery in terms of their mental and physical deterioration. Southern mill children were "stunted, slow, and sad" with "no fragment of education." The spiritual dimensions of child labor took on a new significance in the age of the Social Gospel. Worse than the breakdown of the body and mind in these "God-forgetting mills" was "the breakdown of the soul."[67] The souls of mill children were growing "hardened in crusts of coarseness," resulting in "moral disintegration." This "treason against God" was more offensive than the physical and mental effects of child labor. Not only were children's minds and bodies stunted, but their souls were crushed, robbing them of their human essence. The "church of the South" was "complacent, acquiescent, silent," because its steeples were "in the shadow of the mill." Echoing the religious debates that divided the North and South over slavery, the authors blamed the "icy indifference of organized religion" in the South for not standing "against this treason."[68] The religious dimensions of child labor debates were reminiscent of those that had underpinned the conflict over slavery. As the battle over child labor heated up, Northern reformers claimed God was on their side. Southern opponents would react in kind, deepening sectional divisions along religious lines.

The authors of *Children in Bondage* posed the question, "What Would Christ Have Thought of Child Labor?" The entirety of Christ's life could be understood, they argued, as a "heroic attempt to substitute a more wholesome and brotherly environment for cruel industrial conditions." According to this view, Christ would agitate to rescue the child laborer from bondage: "We can tell authoritatively what He would do if brought face to face with the present child labor problem of the United States. He would sweep through the cotton mills of the Union with a whip in his hand, and the owners of the glass factories, woolen mills, and coal mines, and the operators of sweatshops and all those other agencies for the exploitation of little children would shiver under the passion of his denunciation."[69] For Lovejoy and reformers, abolishing child labor was a necessary step in establishing the Kingdom of God on earth. Concern for children took precedence over other social issues, since it was only "through an uplifted and liberated youth that the kingdom of God on earth would be won."[70] "Spiritual death" awaited a nation that permitted its "industrial machine to mangle nearly two million little children."[71] Complacency was not an option: "Not until Congress and the legislatures are made to take . . . a burning interest in the welfare of children . . . is any decent citizen entitled to rest."[72]

The NCLC oversaw an aggressive outreach to churches as a major component of its effort for a federal law. Since 1905 the NCLC had instituted a Child Labor Day that was observed by participating churches across the country on a given Sunday in January. Initially, the purpose of Child Labor Day was to encourage ministers to make at least one reference to child labor in their sermons. In recent years, however, Child Labor Day had grown into a larger operation. The NCLC had produced sermons on child labor, compiled Bible verses related to children, and solicited hymns about child labor from Christian hymn composers such as Fanny Crosby.[73] In his annual letter to clergymen across the country requesting their observance of Child Labor Day in January 1914, Lovejoy stepped up his religious rhetoric: "The 2,000,000 children working in this country . . . are a mockery of the fact that Christ founded His kingdom on the Child; that he solemnly warned his immediate companions against undervaluation of the child." The participation of "30,000,000 Christians" would be "a force in abolishing child labor, more powerful than any other." This letter was sent to over five thousand clergymen along with pamphlets about the child labor evil. Sermons and instructions for congregations who wanted to help were mailed to ministers on request.[74] In another letter, Lovejoy wrote, "We are eager this year for the widest possible observance of Child Labor Day, because of the federal bill . . . which will be introduced into Congress this December."[75]

In a crucial endorsement from Social Gospel leaders, the Federal Council of Churches of Christ in America (FCCC) endorsed the Palmer-Owen Bill in 1914.[76] Founded in 1908, the FCCC was an association of churches whose famous "Social Creed of the Churches" was the clarion call of the Social Gospel movement.[77] Historians have marked the FCCC's 1908 adoption of the Social Creed as the moment when the Social Gospel became ascendant.[78] With over 17 million members representing at least thirty-three Protestant denominations, the council was a highly influential association that pioneered

Child Labor Abolitionists 97

certain forms of interchurch cooperation.[79] Called the "Magna Charta [*sic*] for church-labor relations," the Social Creed had included from the beginning a commitment to "the abolition of child labor" along with provisions for a living wage for all workers, equal rights for all Americans, old-age insurance, and equitable distribution of wealth.[80] Social Gospel leaders such as Walter Rauschenbusch drew on the child labor issue to explain what he meant by "Christianizing" the social order: "I do not mean putting the name of Christ into the Constitution. . . . Jesus himself does not seem to have cared much about being called 'Lord, Lord,' unless there was substance to the word. To put a stop to child labor in our country would be a more effective way of doing homage to His sovereignty than any business of words and names."[81]

At the height of Social Gospel's popularity, the battle for a federal child labor law became a religious crusade. Ministers preached on the child labor evil, congregations sang hymns about rescuing child workers, Americans wrote letters to Congress urging support for the national child labor law, and *Children in Bondage* became a national sensation. The movement's new tone was reflected at the NCLC's Eleventh Annual Conference in 1915. The opening address was given by Felix Adler, a Jewish social reformer whose views were influenced by the Social Gospel. Chairman of the NCLC since its founding in 1904, Adler had early on in his life rejected the traditional Judaism of his father in favor of religion characterized by "deed not creed."[82] Adler opened the meeting, saying, "The principal point to which I shall call your attention is the aspect of the national child labor movement as intended to contribute to the spiritual awakening and conversion of the American people." While there were many practical reasons to oppose child labor, there were deeper, spiritual issues at stake. Child labor in factories, mills, mines, and fields reflected a spiritually lost nation. It was a symptom of a spiritual disease: moneymaking as the chief end of all life. The "orthodoxy of the market" had taken over the nation. Any market activity that generated profit for a few was not required to pass a spiritual test. "According to the orthodoxy of the market, the chief end of life is not to glorify God but to make money," Adler put it. Americans had grown devoid of spiritual understanding, unable to "comprehend their own condition."[83] Other religious leaders who spoke at the conference echoed Adler's concerns. Edwin H. Hughes of the Methodist Episcopal Church noted that "the ethical and religious side" of the child labor issue had been unusually prominent "in the last two national gatherings."[84]

With the Social Gospel movement buttressing them, reformers focused on a new enemy through sermons, speeches, songs, books, pamphlets, and cartoons: the greedy capitalist. The sinfulness of a capitalism that exploited children for profit formed the core of the national effort to pass a federal child labor bill from 1914 through 1916. "A Little Child Shall Feed Them" was an ironic cartoon in *Life* magazine picturing a small child climbing a ladder to feed cash profits to a giant-size capitalist. "The Biblical Law as Interpreted by Employers of Child Labor," read the caption, suggesting that employers had misinterpreted a verse in Isaiah: "And a little child shall lead them."[85] Another cartoon that appeared in newspapers in 1914 and 1915 depicted Jesus overlooking America while child laborers walked to work. Underneath the picture were child-related verses from the book of Matthew compiled by reformers.[86] "The Money Tree of Child Labor," an illustration that appeared in the *New York Journal* in 1914, emphasized the sinfulness of a capitalism that exploited children for profit. Intoning the righteous anger of the Social Gospel, the authors wrote, "Would that the branches [of this child labor tree] might reach to heaven and stir an avenging justice that would end the system."[87] Other examples of righteous indignation toward a child-exploiting capitalism abounded.[88]

Likening their cause to abolitionism, reformers called the proposed child labor bill a "new Emancipation Proclamation" and argued that federal intervention was necessary to "end child slavery" in America.[89] The greedy capitalist who employed children was a "child slaver," and "immediate action" by the federal government was necessary. Reformers received an additional boost in January 1915 when the most widely observed Child Labor Day to date was held in churches across America.[90] "It is fortunate for us that Child Labor Day falls in January," said Owen Lovejoy, "because it is going to be a big factor in the passage of the federal child labor bill now before Congress. We are asking all who are observing the day to emphasize the need for action in behalf of the bill and the result should be an overwhelming demand for its enactment."[91] Child Labor Day was observed by an unprecedented number of churches and other organizations in at least forty-one states.[92]

The religious dimensions of the child labor debate made its way into the halls of Congress. In February 1915 Representative Mitchell Palmer, the Progressive Democrat who sponsored the bill, spoke to the House of Representatives: "I am very anxious to pass this bill. . . . It is in the platform of all the political parties. The Republican Party, the Progressive Party, and the Democratic Party and the Nation have declared for this kind of legislation. The country is for it, as it is for very few things in either branch of Congress today."[93] The bill, then known as the Palmer-Owen Bill, passed the House after little discussion on February 15, 1915, with a vote count of 233 to 43.[94] Southern congressmen in opposition to the bill had spoken on the House floor, making their usual states' rights arguments. "I am opposed to the Federal Government under the pretense of regulating interstate commerce usurping the powers of the States," said Congressman James F. Byrnes of South Carolina. Congressman Irvine Luther Lenroot of Wisconsin framed his response in moral terms: "All this law says is that if [an individual state] insists on sacrificing the lives of its little children . . . you will keep within the confines of your own State when you do it, and you shall not exercise a right . . . to bring the products of your child labor into competition with other States where they have some respect and some regard for the lives of the little children of the country."[95]

It would be another year and a half before the House and the Senate agreed on a child labor bill. Representative Edward Keating of Colorado sponsored the measure in the House at the next session, and Senator Robert Owen of Oklahoma reintroduced it in the Senate. During both the House and Senate sessions of 1916, opposition to the measure became more pronounced. "Leave us to ourselves. . . . To protect our children is our right; it is our duty. This Congress has neither the power nor the duty," said Congressman Danny Earl Britt of North Carolina in February 1916. At the same session, Congressman Byrnes protested, "My people believe in local self-government; they believe that that legislation is best which is founded upon accurate information, and that accurate information can be secured only by those who are familiar with local conditions." Southern opponents maligned the reformers, calling them "alarmists," "agitators," and "hired mourners." Congressman Edwin Yates Webb of North Carolina said, "I fear there has been a good deal of false sentiment that has been created by a well organized and financed child labor committee, and I fear that many Members are going to vote according to that sentiment." Like other Congressmen in the previous session, Representative Kenneth McKellar of Tennessee focused on the immorality of a capitalism that exploited children: "This fight is a fight of helplessness and innocence on the one side against inhumanity and greed on the other. We have long since made the slaves free. . . . Surely it is time that we were breaking the shackles of slavery from the young children of our land."

Debate on the floor at times sounded like a competition over who could reference the Bible the most. Reminding his colleagues that Jesus was "once a little Lad," Congressman Charles Frank Reavis of Nebraska pointed out that "after the passing of 2,000 years, the civilized world bows in adoration at the feet of the little Lad who followed His father." Congressman Reavis suggested that through the personhood of Jesus, the Bible affirmed that children were sacred and should not be "beasts of burden." Another congressman implored the bill's opponents: "Think well before you cast your votes against the little children." He then reminded them of this verse: "Suffer the little children to come unto me and forbid them not, for such is the kingdom of Heaven." He also warned, "When you vote against this bill, you vote against the teachings of that blessed book; you vote against the teachings of that Divine Savior. . . . You vote to force [children] to lay their young lives as a helpless sacrifice upon the cruel altar of inhumanity and greed. I beg you not to do it." These arguments, which reflected the broader Social Gospel movement, challenged opponents to muster up an equivalent moral fervor for their own position. Pressure to do so was reflected in statements such as one made by Congressman Webb, who defended child labor on the grounds that many children were supporting "widowed mothers" whom the Bible instructs Christians to care for. "I appeal to you on behalf of the tired, saddened, dependent mothers," he said. "I say there is much more Christian spirit, as my friend says, in letting the boy work under these circumstances."[96] A congressman from Florida expressed his view that prohibiting child labor was not biblical, since earning a living by the sweat of one's brow was part of the original curse of man and thus applied to everyone, including children: "[Children] ought to work. The Scripture says, 'In the sweat of thy face shalt thou eat bread.'"[97] Labor was unpleasant, since it was part of the original curse, including child labor. Abolishing child labor was an attempt to overturn divine law.

Southern congressmen had not yet developed a strong moral argument against child labor reformers. Although they defended child labor by pointing to the Bible, they did not muster an equivalent moral fervor to the Social Gospel arguments against child labor. Congressman William Kent of California sensed the opposition's weakness: "I feel almost guilty standing up here and seemingly throwing bricks at those unfortunate Members of the House who feel it necessary to defend child labor. I am sorry for them. I apologize for them if they do not apologize for themselves."[98] Congressman Mahlon M. Garland of Pennsylvania expressed impatience with states' rights excuses: "Let us pass the bill. And if some court declares it unconstitutional, let it do so. . . . If we are going to err, for God's sake, let us err on the side of humanity."[99] Nearing the end of debate, an Alabama congressman made a last-ditch effort to persuade his colleagues: "The American people must sooner or later wake up to a realization of the fact that we have in Congress and elsewhere people who desire the centralization of all power at Washington. Centralization of power here means the destruction of local self-government. . . . I am in favor of all legislation tending to protect the children, but I believe this is a matter that should be dealt with by the States individually, without Federal interference."[100] Representative Henry Barnhart of Indiana responded with a moral imperative: "I believe as firmly as I stand here that the innocent child's blood that bespatters so many windowpanes of the factories of this country is a stain upon the character [of this country] and ought to be abolished . . .

Constitution or no Constitution."[101] With the final votes cast, the bill passed the House, 337 to 46. The majority of the "nay" votes came from Southern states.[102]

Unlike the House, debate in the Senate focused more on whether what was now known as the Keating-Owen Bill fell within the limits of the congressional power to regulate interstate commerce. The senators discussed how the commerce clause had been used previously and compared these precedents to Keating-Owen. But even here the crux of the debate was to what extent the commerce clause gave Congress the power to regulate capitalism on the basis of morality. Senator William Borah of Idaho, who argued in favor of Keating-Owen, likened the bill to the Lottery Act, which the Supreme Court had upheld as constitutional: "The Lottery case cannot be sustained upon any other principle than that of the power of Congress to protect the channels of interstate trade from use by people for immoral purposes." In the case of child labor, the "public morals" were at stake, thus Keating-Owen was on par with the Lottery Act. But Senator John D. Works of California begged to differ. Lottery tickets were subject to regulation under the commerce clause, because their transport across state lines encouraged "immoral behavior" among the residents of another state. But the Keating-Owen Bill was "an entirely different proposition"; "the thing to be carried in this case is not detrimental to health or morals at all." Rather, the bill "prohibits the carrying of goods because they are manufactured in a particular way. . . . That is the troublesome feature of it to me." Senator Borah pointed out that "so long as the Government lends its instrumentalities of government to the use of those who employ child labor, it is augmenting and encouraging the doing of that which is deemed to be immoral." Other precedents debated by the senators included the Mann Act of 1910, which prohibited the transport of prostitutes across state lines. Supporters of Keating-Owen believed the same principle was at stake in regulating child labor. Opponents argued that this bill would "absolutely change our form of government," since the commodity transported across state lines was itself "perfectly innocent."[103] If Keating-Owen passed, opponents feared, Congress could then regulate the transport of any commodity on the basis of the conditions under which it was made.

Senators opposed to Keating-Owen had difficulty countering the Social Gospel rhetoric of the bill's supporters. Debates over constitutionality generally conceded the point that child labor was an "evil" that should be regulated in some manner. At issue among the senators was whether this "evil" had already been committed before the interstate transport had taken place or whether interstate transportation should be considered a "necessary instrument" that enabled the evil. As the Senate neared a vote, momentum was on the side of the bill's supporters. Behind the scenes, President Wilson could see the writing on the wall.[104] Facing reelection in a couple of months, Wilson knew he would need the support of Progressives who had voted for Roosevelt in 1912. The public mood continued to grow in favor of Keating-Owen. Prominent newspapers in at least thirty-two states published editorials supporting Keating-Owen, cartoons depicted the bill as a "New Emancipation Proclamation," and headlines decried "End This Slavery for All Time!"[105] In a move that all but sealed the fate of Keating-Owen, President Wilson urged Democratic Party leaders to "pass the child labor bill at this session."[106] Despite thirty-one senators abstaining from the vote, the Senate managed to pass Keating-Owen with a vote of fifty-two to twelve on August 8, 1916.[107]

President Wilson signed the Keating-Owen Bill into law on September 1, 1916: "I want to say with what real emotion I sign this bill because I know how long the struggle has been to secure legislation of this sort."[108] It is unclear whether Wilson made a political calculation, experienced a change of heart, or both.[109] What is clear is that the decision was politically helpful for him. Though he had jumped onboard the Keating-Owen campaign only at the end, Wilson received much of the credit for signing into law the first federal child labor bill. Taking advantage of the moment, the Democratic Party distributed placards that read "Lincoln freed the slaves; Wilson freed the children." The *Chicago Journal* referred to him as "The Liberator" and pictured him in an illustration, holding the Child Labor Act in one hand as scores of children, presumably freed from labor, surrounded him.[110] In November 1916 Wilson won reelection with the support of Progressives and with the campaign motto "He kept us out of war."[111] But events in Europe would soon prompt Wilson and his administration to reconsider their stance of neutrality in the conflict. Reformers and their supporters celebrated the passage of Keating-Owen. The NCLC called it "the greatest single accomplishment" in the history of the child labor movement.[112] The Social Gospel crusade for a federal law had carried the day.

Occurring on the heels of the most significant legislative victory against child labor in US history, America's entry into the First World War dramatically shifted the ground beneath reformers' feet. Trade tensions among the United States, Britain, and Germany and the sinking of the British passenger liner *Lusitania* in May 1915 had led President Wilson to break diplomatic relations with Berlin. But it was not until after the interception of the notorious Zimmermann Telegram in January 1917 and the sinking of several American ships in February and March of 1917 that Wilson and his administration decided to ask Congress on April 2, 1917, for a declaration of war.[113] "The

Child Labor Abolitionists   103

world must be made safe for democracy," read the front page of the *New York Times* the following day, quoting President Wilson.[114] When the United States entered the war, opponents of Keating-Owen began taking steps to suspend federal, state, and local child labor regulations in the name of "wartime necessity." In many states these efforts included suspending compulsory education laws that would interfere with the ability of minors, especially boys, to contribute to the war effort as laborers in agriculture and industry. In August 1917 the NCLC reported, "In spite of the efforts of our members and many social organizations, several states have succeeded in passing laws which would permit the suspension of child labor [and] education laws."[115] Indeed, a broader effort to suspend all labor laws in the name of wartime necessity was under way. At issue for leaders in Wilson's administration, many state legislatures, and governors was whether child labor laws should be included in this effort.[116] Determined not to allow reversals of hard-won restrictions against child labor, reformers launched a wartime campaign. The purpose of the campaign was to convince President Wilson and his administration, along with supporters of the movement whose resolve was shaken and the American public generally, that the prohibition of child labor was just as important—perhaps even more so—in wartime as in peace time. To accomplish this goal, they needed to address how child labor would actually damage rather than advance the war effort. They published "war pamphlets"; created exhibits; wrote letters and speeches; and reached out to politicians, ministers, educators, and others with their wartime message.[117]

Reformers distributed a pamphlet to hundreds of newspapers arguing that stunting "the future growth and development" of America's boys would lead to the weakening of the American nation and its ability to defend democracy abroad.[118] Now that the nation was at war, reformers were on the defensive. Boys became the focus of a national debate about "wartime necessity" and how they should be contributing to the war effort. Not only the federal Keating-Owen Act but also hard-won state and local laws were suddenly at risk. In this climate they felt pressure to redirect the movement in a way that would address the immediate threats that faced them and their progress. Adapting their movement to wartime aims, reformers drew on a reservoir of institutional knowledge that centered on the relationship of child labor reform to the strength and vitality of the nation.

To make their case about the importance of protecting boys from labor in wartime, reformers looked to Europe. At the start of the conflict, England, Germany, and other nations had asked, "Why shouldn't the children do their bit?" These countries had "rushed children into industry" after war broke out but had since realized that the physical and mental deterioration of children,

Figure 4.2. "His Bit," *New York Call*, June 21, 1917, Cartoon Collection of the National Child Labor Committee, box 48-B, NCLC-LOC. Courtesy of the Library of Congress.

especially boys, was not worth the short-term gains. Reformers argued that increasing the labor of boys during wartime had put the long-term vitality of these nations at risk. As Lovejoy put it, "When the war developed into an endurance test in which the physical fitness, efficiency, and productivity of every individual was increasingly valuable, it began to look as if the children's bit was something more than immediate sacrifice."[119] Putting boys to work in factories during wartime may have seemed to help initially, but as England and Germany had learned, the long-term effects actually decreased the ability of nations to win wars and secure empires. Lovejoy noted that there had been an increase in juvenile delinquency in England and Germany since the start of the conflict, which caused further national deterioration. Imploring federal and state officials alike, the NCLC made this plea in a letter: "At the present time when war is destroying so much of its best manhood, the nation is under special obligation to secure that the rising generation grows up strong and hardy in both body and character."[120]

Despite the NCLC's warnings about the child labor situation in Europe, bills proposing to set aside child labor and compulsory education laws were introduced in state legislatures around the country.[121] One month after America's entry into the war, Connecticut and New Hampshire had given their governors the power to suspend "all labor laws for the duration of the war," Vermont had passed a similar law, and New York had passed two laws that would allow for the suspension of compulsory education laws and child labor laws. In Pennsylvania agricultural work was deemed to be a "valid excuse" for absence from school, and such work would be counted as credit "in lieu of school attendance" for children over the age of twelve.[122] Among certain Southern senators, a more ambitious plan to repeal the Keating-Owen Act was under way, which infuriated the NCLC:

> We of the National Child Labor Committee believe that if [Keating-Owen] was the will of the people before war threatened to take away the men of the nation, it is more than ever their will now. The children cannot actually do the men's work in the factories and mines. To use little children in the place of men would lower the quantity and quality of the output and weaken the future efficiency and health of the race. . . . No matter what excuses of patriotism or expediency the advocates of child labor offer, we must recognize the insidious nature of their proposal.[123]

Reformers' tactics, arguments, and actions dramatically shifted as a result of America's entry into the First World War. During the Keating-Owen campaign, reformers had focused on greedy capitalists exploiting helpless children—especially girls—in the name of profit. This Social Gospel–inspired crusade sought to protect children from the excesses of greedy capitalism. But throughout the duration of America's involvement in World War I, reformers reframed their cause not in terms of the market but in terms of national vitality. Joining them in this campaign were President Wilson and key members of his administration. By December 1917 President Wilson and Secretary of War Newton D. Baker had declared the protection of children a "wartime measure" in the national interest.[124] In a letter, President Wilson wrote, "As the labor situation created by the war develops, I am . . . very glad indeed that the National Child Labor Committee is diligently continuing its labors and extending its vigilance in this important matter. By doing so it is contributing to efficiency and economy of production, as well as to the preservation of life and health."[125] In a speech discouraging the use of child labor in wartime, Secretary Baker said, "We cannot afford, when losing boys in France, to lose children at home."[126] These men joined the NCLC in framing the child labor issue in terms of national interest.

With a renewed focus on boys in the national discourse, Southern opponents of child labor reform saw an opportunity to challenge the Keating-Owen Bill. In the summer of 1917, a North Carolina cotton mill owner and founder of the Southern Textile Association, David Clark, had been strategizing ways to challenge Keating-Owen's constitutionality. Clark sought out a legal case featuring two older boys working on behalf of their father. A North Carolina man, Roland Dagenhart, who worked in a textile mill in Charlotte with his two sons, ages thirteen and fifteen, was being forced under Keating-Owen to take his sons out of the mill. Clark's plan was for Dagenhart to sue for his right to have his sons employed at the mill. Dagenhart agreed to the plan and sued on the grounds that the Keating-Owen Act violated his constitutional right to "due process" under the Fifth Amendment, since it denied him access to his children's earnings. Additionally, Dagenhart's lawyer argued that the Keating-Owen Act was unconstitutional because Congress did not have the power to regulate local labor conditions. The federal court of the Western Judicial District of North Carolina, presided over by Judge James E. Boyd, ruled in favor of Dagenhart on August 31, 1917, declaring the Keating-Owen Act "unconstitutional." District Attorney W. C. Hammer appealed the case to the US Supreme Court, which decided in *Hammer v. Dagenhart* on June 3, 1918, to uphold the ruling of the district court, officially overturning the Keating-Owen Act in a landmark 5–4 decision.[127]

For reformers, this blow could not have come at a worse time. Not only were many local and state laws being suspended in the name of "wartime necessity," but the Social Gospel movement was also gradually disappearing. Federal officials and agencies had determined that protecting the health and well-being of the nation's children should be a wartime priority, but the meaning of child welfare was shifting to accommodate the war effort. Before the war, child welfare had been characterized by a religious urgency to rein in greedy capitalists. But after the war, child welfare came to encompass any effort to preserve the physical and mental fitness of the nation's future citizens. An article in *Red Cross Magazine*, "Look Out for the Children: Measures for the Safeguarding of Young America in Wartime," argued that since America's children were the "future citizens," they must be "safeguarded, developed, and prepared to be fit citizens of the United States."[128] In a letter to NCLC members, Lovejoy reflected on the wartime changes: "Our work has assumed a definite aspect of national patriotism in these days of war pressure. We are aiming to carry out the policy so urgently pressed by President Wilson that industrial resources be conserved, and the health and educational standards of children be maintained in the interest of national defense."[129] In the name of national interest, the Federal Children's Bureau was also taking an active role in wartime child welfare, establishing National Baby Week in May 1917 to increase public awareness of maternal and infant care. One year after America's entry into the war, the bureau announced that 1918 would be Children's Year, which was intended to establish national child welfare as an American war aim.[130] In the first few months of the conflict, the National Council of Defense endorsed child welfare as a wartime measure on the grounds that "the health of the child is the power of the nation."[131]

Alongside federal officials and child welfare agencies, another wartime ally for reformers was the American toy industry. During the war, toy manufacturers were quick to jump aboard the child welfare bandwagon. Consumer culture was relatively new, and toy manufacturers were eager to boost its reputation. As many historians have noted, the corporate reconstruction of American capitalism during these years created a need for not only mass production but also mass consumption.[132] By the time America entered World War I, department stores, chain stores, window displays, mail-order catalogs, movie theaters, hotels, restaurants, billboards, and electric signs were a normal part of the American landscape. This transformation had far-reaching consequences that were not just economic but social and cultural as well. As historian William Leach has described it, the modern consumer society that emerged in early twentieth-century America was a "market-oriented culture, with the exchange and circulation of money and goods at the foundation of its aesthetic life and of its moral sensibility."[133]

A separate consumer culture for children smacked of irony in an age when reformers had defined children as off-limits to capitalism. Displacing the Social Gospel creed was a modern consumerist ethos that defined freedom within market society as the freedom to pursue self-fulfillment and personal growth. Shedding a previous emphasis on capitalism's tragic moral limits, reformers embraced the values of modern industrial society and averted their eyes as spiritual and material progress became one.[134] A separate children's consumer culture was a sign of advancement, encompassing large-scale toy manufacture, children's advertising, entire floors devoted to children in department stores, and independently operated toy stores.[135] Fundamental questions about the moral limits of capitalism faded from public discourse. "How do you calculate . . . a child's worth?" asked an NCLC reformer in 1914. Only those who were "engrossed in the ideals of the marketplace" could ever measure a child's worth "in dollars and cents."[136] Those less at ease with worship of the marketplace had declared "childhood as something precious beyond all money standard."[137]

American toy manufacturers inserted themselves into the child welfare movement by focusing on boys and national vitality. A wartime "made in America" campaign discouraged the consumption of German-made toys, which had constituted the majority of toys bought in America before the war.[138] "The American toy industry came into its own through the war, and American dealers can [now] do a lot to keep out foreign competition," noted a postwar advertisement.[139] Before the war most Americans had seen toys as luxury items to be purchased for children during the Christmas season only.[140] But toy manufacturers in the 1910s promoted the idea that toys were vital to child welfare and should be purchased year-round: "The educational toy had come largely into vogue and this was a decided incentive to foster this all-the-year plan of selling toys."[141] Early twentieth-century toymakers began marketing their toys directly to children rather than to parents.[142] According to one toymaker in 1915, "If the parent purchased the toy, it was the child who was to be pleased, and he was consulted, and he was appealed to by the storekeepers, and his ideas and desires were studied in a way that marked the development of the entire industry."[143] Child consumerism was a type of socialization whereby children learned how to be consumers with desires, tastes, ideas, and behavior shaped by the consumer marketplace. Advertisers and merchants began to consider children a distinctive consumer group with distinctive needs and desires. Though parents or other adults ultimately made the purchase, children were behind the sale.[144]

During the First World War, the American toy industry was uniquely positioned to join the child welfare movement. Trade restrictions with Germany brought on by the war allowed American toy manufacturers to monopolize the domestic market. Since Germany had dominated the American toy market for many years, the wartime rise of the American toy industry was a patriotic victory. Through an intense campaign led by President Wilson's Committee on Public Information (CPI), the once-admired Germans were transformed overnight into savage "Huns," bloodthirsty for world domination.[145] The American toy industry advanced this propaganda themselves. Newspapers across the country ran headlines such as "Supplant German Toys," "Santa Claus Is Beginning to Live in U.S.," "German Toys Called Menace," "Americans to Shun All Toys Made in Germany," and "Into the Ocean with Hun Toys."[146] Toymakers needed to prove that "our particular industry will meet the test which war brings [and that] *we can render our country a service by producing toys.*"[147] The wartime campaign for child welfare—a broad national effort to conserve and protect the nation's children during the war—was just the push they needed. With the wartime retreat of the Social Gospel and greedy capitalism no longer the focus of national discourse, the American toy industry became integral to the child welfare movement.[148] "The necessity of protecting child life is a subject on which the American people are now fully awake," wrote one toymaker in June 1917. The toy industry, he declared, should be "part of the national defense of childhood," since toys "ministered to the growth of children" and were "indispensable to vigorous, healthy life."[149]

Child Labor Abolitionists 109

Through advertisements, window displays, and other forms of public outreach, the American toy industry framed itself as the market antidote to oppressive child labor. "The future of America will soon be in the hands of the children of today," read an advertisement. Since the toy industry worked "to develop children's mental alertness [and] their mechanical natures," it was nothing less than "a national benefit."[150] "American toys," read another ad, "*delight the fancy and develop the mind* of every child."[151] A July 1917 trade journal article connected the aims of the toy industry to the child welfare campaign: "In this day of so-called 'modern warfare' this great thing has dawned upon us: That our children are our future. That we already have with us our tomorrow of national spirit and national life—it is our children. [This] striking hour marks the sunrise for the TOY MAN." In order to seize fully the wartime campaign for child welfare, "The TOY MAN's advertisements should dwell upon the importance of properly training the child's mind [and] of preparing the child for its future place in the national life."[152]

As the American toy industry became an agency of child welfare, it also defined itself as a patriotic, "100 percent American" institution. In April 1917 the Toy Manufacturers of the USA, a trade organization that was barely a year old, sent a resolution to President Wilson approving his decision to enter the war and collectively pledged "to support the President in every act to uphold the honor of the Republic."[153] From the anti-German propaganda campaign led by President Wilson's CPI to the federally backed wartime campaign for child welfare, American toymakers supported the war effort. Toy merchants designed display windows with patriotic themes, encouraged customers to buy Liberty Bonds, and held patriotic plays in their toy departments.[154] They also transformed their stores into public spaces of child welfare education. Toy sellers collaborated with the US Children's Bureau, allowing their toy-store windows to be used as displays for the bureau's National Baby Week during the war.[155] Toymakers also pitched in to help the effort to abolish child labor. In Detroit the J. L. Hudson Co. toy department hosted a child labor exhibit, displaying pictures, posters, and charts in their store window and gaining new customers in the process.[156] Distancing themselves from the use of child labor, toymakers sought to "raise the whole toy industry to a higher ethical standard" and to "correct abuses that may be a menace to the toy industry."[157] They also oversaw the production of patriotic dolls like "Maiden America," "Liberty Boys," and "Uncle Sam's Kids," all the while raising an American flag over their factories each day. A toy factory in Pittsburgh held a ceremony when it raised the flag, including the singing of patriotic songs, prayers for the troops, and a keynote address given by the toy company's president.[158] Other toy manufacturers donated a portion of their operations to the production of ammunition.[159]

Coupled with wartime trade embargoes, the toy industry's ability to link consumerism, patriotism, and child welfare was spectacular for business. By war's end, toymakers were raking in profits that would have made employers of child labor envious. In 1900 the American toy industry was an $8 million industry. But by the end of World War I it had grown into a $70 million industry, a near tenfold increase. Most of this growth occurred during the war years, 1914–1918, as profits from toy sales in 1914 still amounted to just $13.7 million.[160] The toy industry shrewdly defined itself as a benevolent institution of child welfare alongside child labor reformers, public educators, psychologists, and other child welfare experts. Placing the toy industry alongside "the home" and "the school" as the "trinity that builds patriotism," toymakers placed their industry at the heart of child welfare. The "play hour" was an even greater influence on children than the home and the school, they argued. Children who played with "100 percent American made" toys would learn "real Americanism."[161]

Toymakers also shrewdly focused on boys in their wartime arguments about play and leisure. Throughout the war, they emphasized the role of militaristic and mechanical toys in the training of America's middle-class white boys as the future leaders of the country. "America's future depends on her boys," read an advertisement for King Air Rifles that featured middle-class white boys. "Parents today realize the value of having sons know how to handle a gun," the ad read, suggesting that boys who played with King Air Rifles were America's future soldier-citizens.[162] A September 1917 article in *Toys and Novelties* articulated this idea more fully: "The boys who used to play with toys are now our chief defense," wrote one toymaker. Boys who "played with guns and cannon[s]" were "the best America has—in youth, in strength, in her hope of the future."[163] Similarly, mechanical toys for boys were linked to the future vitality of the American nation and the strength of its empire abroad. An ad for Wolverine mechanical toys that included a "Panama Pile Driver" and an "Electric Elevator" read, "The future of America soon will be in the hands of the children of today. Energetic minds in strong little bodies are the best guarantee of our nation's continued development."[164] Another ad for a Structo mechanical engineering set pictured a young white boy playing with a crane. In the background was a vision of his and other young white boys' futures: "EMPIRE BUILDERS."[165]

Although toymakers directed more advertisements to young white boys during the war, they also stepped up their doll advertisements to girls. Unlike female child labor, which harmed the nation's future mothers, playing with dolls could enhance girls' motherly skills and patriotic sentiment. One ad in the "Buy American Toys" campaign pictured "Jane Ann" playing with toys and envisioned her future role as either a Red Cross nurse, who would "take care of our soldiers," or a teacher, who could "tell little children all about patriotism."[166] "Jane Ann is a patriot," the ad read, who "knows all about American-made toys."[167] Other articles and ads suggested that middle-class white girls were "patriots" because they refused to play with anything but "superior" American-made dolls. A young girl in San Francisco was lauded by toymakers for "drowning her German dolls": "A seven-year-old lassie is grieving for three darlings of her heart, but grieving with a patriotic pride that she was able to put duty above her love," reported the *San Francisco Chronicle.*[168] American-made dolls were themselves "100 percent American dolls" with a "peaches and cream complexion."[169] Doll manufacturing companies gave themselves names like Superior Doll Company, the Perfect Doll Company, The Great American Doll, and even The Eugenic Baby. An ad for the Eugenic Baby doll read, "The First Doll Perfect in Mind and Body."[170] Patriotic dolls like "Maiden America" and "Uncle Sam's Kids" reflected and reinforced wartime constructions of national belonging that imagined white, nonimmigrant, middle-class children as the "100 percent American" customers that would patronize toy departments.[171]

By war's end, reformers had lost the religious tone that gave them Keating-Owen, but they had gained new allies in a broad child welfare movement that was rooted in modern industrial society. In 1919 the NCLC reflected on these changes: "The havoc that war has wrought in the adult world has laid additional emphasis on the protection of the coming generation. . . . The real trend of the new 'child labor' movement is the attempt not only to safeguard, but to develop the child along normal lines of education and recreation." Before the war the child labor campaign had "stood in people's minds largely for a negative movement, a plea for the children *not* to go to work prematurely, *not* to break down their health in cotton mills and factories and mines and sweatshops, *not* to grow up uneducated through keeping their noses to the grindstone of monotonous, soul-destroying work." But "today, people are seeking positive measures for child protection."[172] No longer did the child labor campaign concern itself primarily with protecting girls and boys from greedy capitalism. As Lovejoy wrote, "The anti–child labor movement is [now] part of the larger movement for the promotion of child welfare in all of its phases. It is part, indeed, of the whole broad movement for the enhancement of human welfare. . . . It seeks more than laws, it seeks the best development of manhood, womanhood, nationhood."[173] The NCLC changed the name of its major publication from *The Child Labor Bulletin* to the less precise *The American Child*. As the editors explained, the *Child Labor Bulletin* "had entirely out-grown its name, and *The American Child* was chosen as its new title because that seemed best to convey the present purpose of the [movement]."[174]

With America's entry into World War I, child betterment forces united in a campaign to protect and conserve the nation's children, especially white boys, in the name of national interest. Public discourse about child welfare was condensed in a controlled wartime message emphasizing that the "health of the child" was "the power of the nation." As the Social Gospel crusade to protect children from capitalism faded, Northern reformers gained new wartime allies, including the American toy industry, which helped redefine market freedom for white boys in terms of consumerism. The sectionalism of child labor debates also seemed to fade as national unity became a wartime aim. But the postwar years revealed that not all Americans supported the wartime coalition for modern child welfare. The secular orientation of the wartime campaign and its embrace of modern progress created an opening for a cultural backlash. Reformers' faith in federal government grew even as the spiritual underpinnings of that faith diminished. The war had irrevocably changed the movement, recasting child welfare in terms of national interest and setting the stage for the rise of a consumerist ethos. Buttressed by other child welfare efforts, the consumer marketplace was poised to define market freedom for boys and girls as the pursuit of personal growth and self-fulfillment. Labor had nothing to teach boys or girls except drudgery. It was a remarkable shift from an earlier period when reformers fretted over the distinction between free and unfree child labor. Northern reformers steamrolled ahead with a federal agenda to ensure the new definition of child welfare could spread to all parts of the country. But many rural Southerners and their soon-to-be allies saw the new modern child welfare coalition and its secular values as a spiritual threat. Free labor principles were resurrected in America's heartland as assuredly as the Freedmen's Bureau had first delivered them to formerly enslaved people and their former owners. Where market encroachment was not complete, labor still had spiritual value.

5 Cultural Warriors

A Southern Capitalist Vision

> In the sweat of thy face shalt thou eat bread,
> till thou return unto the ground;
> for out of it wast thou taken:
> for dust thou art,
> and unto dust shalt thou return.
> —Genesis 3:19

Reformers emerged from the war with a newfound confidence and sense of inevitability as their cause became swept up in the currents of official culture. Buoyed by a host of new wartime allies, including government and academic experts as well as labor leaders and enlightened businessmen, reformers rode the affirming wave of official sanction and sang a new hymn to the god of modern progress. No longer attached to their quaint portrayals of greedy capitalists, reformers marched into modern industrial America prepared to be its gatekeepers. The spiritual dimensions of child labor reform and emphasis on capitalism's moral limits were eclipsed by the gospel of progress. A modern childhood became the sine qua non of progress, a convenient yardstick that the political establishment could use to measure the right way to live. The new measure revealed that the sinful ways of Southern mill owners barely scratched the surface of inadequacies in rural America, where children, black and white, still labored on farms and where morality was determined by outmoded authorities like family and tradition. For reformers, cataloging and reversing these inadequacies became an official duty rather than a spiritual one. But the righteousness of their effort remained even as their cause adapted to the modern secular order. As the greedy capitalist disappeared, reformers took aim at rural parents who worshiped at the altar of traditional values. Motivated by a new mission, reformers set out to convert those who were resistant to the gospel of progress.[1]

They had their work cut out for them. Southern resentment toward Northern reformers and their habit of framing Southern white factory child labor as the nation's "new slavery" had been building for decades. When reformers diagnosed the rural way of life as a barrier to the march of progress, they spurred a collective protest to child labor reform that was as united as the gatekeepers of modern industrial America. Though initially planned by Southern industrialists to protect their use of child labor, a collective opposition to child labor reform grew into something much larger and more historically significant than mere propaganda. Opponents of reform denied that the secular bureaucratic state could be a chief source of morality. They waged a war against this supposition, striking back with modes of cultural authority that were rooted in an agrarian way of life. Delivering a rebuke to the establishment, opponents of reform defended older sources of morality, such as Scripture, family, and tradition, in a nation that had declared progress the measure of all things. They reasserted the spiritual value of labor for their children, especially boys, in a modern industrial society that had demoted labor's worth in favor of consumerist values. Seventy years after antebellum child rescuers defined honest labor as the heart of the distinction between free and slave society, opponents of reform deployed an ideal of free labor as a weapon against the encroachment of the secular bureaucratic state.

Although antiregulation was a by-product of their aims, Southern opponents of reform were after something much larger. They were rejecting a Northern Progressive vision that looked to the secular bureaucratic state as the guarantor of freedom within market society, and they were denying the prerogative of official experts to establish morality for them. Even in rural America, market capitalism and its secular implications would have to be negotiated. But opponents of reform distrusted the wisdom of official culture to be in charge of such negotiations. Antiregulation became a sacrosanct position, because it meant rejecting secular modes of authority, which were both culturally disparaging and threatening to a rural way of life, while also defending older sources of morality that were sacred in rural communities. It was a Southern capitalist vision that resonated deeply within and beyond the South, picking up supporters across rural America and even urban Catholics who agreed that traditional sources of morality were threatened by the secular bureaucratic state. In the 1920s debates about child labor shaped two distinctive definitions of freedom within market society, redrawing political battle lines around progress and tradition and resulting in opposing cultural visions of how morality should be constituted in the modern industrial age.[2]

Opposition to the regulatory state in favor of private morality depended on, at least to a certain degree, rural white parents' confidence that their children were not in need of government protection from lynching or racial segregation—both primary concerns of rural black parents. Even though they shared many of the same traditional values as opponents to reform, such as a focus on the importance of family, rural black parents were unlikely to wage war against the only entity that had the potential to protect their children from lynching and Jim Crow segregation. At the same time, the new child welfare coalition catered to white boys as the nation's future leaders and empire builders and prioritized the well-being of white children over black children in their reform work. Northern reformers had long argued that physical and mental deterioration of poor white children in the Southern textile industry was a national crisis. Still, given a choice between supporting a movement that sought increased federal authority to protect children over one that denied the state had any role to play in establishing standards of morality, African American parents, commentators, and reformers ultimately lent their support to the NCLC's goals, playing a part in an expanded political base of supporters for federal child labor reform.

By the end of the war, the NCLC had established a new identity as part of a broad-based, American campaign for child welfare, a popular strategy that helped them retain momentum. They distanced themselves from a narrow campaign to end child labor while embracing a newer definition of modern childhood. After renaming its major publication *The American Child* (formerly *The Child Labor Bulletin*), the NCLC even considered renaming itself the National Child Conservation Board, stopping just short of doing so.[3] They would remain the National Child Labor Committee, but they would expand their definition of child labor. Many of the worst abuses of child labor during the war had occurred not in factories and mills but in fields and on farms. Because the nation's food needs increased during the war, children were often excused from school to work in agricultural labor.[4] The census numbers revealed a disturbing trend. While new and improved local and state laws against industrial forms of child labor had helped bring about a decrease in industrial child labor, the numbers of children and youth working in agricultural labor were increasing. In 1900 there were around 1 million child workers in agriculture, which accounted for 66 percent of all child labor in the United States. By 1910 the number had increased to 1.5 million, a staggering 75 percent of all child labor that year.[5]

For reasons both tactical and ideological, the NCLC had always focused on industrial forms of child labor. Industrial development in the post-Reconstruction South and its impact on white civilization initially drove reformers toward a focus on industrial child labor. As a national movement was launched, industrial child labor became a symbol of the worst excesses of capitalism. Although this strategy was effective in garnering public support and securing legislation, it neglected a large and growing child labor problem: children in agriculture. The worsening of agricultural child labor during World War I was an impetus for reformers to address this neglect. In April 1917 the NCLC released a "Plan to Safeguard Children in Farm Work," which proposed regulating child labor in wartime food production. Children under the age of fourteen would be organized by teachers, Boy and Girl Scout leaders, and child welfare leaders to do light work planting and raising potatoes, corn, beans, or other vegetables to help the war effort during the summer months only. Youth between the ages of fourteen and eighteen would be permitted to work no more than eight hours per day from June 1 through October 1 but only if they obtained special work permits.[6] However, as reformers would learn, regulating children in agriculture was a complicated task. Not only was the work irregular and difficult to monitor, but many Americans did not think farm labor for children was as harmful as industrial labor. When it came to agricultural child labor, reformers would have to start anew with a public awareness campaign.

After the war the NCLC announced that agricultural child labor would be its new emphasis. Reformers signaled this change when they selected David F. Houston to replace Felix Adler as the new chairman of the board.[7] The former secretary of agriculture under President Wilson, Houston was a respected economist whose specialty was in agricultural and rural issues.[8] Before stepping down, Adler said, "The next step [of the National Child Labor Committee] should be to give our assiduous attention to child labor in agriculture."[9] Lovejoy wrote of the decision, "No fitter choice for chairman of the Committee as we enter upon this 'next great task' could have been made than was made in the selection of Mr. Houston, a profound and sympathetic student of country life in all its aspects and an authority upon its manifold social and economic problems."[10] The May 1921 issue of *The American Child* featured a farm child in a rural setting on its front cover and published a compilation of several papers by national experts on rural issues, titled "Rural Child Labor: A Symposium." From lack of school attendance in rural America, to migratory farm children in commercialized agriculture, to the family farm child's need for play and recreation, these articles sought to spark public awareness about rural child welfare.[11] The same issue announced that the topic of the upcoming Sixteenth National Conference on Child Labor, held on June 24, 1921, in Milwaukee, Wisconsin, would be "Fair Play for the Country Child." The announcement read that "at Milwaukee it will be shown that there is more child labor in the country than in the city, and that some of

Cultural Warriors 117

it is just as bad." The time had come "for rousing the country to realization of the existence of the child labor evil in forms and places other than urban."[12]

Reformers gathered in Milwaukee to hear papers delivered by rural life experts, to discuss outreach plans to rural areas, and to develop a publicity strategy to spread their message about agricultural child labor.[13] The task before them was tremendous. Investigations into rural child labor were new, and reformers were attacking a form of child labor that most Americans regarded as wholesome and beneficial. The view that farm life and the rural environment produced a physically healthy and morally upright citizenry had a long tradition in American thought, stretching back to Thomas Jefferson.[14] One reformer wrote, "It was generally assumed that farm work was healthful and that children working with their parents learned valuable lessons in family responsibility and also acquired a useful knowledge of farming."[15] Reformers at the 1921 conference in Milwaukee showed awareness of these prevailing views. Lovejoy, who presided over the conference, declared, "The farmer's greatest loss is the loss of his own children to the cities." Rural youth were "flocking from the country to the city," he argued, because they were deprived of adequate educational and recreational activities in the country. "You cannot keep boys and girls on the farm by depriving them of the play and recreation and social life which they instinctively crave."[16]

Reformers evinced a change in how they were thinking about the immorality of child labor. They had already reframed their movement more broadly in terms of modern child welfare. While they never abandoned their concern about labor exploitation, they embraced a modern approach to child welfare, which emphasized the inherent rights of children to health, education, and play. This approach was well suited to the issue of rural child labor, since market exploitation on farms and fields was not always as apparent as it was in mills and factories. "What is rural child labor?" asked reformer Charles Gibbon. "Any work which children do that injures their health, interferes with their education, or robs them of their play, is *child labor*, and as such is to be severely condemned."[17] Children's rights to health, education, and play were "inherent" and "due children simply because they are children," reformers now argued.[18] This formulation—that what defined child labor was the extent to which any aspect of modern childhood was violated—was a departure from the Keating-Owen era, in which reformers had defined child labor in terms of capitalist exploitation. Under the new definition, non-market activities such as chores on the farm before and after school could be considered child labor if the work interfered with a child's health, education, or play. At stake was the disruption of a modern childhood. One reformer suggested that the solution to rural child labor might not be a "legislative program to regulate the hours and conditions under which children work on the farms" but in "getting the parents to see and fully appreciate what *childhood* is."[19] Child welfare expert Sara A. Brown read a paper suggesting that child neglect should become a paramount concern: "Neglect is just as damaging in results, and is quite as *unjust* whether it be willful, due to ignorance or incapacity on the part of a parent, or to lack of opportunity on the part of the community in which the child lives." If for any reason parents or their communities could not provide their children with a modern childhood, Brown asserted, then it was "the responsibility of the state to secure to every child protection from neglect in any form."[20]

Despite these new formulations, there was continuity with past reform efforts. The increasing mechanization of agriculture in the early twentieth century provided reformers with a familiar framework of capitalist exploitation. By 1920 some farms had grown very large and required more labor, especially during harvesting.[21] Lovejoy wrote that Americans needed to recognize that "in many parts of the country conditions of rural labor have greatly changed in recent years," referring especially to "employment of children in gangs, in truck gardens and berry fields, beet sugar fields, cotton picking, onion and tobacco culture, and other specialized farming requiring large numbers of hand-workers." He argued that American farm life should no longer be romanticized as small family operations.[22] The growth of large-scale farming demanded greater numbers of workers, and children were often exploited to meet the demand. In the cotton fields of Arkansas and Texas; the tobacco, vegetable, and fruit farms of Virginia, Maryland, Kentucky, and New Jersey; the sugar beet fields of Colorado and Michigan; and the fruit farms and berry orchards of California and Wisconsin, children under the age of fourteen were working long hours in the spring and summer months doing monotonous, repetitive tasks that interfered with their schooling and play.[23]

The NCLC partnered with the US Children's Bureau, the National Conference of Social Work, the National Council of Rural Agencies, the National Education Association, and the American Country Life Association to raise awareness about rural child welfare.[24] Together they conducted studies about rural child welfare, established state-level Child Welfare Commissions, and collected data on children in agriculture.[25] An investigative report titled "Rural Child Welfare" was published as a book and received a wide readership.[26] Its purpose was "to present to its readers a graphic picture of rural life in America, thus bringing to the general public a realization of the needs of country children," and "to trace the cause of conditions and suggest a definite

Cultural Warriors 119

and practical outline of preventive and remedial policies."[27] An early review of the book said that it would lead "city people who have always looked upon country life as an unmixed blessing for children" to realize "the tremendous handicaps of rural childhood" in many communities.[28] Another reviewer called it "a remarkable book on a vital subject, and one which deserves the widest publicity and attention."[29] Sociology and education professors assigned the book in their classes, and county extension workers made it required reading for employees.[30]

In a collection of essays by many of the same speakers at the NCLC conference in Milwaukee, the introduction, written by reformer Edward N. Clopper, stated, "The fundamental purpose of child welfare work is to prolong the period of childhood." Though much progress in the arena of child welfare had been made, it was "largely for the boys and girls of our cities," while "country children [had] been comparatively neglected." But reformers justified intervention on behalf of rural children differently than they had for industrial child workers. In both instances, reformers argued that childhood was under threat. In the case of industrial child labor, greedy capitalists sacrificed childhood on the altar of profit. Government intervention was needed to protect the nation's children from an unrestrained capitalism. But in the case of the rural child, it was the deficiencies of country life and even the rural family itself that posed a threat to rural children's ability to have a modern childhood. "This volume throws down the gauntlet to all who hold the view that rural child life is safe and needs no care from the state," announced the introduction. Indicting the rural family for its non-modern standards of living and outmoded views about childhood, the book advanced a narrative of neglect of children in rural America that supported the need for state intervention. As Clopper described the problem, "Poor housing, lack of the simplest sanitary devices, failure to observe even elementary health precautions, extra labor made necessary by the absence of conveniences common in cities, lack of recreational life, wretched schooling facilities and poor quality of teachers, burdens prematurely placed upon children in farm- and house-work, the undeveloped social sense of rural folk, and their disinclination to work together for the common good—these are the drawbacks of country life."[31]

In the months following the book's publication, the NCLC and supporting agencies sponsored other exposé-type reports on American rural life. One of the most striking was a series of articles titled "How the Other Half Lives in the Open Country" by professor and writer John F. Smith.[32] An allusion to Jacob Riis's thirty-year-old and widely influential book, *How the Other Half Lives*—which had famously brought to light the squalid living conditions of the slums of New York City in the 1890s[33]—Smith's articles attempted to expose rural life for its unsanitary conditions, ill health, poor diet, lack of education, laboring children, and anti-intellectual Christianity. About rural religion, Smith asked, "How can any great progress ever be made towards bringing the Kingdom nearer in the backward rural sections until highly trained ministers . . . are put in charge of the country pulpits?"[34]

The shift to rural child welfare changed not only the rhetoric but also the actual substance of reformers' investigations to include black children alongside white children. The census of 1920 had revealed that there remained 1,060,858 child laborers in the country in all occupations—from manufacturing, to transportation, to clerical work—but reformers claimed that these estimates were far below actual numbers.[35] Children in agriculture (647,309) comprised the vast majority of child labor, or 61 percent of the total. According to the likely underreported 1920 census numbers, 341,150 were native-born white children (52.7 percent), and 270,265 were native-born black children (41.8 percent). The largest remaining group was white children of foreign birth or foreign parentage (5.2 percent). While previous investigations of the Southern textile industry had concentrated exclusively on poor white children, investigations on agricultural child labor would result in a picture of a rural, backward South where both black and white children worked as agricultural laborers in an outmoded, rural way of life. Child labor in mills remained a problem, but the census showed that both black and white children were more likely to be working in agriculture than in manufacturing. Child labor in factories and mills was still the second-largest category of child labor, according to the 1920 census, but the overall numbers had fallen. Outside of the two largest groups of child labor—agriculture and manufacturing, which together made up nearly 80 percent of child labor—the census accounted for the remaining 20 percent of child labor in "extraction of minerals, transportation, trade, public service, professional service, domestic and personal service, and clerical occupations."[36]

The new child labor investigations of country children, then, included for the first time significant research on black child labor. A study in 1922 of the seasonal demand for farm labor in Virginia, Maryland, and New Jersey—leading states in the production of vegetables and small fruits that were part of the "truck-farming area" stretching along the Atlantic seaboard—revealed that farmers were hiring "family groups" during the harvesting of the crops and that 3,600 children under sixteen years of age—black and white—were found doing most of the hand labor: "Almost three-fifths of all the white children and nearly three-fourths of the Negro children reported that they had started work in the fields before reaching the age of 10; one-fourth of the white and nearly one-third of the Negro children were under 10 years of age when interviewed." They said they picked strawberries, beans, peas, cucumbers, melons, tomatoes, and other plants, and reported weeding and thinning and occasionally planting, plowing, and hoeing.[37]

Another mid-1920s report on rural child welfare was on children living in rural counties in Texas. The investigation covered 998 families, 202 of which were black (20 percent) and 786 of which (80 percent) were white. These rural Texan families were landowners, tenants, or sharecroppers, and their children were "not just temporary or emergency workers, but regular hands." The report lamented that these children had unhealthy diets, were in poor physical health, and lived in "shacks, many of them in such a miserable condition as to be unfit for human habitation." The investigations of rural child welfare inadvertently shined a light on the dismal educational system that had come into being in the racially segregated South. "Over two-fifths of the white children and over two-thirds of the Negro children" were behind in their education; "more than one-fourth of the white children and over one-half of the Negro children [were] retarded three years and more."[38] Other reports on the status of rural education in the South depicted a bleak situation whereby black and white rural children were valued more for their labor in the fields than for their abilities in the classroom.[39]

There were divergent opinions among reformers regarding how to address the rural child labor issue. Some believed it was a matter of educating rural parents about modern childhood. This education would include modern ideals of physical sanitation and health as well as cultural attitudes about play, leisure, and education. If the rural home were improved by modern plumbing; better sanitation, such as screens on doors and windows; a healthier diet; and appreciation for beauty in their homes and yards, rural childhood might also be improved. But rural parents would have to be educated about the value of modern childhood. As one reformer put it, "[Rural parents] are prejudiced against play, recreation, and social life, and cannot see the value of an education if it interferes with their immediate needs, so they often require children to work." Reformers also noted that rural parents had outmoded views regarding the parent-child relationship: "The popular conception in the rural mind is that the child is indebted to the parent for bringing him into this world, that it is the child's duty to make every sacrifice for the parent, that where the interests of the child and parent conflict, those of the former should always be sacrificed." One reformer reported that when he asked a third-grade boy what he would like to be when he grows up, the father interrupted before the boy could speak: "Bill will do just what I tell him to do till he is twenty-one, if he stays under my roof." This view was in conflict with the "newer vision of childhood, in which the parent owes all to the child till he reaches maturity."[40]

Many reformers believed that rural parents could change if educated. A popular educational method was county "extension" programs. Attempting to provide a substitute of wholesome and educative child work to replace rural child labor, boys' and girls' 4-H clubs were aggressively promoted in the most rural areas of the country. These state-funded extension programs were meant to provide both educational and recreational experiences for rural children, giving them projects and activities that promoted the four "H's"—head, heart, hands, and health—under the supervision of a county extension agent who would collaborate with rural child welfare experts.[41] Other reformers wanted to target lax compulsory schooling requirements by making rural schools more accountable for the enforcement of nine months of attendance. Rural primary and secondary schools were often complicit in perpetuating the need for child labor, as they typically opened and closed their doors according to harvest seasons.[42]

Rural American families were living in the past, reformers now argued, and were unaware of the benefits of progress. Rural parents had an outmoded view of childhood that needed correction. According to official experts, children were an investment in the future, not the present. Children's activities should be nonproductive—focused on growth, development, and education—until they reached adulthood and could contribute to society. As Lovejoy wrote, "By a conservative estimate, to give a child a chance to play and develop and go to school is worth at least $100 to his dad, and there are more than a million country children who are not getting that chance. Here is an opportunity for investment where there is no possibility of losing. The whole of America will gain."[43] That modern childhood was an investment in the future of the nation was the official stance taken by the US government and was reflected in federally funded agencies such as the US Children's Bureau. Unlike rural parents, "the state . . . has taken a somewhat different attitude. It regards its children as future citizens, who must be given the chance of normal development so that they can take their proper places later on."[44] While reformers gave lip-service to the home, calling it "the most fundamental of all institutions" and the "natural" agency upon which children's welfare depended, they walked a fine line between respect for the integrity of individual families and enforcing the standards of modern childhood.[45]

It was not only individual families who had a stake in how children were raised, but the entire society had an interest in investing in the future generation. Born out of the First World War, this "national interest" argument had staying power. The state had a claim on children that was separate from parents' rights to children. Children themselves had rights by virtue of being children, and it was in the state's interest to ensure their rights were not violated. As the authors of *Rural Child Welfare* wrote, "Every child should be properly cared for in a good home. When, for any reason, the home fails or breaks down, the state must step in to the aid of the child. Even if there is no break-down, the state has its function in respect to children, to keep watch over them. Then, too, there are many things needful that the home cannot possibly give, as full protection for health, education, and suitable recreation. . . . In the end, it is the business of the state to see that every child gets full and just consideration of his rights."[46]

Pitting the state against parents was not new in the movement against child labor. The notion of regulating child labor had always implied the appropriateness of the state protecting children over and against parents' rights to have their children employed. But the most recent campaign for a federal child labor law had used a different moral calculus for state intervention. Children had to be protected from greedy capitalists. Individual families were not indicted for the persistence of child labor as much as greedy capitalists who put profit above everything. But when the greedy capitalists disappeared, the family became much more visible both as a cause of the problem and as a site of potential solution. The justification for state intervention became more about protecting children's rights within the family than about rescuing children from capitalism. This framework was established during the First World War and found new expression in reformers' postwar emphasis on rural child labor. Their message was beginning to catch on in the national press as newspapers and magazines began publicizing the reformers' findings.[47] In May 1922 reformers had to pivot when the Supreme Court overturned yet another federal child labor law, the Child Labor Tax Law. The decision signaled to reformers that they likely would never gain the Court's approval. Together with new allies, reformers developed a strategy to circumvent the Court by amending the US Constitution. Little did they realize that the issues raised by their rural child welfare campaign had set the stage for the rise of a formidable grassroots opposition in the coming battle over an amendment.

Ironically, the cultural values of rural America helped enable the Lochner era of the Supreme Court.[48] In seeking out test cases to challenge federal child labor legislation, Southern manufacturers like David Clark sought out mill parents who believed their individual liberty to make decisions for their own families had been violated. In *Hammer v. Dagenhart* the Court sided with a working mill father who argued that the Keating-Owen Act violated his right to his children's earnings; the Court overturned Keating-Owen in 1918.

Reformers then consulted with legal advisers to devise another federal bill.[49] With the same Congress that passed Keating-Owen still in place, they decided to try using the federal taxing power to tax the products of child labor. In February 1919 Congress approved the "Tax on Employment of Child Labor," which would levy an excise tax of 10 percent on the profits derived from any mills, factories, or canneries where children under the age of fourteen had been employed during the year. The tax would also apply to any mines or quarries where children under the age of sixteen had been employed, as well as to any industry that had employed children under sixteen for more than eight hours a day or more than six days a week or at night.[50] The bill was to go into effect sixty days later.[51] But Southern manufacturer David Clark already had another working mill parent in mind who could help challenge the bill in court. Employing a similar strategy as before, Clark sought out a North Carolina man, Eugene W. Johnston, whose fifteen-year-old son worked at their local Atherton Cotton Mills. Johnston agreed to request a permanent injunction from Atherton Mills restricting the employer from terminating his son's employment. Judge James E. Boyd of North Carolina ruled in favor of the complainant, declaring the Child Labor Tax Law to be unconstitutional, since it sought to use the federal taxing power to regulate local and state labor conditions rather than to raise revenue.[52] Three years later, in May 1922, the Supreme Court would agree, making the Child Labor Tax Law another dead letter for reformers.[53]

In the face of a Supreme Court that had now struck down federal child labor laws twice, reformers and their allies embraced a constitutional amendment. Just two days after the Court's decision in 1922, Roy G. Fitzgerald of Ohio introduced a resolution for a constitutional amendment that would empower Congress to regulate the labor of children under the age of eighteen. Senator Hiram Johnson of California did the same in the Senate.[54] After the Court's decision in 1922, the national press joined the chorus of amending the Constitution to advance modern childhood. The *New York Times* wrote that the decision was a blessing in disguise, since indirect methods of abolishing child labor—by means of interstate commerce or the taxing power—were actually too limited. By amending the Constitution, a broader and more direct approach would now be possible.[55] The *New York Mail* concurred: "After muddling around for more than ten years with the child labor question, it would seem that even Congress must be convinced by now that the only adequate recourse is to an amendment of the Federal Constitution."[56] Prohibition had recently secured the Eighteenth Amendment, and women had gained suffrage through the Nineteenth Amendment.[57] Many observers believed child labor reform was poised to be the Twentieth. The *San Francisco*

Journal made an explicit connection between Prohibition, women's suffrage, and child labor reform: "By two recent amendments to the Constitution, measures have been taken to make the poisonous liquor traffic a matter of national concern and to secure national recognition of the rights of women as citizens. [We must now] regard the rights of children as an equally important issue and of equal concern to the nation as a whole."[58] As *Survey* magazine put it after the Court's decision was rendered, "The movement for a [child labor] amendment seems inevitable."[59]

The campaign for an amendment included a diverse array of groups. The US Children's Bureau, teachers' federations, women's clubs, religious organizations, the National League of Women Voters, and labor groups all joined the effort. Samuel Gompers, president and founder of the American Federation of Labor (AFL), was the first to arrange a conference. "America must find a way to abolish completely child labor," Gompers told the *New York Times* in advance of the conference.[60] At Gompers's behest, nearly one hundred men and women leaders met at AFL headquarters in Washington, DC, on June 1, 1922, to discuss the possibility of a child labor amendment.[61] "We cannot look for anything to the Supreme Court," Gompers affirmed. "But we can and must secure a constitutional amendment, so that the Supreme Court cannot again refuse freedom to the children."[62] The fight for an amendment would be a "final endeavor to emancipate childhood," said Gompers.[63] Emerging from the meeting was a new organization called the Permanent Conference for the Abolition of Child Labor, of which Gompers agreed to be chairman.[64] The purpose of the organization was to achieve the final elimination of child labor in America by amending the Constitution. Assuming leadership positions in the new organization alongside Gompers were Reverend E. O. Watson of the Federal Council of Churches of Christ in America, Florence Kelley, NCLC leader Rev. Owen Lovejoy, Matilda Lindsay of the National Women's Trade Union League, and Father John A. Ryan of the National Catholic Welfare Council.[65]

The NCLC also reached out to African American reform groups as a potential source of support for the amendment. Child labor reform had not exactly welcomed African American reformers in the past. It was an overwhelmingly white movement due to its origins in rescuing the South's poor white children from racial degeneracy. But the amendment battle came at a time when African American reformers were trying to secure federal antilynching legislation.[66] They could see the amendment's potential to give Congress authority to protect black children and youth. In June 1922 the Indiana Federation of Colored Women endorsed the Dyer antilynching bill and the federal Child Labor Amendment at the same meeting.[67] Their resolution read: "Be it further resolved that an amendment to the Constitution be such that it will protect *all children in all parts of the country alike.*"[68] Many African American reformers had come to embrace federal authority because of resistance they had encountered with antilynching legislation. An article about a lynching mob in southern Illinois explained that the "doctrine of states' rights" permitted "the mob spirit to dominate any one particular locality" so that "the citizens thereof must necessarily be at the mercy of the mob." This "mob doctrine," or "states' rights" as legislators referred to it, was what permitted barbarities such as lynching and child labor to continue unimpeded in the South, the article argued. Attempts to prohibit either of these evils through protection by the federal government were always declared "unconstitutional."[69] The *Chicago Defender* endorsed the amendment on the grounds that "the youth of our group live in states that offer them little protection for *life*, much less in their work." Thus, "we are heartily in favor of the proposed amendment."[70]

In 1924 Lovejoy attended a meeting of the Urban League, urging their support for ratification of the amendment on the grounds that "under present conditions in the South," black children were "more crushed down by the exploitations of business and industry than the white children."[71] Other African American groups supported the amendment because of its potential to help achieve better schooling for black children. The prominent African Methodist Episcopal Zion Church, for instance, endorsed the amendment on the grounds that such federal legislation would likely be accompanied by federal involvement in "compulsory education," one of the Church's "chief aims" for black children.[72]

Riding a wave of public recognition and endorsements, the national movement was confident in its ability to amend the Constitution, first by congressional approval and then by state-by-state ratification. After having twice secured federal child labor laws in Congress, federal regulation seemed almost pedestrian. A committee of ten members chosen by the Permanent Conference began drafting an amendment in regular meetings with Roscoe Pound, Newton D. Baker, Ernest Freund of the University of Chicago Law School, and Joseph Chamberlain of Columbia University Law School.[73] Inevitability was a universal sentiment. At the NCLC's annual conference in 1922, attendees showed "no sign of pessimism" about the future of reform. Some reformers argued that the Court's decision to overturn their federal laws was preferable, since reformers could now "clear away their difficulties by amending the Constitution." Lovejoy admitted he had never been satisfied with federal laws, since they "did not reach children in agriculture, street trades, the movies, tenement homework, or stores."[74] A child labor amendment to the Constitution was viewed as an opportunity to achieve more meaningful and far-reaching change. It seemed like a foregone conclusion. Congress was no stranger to federal child labor legislation, and reformers had support from a wide array of organizations and federal agencies.

Though they had reason to believe the path would be smooth, reformers misjudged the moment. They did not foresee the deep divisions in American society that their campaign would bring to the fore in the mid-1920s. From their perspective, amending the Constitution was a sensible means of achieving what Congress had twice determined was the will of the American people. But for many other Americans, the reformers' amendment campaign was a breaking point, a last straw that provoked them to rise up in opposition. Just as the coalition for an amendment was more varied and diverse than the previous reform movement, so too was the coalition that mobilized to defeat the amendment. The new opposition movement included not only Southern textile owners and business interests but also farm families, working-class urban Catholics, traditionalist women, localist Progressives, and conservative intellectuals. Motivated by a collective distrust of the modern bureaucratic state and secular consumerist values, opponents of the amendment mounted a collective protest that overwhelmed reformers. Before the end of the decade, opponents were able to block an amendment that was regarded as more or less inevitable by the political establishment.

The amendment debates reflected a profound shift in public rhetoric regarding children, capitalism, and the state. When reformers secured Keating-Owen in 1916, the heart of their rhetoric was a Social Gospel critique of greedy capitalism. The Keating-Owen campaign argued that callous market logic should not invade the sacred realm of childhood. As one of capitalism's most conspicuous evils, child labor proved that the capitalist system, if left to its own devices, would not engender morality. Restraining capitalism's sinful ways through federal intervention was a religious duty. Debates over Keating-Owen reflected this framing of the issue and led reformers to a sweeping victory in 1916. A new political and religious climate in the 1920s would turn this paradigm on its head. As reformers shifted their focus away from urban industrial capitalism to rural child welfare, battle lines were drawn around progress and tradition. Opponents interpreted the campaign for an amendment as a power grab to seize control of children whose parents did not embrace the modern secular order. The modern bureaucratic state that reformers used to wield power over a traditional way of life was the real threat, opponents argued. Their effort to quash the amendment had a moral urgency that was missing in previous antiregulation efforts. The result was a collective protest against the gatekeepers of modernity that aligned itself with business interests in order to defend older cultural authorities such as family and tradition that were rooted in an agrarian way of life.

The battle over the amendment occurred in a broader climate of economic, social, and political unrest. Economic and military demobilization had led to staggering inflation while the wartime experience produced public disillusionment regarding involvement in international affairs.[75] The postwar mood of the country fostered both an isolationist stance and a general apprehension regarding perceived outsiders or foreigners. As one historian has argued, "The League of Nations proved vulnerable to the same forces that would feed the Red Scare, the Ku Klux Klan's revival, and nativism."[76] Wilson himself predicted that if the United States entered the war, "a wave of intolerance would sweep the nation."[77] The Espionage Act of 1917, the Sedition Act of 1918, the Committee on Public Information, and other efforts by the federal government to squelch dissent led to a repressive wartime regime that imprisoned dissenters, stimulated hatred of Germans, and banned antiwar literature.[78] Fears of communism sparked by the Bolshevik Revolution of 1917 enhanced this already existing wartime paranoia.[79] An English journalist passing through America in the fall of 1919 described the "feverish condition of the public mind" as "hag-ridden by the spectre of Bolshevism." As he put it, "the horrid name 'Radical' covered the most innocent departure from conventional thought."[80] Indeed, during the so-called Red Scare of 1919, anti-Red campaigns were taken up by quasi-governmental groups like the National Security League while business interests warned about "the Grasping Hand of the Bolshevik" in a nationwide campaign to discredit labor unions.[81]

In this postwar climate, many American voters turned away from Wilson's Democratic Party—which had come to be associated with out-of-control Progressive reform, growth of big government, and crusading wars—and toward the Republican candidate for president in 1920, Warren G. Harding, who launched a "Return to Normalcy" campaign. Appealing to an "America first" sentiment, the Republican National Committee announced that its party stood for "absolute control of the United States by the United States" and pledged that "this country will remain American" with "no foreign control expressed or implied."[82] During the campaign, Harding pledged a return to "normalcy" with regard to the government activism of the Progressive era, including a scale-back of social reform and economic regulation. Pledging tax cuts, immigration restrictions, reduction of government spending, and protective tariffs, Harding's campaign framed the election as a choice between Wilson's "progressive ideology" and Harding's "normalcy." With Republican Calvin Coolidge as his vice-presidential running mate, Warren G. Harding sailed to victory in 1920 over Democratic nominee James M. Cox and his running mate, Franklin Delano Roosevelt, with 60 percent of the popular vote, the largest margin in electoral history to that point.[83]

America was poised for a coming decade of Republican rule that would attempt to undo many reforms and regulations of the Progressive era. Culturally, the consequences of the Red Scare and nativism resonated throughout the 1920s as the second Ku Klux Klan gained millions of new members, and the draconian Immigration Act of 1924 was signed into law.[84] Like immigrants, African Americans experienced new kinds of hostilities in the postwar decade, many of them as they settled into Northern cities after migrating during the war.[85] Race riots, spurred by job competition and the threat of thousands of returning black soldiers who demanded better treatment, occurred in towns and cities across the country in 1919, leaving 120 black Americans dead.[86] During the same year, the Prohibition Amendment was ratified, a measure that would symbolize the failure of federal government to remedy social problems. And the Nineteenth Amendment, granting women the right to vote, in 1920 was ratified in the midst of a growing cultural backlash against changes in the traditional male-headed family. Women's political influence was also associated with Progressive reform, and many postwar Americans were wary of the changes that newly enfranchised women might attempt. For instance, when Congress enacted the Sheppard-Towner Act of 1921—a bill that provided federal funding for prenatal and maternity care—opponents charged that the measure was a "Bolshevistic" scheme devised by radical women.[87] Organized labor was also weakened in the 1920s as labels like "Red" and "Radical" were used effectively against labor activists while three successive Republican administrations—Harding, Coolidge, and Hoover—enacted policies that favored big business over labor.[88]

The Social Gospel also took a hit in the postwar decade. In the first two decades of the twentieth century, leading Progressive reformers had embraced the Social Gospel as granting moral and scriptural sanction for their social causes. As historian Henry F. May put it, "Undoubtedly, the ability to justify social change in terms of Christian doctrine [gave] American progressivism authority, power, and a link with tradition."[89] But the experience of the First World War cast doubt on the Social Gospel's faith in progress while also serving as an impetus for a renewed interest in premillennialist theology, which flourished during wartime.[90] Premillennialism, the belief that Christ's return to earth would occur before a literal thousand-year reign on earth, differed from postmillennialism, which held that Christ's thousand-year reign was figurative and manifested by Christians' ability to create the Kingdom of God on earth, a hope that seemed increasingly naïve during the war.[91] During World War I, anti-German sentiment also led to renewed attacks on German higher criticism, the major theological influence on the Social Gospel.[92] In its rejection of biblical literalism, German higher criticism had led to "the destruction of Christianity itself," decried wartime critics.[93] As attacks on German biblical scholarship became part of American wartime patriotism, adherents of the Social Gospel were placed on the defensive.

The postwar mood conditioned many Americans to question the Social Gospel. While the Social Gospel never died completely, it lost much of the influence it had formerly enjoyed. One response to the Social Gospel was fundamentalist Christianity, which promised a "return to the fundamentals," including a literalist reading of Scripture and a renewed commitment to individual rather than social salvation. Fundamentalist Christianity promised to restore the Bible to its historic place in the family, public schools, churches, and colleges and universities as the "only hope" for America."[94] Like other Americans who supported Harding in 1920 on the basis of his "return to normalcy" campaign, fundamentalist Christians were wary of putting faith in government to solve social problems. For answers, they preferred looking backward rather than forward.[95] But as historian George Marsden has pointed out, fundamentalists also "wished to revive an evangelical theological consensus that had in fact been gone for at least a generation."[96] In that regard, they wanted more than what the election of President Harding could give them. They were after the unseating of the Social Gospel as the major influence on Christians in America. The rise of fundamentalism as a cultural force was the theological expression of a broader cultural impulse to recapture the "old moral values" of a previous time. In a study of cultural movements in the 1920s, Lawrence W. Levine noted that although Prohibition, fundamentalist Christianity, and the second Klan did not always overlap, they arose in a similar cultural milieu that "promised a real or symbolic flight from the new America back to the familiar confines of the old."[97] It was in this postwar environment that the battle over a child labor amendment got under way.

The Permanent Conference for the Abolition of Child Labor drafted an amendment to be introduced by US senator Medill McCormick of Illinois—formerly of the Progressive Party but now Republican—on July 26, 1922. The draft read:

> The Congress shall have the power to limit or prohibit the labor of persons under eighteen years of age, and power is also reserved to the several states to limit or prohibit such labor in any way which does not lessen any limitation of such labor or the extent of any prohibition thereof of Congress. The power vested in the Congress by this article shall be additional to and not a limitation on the powers elsewhere vested in the Congress by the Constitution with respect to such labor.[98]

The wording of the amendment generated much debate. Using the word "labor" instead of "employment" was a sticking point. Reformers wanted "labor," as they thought "employment" would leave too many loopholes. Children who worked on family farms would not be included nor would children who "helped" their parents in factories or tenements. The age limit of eighteen was also controversial, but reformers wanted it at eighteen since many sixteen- and seventeen-year-olds were recruited into hazardous jobs in mines and fields. Neither the word "child" nor "children" appeared anywhere in the amendment, as its framers noted that these categories were prone to uncertainty. Since the amendment was meant to grant a new power to Congress rather than to specify a new prohibition, reformers felt the wording of the amendment should be as broad as possible. They did make a point to safeguard the rights of states to set child labor standards as long as they were stricter than federal standards.[99]

By the fall of 1922 some journalists were inaccurately reporting that the amendment would prohibit the labor of children and youth. The *New York Times* ran a piece in October asserting that "a misconception with regard to the proposed child labor amendment to the Federal Constitution needs to be cleared up. The NCLC has noted that there is a misapprehension current, arising from the belief that the child labor amendment is a bill before Congress designed to limit or prohibit the employment of children under 18 years of age."[100] The Child Labor Amendment was not the equivalent of a legislative act. It merely empowered Congress to pass such legislation: "Thus, even though the amendment [can] be incorporated into the Constitution, no change in the status of child labor . . . is possible until legislation based on the amendment is passed by Congress."[101] Early opposition raised questions about how much power the amendment would grant to Congress and mounted familiar states' rights arguments, mostly from Southerners. But this initial opposition was relatively mild.[102] Representatives from the Permanent Conference for the Abolition of Child Labor testified on behalf of the amendment—known as the McCormick-Foster measure—in January 1923 and, for the most part, dominated the debate. On February 19, 1923, they won the first stage of their fight when the Senate Judiciary Committee reported favorably on the resolution. Accounting for several resolutions debated by the Judiciary Committee, the final wording of the amendment would read, "That Congress shall have power, concurrent with the several States, to limit or prohibit the labor of persons under the age of 18 years."[103]

It would be another year before the House held hearings on the amendment. Meanwhile, reformers prepared for the battle in Congress. Much of the material they prepared reflected their recent investigations on rural child welfare. One of their first public outreaches was a Thanksgiving holiday campaign called "What Thanksgiving Day Cost." They distributed a pamphlet titled "The Children Who Picked Your Cranberries" and another, "The Children Who Worked in the Sugar-Beet Fields to Supply Your Sweets."[104] The purpose of the campaign was to encourage Americans at the Thanksgiving holiday to think of the children who picked their cranberries and hoed their sugar beets by writing to their congressmen in support of the Child Labor Amendment. "Approximately 1,044 children were absent from school during September and October in the school district of Philadelphia, due to working on the cranberry bogs in New Jersey," another pamphlet read. These children had picked berries "ten hours a day" and "crawled through the wet marsh on hands and knees."[105] NCLC reformers continued sponsoring Child Labor Day by sending posters, fact sheets, pamphlets, speeches, and sermons to churches, schools, clubs, and any groups interested in observing Child Labor Day. A Child Labor Constitutional Amendment Fund was established for monetary donations. Child Labor Amendment Dime Banks were distributed in public places such as libraries, schools, and churches.[106]

When Congress reconvened early in 1924, the House Judiciary Committee was scheduled for hearings on the amendment. Supporters in attendance represented an array of organizations, from Grace Abbott of the Federal Children's Bureau, Owen Lovejoy of the NCLC, and Edgar Wallace of the American Federation of Labor to E. O. Watson of the Federal Council of Churches of Christ and Agnes Regan of the National Council of Catholic Women. Alongside other supporters, these individuals testified as to why they believed an amendment to the US Constitution was necessary. During questioning, the House Judiciary Committee was especially interested in the power the amendment would give Congress to regulate farm labor. Grace Abbott and Owen Lovejoy, the avowed experts at the hearings, were especially interrogated on this point. Representative Hatton W. Sumners of Texas raised the question of whether "this resolution puts the power of the Federal Government on every farm and in every home."[107] Lovejoy replied that most of the advocates of this amendment believed that "the child on the farm can best be protected not directly by prohibitive child-labor laws but by better health and educational and other social facilities originating in the community."[108] But his response did not satisfy some of the members, especially from rural districts. Citing the 1920 census numbers, Rep. George S. Graham of Pennsylvania asked a supporter if he was aware that "61 percent of the child-labor employment is engaged in agriculture?" When the supporter said yes, Graham pressed the matter: "Well, how far is the State going to be called upon to pass coercive legislation to control the power of the parents over their children [on the farms]?"[109] Representative Sumners continued this line of questioning with Abbott: "Do you, at this point, desire to express an opinion as to the wisdom of having the National Government leave to the States the matter of regulating the labor of children on the farms?" Abbott explained that an exception for farm labor in the amendment would be unwise, since "we do not know what will develop with reference to agricultural labor in the future."[110] Rep. Andrew J. Montague of Virginia chimed in, saying, "You would give [the federal government] just as much regulatory power as to farming as you would to mines, or any other work or occupation?" Abbott minced no words: "Yes, as far as the power goes."[111]

Reformers had not anticipated the number of attendees who came to testify in opposition to the amendment. Unlike well-known opponents in attendance, such as Southern Textile Association president David Clark and general counsel of the National Association of Manufacturers James A. Emery, many were unfamiliar to reformers. Reformers had gotten to know Clark and Emery and the groups they represented as the core opposition to child labor reform. Various manufacturing interests led by the Southern textile industry had always been major opponents of federal child labor laws, claiming the rights of local and state jurisdictions in an attempt to forestall federal interference with their labor practices. But at the House hearings in February 1924, there were unfamiliar faces on the scene motivated by new reasons. Representing groups such as the Sentinels of the Republic, the Woman's Patriotic Publishing Company, the Women's Constitutional League of Maryland, and the Moderation League, these groups were mobilized to bring down the amendment in defense of traditional values.

Many of the oppositional groups that testified at the hearings were outgrowths of the post–World War I antigovernment conservative ethos of the 1920s. The Women's Constitutional League of Maryland, for instance, was founded in December 1922 as a protest movement against the passage of the Sheppard-Towner Act of 1921, a bill signed into law by President Harding that provided federal funding for maternity and child care.[112] The group's spokeswoman, Mrs. Ruben Ross Holloway, explained at the hearings that her organization "came into birth because we resented being absolutely all the time quoted as being represented by the women of America."[113] Channeling a broader cultural impulse to recapture the "fundamentals" of an older America, Holloway opposed the Child Labor Amendment, saying:

> We are opposed to any further power being granted to the Government. . . . The very foundation of our Government is the Constitution of the United States. . . . We stand for the preservation of the principles of the Constitution and the

134   CHAPTER 5

> Bill of Rights of the States and the United States in letter and in spirit, against
> violation, whether by direct assault or indirect invasion, whether in the name
> of socialism, feminism, or in the name of humanity, or in whatever guise the
> effort is made to subvert the system of ordered progress under the forms of law
> ... that we have inherited from the founders of the American Constitution.[114]

Holloway noted that the league's members were "married women with children" who were tired of "being constantly quoted as among the thousands who are supporting a great many bills that are being forced upon our country."[115] A legal representative for the Women's Constitutional League, Willis R. Jones, testified that the group's purpose was "to preserve the constitutional liberties as they were created by the original Constitution." When asked if he was aware that most "women's organizations" were in favor of the amendment, Mr. Jones replied, "My observation of the women's organizations is that those that have the largest numbers and pass the most resolutions and spread their names in the papers more prominently than the others are, generally speaking, composed of maiden ladies and unmarried ladies without children." Traditional family women, Jones argued, did not want a child labor amendment and trusted "the mothers and fathers of the community to that of some governmental agency."[116]

Like the Women's Constitutional League, the Sentinels of the Republic was a group formed in 1922 in response to what its members perceived as threats to the original Constitution, especially federal encroachment on the rights of the states and individual families.[117] The group's founding purposes were "to maintain the fundamental principles of the American Constitution; to oppose further Federal encroachment upon the reserved rights of the States; to stop the growth of Socialism; to prevent concentration of power in Washington; and to help preserve a free republican form of government in the United States."[118] The chairman of the Sentinels, Louis A. Coolidge, attended the House hearings on the Child Labor Amendment and testified in opposition. Coolidge said the amendment "is the attempted continuation of a tendency which has been getting stronger and stronger for the last 20 years, to subordinate to Federal control all local activities . . . in order to concentrate everything here in Washington."[119] For Coolidge, the Child Labor Amendment was the final straw in this disturbing trend. Not only was it a new concentration of power in Washington, but it was also an attempted federal takeover of Americans' most sacred possession: their children. The Sentinels of the Republic feared that if this particular amendment passed, there would be "practically nothing [Congress] could not do with regard to children. They can determine how children shall be educated; they can determine the moral character of parents and guardians; whether they shall be Roman Catholics, or Protestants, or Jews."[120]

Other organizations testifying against the amendment represented various spin-offs of anti-suffrage groups such as the Woman's Patriotic Publishing Company, previously the Anti-Suffrage Association, which was devoted to "the defense of the family and the state against feminism and socialism."[121] This organization, represented by its president, Mary G. Kilbreth, opposed the creation of the Federal Children's Bureau, Sheppard-Towner, and other welfare measures relating to children, mothers, and families. Kilbreth testified, "As women, we are particularly concerned in violation of the right of castle aspect of this amendment—possibly even more than in any other constitutional aspect of it. As women, that is very immediate to us. And we are opposed to the vast increase in bureaucracy and Federal job holders the administration of this measure would entail." Linking the recapturing of an older America when "the Federal Government kept within the bounds . . . prescribed for it" with a traditional, male-headed family, Kilbreth defined as the enemy of children and families the federal government rather than capitalism. In farm families, Kilbreth argued, labor still had instructive value for both boys and girls: "The daughter could be prevented [from] helping her mother with the housework and the son forbidden to help his father on the farm . . . allowing an invasion of the home." Kilbreth also connected the amendment with federally mandated public education, which she believed focused too much on "intellectual standards" and "theoretical brain stuffing from books" instead of the "practical moral training inherent in work." The spiritual value of labor and the values learned from it had been demoted by child labor bureaucrats and self-proclaimed "experts." If nothing were done to stop this encroachment, Kilbreth forecasted a nation "tending in the direction of communistic regulation of children by the State."[122]

The amendment's supporters left the hearings relieved that their new opponents seemed backward and out of step with official culture. As Lovejoy put it, "We returned today from Washington after listening to testimony before the House Judiciary Committee. . . . If a cause is known by the enemies it makes, then the proposed Amendment is to be congratulated."[123] Noting that the opponents represented marginalized groups who opposed popular measures like women's suffrage and public education, reformers dismissed them as antimodern cranks. But if reformers had listened more closely to the testimony of the business interests that followed—the Southern Textile Association and the National Association of Manufacturers—they would have caught a glimpse of the new strategy to be used against them. The business interests in attendance took a cue from the fiery cultural warriors and incorporated some of the same arguments into their own testimonies. Clark and Emery had learned in the Keating-Owen battle that opponents needed a moral urgency that could compete with the sanctimonious rhetoric of the Social Gospel. They had emerged wiser from that battle, ready to equip the cultural warriors with weapons to fight their true enemy. Naked business opposition to child labor reform would not suffice. "There is a natural suspicion that when the manufacturer appears in opposition to child-labor legislation, [then] he is opposed to the proper protection of children in industry—a position which I absolutely reject," said Emery. After referencing James Madison's Federalist Papers, Emery claimed his organization was opposing the amendment not as businessmen but as citizens who were concerned "about a principle of government." If the "child life of the Nation" were placed under the authority of the federal government, then "you are [undertaking] to substitute a distant, remote, irresponsible, unsympathetic, unreachable authority *for the local authority which controls that life today*, which is within easy reach of the citizenship which lives in the community."[124]

Not only did Emery define the modern bureaucratic state as the new enemy of children and families, but he also defended a more traditional, rural America whereby "the local control of life [was] the very basis of self-government, upon which our fathers were determined to rest this Government."[125] Representative Sumners of Texas extended this line of reasoning, describing two kinds of government: "One is that you should have government come up from the people; and the other is that the Federal Government, with an elected personnel of less than 600 and between five and six hundred thousand appointed officials should substitute its will and government for the will and government of the people of the States or citizens of the States." By shifting the terms of debate to who should have moral authority in modern industrial society—local communities or a distant bureaucratic state—opponents were planting the seeds of an enduring collective protest to the secular state. Antiregulation was not about business interests increasing their profits; it was a sacred position that rejected the moral authority of the modern secular bureaucratic state. The elevation of rural child welfare to the center of national child labor discussions had diminished reformers' claim to be protecting children from anything other than traditional values and their own parents. To secure grassroots support, business interests would turn to rural white farmers in their quest to rescue children from the threat of government rule.

The resolution made it out of committee and was debated in the House in April 1924. Nearly one hundred members of the House spoke, echoing many of the same arguments made in the hearings. The spiritual value of labor, especially for boys, and the US Constitution emerged as focal points. Opponents cited the founding fathers and decried what they perceived as ongoing "tampering" with the sacred Constitution. As Rep. Hampton Pitts Fulmer of South Carolina put it, "I think it high time that we should hark back to the principles of the fathers. . . . In this hour when wild and radical legislation is being offered, I do not think it timely to tamper with the Constitution of the United States."[126] Representative Fulmer reflected nostalgically about his "boyhood days on the farm" when he "followed the plow handles at 12 years of age": "If I have made any success in life, I believe it [was] because of those years spent on the farm, where I was permitted to follow the leading of an honest and hardworking father unmolested under the law."[127] Other congressmen linked the sacredness of the Constitution with a literal reading of the Bible. Both the Constitution and the Bible were cast as sacred documents that demanded literalist readings respecting their content rather than "amendments" of the timeless truths they contained. As Rep. Charles Brand of Ohio suggested, "On general principles, I am not inclined to change the Constitution. Neither am I inclined to have the Bible and the Constitution take issue with one another. The original man was told, 'In the sweat of thy brow shalt thou eat bread,' and that has been an abiding rule of life since."[128] Both the Bible and the Constitution recognized the spiritual value of labor. Just as the Bible decreed that labor was superior to idleness, for both young and old, so too did "the original framers of the Constitution refrain from interfering with the right of youth to develop itself by industry."

Nowhere was the spiritual value of labor more sacred than in the rural farm family. "The principal complaint with reference to child labor seems to be directed against those who work in agriculture, and the outstanding purpose seems to be to make of Federal agents the lares and penates of the rural home," said Rep. Fritz G. Lanham of Texas.[129] Representative Lanham spun a hypothetical tale about a federal agent who entered a rural home under the provisions of the newly adopted amendment. In Lanham's tale, delivered on the House floor, the agent conducts a family devotional but "does not read, to be sure, from the good old family Bible on the table beside him." Instead he "substitutes for it an illuminating volume of his own," a Bible containing the precepts of the federal government:

> Children, obey your agents from Washington, for this is right.
> Honor thy father and thy mother, for the Government has created them but a little lower than the Federal agent. Love, honor, and disobey them [Laughter].
> Whatsoever thy hand findeth to do, tell it to thy father and mother and let them do it.

Six days shalt thou do all thy rest, and on the seventh day thy parents shalt rest with thee [Laughter].

Go to the bureau officer, thou sluggard; consider his ways and be idle.

Toil, thou farmer's wife; thou shalt have no servant in thy house, nor let thy children help thee.

And all thy children shall be taught of the Federal agent, and great shall be the peace of thy children.

Thy children shall rise up and call the Federal agent blessed [Laughter].[130]

In this parody of a federal agent's "Bible reading," Lanham captured many of the elements of grassroots opposition to the amendment. The concern being satirized was federal takeover of the home, of children, even of the Bible, which had been substituted by the agent's version of Scripture. Lanham's vision was echoed by other Southern congressmen, such as Henry St. George Tucker of Virginia. "Under [this amendment] Congress would have the power to declare that no boy or girl under 18 years of age could do any work in the home of the family, in the garden, at the stable, in the harvest field, or in the cornfield; taking away from the parents the right to control the domestic work of their children," said Tucker. "When I think of such a provision . . . I feel like exclaiming in the language of the great Virginian orator, who fired the hearts of our people in resistance to tyranny, 'Give me liberty or give me death!'"[131]

Many congressmen from rural areas argued that farm labor was healthy and beneficial for boys, especially. Along with other Southern congressmen, Rep. John J. McSwain of South Carolina pointed out that the majority of the so-called child labor in America was on farms and in fields rather than in factories and mills: "Everybody with common sense will admit that farm labor does not hurt children—physically, morally, or intellectually. It is out in [the] open and in the sunshine where health and strength are gained." Empowering Congress to prevent boys from working on farms was not only against the interests of children, McSwain argued, but was also blatantly "un-American." "This is Prussianism, pure and simple," he said.[132] The possibility of a federal standard for all children and youth, including those in rural areas, also brought out racial anxieties among various congressmen. Perhaps because the recent investigations of rural child labor had focused on the working and schooling conditions of both black and white children, some congressmen from farming districts expressed thinly veiled racist concerns about the potential of a child labor amendment to bring black and white children of their rural districts under federal jurisdiction, which would usurp the white-controlled, local prerogatives of their communities. Rep. Millard Tydings of Maryland, for instance, asked Congress to consider "just a few of the things that could take place" if the amendment were adopted and carried out in the several states. Among other things, he asked, "How about the colored people, male and female? The colored schools in Maryland of the better sort run up to the ninth grade. So after these colored people finish these grades they must remain idle until they are 18 years old. Is this conducive to good citizenship for either the white man or the black man? Yet that is what we do here by adopting this amendment."[133]

The amendment's supporters challenged what might be deemed a kind of constitutional fundamentalism. Rep. Fiorello LaGuardia of New York, a staunch Progressive, was irked by the suggestion that the Constitution was meant to be followed as if it were a static document containing timeless, divine truths: "I fail to find any provision or word in the Constitution of finality. To the contrary, the far-sighted men of vision who framed that remarkable document realized that they could not speak for a century ahead of them and therefore provided the very means by which the Constitution could be amended, altered, or enlarged."[134] Constitutional limitations should "be construed in the light of changed times and changed conditions," he argued. In a break with other North Carolina representatives, Rep. Zebulon Weaver argued, "I love the Constitution as much as any of my colleagues. . . . It was wonderfully conceived by our forefathers, but it is evident . . . they expected that as time passed and new problems confronted the people affecting their lives, their pursuits, and their happiness, that it would be necessary to amend it."[135] Rep. Knud Wefald of Minnesota argued that slave emancipation, rather than the original founding of the country, should be the model for the present. The "great immortal" who had "made the Constitution a living thing" in the first place, said Wefald, was Abraham Lincoln. Wefald reminded his colleagues that Lincoln believed "the heart of the Constitution [was] that phrase in the Declaration of Independence that says there shall be guaranteed to everybody 'life, liberty, and the pursuit of happiness.'" "When we pass this resolution we bring the dreams of the forefathers closer to realization than many will imagine. We abolished chattel slavery with a bloody conflict that shook the world; today we take a step toward the abolishment of the industrial slavery of childhood." Wefald was also laying claim to a different version of America, a narrative of the nation's past that had at its center the abolition of slavery rather than the overthrow of government tyranny. This history, he suggested, would support a federal grant of power to abolish child labor. "While the passage of this constitutional amendment will not affect my child, I feel that I am my brother's keeper."[136]

Debate in the Senate covered much of the same territory. Senator Hubert Stephens of Mississippi asserted, "This is a socialistic movement that has

for its end purposes far deeper and more radical than appear on the surface
... the child becomes the absolute property of the Federal Government."[137]
Ultimately, the *Congressional Record* was filled with over a hundred pages of
speeches, arguments, and other evidence related to the Child Labor Amendment proposal. Though many congressmen expressed skepticism about the
amendment, the majority was not convinced by the opposition and voted
to pass the measure. The final vote in the House was 297 to 69 and was cast
on April 26, 1924. Of the 69 votes cast against the amendment, 48 of them
were cast by Southerners (13 Republicans and 56 Democrats opposed the
measure).[138] The Senate approved the resolution on June 2, 1924, by a vote of
61 to 23. Of the 23 no votes, 14 were cast by Southern senators (6 Republicans
and 17 Democrats opposed the resolution).[139] Following was the amendment's
final wording:

> Section I. The Congress shall have power to limit, regulate, and prohibit the
> labor of persons under eighteen years of age.
> Section II. The power of the several States is unimpaired by this article except
> that the operation of State laws shall be suspended to the extent necessary to
> give effect to legislation enacted by the Congress.[140]

Having been approved by Congress, the amendment would now be sent to
the states for ratification. The support of thirty-six states—or three-fourths of
them—would be required. The amendment's supporters prepared for the fight
ahead. So too did opponents. Just weeks after the amendment passed Congress, the state of Arkansas ratified the amendment, a seemingly encouraging
sign for reformers—though the close vote in the Arkansas legislature (60–53)
was a harbinger of difficulties to come.[141] All three presidential candidates of
1924—Republican candidate Calvin Coolidge, Democratic candidate John
W. Davis, and Progressive candidate Robert M. LaFollette—supported the
amendment. As the Arkansas vote suggested, however, the spark of a powerful collective protest had already begun. Leading business interests fanned
the flames to ensure it would spread far and wide.

The proposed child labor amendment was one of the most debated political issues of the 1920s. The nation was flooded with propaganda from
both sides, in newspapers, magazines, printed leaflets, speeches, lectures,
and, for the first time in the history of the movement, over the radio.[142] The
Permanent Conference for the Abolition of Child Labor redoubled its efforts
by establishing its central headquarters in Washington, DC, at the office of
the National League of Women Voters, which endorsed the amendment.[143]
Despite the early victory in Arkansas, momentum for ratification was short-
lived, as an anti-amendment campaign was mounted in the summer of 1924.

Manufacturing and textile interests and chambers of commerce provided the financial resources while traditionalist women, defenders of the Constitution, and farm bureaus remained highly involved and influential.[144] As in previous fights, Southern Textile Association president David Clark provided leadership and resources to the anti-amendment campaign. Clark's first move was to reach out to Southern farmers with a message about the amendment. In the summer of 1924, he sent an estimated fifty thousand pieces of literature to Southern farmers, emphasizing that the proposed amendment would invade their homes and give the federal government control over their children.[145]

The *Southern Textile Bulletin* also became a major organ of the anti-amendment campaign. To encourage farmers' participation, Clark organized the Farmers' States Rights League in Troy, North Carolina, for the purpose of protecting farmers against the encroachment of a federal bureaucracy on their homes and families.[146] This organization flooded not only Southern newspapers but also newspapers and agricultural publications in the West to reach rural farmers with articles denouncing the measure.[147] Similar to Clark's organization, the National Association of Manufacturers (NAM) made defeat of the amendment its major policy agenda of 1924. Like the Southern Textile Association, NAM also founded an organization to gain popular support, the National Committee for the Rejection of the 20th Amendment. This organization was broad in outreach, preparing special publications that targeted small towns and rural areas while also preparing articles for select academic journals and large urban newspapers.[148]

The amendment's supporters spent much of their time rebutting misinformation about the amendment.[149] Much of their efforts were aimed at shifting focus away from boys on the farm and toward girls in the factory. To this point, reformers answered letters to editors in newspapers, distributed informational leaflets, bought radio spots, and hired artists to paint posters for national distribution. Reformers promised they would not use the amendment to disrupt healthy farm labor for boys. Reflecting the shifting gender dynamics of the child labor debate, they tried desperately to shift the focus back to capitalist exploitation of "helpless" girls. A widely distributed poster argued that girls in industrial labor were the target of the amendment, not boys engaged in healthy farm labor. The amendment "will not take children off their home farms," the poster read. Juxtaposing two images—a textile mill girl worker and a happy farm boy—reformers tried to neutralize the claim that boys would be prevented from working on the family farm. An NCLC pamphlet titled "Brass Tacks on the Pending Child Labor Amendment" contained a special section on "Children on Farms," which backed off the notion that reformers were interested in farm child labor. No attempts had ever been

Figure 5.1. "Stop This! Let This Continue!" *American Child* 6, no. 11 (1924), 8. Courtesy of the University of Chicago Regenstein Library.

made by Congress in the first two federal child labor laws "to control the labor of any child on any farm." Thus it was "unlikely" that Congress would legislate "to control the work of children on their parents' farms."[150] Educator E. C. Lindeman's article "Child Labor Amendment and the Farmers" tried to put to rest accusations that the pending amendment was designed to control the labor of boys on family farms.[151] But the votes from Southern states in the summer of 1924 indicated that reformers' concessions were too little, too late. Any hopes for Southern ratification were dashed after the Louisiana House almost unanimously rejected the amendment in late June, followed by the Georgia legislature in early July and the North Carolina Senate in August.[152] Characteristic of other Southern states, the formal resolution of the Georgia legislature declared that the amendment "would place Congress in control in every home in the land between parent and child."[153]

Southern congressmen had long resented Northern reformers' depictions of the Southern textile industry and regarded child labor reform as "Northern interference." But reformers' recent rural child welfare campaign was a final straw that confirmed many opponents' worst suspicions about reformers' intentions. While Southern states' overwhelming rejection of the amendment was not surprising given this background, the Farmers' States Rights League and the National Committee for the Rejection of the 20th Amendment were planning something bigger than a Southern rout. To expand the opposition beyond the South, they were reaching out to working-class urban Catholics in Massachusetts. Since Massachusetts had the most advanced child labor laws in the country, opponents believed that if this "enlightened" state were to reject ratification, reformers would be forced to accept that the country did not want a child labor amendment. It would be difficult for reformers to paint Massachusetts as a "backward" state as they had done with Southern states. A Massachusetts rejection would be the amendment campaign's "waterloo." The opposition had several months to organize, since the Massachusetts legislature decided to hold a popular referendum on the amendment in November. The Associated Industries of Massachusetts (AIM), headed by Clifton Anderson, who was also a member of the National Committee for the Rejection of the 20th Amendment, founded an organization that would work to defeat the amendment in Massachusetts: the Citizens' Committee to Protect Our Homes and Children.[154] Similar organizations were founded around the same time, arranging radio broadcasts against the amendment, cooperating with the Sentinels of the Republic (who were based in Massachusetts), and circulating material to both legislators and regular citizens.[155] Targeting the large population of Catholics in the state with the message that an enlarged federal government threatened the sanctity of the home, parental authority, and especially the education of Catholic children, opponents placed their bets that it would work. One pamphlet declared that the amendment would "take away from you the control of the education of your children and give it to a political bureau in Washington."[156]

The message targeting Catholics seemed to catch on quickly. In October the Boston prelate instructed the pastors in his archdiocese to warn their parishioners of the dangers of the Child Labor Amendment.[157] The archdiocese's official publication, the *Boston Pilot*, announced that the amendment would "substitute the will of Congress and the dictate of a centralized bureaucracy, more in keeping with Soviet Russia than with the fundamental principles of American Government" in place of the "parental control over children."[158] Cardinal William Henry O'Connell, archbishop of Boston, recommended that pastors bring to the attention of their parishioners "at all Masses on Sunday, October 5th, the dangers hidden in the child labor proposed amendment" and "the necessity of their voting on election day to protect the interests of their children."[159] Many Catholics in the state, clergy and laymen, came to oppose ratification. The Catholic Church in the state never took an official stance, and several prominent Catholic individuals and groups continued to support the amendment, including leading progressive Father John A. Ryan, the National Council of Catholic Women, and the National Catholic Welfare Council.[160] Father Ryan, in particular, tried to convince Catholics in

144   CHAPTER 5

Massachusetts they had nothing to fear from the proposed amendment.[161] But the majority of Catholics in both Massachusetts and New York were persuaded that the proposed amendment had broad implications for controlling not only the labor of their children but their schooling as well. For these Catholics, federal control of their children's education threatened a future prohibition of Catholic education.[162]

Joining Catholics for rejection of the amendment were other prominent Massachusetts citizens such as attorney Moorfield Storey, Harvard University president A. Lawrence Lowell, and Boston mayor James M. Curley.[163] Both sides in the debate had come to regard Massachusetts as a key state in the amendment battle. By late October those in favor of the amendment worried that the tide was turning against them. On November 4, 1924, by popular referendum, the voters of Massachusetts opted against ratification of the Child Labor Amendment by a margin of nearly 3 to 1. Massachusetts lawmakers followed the outcome of the popular referendum, officially rejecting ratification in February 1925.[164] For reformers, the Massachusetts defeat was devastating, as it influenced other states. By the end of February, only four states (Arkansas, Arizona, California, and Wisconsin) had ratified the amendment, whereas twelve (Connecticut, Delaware, Georgia, Kansas, Massachusetts, North Carolina, South Carolina, South Dakota, Tennessee, Texas, Utah, and Vermont) had rejected it. Eleven other states rejected the amendment in at least one House, whereas only one other state (New Mexico) had one House that had ratified it. Elsewhere in the country, the amendment was either pending or legislatures were not in session.[165] Some journalists began declaring the amendment "dead" by March 1925. Herbert Croly of the *New Republic* wrote that "the only aspect of [the amendment] which is worth discussing now is what the effect of the defeat will be and what the causes of it were."[166]

Reformers had a hard time accepting defeat. Instead of considering the possibility that rural white farm families and urban Catholics did not want a child labor amendment, they blamed business interests for orchestrating the amendment's demise. They were stunned to learn that the National Committee to Protect Our Homes and Children had spent $15,522 in Massachusetts alone to defeat the amendment. The major source of the contributions was manufacturing and business corporations.[167] Child welfare expert Katharine Lumpkin blamed Massachusetts manufacturers for the defeat in that state:

> While I do not understand just how I came to this belief, I know that I thought the manufacturers of Massachusetts as a rule had more social vision than manufacturers in my own state [North Carolina] and adjoining states in the South. I was wrong. After a number of my experiences in the campaign for the

Cultural Warriors 145

ratification of the Child Labor Amendment in Massachusetts I am thoroughly convinced that the average manufacturer of Massachusetts wants to be let alone to do as he pleases on the matter of working children just as much as does the average manufacturer of North Carolina.[168]

Whenever they acknowledged grassroots opposition, reformers argued that opponents had been duped by business interests. In a radio talk in March 1925, a labor organizer argued that rural farmers had been hoodwinked into fighting the battles of manufacturers: "Until the farmers have fought their way to victory on such issues as lower taxes, lower freight rates, [and] better credit facilities, clearly they would do well to waste no further time fighting the battles of the eastern and southern manufacturers against the regulation of admitted child labor abuses—especially when those same manufacturers and their financial allies are profiteering not only on unregulated child labor but on everything the farmer has to buy and everything he has to sell."[169] In January 1925, *Labor*, the official publication of several railroad labor organizations, published an expose of the "fake farmers' league" led by David Clark. *Labor* magazine sent a staff representative to North Carolina to investigate the so-called Farmers' States Rights League. Among the investigator's findings were "the League is not a farmers' organization. Its president is the cashier of a cotton mill bank. Its vice president is an employee of a cotton mill store." The men in charge of the Farmers' States Rights League admitted that they did not collect dues from their members, refused to reveal how they paid for their advertisements, and were unable to produce a membership roll.[170]

Other observers perceived a more profound shift in politics and ideas. In January 1925 journalist William L. Chenery penned a perceptive piece titled "Child Labor—The New Alignment." Chenery argued that the battle over the Child Labor Amendment marked the beginning of a new alignment in American politics. The core of the opposition, he noted, was "well-organized associations of manufacturers." But these manufacturers had brought into their fold "a new body of independents," millions of "rural farmers" and "anti-suffragists" under an ideological covering that included the sanctity of the family, parental authority, agrarian values, and distrust of the federal bureaucratic state. These business interests had also brought together Catholics and fundamentalist Christians who were concerned about a federal takeover of the education of their children.[171] These new opponents also tended to believe that labor had spiritual value. As Georgia statesman S. G. McLendon explained in the *Manufacturers' Record*, the Twentieth Amendment was unbiblical because God's law stated, "In the sweat of thy brow shalt thou eat bread, and six days shalt thou labor."[172] Another fundamentalist

146   CHAPTER 5

Christian argued that the amendment was unbiblical since "Christ worked in a carpenter shop at the age of fourteen."[173] Fundamentalist Christians also worried that the federal government would replace the biblical authority of parents. McLendon noted that "the 20th amendment would annul the commandment, 'Thou shalt honor thy father and thy mother,'" by making children obey the laws of the federal government rather than their parents.[174]

On the other side of Chenery's "new alignment" was a new guard of pro-federal government reformers and activists, organized labor unions, organized teachers, reform-minded women, and liberal Christians, including liberal Catholics. Intoning the fundamentalist-modernist controversy within 1920s Christian circles, some Christian commentators noted that the Child Labor Amendment battle reflected a fight for the "soul" of Christianity. Massachusetts had "failed in her hour of privilege," lamented *Christian Century* magazine. Both Catholics *and* Protestants had voted down the amendment, the author noted. The church had seemingly stopped "caring about the major social issues of our day."[175] The *Federal Council Bulletin*, the official publication of the Social Gospel organization, the FCCC, continued to decry child labor and called for ratification of the amendment. An article in June 1925 compared the Child Labor Amendment debate to the proslavery and antislavery debates of the mid-nineteenth century. "There were religious and Christian people on both sides," the author wrote. Just like debates over child labor, both factions "pointed to the Bible" to support their conclusions. But "the people who were on the side of slavery . . . *were wrong*."[176] Similarly, the people who believe that America must "build her prosperity on the work of children . . . *are wrong*," the author argued.[177]

The amendment's defeat signaled not only a rejection of federal authority over child labor but also the emergence of a collective resistance to the modern bureaucratic state that would persist for decades to come.[178] Southern manufacturers' most powerful allies were, ironically, in rural regions where the market had not yet triumphed. Whereas laissez-faire capitalists and their allies on the Supreme Court had defined free labor in modern industrial society as the ability to contract freely without government interference, rural Americans claimed their right to appeal to the authority of Scripture, tradition, and the family without government interference. It was a powerful argument that Southern manufacturers learned to wield by taking seriously the values of the people whose support they needed to be successful. Stung by defeat, reformers blamed manufacturers for duping rural white farmers and other amendment opponents into fighting against their own interests. It was not the right lesson. Southern manufacturers learned they could gain powerful allies by arming these cultural warriors in a battle against modern

Cultural Warriors   147

secular bureaucracy. From the ground, this battle was not economic but spiritual. An astute observer in 1924 reflected on the conflict: "In the current propaganda against the child labor amendment," he wrote, "the economics of the issue is strangely subordinated. We are gravely assured . . . that what is at stake is our *sacred liberty, the sanctity of our homes.*" Defeating the Child Labor Amendment had become synonymous with preserving "American liberty and the sacredness of the American home."[179]

In the amendment battle, antiregulation had acquired sacred meaning. It was not antiregulation per se that motivated opponents but rather addressing a spiritual threat to their way of life. This threat was made all the more urgent by the continual missteps of reformers whose actions affirmed their opponents' worst suspicions. Rallying against the amendment gave opponents a chance to reassert cultural modes of authority that reformers had declared obsolete. In the 1920s a Northern Progressive vision of modern child welfare emerged as a violation of rural Americans' most cherished principles. As reformers increasingly condemned the rural way of life, opponents struck back with a defense of their traditional values as the essence of freedom. Reformers also claimed the mantle of freedom, arguing that it was "child labor, not any law restricting it, that is destructive of liberty."[180] Debates about children and their labor had once again brought to the fore opposing visions of freedom in American society, this time around progress and tradition in the modern industrial age. Though anti–child labor reform had deep roots in the South, the 1920s amendment battle spurred the opposition's maturation into a social movement of its own. An imaginary new Mason-Dixon Line was drawn within capitalist society that divided the gatekeepers of modernity from the cultural warriors who resisted them. In allying themselves with the forces of antiregulation, the cultural warriors did not impede the encroachment of the market but that of the modern bureaucratic state. Their enduring protest insisted that spiritual values, not secular ones, should be the measure for determining how to negotiate the changes wrought by capitalism.

Conclusion

On December 16, 1929, the National Child Labor Committee gathered to celebrate its twenty-five-year anniversary in the ballroom of the Roosevelt Hotel on Madison Avenue in New York City. The program of the evening dinner included a keynote address by the governor of New York, Franklin Delano Roosevelt.[1] While reformers sat around formal dining tables exchanging toasts, FDR delivered sobering remarks on how much work remained. "Many great strides" had been made "in the regulation and prevention of child labor," he noted. "And yet it seems to me that we have, in this country, gone perhaps *half of the way towards our goal*."[2] In the committee's twenty-five years, much regulation had been achieved. Every state had some regulation on the hours of work for children, restrictions on night work, and a minimum age of fourteen for entering most types of industrial labor.[3] But loopholes in child labor laws, lax schooling requirements, and resistance to federal intervention remained major obstacles. The eight-hour day was not universal, and enforcements of minimum age requirements varied greatly from state to state.[4] Moreover, child labor in agriculture, canneries, street trades, and tenements remained largely unregulated. As Roosevelt remarked, the child labor issue had revealed major divisions in the country. As he saw it, this division was between those who, "from the point of view of the moment," emphasized short-term market prosperity for the few and those who took a "long-range view" that emphasized social protection and well-being for the many.[5]

When FDR spoke at the anniversary dinner, it had been only two months since the stock market crash that, as he did not then realize, would lead to the most severe economic depression of the twentieth century. He also could not have then realized that he would lead the country through this difficult period as its president and that one result of his presidency would be higher child labor standards for the nation as a whole. Conditions brought on by the Great Depression both improved and worsened the problem of child labor. On the one hand, child labor declined overall as unemployment spread everywhere. On the other hand, desperation led many employers to replace adult workers with children.[6] By 1933 sweatshop conditions were once again widespread, especially in the industrial East. Manufacturers were crossing state lines to take advantage of lower regulatory standards in the South. These conditions brought about renewed interest in the Child Labor Amendment. According to *Collier's* magazine, "The whole situation changed with the depression. Labor's demand that all available jobs should go to adult workers gained general support and a new appreciation of the importance of national action for social welfare developed."[7] Between February 1 and July 15, 1933, nine more state legislatures—Illinois, Michigan, New Hampshire, New Jersey, North Dakota, Ohio, Oklahoma, Oregon, and Washington—ratified the amendment.[8] Over the next five years, reformers would divide their time between advising FDR on regulations to be included in his emergency recovery provisions and campaigning for the Child Labor Amendment.

President Roosevelt supported the inclusion of federal child labor provisions as part of his National Recovery Administration (NRA). The NRA's child labor provisions established a federal minimum age standard of sixteen for manufacturing and mercantile employment.[9] This standard remained in effect until the Supreme Court declared the NRA unconstitutional on May 27, 1935.[10] Meanwhile, five more states—Iowa, Maine, Minnesota, Pennsylvania, and West Virginia—voted to ratify the Child Labor Amendment, bringing the total to twenty.[11] But even the urgencies of the Depression did not eclipse concerns that the Child Labor Amendment presented a threat to older cultural modes of authority. The chief organization opposed to ratification in the 1930s was the National Committee for the Protection of Child, Family, School, and Church, which was set up in January 1934.[12] It revived familiar arguments against the amendment, including government interference with parental authority, an agrarian way of life, and religious education. In a departure from the 1920s, the national press turned against the amendment in the 1930s as the provisions of the NRA made them concerned about a prohibition of newsboys selling and delivering their papers.[13] The American Bar Association also took a strong stand against the amendment in the 1930s, arguing that the amendment was dead and was no longer open for ratification.[14]

While reformers strongly preferred a child labor amendment—believing it was the only comprehensive solution to child labor—they were committed

Conclusion

to supporting federal child labor provisions in FDR's ongoing recovery and reform measures. After the Supreme Court struck down the NRA and other New Deal measures, President Roosevelt proposed a Judicial Procedures Reform Plan, known as his "court-packing plan," to Congress in 1937. However, the retirement of conservative justice Willis Van Devanter in June 1937 along with a jurisprudential shift by associate justice Owen J. Roberts in *West Coast Hotel Co. v. Parrish* (1937)—a case that effectively ended the Lochner era by upholding minimum wage legislation—made FDR's plan to stack the Court unnecessary.[15] The Fair Labor Standards Act (FLSA), which was primarily a minimum-wage and maximum-hours measure for adult workers, would be the next attempt at federal child labor regulation.[16] Since the new Supreme Court had broadened the interpretation of the commerce clause, Congress based the FLSA's child labor provisions on it.[17] Reformers endorsed the measure with reluctance. Without a child labor amendment, they worried that the child labor provisions of the FLSA would be inadequate. Applicable only to "shipment in interstate commerce goods produced in establishments where oppressive child labor conditions have prevailed within 30 days prior to shipment," the FLSA provisions would exempt child-employing establishments that handled but did not produce goods, such as transportation, domestic service, and communications. The provisions also exempted "children under 16 employed in agriculture," "children employed as actors in motion picture or theatrical productions," and "children working for their parents in any occupation other than manufacturing or mining."[18]

In 1937 the Children's Bureau estimated that only one-fourth of child labor in the United States would be affected by the provisions of the FLSA.[19] Grace Abbott expressed her "disappointment" in the measure, noting that a recent survey by the bureau found that "now the concentration [of child employment] is in service, trade, and miscellaneous occupations, and fewer children are in industrial occupations."[20] The FLSA was a "mines and factories" bill.[21] Agricultural child labor—the largest category of child labor—remained largely unregulated.[22] The *Christian Science Monitor* published a piece in support of reformers that called the FLSA a "conservative measure" that "came as something of a shock" to supporters of federal child labor regulation.[23] But the child labor provisions of the FLSA were important despite limitations, and the measure represented a possible constitutional test for future regulation. On February 3, 1941, the Supreme Court upheld the FLSA's constitutionality, overturning the *Hammer v. Dagenhart* case, which had invalidated Keating-Owen. The *New York Times* praised the FLSA as a sign that "oppressive child labor is on the way out in the United States of America," while reformers continued to hope for ratification of the Child Labor Amendment.[24] Other responses revealed that strong opposition to federal child labor regulation remained alive and well. The National Association of Manufacturers denounced the FLSA as "a step in the direction of Communism, bolshevism, and Nazism," and the Cotton Textile Institute said that the measure was "not indigenous to America."[25]

Historically, the elements of the New Deal that pertained to child labor were not new. Substantively identical to the Keating-Owen Act of 1916, the child labor provisions of the FLSA did not reflect any advancement in approach or policy. These provisions did, however, reflect the legacy of the movement to end child labor. From the height of the nation's sectional crisis over slavery through the early twentieth century, debates about children and their labor shaped how Americans on both sides of the Mason-Dixon Line defined such fundamental issues as work, freedom, morality, the market, and the state. Distinguishing between free and unfree labor for children defined the first phase of the movement in the aftermath of the Civil War. But neither the types of child labor that constituted unfree labor nor the meaning of emancipation for child laborers was ever self-evident. Unfree labor for children had been defined as the white racial degeneration of Southern mill children, industrial child labor exploited in the name of profit, and farm children denied the trappings of a modern childhood. Emancipating the child laborer had just as many meanings, from strengthening American empire, to liberating children in the consumer marketplace, to converting rural parents to the gospel of progress. On a certain level, reformers were merely fighting to end a practice they thought was wrong. But historically, the consequences of that struggle were much larger than they likely realized. Both ideologically and materially, reformers created a new world in their decades-long battle against child labor. As the first federal child labor provisions to be upheld by the Supreme Court, the FLSA reflected both the successes and limitations of that movement. In the end the FLSA empowered the federal government to intervene in certain instances of industrial child labor, but child labor was assigned a much narrower definition than reformers sought. When the reformers' ultimate aim, a constitutional amendment, was defeated a second time in the 1930s, the effort faltered on the same disagreements that had dominated in the 1920s. Once again the modern bureaucratic state would not be empowered to displace older sources of morality such as tradition, parental authority, and honest labor. Opponents insisted that these values would not only survive modern capitalist society but would also thrive as key weapons against the modern secular order. Even at a point of maximum federal intervention in the economy, therefore, a barrier had been raised to subsequent state initiatives that reflected the legacy of a new imaginary Mason-Dixon Line.

Notes

Introduction

1. See Laura F. Edwards, *Gendered Strife and Confusion: The Political Culture of Reconstruction* (Urbana: University of Illinois Press, 1997); Eric Foner, *The Story of American Freedom* (New York: W. W. Norton, 1998); Eric Foner, *Free Soil, Free Labor, Free Men: The Ideology of the Republican Party before the Civil War* (New York: Oxford University Press, 1970); Steven Hahn, *The Roots of Southern Populism: Yeoman Farmers and the Transformation of the Georgia Upcountry, 1850–1890* (New York: Oxford University Press, 1983); Stephanie McCurry, *Masters of Small Worlds: Yeoman Households, Gender Relations, and the Political Culture of the Antebellum South Carolina Low Country* (New York: Oxford University Press, 1995); James M. McPherson, *Battle Cry of Freedom: The Civil War Era* (New York: Oxford University Press, 1998); Edmund S. Morgan, *American Slavery, American Freedom* (New York: W. W. Norton, 1975); Heather Cox Richardson, *The Death of Reconstruction: Race, Labor, and Politics in the Post–Civil War North, 1865–1901* (Cambridge, MA: Harvard University Press, 2001); Julie Saville, *The Work of Reconstruction: From Slave to Wage Labor in South Carolina, 1860–1870* (New York: Cambridge University Press, 1994); Amy Dru Stanley, *From Bondage to Contract: Wage Labor, Marriage, and the Market in the Age of Slave Emancipation* (New York: Cambridge University Press, 1998); C. Vann Woodward, *Origins of the New South, 1877–1913* (Baton Rouge: Louisiana State University Press, 1951).

2. See Barbara Jeanne Fields, *Slavery and Freedom on the Middle Ground: Maryland during the Nineteenth Century* (New Haven, CT: Yale University Press, 1987); Eric Foner, *Nothing but Freedom: Emancipation and Its Legacy* (Baton Rouge: Louisiana State University Press, 1983); Thomas C. Holt, *The Problem of Freedom: Race, Labor, and Politics in Jamaica and Britain, 1832–1938* (Baltimore: Johns Hopkins University Press, 1992); Rebecca J. Scott, *Degrees of Freedom: Louisiana and Cuba after Slavery* (Cambridge, MA: Harvard University Press, 2005).

Notes to Introduction

3. There is a rich literature on children and labor in early America and the legal and cultural underpinnings of that labor. See Ruth Wallis Herndon and John E. Murray, eds., *Children Bound to Labor: The Pauper Apprentice System in Early America* (Ithaca, NY: Cornell University Press, 2009); Christopher L. Tomlin, *Law, Labor and Ideology in the Early American Republic* (New York: Cambridge University Press, 1993); and Robert J. Steinfeld, *The Invention of Free Labor: The Employment Relation in English and American Law and Culture* (Chapel Hill: University of North Carolina Press, 2002).

4. See Hugh D. Hindman, *Child Labor: An American History* (Armonk, NY: M. E. Sharpe, 2002); Walter I. Trattner, *Crusade for the Children: A History of the National Child Labor Committee and Child Labor Reform in America* (Chicago: Quadrangle Books, 1970); John A. Fliter, *Child Labor in America: The Epic Legal Struggle to Protect Children* (Lawrence: University Press of Kansas, 2018).

5. See Clark Nardinelli, *Child Labor and the Industrial Revolution* (Bloomington: Indiana University Press, 1990); Philippe Ariès, *Centuries of Childhood* (New York: Vintage, 1962); Peter Uhlenberg, "Death and the Family," in *The American Family*, ed. Michael Gordon, 157–65 (New York: St. Martin's Press, 1978); Theodore W. Schultz, "The Value of Children: An Economic Perspective," *Journal of Political Economy* 81 (Mar.–Apr. 1973): 2–13; Gary S. Becker, *A Treatise on the Family* (Cambridge: Harvard University Press, 1981); Isabel Sawhill, "Economic Perspectives on the Family," *Daedalus* 106 (Spring 1977): 116–25; Fred Arnold, et al., *The Value of Children* (Honolulu: East-West Population Institute, 1975); and Carl Degler, *At Odds: Women and the Family in America from the Revolution to the Present* (New York: Oxford University Press, 1980). A notable exception is Christopher Lasch, who has argued that the removal of children from the labor market deteriorated family ties rather than strengthening them as new "agencies" tried to take the place of parents. See Lasch, *Haven in a Heartless World* (New York: Basic Books, 1979). For scholarship emphasizing cultural factors, see Viviana A. Zelizer, *Pricing the Priceless Child: The Changing Social Value of Children* (New York: Basic Books, 1985), and Philip Greven, *The Protestant Temperament* (New York: Signet, 1977).

6. William A. Link, *The Paradox of Southern Progressivism, 1880–1930* (Chapel Hill: University of North Carolina Press, 1992), 182. A recent treatment of the sectional differences in child labor debates is Gwendolyn Alphonso, "Of Families or Individuals? Southern Child Workers and the Progressive Crusade for Child Labor Regulation, 1899–1920," in *Child and Youth during the Gilded Age and Progressive Era*, ed. James Marten (New York: New York University Press, 2014), 59–80. Alphonso argues that Northern proponents and Southern opponents of child labor regulation had differing understandings of children and families, one that defined the child as an "individual" and the other defining the child as "relational" within family units. In a similar vein, James Schmidt demonstrated how court battles over industrial accidents incurred by young workers in the Appalachian South between the 1880s and 1920s reveal that Appalachian families defined child labor in terms of workplace safety rather than in terms of childhood incapacity, which was the legal definition pushed by reformers.

Notes to Introduction and Chapter 1   155

See James Schmidt, *Industrial Violence and the Legal Origins of Child Labor* (New York: Cambridge University Press, 2010).

7. Link, *Paradox of Southern Progressivism*, 176.

8. To be sure, there were other antireform movements including national anti-suffrage, which defended traditional values against modern Progressivism. However, none of them displayed the same level of sectional hostilities that marked the child labor battle. See, for instance, Susan Goodier, *No Votes for Women: The New York State Anti-Suffrage Movement* (Urbana: University of Illinois Press, 2013).

9. Shelley Sallee's *The Whiteness of Child Labor Reform in the New South* (Athens: University of Georgia Press, 2004) broke new ground as the first book-length study on the "whites-only" route taken by Progressive reformers in the South.

10. The work of T. J. Jackson Lears on antimodernism in the consumer age sparked my interest in exploring rural opposition to child labor reform as a type of antimodernist movement. The Southern-led opposition to reform coalesced as child labor reformers embraced a secular, progress-oriented campaign that explicitly endorsed consumerist values. Whereas Lears examined antimodernists among the educated Northern bourgeoisie, I examine a group of antimodernists in rural America that mobilized against the encroachment of consumerist values and modern secular bureaucracy by reasserting the spiritual value of farm labor for their children. See Lears, *No Place of Grace: Antimodernism and the Transformation of American Culture, 1880–1920* (Chicago: University of Chicago Press, 1981).

Chapter 1. Fields of Free Labor

1. "Office-Journal," in appendix to Children's Aid Society (CAS), *Sixth Annual Report of the Children's Aid Society, February 1859* (New York: Wynkoop, Hallenbeck, and Thomas, 1859), 61–62.

2. Ibid., 62–64.

3. The landscape of moral reform shifted dramatically between 1830 and 1860. As Paul Boyer has argued, if a tourist in 1830 wished to visit the most active and influential moral reform agencies in New York City, he or she would have visited "the Bible society, the Tract Society, the City Mission Association, and the local Sunday School Union." By 1860, however, the same tourist would have visited the headquarters of three organizations that were unknown in 1830: "the Association for Improving the Condition of the Poor, the Children's Aid Society, and the Young Men's Christian Association." See Paul Boyer, *Urban Masses and Moral Order in America, 1820–1920* (Cambridge: Harvard University Press, 1978), 85.

4. Historically, antislavery and capitalism have a complicated relationship. The rise of antislavery had much to do with the growth of capitalism. Even when historians disagree about how the two developments are connected, they tend to agree the market played an important role in shaping the perception that slavery was wrong. The best example of this debate is between Thomas Haskell, David Brion Davis, and John Ashworth that appeared in the *American Historical Review* in the 1980s and was reprinted in Thomas Bender, ed., *The Antislavery Debate: Capitalism and Abolitionism*

156   *Notes to Chapter 1*

as a Problem in Historical Interpretation (Berkeley: University of California Press, 1992). David Brion Davis, for instance, has argued that the emergence of antislavery represented a "momentous turning point in the evolution of man's moral perception" that "reflected the ideological needs of various groups and classes." See Davis, *The Problem of Slavery in the Age of Revolution, 1770–1823* (Ithaca, NY: Cornell University Press, 1975), 42.

5. See Eric Foner, *Free Soil, Free Labor, Free Men: The Ideology of the Republican Party before the Civil War* (New York: Oxford University Press, 1995), Julie Saville, *The Work of Reconstruction: From Slave to Wage Laborer in South Carolina, 1860–1870* (New York: Cambridge University Press, 1996), especially pp. 2–4, 46–47, and 157–58; and Jonathan A. Glickstein, *Concepts of Free Labor in Antebellum America* (New Haven, CT: Yale University Press, 1991). For Abraham Lincoln's views of "free labor," see Lincoln, "Sept. 30, 1859—Annual Address before the Wisconsin State Agricultural Society, at Milwaukee, Wis.," in *Abraham Lincoln: Complete Works, Comprising His Speeches, Letters, State Papers, and Miscellaneous Writings*, vol. 1, ed. John George Nicolay and John Hay (New York: Century Co., 1907), 576–84. See also Lincoln, "February 27, 1860—Address at Cooper Institute, New York," in *Abraham Lincoln: Complete Works*, especially pp. 611–16. "Advancement—improvement in condition—is the order of things in a society of equals. . . . Free labor has the inspiration of hope; pure slavery has no hope" (Lincoln, "July 1, 1854—Fragment. On Slavery," in *Abraham Lincoln: Complete Works*, 179). "When one starts poor, as most do in the race of life, free society is such that he knows he can better his condition; he knows that there is no fixed condition of labor for his whole life" (Lincoln, "March 6, 1860—Speech at New Haven, Conn.," in *Abraham Lincoln: Complete Works*, 625).

6. See Foner, *Free Soil, Free Labor*. See also Alexis de Tocqueville, who recorded similar observations about the South in *Democracy in America*. For Tocqueville, the danger to the Union was not that the North and South had different "interests" but that slavery had produced a distinctive character and way of life in the South: "In the Southern States, the more immediate wants of life are always supplied. . . . The American of the South is fond of grandeur, luxury, and renown, of gaiety, of pleasure, and, above all, of idleness; nothing obliges him to exert himself in order to subsist; and he has no necessary occupations, he gives way to indolence, and he does not even attempt what would be useful." Tocqueville, *Democracy in America*, vol. 2, trans. Henry Reeves (New York: D. Appleton, 1904), 433–34.

7. Quoted in Foner, *Free Soil, Free Labor*, 46.

8. Quoted in ibid., 297.

9. Ibid. See also Tocqueville, *Democracy in America*, 438. "We have already seen that slavery, which is abolished in the North, still exists in the South. . . . The North is therefore superior to the South both in commerce and manufacture; the natural consequence of which is the more rapid increase of population and of wealth within its borders."

10. The Southern proslavery movement reached its height in the 1850s. James Henry Hammond, John C. Calhoun, and George Fitzhugh were some of the move-

Notes to Chapter 1 157

ment's most prominent leaders. In addition to mounting a full-blown defense of slave society, these men also offered a scathing critique of capitalism and free society. See especially George Fitzhugh, *Cannibals All! Or Slaves without Masters* (Richmond, VA: A. Morris, 1857). For scholarship on American proslavery, see William Jenkins, *Proslavery Thought in the Old South* (Chapel Hill: University of North Carolina Press, 1935); Drew Gilpin Faust, "A Southern Stewardship: The Intellectual and the Pro-slavery Argument," *American Quarterly* 31, no. 1 (1979): 63–80; and Paul Finkelman, *Defending Slavery: Proslavery Thought in the Old South* (Boston: Bedford Press, 2003).

11. Fitzhugh, *Cannibals All!*, 332.

12. Ibid.

13. Foner, *Free Soil, Free Labor*.

14. Children's Aid Society, *First Annual Report of the Children's Aid Society, February, 1854* (New York: C. W. Benedict, 1854), 3, 4.

15. Ibid., 3. Brace discusses "overcrowding" and its social results in his correspondence and later publications. See Brace and Brace, The *Life of Charles Loring Brace, Chiefly Told in His Own Letters* (New York: Charles Scribner's Sons, 1894), 202. The emigration plan would "help to solve, in the only feasible mode, the great economic problem of poverty in our cities, for it sends future laborers where they are in demand, and relieves the overcrowded market in the city." See also Charles Loring Brace, *The Dangerous Classes of New York and Twenty Years' Work among Them* (New York: Wynkoop and Hallenbeck, 1872). "The source of juvenile crime and misery in New York, which is the most formidable, and, at the same time, one of the most difficult to remove, is the *overcrowding* of our population" (51).

16. *CAS, First Annual Report*, 4.

17. Ibid., 3–4.

18. In 1858 Brace reported, "There is not yet, we confidently hope, such an ingrained, inveterate, transmitted condition of pauperism and crime as in the cities of the Old World. The tendency of our whole life and society in America is to break up classes; and we may believe—with much encouragement—that this effect has been felt even among the lowest ranks of our vagrant and destitute. There is every reason in all these operations, we are confident, for hopeful work." Children's Aid Society, *Fifth Annual Report of the Children's Aid Society, February 1858* (New York: Wynkoop, Hallenbeck, and Thomas, 1858), 12.

19. For more on other antebellum approaches to aiding the poor, see Walter I. Trattner, *From Poor Law to Welfare State: A History of Social Welfare in America* (New York: The Free Press, 1974); Michael B. Katz, *In the Shadow of the Poorhouse: A Social History of Welfare in America* (New York: Basic Books, 1986); and Timothy A. Hacsi, *Second Home: Orphan Asylums and Poor Families in America* (Cambridge; Harvard University Press, 1998).

20. Brace and Brace, *Life and Letters*, 170. See also *Second Annual Report of the Children's Aid Society, February 1855* (New York: M. B. Wynkoop, Book, and Job, 1855), 5. "No relief can be of permanent value to society, or to the poor themselves, without influence in some form, on character. . . . Such children cannot all be shut up

158   *Notes to Chapter 1*

in Asylums, and indeed, it may be doubted, whether they are, even the best Institutions, improved, by the crowding of numbers together."

21. The first lodging house was opened in 1854 on the corner of Nassau and Fulton streets. It was meant especially for the "newsboys," as they were thought to have lived a "homeless, vagabond life," sleeping mostly "in the open air" or in "boxes and alleys" (*First Annual Report*, 11–12).

22. Ibid., 169. See also Children's Aid Society, *Fourth Annual Report of the Children's Aid Society, February 1857* (New York: John P. Prall, 1857). "One thing is more and more impressed on our minds as this labor continues—that is—that for the permanent cure of the evils which afflict the city, mere charity, the giving of food and shelter and clothing is of little account. It belongs to the duties of humanity—it is part of mercy and compassion . . . but as a permanent, thorough philosophic means of remedy, which shall prevent and remove moral evils . . . it is not to be highly estimated" (7).

23. Ibid., 294.

24. Ibid., 312.

25. CAS, *Second Annual Report*, 18–19.

26. For a starting point on antislavery scholarship, see Louis Filler, *Crusade against Slavery: Friends, Foes, and Reforms, 1820–1860* (New York: Harper, 1960); Gilbert H. Barnes, *The Anti-Slavery Impulse, 1830–1844* (New York: Harcourt Brace, 1964); David Brion Davis, *The Problem of Slavery in Western Culture* (Ithaca, NY: Cornell University Press, 1966); James Brewer Stewart, *Holy Warriors: The Abolitionists and American Slavery* (New York: Hill and Wang, 1976); Lewis Perry, *Antislavery Reconsidered: New Perspectives on the Abolitionists* (Baton Rouge: Louisiana State University Press, 1979); Ronald G. Walters, *The Antislavery Appeal: American Abolitionism after 1830* (New York: W. W. Norton, 1984); Henry Mayer, *All on Fire: Henry Lloyd Garrison and the Abolition of Slavery* (New York: W. W. Norton, 1998); Mason Lowance, ed., *Against Slavery: An Abolitionist Reader* (New York: Penguin Books, 2000).

27. Brace and Brace, *Life and Letters*, 1–2. On revivalism and reform in antebellum America, see Paul E. Johnson, *A Shopkeeper's Millennium: Society and Revivals in Rochester, New York, 1815–1837* (New York: Hill and Wang, 1978); Ronald G. Walters, *American Reformers, 1815–1860* (New York: HarperCollins, 1978); John Butler, *Awash in a Sea of Faith: Christianizing the American People* (Cambridge: Harvard University Press, 1990); Nathan O. Hatch, *Democratization of American Christianity* (New Haven, CT: Yale University Press, 1991); Charles Sellers, *The Market Revolution: Jacksonian America, 1815–1846* (New York: Oxford University Press, 1991); Lori Ginzberg, *Women and the Work of Benevolence: Morality, Politics, and Class in the Nineteenth-Century United States* (New Haven, CT: Yale University Press, 1992); Robert H. Abzug, *Cosmos Crumbling: American Reform and the Religious Imagination* (New York: Oxford University Press, 1994); Whitney R. Cross, *The Burned-Over District: The Social and Intellectual History of Enthusiastic Religion in Western New York, 1800–1850* (Ithaca, NY: Cornell University Press, 2006); and Daniel Walker

Howe, *What God Hath Wrought: The Transformation of America, 1815–1848* (New York: Oxford University Press, 2007).

28. Foner, *Free Soil, Free Labor*, 9–12. See also Daniel T. Rodgers, *The Work Ethic in Industrial America, 1850–1920* (Chicago: University of Chicago Press, 1979), especially pp. 31–34; John Ashworth, *Slavery, Capitalism, and Politics in the Antebellum Republic*, vol. 2, *The Coming of the Civil War, 1850–1861* (New York: Cambridge University Press, 1995); and John Ashworth, "Free Labor, Wage Labor, and the Slave Power: Republicanism and the Republican Party in the 1850s," in *The Market Revolution in America: Social, Political, and Religious Expressions, 1800–1860*, ed. Melvyn Stokes and Stephen Conway, 128–46 (Charlottesville: University Press of Virginia, 1996).

29. Brace and Brace, *Life and Letters*, 55–56.

30. Horace Bushnell, *The Northern Iron: A Discourse Delivered in the North Church, Hartford, On the Annual State Fast, April 14, 1854* (Hartford, CT: L. E. Hunt, 1854). Bushnell forcefully expressed his pro–free labor views in this sermon: "Thus it will be seen that wealth is the natural fruit of free labor, poverty of slave labor. Freedom unites motives to industry. The slavery of labor is work without industry" (20). However, Bushnell is most famous for his views about Christian child rearing and the nature of children. One historian has called Bushnell "the quintessential American theologian of childhood." See Margaret Bendroth, "Horace Bushnell's *Christian Nurture*," in *The Child in Christian Thought*, ed. Marcia JoAnn Bunge (Grand Rapids, MI: William B. Eerdmans Publishers, 2001), 350. For Brace's relationship with Bushnell, see Stephen O'Connor, *Orphan Trains: The Story of Charles Loring Brace and the Children He Saved and Failed* (Boston: Houghton Mifflin, 2001), especially pp. 18–22. As O'Connor put it, "Apart from his father, the single most important figure in Charles Loring Brace's early education was Horace Bushnell" (18).

31. Foner, *Free Soil, Free Labor*, 42–43.

32. Brace and Brace, *Life and Letters*, 90.

33. By far the most important figure in this regard was Horace Bushnell (1802–1876), minister of the North Congregational Church in Hartford, Connecticut, which the Brace family attended. In addition to imbibing Bushnell's free labor ideology, Brace was influenced by Bushnell's ideas about children and sin, which Bushnell described most comprehensively in his 1847 book, *Views of Christian Nurture*. This book was "one of the first extended reflections on the religious lives of infants and young children." Bunge, *Child in Christian Thought*, 350. Bushnell helped to overturn Calvinistic understandings of the child's sinful nature, emphasizing the innocence, purity, and plasticity of childhood (ibid). Salvation, according to Bushnell, was the process of developing Christian character within children. Brace would apply many of Bushnell's ideas about children in his work with the Children's Aid Society. See Bushnell, *Views of Christian Nurture, and of subjects adjacent thereto* (Hartford, CT: E. Hunt, 1847).

34. The Children's Aid Society as a whole held strong views about the malleability of childhood, believing that all meaningful reform of society must begin with children: "The children are so much superior to the parents. It needs time for vice and beggary,

160 *Notes to Chapter 1*

and filth to degrade childhood. God has given every fresh human soul something, which rises above its surroundings, and which even Want and Vice do not at once wear away. . . . The old heart of man is a hard thing to change. In any comprehensive view, the only hopeful reform through society must begin with *childhood*—basing itself on a change of circumstances and on religious influences." In appendix to CAS, *Second Annual Report*, 35.

35. Brace and Brace, *Life and Letters*, 154–56. In the early years of New York City, when poverty arose as a visible problem, the city dealt with poor and "vagrant" children mainly by incarcerating them in adult prisons and almshouses. Beginning in the 1820s, the city built juvenile asylums and juvenile prisons, essentially institutionalizing the children in a punitive fashion, generally without systematic attempts to reform them. Brace's society was one of the first organizations that focused its efforts primarily on reforming children. See O'Connor, *Orphan Trains*, xiv–xv.

36. Children's Aid Society, *Seventh Annual Report of the Children's Aid Society* (New York: Wynkoop, Hallenbeck, and Thomas, 1860), 10–11, 52.

37. Appendix to CAS, *Second Annual Report*, 23, 14.

38. Children's Aid Society, *Third Annual Report of the Children's Aid Society, February, 1856* (New York: M. B. Wynkoop, Book, and Job, 1856), 18–19.

39. Ibid., 6.

40. Ibid., 5.

41. "Smashing baggage" referred to pretending to carry someone's baggage for them and then running off with that individual's belongings. "Book-bluffing" was a form of cheating by selling a book for more than what it was probably worth. The more general activity was referred to as "bluffing," which meant selling any item for more than what it was worth, "such as galvanized watches for gold, mock jewelry for genuine," or "old newspapers for latest issue, etc." CAS, *Third Annual Report*, 26, 6.

42. In the 1855 annual report, it was suggested that businessmen in the city with child laborers should consider mingling instruction with their industry. "Better than any work of a society, would be the attempt of a business man, who has children in his employ, and who believes in his responsibility to God for their improvement, to mingle instruction with his business, as has been so successfully done by Mr. Wilson, in Price's Candle Factory, London, and to raise up intelligent and Christian men from his own 'hands'" (6). Mr. Wilson had apparently opened up a school and a chapel inside the factory for the child workers, which introduced "order, and cleanliness, and sobriety among [the children]" (6–7).

43. Brace and Brace, *Life and Letters*, 209, 210.

44. "Speech of the Honorable William H. Seward, In the Senate, Feb. 17, 1854, 'Freedom and Public Faith,'" in *The Nebraska Question: Comprising Speeches in the United States Senate by Mr. Douglas, Mr. Chase, Mr. Smith, Mr. Everett, Mr. Wade, Mr. Badger, Mr. Seward and Mr. Sumner, Together with The History of the Missouri Compromise, Daniel Webster's Memorial in Regard to It—History of the Annexation of Texas—The Organization of Oregon Territory—and The Compromise of 1850* (New York: Redfield, 1854), 102.

Notes to Chapter 1   161

45. Brace and Brace, *Life and Letters*, 210.

46. James McPherson, *Battle Cry of Freedom: The Civil War Era* (New York: Oxford University Press, 1988), 121.

47. Foner, *Free Soil, Free Labor*, 73. "The American antislavery movement, which began as a moral crusade, eventually found that it would have to turn to politics to achieve its goals."

48. The Missouri Compromise was an agreement that proslavery and antislavery forces in the United States Congress made with each other in 1820 regarding the spread of slavery in the Western territories. The compromise prohibited slavery in the former Louisiana Territory north of the parallel 36°30' north except within the state of Missouri. See Robert Pierce Forbes, *The Missouri Compromise and Its Aftermath: Slavery and the Meaning of America* (Chapel Hill: University of North Carolina Press, 2007); quote on p. 95. See also McPherson, *Battle Cry of Freedom*, 128.

49. Horace Greeley of the *New York Tribune* coined the term "Bleeding Kansas" to refer to the turbulent period of violence and unrest in the Kansas territory that lasted from 1854 to 1861, when Kansas was finally admitted to the Union as a free state. Much of the drama occurred along the Kansas-Missouri border, where "Border Ruffians" (Missourians who were sympathetic to slavery) would cross the border to stuff ballot boxes or, as they did in 1856, stage an attack against Lawrence, Kansas—a community of "free-soilers." In response to the raid on Lawrence, abolitionist John Brown led a group of his supporters in a massacre of five proslavery Southerners at Pottawatomie Creek the same year. Because of sharp disagreement over the future of slavery in the territory, several constitutions were drafted, both proslavery and antislavery. One, the Lecompton Constitution, a proslavery document, was recognized and endorsed by President James Buchanan but soundly defeated when put to a referendum by Kansas voters. The Wyandotte Constitution, an antislavery document, was approved by Kansas voters in 1859. See James A. Rawley, *Race and Politics: "Bleeding Kansas" and the Coming of the Civil War* (Lincoln: University of Nebraska Press, 1980); Stephen B. Oates, *To Purge This Land with Blood: A Biography of John Brown* (Amherst: University of Massachusetts Press, 1984); Thomas Goodrich, *War to the Knife: Bleeding Kansas, 1854–1861* (Lincoln: Bison Books, 1998); Nicole Etcheson, *Bleeding Kansas: Contested Liberty in the Civil War Era* (Lawrence: University Press of Kansas, 2004).

50. Quoted in Foner, *Free Soil, Free Labor*, 96.

51. Ibid., 97. *Dred Scott v. Sandford* (1857) was a decision handed down by the Supreme Court, which ruled that persons of African descent, and their offspring, did not have constitutional rights and therefore could not be considered citizens of the United States. Significantly, the decision also determined that the federal government could not interfere in the expansion of slavery into federal territories. Finally, the ruling handed down a final victory for slaveholders, as it declared that slaves were by definition property that must be protected by the Constitution. See Don E. Fehrenbacher, *The Dred Scott Case: Its Significance in American Law and Politics* (New York: Oxford University Press, 1978).

162 *Notes to Chapter 1*

52. Foner, *Free Soil, Free Labor*, 97.

53. See Robert M. Taylor, ed., *The Northwest Ordinance, 1787: A Bicentennial Handbook* (Ann Arbor: University of Michigan Press, 1987). By 1804 every Northern state had committed itself to emancipation in one form or another, though slavery stubbornly persisted in some Northern areas for years thereafter. See Ira Berlin, *Many Thousands Gone: The First Two Centuries of Slavery in North America* (Cambridge: Harvard University Press, 1998): 234–35.

54. For an in-depth and insightful discussion of the Missouri Compromise and its historical consequences, see Forbes, *Missouri Compromise.*

55. As Robert V. Hine and John Mack Faragher have argued about the Mexican War, "The Democrats had anticipated that a patriotic war for territorial expansion would unify the country. It did not work that way. Instead, the Mexican War opened a divisive and violent new conflict on the question of slavery's extension that led directly to the Civil War." See Hine and Faragher, *The American West: A New Interpretive History* (New Haven, CT: Yale University Press, 2000), 219.

56. Ibid., 220–21.

57. Though Frederick Jackson Turner would popularize the "safety-valve" conception of the West half a century later, free labor Republicans in the antebellum period accepted this idea as a reality. See Foner, *Free Soil, Free Labor*, 27.

58. Ibid., 27–28. Though Greeley probably did not coin the phrase "Go West, Young Man!," which has famously been attributed to him, he did espouse that message from 1837 until the end of his life in 1872. See Robert Chadwell Williams, *Horace Greeley: Champion of American Freedom* (New York: NYU Press, 2006), 40.

59. Foner, *Free Soil, Free Labor*, 28.

60. "First Circular of the Children's Aid Society" in Brace, *Dangerous Classes*, 90–92.

61. CAS, *First Annual Report*, 8.

62. Brace and Brace, *Life and Letters*, 260. For more on Brace's understanding of the importance of "environment," see Barry Gewen, "The Intellectual Foundations of the Child Labor Reform Movement," PhD diss., Harvard University, Boston, 1972.

63. Brace and Brace, *Life and Letters*, 260.

64. Children's Aid Society, *Eleventh Annual Report of the Children's Aid Society, February, 1864* (New York: Press of Wynkoop, Hallenbeck, and Thomas, 1864), 8.

65. CAS, *Second Annual Report*, 5–6.

66. CAS, *Sixth Annual Report*, 9.

67. CAS, *Fourth Annual Report*, 9. It is important to note that the emigration plan was not Brace's unique invention. According to Stephen O'Connor:

> Although the CAS habitually portrayed its "Emigration Plan" as a unique revolutionary innovation, the idea had numerous precedents. The most striking of these was the work of the Children's Mission to the Children of the Destitute in Boston. Beginning in 1850, the mission sent quarterly parties of thirty or forty destitute children by train to western New England and the near Midwest to be indentured to local farmers and merchants. Brace certainly knew about

Notes to Chapter 1

these trains, and they may even have been his inspiration: the mission's original president, John Earl Williams, moved to New York in 1851 and was a founding member of the CAS.... There were also foreign precedents: a German charity, "The Friends in Need," placed vagrant city children with country families. Brace also knew about this organization, having visited it during his European tour. The only antecedent Brace ever acknowledged publicly was the French practice of placing abandoned and destitute infants with rural wet nurses, who often ended up adopting them. [See O'Connor, *Orphan Trains*, 94–95.]

68. CAS, *First Annual Report*, 13.

69. See the "Emigration Plan" sections of the "Secretary Reports" in the *Annual Reports of the Children's Aid Society* from 1855 through 1865.

70. In appendix to CAS, *Fourth Annual Report*, 28–30.

71. Scholars have noted that racial attitudes in the North hardened during this period, especially with the rise of antiblack riots and the American, or Know-Nothing, Party. In the 1850s the reformers of the Children's Aid Society were most closely aligned with the views of Abraham Lincoln regarding the scourge of unfree labor and the potential of free labor for uplift. For more on racial attitudes in the antebellum North, see Tyler Anbinder, *Nativism and Slavery: The Northern Know Nothings and the Politics of the 1850s* (New York: Oxford University Press, 1992); and John Wood Sweet, *Bodies Politic: Negotiating Race in the American North, 1730–1830* (Baltimore: Johns Hopkins University Press, 2003).

72. CAS, *Fifth Annual Report*, 7–8.

73. In appendix to CAS, *First Annual Report*, 20.

74. In appendix to CAS, *Second Annual Report*, 43.

75. For more on the CAS's treatment of girls as well as the marginalized role of female reformers in the CAS, see Christine Stansell, *City of Women: Sex and Class in New York, 1789–1860* (Urbana: University of Illinois Press, 1987), especially pp. 212–14.

76. In appendix to CAS, *First Annual Report*, 21.

77. CAS, *Sixth Annual Report*, 10.

78. In appendix to CAS, *Sixth Annual Report*, 68.

79. O'Connor, *Orphan Trains*, 158. Rhetorically, reformers used the term "Asylum-Interest" in a way that paralleled Republicans' use of "Slave Interest" to describe slaveholding Southerners in the 1850s.

80. CAS, *Seventh Annual Report*, 32.

81. CAS, *Sixth Annual Report*, 7.

82. CAS, *Seventh Annual Report*, 33.

83. Ibid., 33.

The contrast is most striking and most favorable to them. Every feature in this sudden transition is calculated to make them happier and better children. The change leaves them nothing to regret, but everything to be thankful for. They are not indentured, but they are put under a *moral bond to themselves* not to be

164 *Notes to Chapter 1*

unworthy or ungrateful. . . . *Self-respect* is awakened within them. They find they *can* do right. They can tell the truth. They can grow in usefulness and honor, and, moreover, they have found out that this course promotes peace of mind and true happiness, and they are *tempted* to try it. [Ibid., 32–33]

84. O'Connor, *Orphan Trains*, 156–62.

85. See especially the "Treasurer's Tenth Annual Report," in Children's Aid Society, *Tenth Annual Report of the Children's Aid Society, February 1863* (New York: Press of Wynkoop, Hallenbeck, and Thomas, 1863), 35–36; "Treasurer's Eleventh Annual Report," in CAS, *Eleventh Annual Report, February 1864*, 34–36; and "Treasurer's Twelfth Annual Report," in CAS, *Twelfth Annual Report, February 1865*, 37–38. According to O'Connor, "By the end of the 1850s the belief that children were better cared for in families than institutions had received considerable attention, and many experts on the treatment of dependent and criminal children had come to believe that the 'cottage' or 'family' system, as innovated by the *Rauhe Haus* in Germany, was the best model for congregate care" (*Orphan Trains*, 157). See also Charles Loring Brace, *Home-Life in Germany* (New York: Charles Scribner, 1853), in which Brace describes some of his observations about the Rauhe Haus after visiting Germany.

86. See Catherine A. Brekus, "Children of Wrath, Children of Grace: Jonathan Edwards and the Puritan Culture of Child Rearing," in Bunge, *Child in Christian Thought* 300–328. The reasons for shifting understandings of human nature are part of a larger transformation in social and economic organization in the eighteenth and early nineteenth centuries. On the religious and cultural implications of the market economy, see Sellers, *Market Revolution*; Johnson, *Shopkeeper's Millennium*; Mark A. Noll, ed., *God and Mammon: Protestants, Money, and the Market, 1790–1860* (New York: Oxford University Press, 2001); Scott C. Martin, ed., *Cultural Change and the Market Revolution, 1790–1860* (New York: Rowman and Littlefield, 2004); and Stokes and Conway, *Market Revolution*. For the market revolution's effect on gender roles, see Jeanne Boydston, *Home and Work: Housework, Wages, and the Ideology of Labor in the Early Republic* (New York: Oxford University Press, 1994); Nancy Cott, *The Bonds of Womanhood: "Woman's Sphere" in New England, 1780–1835* (New Haven, CT: Yale University Press, 1977); Stansell, *City of Women*; Amy Dru Stanley, "Home Life and the Morality of the Marketplace," in Stokes and Conway, *Market Revolution*; and Catherine E. Kelley, *In the New England Fashion: Reshaping Women's Lives in the Nineteenth Century* (Ithaca, NY: Cornell University Press, 1999). On the effects of romanticism, see Michael T. Gilmore, *American Romanticism and the Marketplace* (Chicago: University of Chicago Press, 1985). On the effect of Enlightenment ideals, see Mark A. Noll, *America's God: From Jonathan Edwards to Abraham Lincoln* (New York: Oxford University Press, 2002), and Henry May, *The Enlightenment in America* (New York: Oxford University Press, 1976), especially chapter 3, "The Age of Reason and the Age of Enthusiasm," pp. 42–65. See Nathan O. Hatch, *The Democratization of American Christianity* (New Haven, CT: Yale University Press, 1989) for more on the effect of democratic ideals after the Revolution, and Bernard Bailyn, *The Ideological Origins of the American Revolution* (Cambridge: Harvard University Press, 1967),

Notes to Chapter 1   165

especially pp. 232–46, for an account of the "contagion of liberty" that swept the new nation.

87. These institutions developed methods around the belief that human beings, especially the poor, were depraved individuals who could best be helped through rigid discipline and punishment. See M. B. Katz, *Shadow of the Poorhouse*; Joseph M. Hawes, *Children in Urban Society: Juvenile Delinquency in Nineteenth-Century America* (New York: Oxford University Press, 1971); Robert M. Mennel, *Thorns and Thistles: Juvenile Delinquents in the United States, 1825–1940* (Hanover, CT: University Press of New England, 1973); David J. Rothman, *The Discovery of the Asylum: Social Order and Disorder in the New Republic* (Boston: Little, Brown, 1990); and David Wagner, *The Poorhouse: America's Forgotten Institution* (Lanham, MD: Rowman and Littlefield, 2005). See also O'Connor, *Orphan Trains*, especially p. 156.

88. See O'Connor, *Orphan Trains*, 177; and Stansell, *City of Women*, 211. See also Natan Sznaider, *The Compassionate Temperament: Care and Cruelty in Modern Society* (New York: Rowman and Littlefield, 2000), especially pp. 49–52.

89. "Letters in Regard to Children Sent West," in Appendix, *Seventh Annual Report*, 84–85.

90. Not all children who were "placed out" were grateful and happy; some of them hated their situation and ran away. Others reported abuse from the families they were placed with. Brace and his fellow reformers were inclined to exaggerate the "success" of the emigration plan for fund-raising purposes, omitting from the records instances in which placed-out children returned to New York, ran away, or caused trouble. See O'Connor, *Orphan Trains*, 160–61.

91. "Incidents of the News-boys' Lodging-House," in Children's Aid Society, *Eighth Annual Report of the Children's Aid Society, February, 1861* (New York: Wynkoop, Hallenbeck and Thomas, 1861), 73–74.

92. Ibid., 240.

93. Children's Aid Society, *Ninth Annual Report of the Children's Aid Society, February, 1862* (New York: Wynkoop, Hallenbeck and Thomas, 1862), 5.

94. Ibid., 5, 10, 27–28.

95. CAS, *Tenth Annual Report*, 6.

96. CAS, *Ninth Annual Report*, 49–50.

97. CAS *Tenth Annual Report*, 59–60.

98. Appendix to CAS, *Tenth Annual Report*, 72.

99. "Treasurer's Tenth Annual Report," in CAS, *Tenth Annual Report*, 39.

100. CAS, *Tenth Annual Report*, 6.

101. Appendix to CAS, *Tenth Annual Report*, 64.

102. CAS, *Eleventh Annual Report*, 58–59.

103. CAS, *Twelfth Annual Report*, 9, 11, 22, 71, 73.

104. CAS, *Ninth Annual Report*, 3, 24, 25.

105. CAS, *Tenth Annual Report*, 39.

106. Appendix to CAS, *Ninth Annual Report*, 54–55.

107. CAS, *Eleventh Annual Report*, 33.

166 *Notes to Chapter 2*

Chapter 2. Testing Ground of Freedom

1. As Steven Hahn has argued, the channels of enslaved people's communication with one another were vast. A primary way by which enslaved people kept themselves informed and built community, these channels constituted a vast interchange of information, gossip, and rumor. A Northern teacher referred to the channels as "an underground telephone" much "like the underground railroad." These informal networks provided enslaved people with "their own way of gathering news from the whole country." Hahn, *Nation under Our Feet: Black Political Struggles in the Rural South from Slavery to the Great Migration* (Boston: Harvard University Press, 2003), 41. During the Civil War, enslaved people famously provided the Union Army with vital information using these informal channels. See Hahn, *Nation under Our Feet*, especially pp. 6–7, 15, 41–43, 89, 129, 132–34, 142.

2. "Affairs in the South—Affairs in Louisiana—The Freedmen—Troublesome Times and Dismal Prospects," *New York Times*, October 27, 1865. See also John Blassingame, *Black New Orleans, 1860–1880* (Chicago: University of Chicago Press, 1973), 170–71; and William S. McFeely, *Yankee Stepfather: General O. O. Howard and the Freedmen* (New Haven, CT: Yale University Press, 1968), 178–79.

3. "Affairs in the South." See also McFeely, *Yankee Stepfather,* 178–79.

4. Children's Aid Society, *Sixteenth Annual Report of the Children's Aid Society, February 1869* (New York: Press of Wynkoop and Hallenbeck, 1869), 41–42.

5. Charles Loring Brace, *The Dangerous Classes of New York and Twenty Years' Work among Them* (New York: Wynkoop and Hallenbeck, 1872), 350. See also pp. 355–56.

6. The text of the Thirteenth Amendment to the US Constitution, which was adopted on December 6, 1865, reads as follows: "Neither slavery nor involuntary servitude, except as a punishment for crime whereof the party shall have been duly convicted, shall exist within the United States, or any place subject to their jurisdiction. Congress shall have the power to enforce this article by appropriate legislation." (For full text of the amendment, see http://caselaw.lp.findlaw.com/data/constitution/amendment13, retrieved September 17, 2019.) For more on the Thirteenth Amendment and its social, legal, and political consequences, see Michael Vorenberg, *Final Freedom: The Civil War, the Abolition of Slavery, and the Thirteenth Amendment* (New York: Cambridge University Press, 2001); Alexander Tsesis, *The Thirteenth Amendment and American Freedom: A Legal History* (New York: New York University Press, 2004); and Harold Holzer and Sara Vaughn Gabbard, eds., *Lincoln and Freedom: Slavery, Emancipation, and the Thirteenth Amendment* (Carbondale: Southern Illinois University Press, 2007).

7. See Eric Foner, *Reconstruction: America's Unfinished Revolution, 1863–1877* (New York: Harper and Row, 1988); W.E.B. Du Bois, *Black Reconstruction in America, 1860–1880* (New York: Harcourt and Brace, 1935); Julie Saville, *The Work of Reconstruction: From Slave to Wage Laborer in South Carolina, 1860–1870* (New York: Cambridge University Press, 1996); and Thomas C. Holt, *Black over White: Negro Political*

Leadership in South Carolina during Reconstruction (Urbana: University of Illinois Press, 1979).

8. The sample of records from the US National Archives that form the Freedmen and Southern Society Project has had a tremendous influence on changing our perceptions of enslaved people's influence on the war's outcome and aftermath. For scholarship in this vein, see Saville, *Work of Reconstruction*; Eric Foner, *Nothing but Freedom: Emancipation and Its Legacy* (Baton Rouge: Louisiana State University Press, 1983); Barbara Jeanne Fields, *Slavery and Freedom on the Middle Ground: Maryland during the Nineteenth Century* (New Haven, CT: Yale University Press, 1985); and Hahn, *Nation under Our Feet.*

9. For some time, Rebecca Scott's excellent article "The Battle over the Child: Child Apprenticeship and the Freedmen's Bureau in North Carolina," *Prologue* 10 (1978): 101–13, was one of the only systematic treatments of this subject, but historians have recently shown renewed interest in the topic. See Catherine A. Jones, *Intimate Reconstructions: Children in Postemancipation Virginia* (Charlottesville: University of Virginia Press, 2015); Karin L. Zipf, *Labor of Innocents: Forced Apprenticeship in North Carolina, 1715–1919* (Baton Rouge: Louisiana State University Press, 2005); and Mary Niall Mitchell, *Raising Freedom's Child: Black Children and Visions of the Future after Slavery* (New York: New York University Press, 2008).

10. See *Freedom: A Documentary History of Emancipation, 1861–1867*, ser. 3, vol. 1, *Land and Labor, 1865*, eds. Steven Hahn, Steven F. Miller, Susan E. O'Donovan, John C. Rodrigue, and Leslie S. Rowland (Chapel Hill: University of North Carolina Press, 2008), 922.

11. "Affidavit of Derinda Smothers, 18 Sept. 1865," in Hahn et al., *Freedom*, ser. 1, vol. 2, 546.

12. "Joseph Hall to General Howard or those having charge of freedmen at Washington D.C., 14 Sept. 1865," in Hahn et al., *Freedom*, ser. 1, vol. 2, 544–55.

13. "Affidavit of Danl. Chase, 24 Aug. 1865, enclosed in Col. John Eaton, Jr., to Maj. Genl. O. O. Howard, 18 Sept. 1865," in Hahn et al., *Freedom*, ser. 1, vol. 2, 543–44.

14. "Lucy Lee to Lt. Col. W.E.W. Ross, 10 Jan. 1865," in "Communication from Major Gen'l Lew. Wallace, in Relation to the Freedmen's Bureau, to the General Assembly of Maryland," Maryland House Journal and Documents (Annapolis 1865), document J, 68–69. Quoted in Hahn et al., *Freedom*, ser. 1, vol. 2, 498.

15. "Statement of Jane Kamper, 14 Nov. 1864," in Hahn et al., *Freedom*, ser. 1, vol. 2, 519.

16. Quoted in Mitchell, *Raising Freedom's Child*, 145.

17. "S. H. Melcher to Lieut, 27 Dec. 1865," in Hahn et al., *Freedom*, ser. 3, vol. 1, 982.

18. "Carter Holmes to Lieut. Col. Wm. M. Beebe, 22 Apr. 1867," in Hahn et al., *Freedom*, ser. 1, vol. 2, 346.

19. "John B. Walker to Genrl. Tillson, 17 Nov. 1865," in Hahn et al., *Freedom*, ser. 3, vol. 1, 670, 671.

20. Ibid., 671.

168   *Notes to Chapter 2*

21. "Col. E. Whittlesey, Circular, No. 4, Bureau of Refugees. Freedmen &c, Hd. Qrs. Asst. Comsr. State of N.C., 10 Nov. 1865," in Hahn et al., *Freedom*, ser. 3, vol. 1, 667–68.

22. Ibid., 668.

23. "Major General O. O. Howard, Circular Letter, 4 Oct. 1865," in Hahn et al., *Freedom*, ser. 3, vol. 1, 645.

24. Quoted in Zipf, *Labor of Innocents*, 68. For a nuanced discussion of Eliphalet Whittlesey and his role in undermining apprenticeship in North Carolina, see Zipf's chapter 3, "Free Labor Ideology, Apprenticeship, and the Freedmen's Bureau," 68–83.

Free-labor ideology often shaped agents' knowledge, understanding, and approach to apprenticeship cases. Their sometimes ad hoc treatment of apprenticeship also bewildered African Americans, who faced many odds in their struggle to preserve their families. Yet Freedmen's Bureau officials such as Eliphalet Whittlesey struck at the heart of apprenticeship by declaring that in most cases children should not be apprenticed without their parents' consent. As a result, the Freedmen's Bureau had opened the door to African American challenges to the institution. In 1867, mothers and fathers, recognizing the bureau's power and its willingness to defend free labor, enlisted its agents as their legal counsel to retrieve their children. [83]

25. See Hahn et al., *Freedom*, ser. 1, vol 2, I, 481. The Emancipation Proclamation, issued by President Abraham Lincoln on January 1, 1863, applied only to enslaved people in the Confederacy with the exception of those in Tennessee and in the Union-occupied areas of Louisiana and Virginia. Other wartime measures had anticipated Lincoln's now-famous proclamation. Early in the war, the First Confiscation Act of 1861 permitted enslaved persons to be seized by the Union as an act of war while the Militia Act of 1862 freed enslaved persons who worked for the Union Army. The most radical of these wartime measures preceding Lincoln's proclamation was the Second Confiscation Act, which was approved by Congress on July 17, 1862. It declared that any enslaved persons who sought refuge behind Union lines would be emancipated and "not again held as slaves." For more on wartime measures, see John Syrett, *The Civil War Confiscation Acts: Failing to Reconstruct the South* (New York: Fordham University Press, 2005).

26. "Capt. Andrew Stafford to General H. H. Lockwood, 4 Nov. 1864," in Hahn et al., *Freedom*, ser. 1, vol. 2, 510, 511, 520.

27. "Philip Pettebone and Chas. S. Welch to Geo. W. Curry Esq., 30 Nov. 1864," in Hahn et al., *Freedom*, 520–21.

28. Ibid., 521.

29. Ibid. The law to which the judges referred was a statute that had been used to apprentice the children of free blacks in Maryland prior to the Civil War. According to the particular law cited, the orphans courts could decide to bind out children—to the age of twenty-one for boys, and eighteen for girls—if it deemed "that it would be better for the habits and comfort of such child that it should be bound as an apprentice to some white person to learn to labor." However, no child was to be bound

Notes to Chapter 2 169

if the parents "have the means and are willing to support such child, and keep the same employed so as to teach habits of industry." Quoted in Hahn et al., *Freedom*, 494.

30. "Capt. Andrew Stafford to General H. H. Lockwood, 4 Nov. 1864," in Hahn et al., *Freedom*, 511.

31. Ibid., 974.

32. "Capt. Andrew Stafford to General H. H. Lockwood, 4 Nov. 1864," in Hahn et al., *Freedom*, ser. 1, vol. 2, 511.

33. Quoted in ibid., 494.

34. Former owners sometimes claimed that the relatives of formerly enslaved children wanted custody of them only to use them for their labor. See Mitchell, *Raising Freedom's Child*, 177.

35. For more on black families in slavery and freedom, see Herbert G. Gutman, *The Black Family in Slavery and Freedom, 1750–1925* (New York: Pantheon Books, 1976); Leon F. Litwack, *Been in the Storm So Long: The Aftermath of Slavery* (New York: Alfred A. Knopf, 1979); and John W. Blassingame, *The Slave Community: Plantation Life in the Antebellum South* (New York: Oxford University Press, 1972).

36. "Joseph Hall to General Howard or those having charge of freedmen at Washington, DC, 14 Sept. 1865," in Hahn et al., *Freedom*, ser. 1, vol. 2, 545.

37. "Joseph Hall to Lieut General S. N. Clark, 4 Nov. 1865," in Hahn et al., *Freedom*, ser. 3, vol. 1, 567. In some cases, formerly enslaved women agreed to the temporary apprenticing of their children to former owners while they left to find a means of support. When these women returned, they would make application for custody of their children through the Freedmen's Bureau. (See Mitchell, *Raising Freedom's Child*, 184.)

38. The Fourteenth Amendment, adopted on July 9, 1868, also provided for voting rights for the male inhabitants twenty-one years of age in every state. (For full text of the amendment, see http://caselaw.lp.findlaw.com/data/constitution/amendment14, retrieved September 17, 2019.)

39. See Mitchell, *Raising Freedom's Child*, 153. The so-called Black Codes were a series of laws passed in Southern states after the Civil War to restrict the freedom of emancipated persons, particularly regarding their labor and freedom of movement. See Theodore Brantner Wilson, The *Black Codes of the South* (Tuscaloosa: University of Alabama, 1965).

40. For instance, *In the Matter of Harriet Ambrose and Eliza Ambrose* was a case decided in 1867 by the North Carolina State Supreme Court. For more on this case, see Scott, "Battle over the Child," 205.

41. See Scott, "Battle over the Child," 201, 206.

42. See Zipf, *Labor of Innocents*, 82–83.

43. "Children as Slaves—The Little Ones Kidnapped in Italy and Sold in New York—Horrible Treatment by their Masters," *New York Times*, June 17, 1873, 1.

44. As historian John Zucchi's excellent research on the 1870s padrone trade in Italian children has shown, "Most of the children were from towns south of Po-

170   *Notes to Chapter 2*

tenza: Laurenzana, Viggiano, Corleto Perticara, and Marsiconuovo. Many traveled to Philadelphia, Chicago, Cincinnati, Baltimore, and San Francisco. Others went to Charleston, Providence, Buffalo, New Orleans, Louisville, and Troy. Over half of the street musicians, however, settled in New York City. In 1868, a man from Viggiano informed the Italian consul that 72 padroni operated from that city; 153 adults and 198 children and teenagers worked under them." See John E. Zucchi, *The Little Slaves of the Harp: Italian Child Street Musicians in Nineteenth-Century Paris, London, and New York* (Montreal: McGill-Queen's University Press, 1992), 115. The *New York Times* regularly estimated the total number of Italian padrone children in the city at seven thousand to eight thousand. However, these numbers may have been exaggerated. Ibid., 115.

45. See Zucchi, *Little Slaves*, 4–5. For more on nineteenth-century immigration to the United States, see Roger Daniels, *Coming to America: A History of Immigration and Ethnicity in American Life* (New York: Harper Perennial, 1991); Thomas Dublin, ed., *Immigrant Voices: New Lives in America, 1773–1986* (Urbana: University of Illinois Press, 1993); and Jon Gjerde, ed. *Major Problems in Immigration and Ethnic History* (New York Houghton Mifflin, 1998).

46. Luciano J. Iorizzo and Francesco Cardasco, *Italian Immigration and the Impact of the Padrone System* (New York: Arno Press, 1980), 74.

47. See Zucchi, *Little Slaves*, 39; and Iorizzo and Cardasco, *Italian Immigration*, 80.

48. Iorizzo and Cardasco, *Italian Immigration*, 74–75.

49. Zucchi, *Little Slaves*, 38–41. See also Iorizzo, *Italian Immigration*, 47–48.

50. Zucchi, *Little Slaves*, 17–18. Zucchi argues that while there were undoubtedly many cases of violence against padrone children, the press "presented the extreme cases as the norm" (11).

51. While padroni employed both boys and girls as street musicians, boys were more often the subject of news reports in the New York press. See Zucchi, *Little Slaves*, 115–125. See *Annual Reports of the Children's Aid Society*, 1855–1870, especially A. E. Cerqua's reports on the Italian School in the Five Points district, which was founded in 1855. See also Brace, *Dangerous Classes*, 197–200.

52. See Cerqua's regular reports in *Annual Reports of the Children's Aid Society*. See also Brace, *Dangerous Classes*, 195–200; and Zucchi, *Little Slaves*, 112–14.

53. "The Little Italian Harpers—To the Editor of the New York Times," *New York Times*, February 1, 1869, 5.

54. See Children's Aid Society *Twentieth Annual Report of the Children's Aid Society, November 1872* (New York: Press of Wynkoop and Hallenbeck, 1872), 20–21; *Twenty-First Annual Report of the Children's Aid Society, November 1873* (New York: Wynkoop and Hallenbeck, 1873), 29–36; and *Twenty-Second Annual Report of the Children's Aid Society* (New York: Wynkoop and Hallenbeck, 1874), 33–34.

55. "The Italian Slave-Trade: How Boy Musicians Are Entrapped and Imported— Sufferings and Trials of the Unfortunates—A Shameful Practice," *New York Times*, July 7, 1872, 3.

Notes to Chapter 2

56. "Slavery of the Street Minstrels," *New York Times*, June 18, 1873, 4. The interest of the New York press in the "child slave" issue was sparked by "an Italian soldier of fortune, formerly a parliamentarian, Celso Caesar Moreno. . . . In May 1873, Moreno published a letter in San Francisco's Italian newspaper, *La Voce del Popolo*, in which he accused the Italian consul in New York, Ferdinando De Luca, of responsibility for the child slave trade. The communication was reprinted in the *New York Times*." Because of the accusations involved, the *Times* decided to launch an investigation into the padrone trade. See Zucchi, *Little Slaves*, 117.

57. Quoted in Zucchi, *Little Slaves*, 118.

58. CAS, *Twenty-First Annual Report*, 31.

59. "The Italian Boys," *Harper's Weekly*, September 13, 1873, 802.

60. See "The Italian Boys in New York—Tortures of the Training Room," *Harper's Weekly*, September 13, 1873, 801.

61. "The Italian Slaves: Interesting Interview with Three of the Little Ones—A Tale of Degradation and Suffering," *New York Times*, June 19, 1873, 5. See also "The Italian Slaves—Another Visit to Crosby Street—The Condition and Appearance of the Little Ones," *New York Times*, June 23, 1873, 8.

62. Ibid.

63. "The Italian Slaves: Hunting Down the Boy Joseph—Latest Incidents and Disclosures—The Trade Going to Chicago," *New York Times*, June 28, 1873, 1.

64. "The Italian Slaves: Arrest of a Padrone—Action of the New Haven Authorities—Antecedents of the Prisoner—Barbarous Practices," *New York Times*, July 22, 1873, 5. "To their credit . . . they have refused to accept the bribe, and Joseph still remains in safe hands to become a witness as soon as the authorities need him" (ibid).

65. Personal liberty laws were a series of laws passed in Northern states as early as 1780 to protect runaway slaves and free blacks after the passage of fugitive slave acts that would apply to all states. For an incisive account of the personal liberty laws passed in Northern states before the Civil War, see Thomas D. Morris, *Free Men All: The Personal Liberty Laws of the North, 1780–1861* (Baltimore: Johns Hopkins University Press, 1974).

66. Ibid.

67. Zucchi, *Little Slaves*, 122.

68. Ibid.

69. "Selling Italian Children: Padrone Glione Held to Answer—The Contracts under Which the Children Were Held—An Old Law," *New York Times*, July 23, 1873, 4.

70. Ibid.

71. "Italian Slave Children," *New York Times*, July 25, 1873, 1. Though the padrone Michael Carcone was never found by the authorities, Vito and Giuseppe's escape caused quite a sensation in the press nonetheless.

72. "Italian Slaves: Proposed Action by Italian Consul General," *New York Times*, August 1, 1873, 5.

172   *Notes to Chapter 2*

73. See CAS, *Twenty-First Annual Report*, 36.

74. "The Italian Slaves," *New York Times*, August 2, 1873, 5.

75. Ibid.

76. CAS, *Twenty-First Annual Report*, 6.

77. "The Italian Slaves: Justice at Last—Arrest of the Padrone Vincenzo Motto—Two Nights' Adventures in Crosby Street," *New York Times*, August 20, 1873, 5.

78. Ibid.

79. "The Civil Rights Act of 1866—An Act to Protect All Persons in the United States in Their Civil Rights, and Furnish the Means of Their Vindication," *U.S. Statutes at Large*, vol. 14, Stat. 27–30, April 9, 1866.

80. "The Italian Slaves: Justice at Last," 5.

81. "Slavery in New York: The Italian Task-Master—Examination of the Captured Padrone in the United States Court—The Boy Joseph's Abduction and Sufferings," *New York Times*, August 21, 1873, 8.

82. "The Case of Vincenzo Motto," *New York Times*, August 27, 1873, 5.

83. Ibid.

84. "The Italian Children and Senator Sumner," *New York Times*, December 4, 1873, 2.

85. Ibid.

86. "Relief for the Italian Slaves," *New York Times*, January 11, 1874, 4.

87. Zucchi, *Little Slaves*, 138.

88. Ibid., 125–26.

89. "Relief for the Italian Slaves," 4.

90. Zucchi, *Little Slaves*, 139–41. See also Shauna Vey, "Good Intentions and Fearsome Prejudice: New York's 1876 Act to Prevent and Punish Wrongs to Children," *Theatre Survey* 42, no. 1 (2001): 53–68; and Timothy J. Gilfoyle, "Street Rats and Gutter-Snipes: Pickpockets and Street Culture in New York City, 1850–1900," *Journal of Social History* 37, no. 4 (2004): 853–62.

91. "A Padrone Convicted: The Keeper of Seven Little Italian Boys," *New York Times*, December 20, 1879, 8.

92. For more on the padrone system and adult immigrants in the late nineteenth and early twentieth century, see Gunther Peck, *Reinventing Free Labor: Padrones and Immigrant Workers in the North American West, 1880–1930* (New York: Cambridge University Press, 2000).

93. Horatio Alger Jr., *Phil, the Fiddler; or, the Story of a Young Street Musician* (Philadelphia: Porter and Coates, 1872), viii, 122, 127, 130, 131.

94. See Melvin Thomas Copeland, *The Cotton Manufacturing Industry of the United States* (Cambridge: Harvard University Press, 1912); and Laurence F. Gross, *The Course of Industrial Decline: The Boott Cotton Mills of Lowell, Massachusetts, 1835–1955* (Baltimore: Johns Hopkins University Press, 1993).

95. "After the Calamity: The Excitement in Fall River, Yesterday—Full List of the Killed, Missing, and Wounded—Funerals of the Victims—Statement of the Chief Engineer," *Boston Daily Globe*, September 21, 1874, 1; and "Fire and Death: A Fearful

Notes to Chapter 2 173

Disaster in Fall River," *Boston Daily Globe*, September 21, 1874, 1. See also "Sad Calamity: Burning of a Large Cotton Mill in Fall River, Mass—Forty Young Girls Lose Their Lives and Eighty More or Less Injured," *Chicago Daily Tribune*, September 20, 1874, 1; "Fall River: The Granite Mill Holocaust," *Chicago Daily Tribune*, September 23, 1874, 8; "A Complete Review of the Disaster: How the Fire Began and Spread," *New York Times*, September 20, 1874, 1; and "A Shocking Calamity: A Woolen Mill Burned and Forty Lives Lost," *New York Times*, September 20, 1874, 1.

96. As historian Rebecca Edwards articulated in her recent monograph, *New Spirits: Americans in the Gilded Age, 1865–1905* (New York: Oxford University Press, 2006), "In the last half of the nineteenth century, a new United States emerged out of a crucible of fire. Literally as well as figuratively, fire shaped Americans' destinies" (1–4).

97. "Editorial," *New York Times*, September 20, 1874, 4.

98. Ibid.

99. "The Fall River Disaster," *Boston Daily Globe*, September 21, 1874, 4.

100. "Notes and Extracts," *Boston Daily Globe*, September 22, 1874, 4.

101. "The Fall River Disaster," *Chicago Daily Tribune*, September 21, 1874, 4.

102. The US Federal Census of 1870 was the first census to report child labor numbers. The 750,000 figure was almost certainly an underestimate, however, since it did not include children who worked for their families in businesses or on family farms.

103. Though a few states in New England had some antebellum protective statutes regarding child labor, these statutes were notoriously weak and often ignored. For instance, many of them required a minimum age of ten or twelve for children to be employed in industry but included exceptions such as parents needing the income or the children being orphaned. A major loophole in these statutes was that employers had to "knowingly" employ children who did not meet the proper criteria in order to be held accountable. As long as manufacturers could claim ignorance, they were off the hook. See Brace, *Dangerous Classes*, 353–65; Edith Abbot, "A Study of the Early History of Child Labor in America," *American Journal of Sociology* 14, no. 1 (1908): 15–37; Florence Kelley, *Some Ethical Gains through Legislation* (New York: Macmillan, 1905); and Walter I. Trattner, *Crusade for the Children: A History of the National Child Labor Committee and Child Labor Reform in America* (Chicago: Quadrangle Books, 1970), 27–32.

104. Brace, *Dangerous Classes*, 353–57.

105. "An Act for the Protection of Factory Children," in Brace, *Dangerous Classes*, 362–65.

106. Ibid., 362.

107. Trattner, *Crusade for the Children*, 30–31. Typical statutes of this kind include the New Hampshire and Maine laws of 1847–1848. For discussions of the antebellum child labor statutes of Massachusetts, Rhode Island, and Connecticut, see Brace, *Dangerous Classes*, 357–62.

108. For historians who make this point in their work, see Amy Dru Stanley, *From Bondage to Contract: Wage Labor, Marriage, and the Market in the Age of Slave Eman-*

174   *Notes to Chapter 2*

cipation (New York: Cambridge University Press, 1998); Thomas C. Holt, *The Problem of Freedom: Race, Labor, and Politics in Jamaica and Britain, 1832–1938* (Baltimore: Johns Hopkins University Press, 1992); Saville, *Work of Reconstruction*; and Foner, *Reconstruction*; and Fields, *Slavery and Freedom*.

109. Massachusetts, Bureau of Statistics of Labor, *Report of the Bureau of Statistics of Labor*, Sen. No. 120 (Boston: Wright and Potter, State Printers, 1870), 107. See also Massachusetts, Bureau of Statistics of Labor, *Report of the Bureau of Statistics of Labor*, Sen. No. 150 (Boston: Wright and Potter, State Printers, 1871), 489.

110. Massachusetts, *Report of the Bureau of Statistics of Labor* (1871), 489.

111. "Oppression of Poor Children," *New York Times*, March 15, 1872, 4.

112. Julia A. Holmes, "Children Who Work," *Scribner's Monthly*, vol. 1, no. 6 (1871), 607–8.

113. "Poor Children," *New York Times*, June 19, 1873, 4.

114. "The Employment of Children in Factories, *New York Times*, October 1, 1871, 4.

115. "Little Slaves of Capital," *New York Times*, January 26, 1873, 4.

116. Children's Aid Society, *Nineteenth Annual Report of the Children's Aid Society, November 1871* (New York: Press of Wynkoop and Hallenbeck, 1871), 35.

117. Brace, *Dangerous Classes*, 353.

118. Holmes, "Children Who Work," 611.

119. Brace, *Dangerous Classes*, 353.

120. "The Protection of Factory Children—Proper Legislation," *New York Times*, October 8, 1871, 4.

121. "Oppression of Poor Children," 4.

122. Brace, *Dangerous Classes*, 353.

123. On the development of universal compulsory education in the United States, see David B. Tyack, "Ways of Seeing: An Essay on the History of Compulsory Schooling," *Harvard Educational Review* 46, no. 3 (1976): 355–89; Charles Burgess and Merle L. Borrowman, *"What Doctrines to Embrace": Studies in the History of American Education* (Glenview, IL: Scott, Foresman, 1969); Lawrence A. Cremin, *American Education: The National Experience, 1783–1876* (New York: Harper and Row, 1982); and Michael S. Katz, *A History of Compulsory Education Laws* (Bloomington: Phi Delta Kappa Educational Foundation, 1976).

124. "Compulsory Education," *New York Times*, February 28, 1872, 4.

125. Ibid. According to the report, the number of persons over the age of ten in the state of New York who could be classified as "illiterate" was 241,152. In Pennsylvania the number was 222,356; in Ohio, 173,172; and throughout the Union, 5,660,074.

126. It should be noted that the discovery of a "literacy problem" corresponded with both slave emancipation and an influx of non–English speaking immigrants to the United States at the moment the franchise was extended to all male citizens twenty-one years of age. Thus, concerns about a national literacy "problem" should not be taken at face value, as they often concealed anti-immigrant and antiblack sentiment. The meanings of "literate" and "illiterate" were not always clear either, and native-born whites often failed to disclose their inability to read and write. See

Notes to Chapters 2 and 3

Harvey J. Graff, *The Literacy Myth: Cultural Integration and Social Structure in the Nineteenth Century* (New York: Academic Press, 1977); and Carl F. Kaestle, Helen Damon-Moore, and Katherine Tinsley, *Literacy in the United States: Readers and Reading since 1880* (New Haven, CT: Yale University Press, 1993).

127. Brace, *Dangerous Classes*, 33.

128. CAS, *Twenty-Second Annual Report*, 7–8.

129. CAS, *Nineteenth Annual Report*, 35. See also Brace, *Dangerous Classes*, 362.

130. Brace, *Dangerous Classes*, 362–65.

131. See CAS, *Nineteenth Annual Report*; *Twentieth Annual Report*, 25–26; *Twenty-First Annual Report*, 8; and *Twenty-Second Annual Report*, 6. See also *Journal of the Senate of the State of New York, at their Ninety-Seventh Session, begun and held at the capitol, in the city of Albany, on the sixth day of January, 1874* (Albany: Weed, Parsons and Co, 1874), 251–52, 350, 507, 521–22; and Jeremy P. Felt, *Hostages of Fortune: Child Labor Reform in New York State* (Syracuse, NY: Syracuse University Press, 1965), 3–4.

132. CAS, *Twenty-First Annual Report*, 8.

133. "Oppression of Poor Children," 4.

134. "Protection of Factory Children—Argument on the Bill for Protecting Factory Children," *New York Times*, January 30, 1874, 1.

135. "Factory Children," *New York Times*, February 5, 1874, 4.

136. Ibid.

137. *Journal of the Senate of the State of New York*, 507, 251–52.

138. "Working Children," *New York Times*, January 29, 1874, 4.

139. "Article 1—No Title," *New York Times*, February 1, 1874, 4.

140. "Editorial Article 4—No Title," *New York Times*, February 20, 1874, 4.

141. "Factory Children," *New York Times*, March 20, 1874, 4.

142. *Journal of the Senate of the State of New York*, 521–22; and Brace, *Dangerous Classes*, 364–65.

143. "Factory Children," 4.

144. Ibid.

Chapter 3. Seeds of a New Sectionalism

1. Elizabeth Huey Davidson, "Early Development of Public Opinion against Southern Child Labor," *North Carolina Historical Review* 14, no. 3 (1937): 237. According to Davidson, there was no widespread demand for reform in the South at this time. "A number of labor measures" were proposed in the South in the 1880s due to "new industrial trends," but there was no strong group to demand legislation, nor were there many textile manufacturers yet to oppose such legislation. She wrote in reference to the Alabama law, "The new law received scant attention from the press and public, and proved to be a false start" (237).

2. Ibid. See also B. J. Baldwin, "History of Child Labor Reform in Alabama," *Annals of the American Academy of Political and Social Science* 38 (July 1911): 111.

3. Hugh C. Bailey, *Edgar Gardner Murphy: Gentle Progressive* (Coral Gables, FL: University of Miami Press, 1968), 65.

176   *Notes to Chapter 3*

4. Ibid.

5. Elizabeth H. Davidson, *Child Labor Legislation in the Southern Textile States* (Chapel Hill: University of North Carolina Press, 1939), 1.

6. The classic work on the post-Reconstruction South is C. Vann Woodward, *Origins of the New South, 1877–1913* (Baton Rouge: Louisiana State University Press, 1951). See also Woodward, *Strange Career of Jim Crow* (New York: Oxford University Press, 1955).

7. Edgar Gardner Murphy, *Problems of the Present South: A Discussion of Certain of the Educational, Industrial, and Political Issues in the Southern States* (New York: Macmillan, 1904), 10. For more on the "best man" paradigm, see Glenda Elizabeth Gilmore, *Gender and Jim Crow: Women and the Politics of White Supremacy in North Carolina, 1896–1920* (Chapel Hill: University of North Carolina Press, 1996), 62–63; and Laura Edwards, *Gendered Strife and Confusion: The Political Culture of Reconstruction* (Urbana: University of Illinois Press, 1997), 218–19.

8. In late nineteenth- and early twentieth-century America, "whiteness" was redefined as "pan-white supremacy"—"a single, consanguine race of Caucasians"—even though American imperialism was often carried out under the banner of "Anglo-Saxon" entitlement. This redefining of "whiteness" was reinforced by naturalization case law and the binary logic of the Jim Crow system of segregation. See Matthew Frye Jacobson, *Whiteness of a Different Color: European Immigrants and the Alchemy of Race* (Cambridge: Harvard University Press, 1998), 201. The classic economic explanation of the rise of American imperialism is William LeFeber, *The New Empire: An Interpretation of American Expansion, 1860–1898* (Ithaca, NY: Cornell University Press, 1963). For the religious, moral, and racial motivations behind expansion, see Richard Hofstadter, "Cuba, the Philippines, and Manifest Destiny," in *The Paranoid Style in American Politics* (New York: Alfred A. Knopf, 1965), 145–87; and Rubin Francis Weston, *Racism in U.S. Imperialism: The Influence of Racial Assumptions on American Foreign Policy, 1893–1946* (Columbia: University of South Carolina Press, 1972).

9. See note 8 above. At the turn of the century, "whiteness" itself was being nationally redefined as "pan-white supremacy" in the age of imperialism and the rise of the binary system of Jim Crow segregation in the South. Indeed, a nationally condoned "enlightened" white supremacy undergirded racial oppression in the South. See Edward L. Ayers, *Promise of the New South: Life after Reconstruction* (New York: Oxford University Press, 1992), 418–419. See also Mary Frances Berry, "Repression of Blacks in the South, 1890–1945: Enforcing the System of Segregation," in *The Age of Segregation: Race Relations in the South, 1890–1945*, ed. Robert Haws (Oxford: University of Mississippi Press, 2008), especially pp. 39–40; and David W. Southern, *The Progressive Era and Race: Reaction and Reform, 1900–1917* (Wheeling, IL: Harlan Davidson, 2005).

10. Davidson, *Child Labor Legislation*, 3. See also Ayers, *Promise of the New South*, 111.

11. Ayers, *Promise of the New South*, 111; and Eric Foner, *Reconstruction: America's Unfinished Revolution, 1863–1877* (New York: Harper and Row, 1988), 596. On the rise

Notes to Chapter 3   177

of the corporation and the restructuring of American capitalism in this period, see Alan Trachtenberg, *The Incorporation of America: Culture and Society in the Gilded Age* (New York: Hill & Wang, 1982); Martin Sklar, *The Corporate Reconstruction of American Capitalism, 1890–1916: The Market, The Law, and Politics* (New York: Cambridge University Press, 1988); and Sven Beckert, *The Monied Metropolis: New York City and the Consolidation of the American Bourgeoisie, 1850–1896* (New York: Cambridge University Press, 2003).

12. Ayers, *Promise of the New South,* 111.

13. Davidson, *Child Labor Legislation,* 8; and Hugh D. Hindman, *Child Labor: An American History* (New York: M. E. Sharpe, 2002), 153.

14. Jacquelyn Dowd Hall et al., *Like a Family: The Making of a Southern Cotton Mill World* (New York: W. W. Norton, 1987), 61. A "doffer's" job was to replace whirling bobbins that were full of thread with empty ones. See Russell Freedman, *Kids at Work: Lewis Hine and the Crusade against Child Labor* (New York: Houghton Mifflin, 1998), 3.

15. Ibid.

16. Ibid., 64–65.

17. Foner, *Reconstruction,* 581, 587–88.

18. Ibid., 588.

19. Ibid., 588–90.

20. See Paul M. Gaston, *The New South Creed: A Study in Southern Mythmaking* (New York: Alfred A. Knopf, 1970).

21. Quoted in C. Vann Woodward, *Origins of the New South, 1877–1913* (Baton Rouge: Louisiana State University Press, 1951), 112.

22. Foner, *Reconstruction,* 596–97.

23. Ibid. Impersonal forces also played a role in Southern industrialization, including the end of a great depression in 1879 that released Northern and English capital for investment in the South. Woodward, *Origins of the New South,* 113.

24. Bailey, *Edgar Gardner Murphy,* 4–5.

25. Murphy, *Problems of the Present South,* 10. For more on the "best man" paradigm, see Gilmore, *Gender and Jim Crow,* 62–63; and Edwards, *Gendered Strife and Confusion,* 218–19.

26. "Backward or Forward?," January 1909, Edgar Gardner Murphy Papers, University of North Carolina Louis Round Wilson Library, Southern Historical Collection; hereafter cited as Murphy Papers–UNC, series 1, part 1, General Papers and Correspondence.

27. Ibid. For an in-depth study of antiblack lynchings in the South during this period, see W. Fitzhugh Brundage, *Lynching in the New South: Georgia and Virginia, 1880–1930* (Urbana: University of Illinois Press, 1993).

28. "Resolutions on Paris Lynching, 1893," Murphy Papers–UNC, series 1, part 1, General Papers and Correspondence. For newspaper coverage of the Smith lynching, see "Another Negro Burned—Henry Smith Dies at the Stake," *New York Times,* Thursday, February 2, 1893, 1. For scholarly treatments of the Smith lynching and its

178 *Notes to Chapter 3*

context in a broader history of late-nineteenth century racial violence in the South, see Amy Louise Wood, *Lynching and Spectacle: Witnessing Racial Violence in America, 1890–1940* (Chapel Hill: University of North Carolina Press, 2009), 71–77; and Walter Louis Buenger, *The Path to a Modern South: Northeast Texas between Reconstruction and the Great Depression* (Austin: University of Texas Press, 2003), 19–21. For more context on Texas lynchings in particular, see Cynthia Skove Nevels, *Lynching to Belong: Claiming Whiteness through Racial Violence* (College Station: Texas A&M University Press, 2007).

29. See Bailey, *Edgar Gardner Murphy*. See also Maud King Murphy, *Edgar Gardner Murphy: From Records and Memories* (New York, 1943).

30. Gail Bederman, *Manliness and Civilization: A Cultural History of Gender and Race in the United States, 1880–1917* (Chicago: University of Chicago Press, 1995), 25. On the influence of social Darwinism in American life and thought, see Richard Hofstadter, *Social Darwinism in American Thought* (Philadelphia: University of Pennsylvania Press, 1944); Richard Bannister, *Social Darwinism: Science and Myth in Anglo-American Social Thought* (Philadelphia: Temple University Press, 1979); and Carl Degler, *In Search of Human Nature: The Decline and Revival of Darwinism in American Social Thought* (New York: Oxford University Press, 1992). On the history of scientific racism in American life, see Stephen Jay Gould, *The Mismeasure of Man* (New York: W. W. Norton, 1981).

31. Bederman, *Manliness and Civilization*, 25. See also Audrey Smedley, *Race in North America: Origin and Evolution of a Worldview* (Boulder, CO: Westview Press, 2007), especially 235–80.

32. Ibid., 29.

33. Murphy, *Problems of the Present South*, 10–11.

34. Ibid., 14.

35. Ibid., 10–11.

36. Ibid., 16.

37. Shelley Sallee, *The Whiteness of Child Labor Reform in the New South* (Athens: University of Georgia Press, 2004), 79.

38. Influential works include Dewey W. Grantham, *Southern Progressivism: The Reconciliation of Progress and Tradition* (Knoxville: University of Tennessee Press, 1983); Jack T. Kirby, *Darkness at the Dawning: Race and Reform in the Progressive South* (Philadelphia: J. B. Lippincott, 1972); and William A. Link, *The Paradox of Southern Progressivism, 1880–1930* (Chapel Hill: University of North Carolina Press, 1992).

39. See especially W. Link, *Paradox of Southern Progressivism*.

40. See Murphy, *Problems of the Present South*, 232–38. See also Louis R. Harlan, "The Southern Education Board and the Race Issue in Public Education," *Journal of Southern History* 23, no. 2 (1957): 189–202; and Michael Dennis, "Schooling Along the Color Line: Progressives and the Education of Blacks in the New South," *Journal of Negro Education* 67, no. 2 (1998): 142–56.

Notes to Chapter 3 179

41. See Paul M. Gaston, *The New South Creed: A Study in Southern Mythmaking* (New York: Alfred A. Knopf, 1970).

42. The most influential proponent of the New South Creed of progress and modernization was Henry W. Grady, a Southern journalist and orator. See Henry W. Grady, *The New South* (New York: Robert Bonner's Sons, 1890). See also Raymond Nixon, *Henry W. Grady: Spokesman of the New South* (New York: Alfred A. Knopf, 1943).

43. Murphy, *Problems of the Present South*, 147, 148. For Murphy, the evolutionary march toward advancement was not merely a natural process but also a divine one. The Kingdom of God could be realized on earth through Nature's processes, but Christians were responsible for changing earthly conditions to promote the divine fulfillment of natural human potential. And in his view, human potential—or in evolutionary terms, the capacity for advancement—could not be separated from race. See Edgar Gardner Murphy, *The Larger Life: Sermons and an Essay* (New York: Longmans, Green, 1897), 149, 151, 153–54.

44. Davidson, *Child Labor Legislation*, 21.

45. Ibid.

46. Sallee, *Whiteness of Child Labor Reform,* 45. Organized labor held various positions on the issue of child labor. For more on the relationship of organized labor to child labor reform in the United States, see Hugh D. Hindman, *Child Labor: An American History* (Armonk, NY: M. E. Sharpe, 2002), especially pp. 49–50, 140, 149–51. For more on Samuel Gompers, see Nick Salvatore, ed. *Seventy Years of Life and Labor: An Autobiography* (Ithaca, NY: ILR Press, 1984); and Rowland Hill Harvey, *Samuel Gompers: Champion of the Toiling Masses* (Palo Alto, CA: Stanford University Press, 1935).

47. Walter I. Trattner, *Crusade for the Children: A History of the National Child Labor Committee and Child Labor Reform in America* (Chicago: Quadrangle Books, 1970), 32–33.

48. Sallee, *Whiteness of Child Labor Reform,* 45.

49. Ibid.

50. Davidson, *Child Labor Legislation*, 24–25.

51. Sallee, *Whiteness of Child Labor Reform,* 61.

52. Davidson, *Child Labor Legislation*, 26. See also Bailey, *Edgar Gardner Murphy,* 68.

53. Davidson, *Child Labor Legislation*, 31.

54. Ibid., 30.

55. The Child Labor Bill Adversed by Committee, February 5, 1901, Murphy Papers–UNC, series 2, scrapbook.

56. Ibid.

57. Ibid.

58. Davidson, *Child Labor Legislation*, 31.

59. Ibid., 32.

180 *Notes to Chapter 3*

60. Davidson, "Early Development of Public Opinion," 235.

61. Ibid., 31–32.

62. Sallee, *Whiteness of Child Labor Reform*, 79–80.

63. For a classic study of the Spanish-American War, see Ernest R. May, *Imperial Democracy: The Emergence of America as a Great Power* (New York: Harcourt, Brace, and World, 1961). For a detailed military history of the conflict, see Joseph Smith, *The Spanish-American War: Conflict in the Caribbean and the Pacific, 1895–1902* (New York: Longman Publishers, 1994). For a gender analysis of the conflict, see Kristin L. Hoganson, *Fighting for American Manhood: How Gender Politics Provoked the Spanish-American and Philippine-American Wars* (New Haven, CT: Yale University Press, 2000).

64. David W. Blight, *Race and Reunion: The Civil War in American Memory* (Boston: Harvard University Press, 2002), 351.

65. Nina Silber, *The Romance of Reunion: Northerners and the South, 1865–1900* (Chapel Hill: University of North Carolina Press, 1997), 180.

66. The rich literature on "whiteness" in this period has shown that whiteness itself was being remade at the turn of the century. A reforging of a unified whiteness—rather than hierarchically ordered white races—was spurred by American imperialism, naturalization case law, and civil rights politics. M. Jacobson, *Whiteness of a Different Color*, 201–2. Though American imperialism was often carried out under the banner of "Anglo-Saxon" entitlement, the discourse of empire "conferred its benefits by a logic of pan-white supremacy" (201–2).

67. Ibid., 180–81.

68. Blight, *Race and Reunion*, 348. For more on black soldiers' military participation in the war, see *African Americans at War: An Encyclopedia*, vol. 1, ed. Jonathan D. Sutherland (Santa Barbara: ABC-CLIO, 2004), 327–28, 368–75, and 440–42.

69. Quoted in Sutherland, *African Americans at War*, 350–51. For more on the historical relationship between the Spanish-American War and Jim Crow in the South, see Willard B. Gatewood Jr., *Black Americans and the White Man's Burden, 1898–1903* (Urbana: University of Illinois Press, 1975); Scot Ngozi-Brown, "African-American Soldiers and Filipinos: Racial Imperialism, Jim Crow, and Social Relations," *Journal of Negro History* 82, no. 1 (1997): 42–53; and Richard E. Welch, *Response to Imperialism: The United States and the Philippine-American War, 1899–1902* (Chapel Hill: University of North Carolina Press, 1979).

70. Edgar Gardner Murphy, "The Pulpit and the War," June 1898, Murphy Papers–UNC, series 2, scrapbook.

71. Ibid.

72. "The White Man and the Negro," speech at Philadelphia, March 8, 1900, Murphy Papers–UNC, series 2, scrapbook.

73. Ibid. Murphy's invitation to speak had been extended by the American Academy of Political and Social Science, the American Society for the Extension of University Teaching, and the "Civic Club." See "Correspondence," Murphy Papers–UNC, series 2, scrapbook.

Notes to Chapter 3

74. "White Man and the Negro."

75. Ibid.

76. See Kofi Lomotey, ed., *Encyclopedia of African American Education* (Thousand Oaks, CA: Sage Publications, 2010), 75–76, 365–66. See also Marybeth Gasman and Katherine Sedgwick, eds., *Uplifting a People: African American Philanthropy and Education* (New York: Peter Lang Publishers, 2005).

77. "White Man and the Negro."

78. Ralph Luker, *A Southern Tradition in Theology and Social Criticism, 1830–1930: The Religious Liberalism and Social Conservatism of James Miles, William Porcher Dubose, and Edgar Gardner Murphy* (New York: Edwin Mellen Press, 1984), 341–42; and Bailey, *Edgar Gardner Murphy*, 76. Bailey explained Murphy's decision to resign from the ministry as a "reflection of his growing awareness of the Christian's responsibility to see that God's will is done in society." The bishop of Alabama regarded Murphy's resignation as a "calamity." Bailey, *Edgar Gardner Murphy*, 148.

79. "Mr. Murphy Resigns to be Executive Secretary of Southern Education Board," November 28, 1901, *Montgomery Advertiser*, Murphy Papers–UNC, series 2, scrapbook.

80. Ibid.

81. Ibid.

82. Historians have only recently considered the role of late nineteenth-century moral reform in the creation of white racial solidarity and the symbolic moral reunification of North and South in post-Reconstruction America. Edward J. Blum, for example, has recently suggested that the temperance movement reinforced white solidarity and contributed to the moral reunification of North and South. See Edward J. Blum, *Reforging the White Republic: Race, Religion, and American Nationalism, 1865–1898* (Baton Rouge: Louisiana State University Press, 2007). Blum's broader argument is that Protestant Christianity served as a force of moral reunification by conflating whiteness, Godliness, and nationalism. For a similar approach to the role of moral reform and Christianity in this period, see Gaines M. Foster, *Moral Reconstruction: Christian Lobbyists and the Federal Legislation of Morality, 1865–1920* (Chapel Hill: University of North Carolina Press, 2007).

83. Sallee, *Whiteness of Child Labor Reform*, 3–8.

84. An index to periodical literature listed sixty-nine articles under the heading of "child labor" from 1902 to 1906, whereas only four such articles were listed for 1897 to 1901. See Trattner, *Crusade for the Children*, 48.

85. See John Spargo, *Bitter Cry of the Children* (New York: Macmillan, 1906); and Mary Van Vorst, *The Cry of the Children: A Study of Child Labor* (New York: Moffat, Yard and Co., 1908).

86. Edwin Markham, "The Child at the Loom," *The Cosmopolitan: A Monthly Illustrated Magazine*, vol. 41, issue 5 (1906), 484.

87. Davidson, "Early Development of Public Opinion," 248.

88. "Child Labor in Factories," *Harper's Weekly*, vol. 46, part 2 (1902), 1280.

89. Davidson, "Early Development of Public Opinion," 247–49.

Notes to Chapter 3

90. See Irene M. Ashby, "Child Labor in Southern Cotton Mills: A Personal Investigation of Its Extent and Abuses—The South Going through the Barbarous Experience of England and New England—Abuses that Cry to Heaven for Correction," *World's Work* 2 (May 1901–October 1901): 1290–95.

91. Davidson, *Child Labor Legislation*, 64–66.

92. "Child Labor at the North," February 14, 1903, *The Outlook*, Murphy Papers–UNC, series 1, part 1, General Papers and Correspondence.

93. Ibid.

94. Davidson, *Child Labor Legislation*, 33.

95. "An Appeal to the People and Press of New England," November 2, 1901, Murphy Papers–UNC, series 2, scrapbook.

96. Ibid.

97. J. Howard Nichols, "A Reply to the Committee," reprinted in E. Murphy, *Problems of the Present South*, 310.

98. E. Murphy, "A Rejoinder from Alabama," in *Problems of the Present South*, 314, 325–36, 328.

99. The National Conference on Charities and Corrections, *The Social Welfare Forum—Official Proceedings of the Annual Forum* (New York: American Social Science Association, 1885).

100. Robert W. DeForest, "President's Address," Official Proceedings of the Annual Meeting of the National Conference on Charities and Corrections at the Thirtieth Annual Session held in the city of Atlanta, May 6–12, 1903, 1.

101. "Preface," in ibid., iii.

102. A. J. McKelway, "Edgar Gardner Murphy: Memorial Meeting," December 7, 1913, Murphy Papers–UNC, series 1, part 1, General Papers and Correspondence.

103. Edgar Gardner Murphy, "Child Labor as a National Problem; with especial reference to the Southern states," in "Proceedings of the Annual Meeting" (1903), 121–22.

104. Ibid., 129, 130, 132–33.

105. Ibid., 122.

106. Ibid.

107. Edgar Gardner Murphy, "The National Child Labor Committee," *Charities Review* (1904), Murphy Papers–UNC, series 1, part 1, General Papers and Correspondence.

108. National Child Labor Committee—A Suggested Organization, April 1904, Murphy Papers–UNC, series 1, part 1, General Papers and Correspondence.

109. Ibid.

110. Trattner, *Crusade for the Children*, 55–56.

111. Ibid., 56–57. Other charter members of the New York Child Labor Committee included Mary K. Simkhovitch of Greenwich House; Pauline Goldmark of the National Consumers' League; James G. Stokes, founder of Hartley House settlement; William H. Baldwin; V. Everit Macy, director of the Title Guarantee and Trust Company; and Paul M. Warburg and Jacob A. Schiff, partners in the Kuhn-Loeb Investment Banking Company.

Notes to Chapter 3   183

112. Trattner, *Crusade for the Children*, 57.

113. Minute Book, April 15, 1904, box 6, Records of the National Child Labor Committee, Library of Congress; hereafter cited as NCLC-LOC. See also Davidson, *Child Labor Legislation*, 123–24.

114. Trattner, *Crusade for the Children*, 58.

115. Minute Book, April 15, 1904, box 6, NCLC-LOC.

116. Ibid. An executive committee was also appointed at the meeting. This committee included Felix Adler, William H. Baldwin, Robert W. DeForest, Edward T. Devine, John S. Huyler, Florence Kelley, V. Everit Macy, Edgar Gardner Murphy, Isaac T. Seligman, Paul M. Warburg, and John W. Wood.

117. Ibid.

118. Bailey, *Edgar Gardner Murphy*, 90.

119. National Child Labor Committee—A Suggested Organization, April 1904, Murphy Papers–UNC, series 1, part 1, General Papers and Correspondence.

120. Ibid.

121. "Conference for Education in the South," March 18, 1903, Murphy Papers–UNC, series 1, part 1, General Papers and Correspondence.

122. "Conference for Education in the South."

123. Ibid.

124. See Edgar Gardner Murphy, "Shall the Races Be Separated?" January 1907, Murphy Papers–UNC, series 1, part 1, General Papers and Correspondence. For a broader sampling of Murphy's moral and intellectual justifications for Jim Crow, see E. Murphy, *Problems of the Present South* (1904) and Edgar Gardner Murphy, *The Basis of Ascendancy: A Discussion of Certain Principles of Public Policy Involved in the Development of the Southern States* (New York: Longmans, Green, 1909).

125. See *Plessy v. Ferguson: A Brief History with Documents*, ed. Brook Thomas (New York: Bedford/St. Martin's Press, 1997).

126. Minutes of Executive Committee Meeting, May 4, 1904, box 6, NCLC-LOC.

127. Bailey, *Edgar Gardner Murphy*, 86–90.

128. NCLC Minute Book, November 16, 1905, box 6, NCLC-LOC.

129. Ibid.

130. Proceedings of the Second Annual Meeting, Supplementary Sessions, "Child Labor: A National Problem," December 7, 1905, box 10, NCLC-LOC.

131. On turn-of-the-century anxieties regarding "nature" in the face of advancing civilization, see T. J. Jackson Lears, *No Place of Grace: Antimodernism and the Transformation of American Culture, 1880–1920* (Chicago: University of Chicago Press, 1981). See also Bederman, *Manliness and Civilization*. The classic work on this topic is Richard Hofstadter, *The Age of Reform: From Bryan to FDR* (New York: Vintage Books, 1955).

132. "Child Labor: A National Problem."

133. Proceedings of the Second Annual Meeting, "The Child Labor Problem—A Study in Degeneracy," December 8, 1905, box 10, NCLC-LOC.

134. "Child Labor: A National Problem."

135. Minutes of Executive Committee Meeting, May 4, 1904, box 6, NCLC-LOC.

184 *Notes to Chapter 3*

136. Davidson, *Child Labor Legislation*, 127.

137. Proceedings of the First Annual Meeting, February 14, 1905, box 10, NCLC-LOC.

138. Proceedings of the First Annual Meeting, "The Church and Child Labor," February 14, 1905, box 10, NCLC-LOC.

139. Ibid.

140. Ibid.

141. Proceedings of the Second Annual Meeting, December 1905, box 10, NCLC-LOC.

142. After William Randolph Hearst bought Cosmopolitan in 1905 and transformed it into the model of sensational journalism, circulation numbers soared. By 1915 circulation reached one million copies per month. See *The Encyclopedia of American Journalism*, ed. Stephen L. Vaughn (New York: Routledge Press, 2008), 121–22.

143. Edwin Markham, "The Child at the Loom," *Cosmopolitan*, vol. 41, issue 5 (1906), 480, 482, 486–87.

144. See Vaughn, *Encyclopedia of American Journalism*, 121–22.

145. See Ben H. Proctor, *William Randolph Hearst: The Early Years, 1863–1910* (New York: Oxford University Press, 1998). See also Vaughn, *Encyclopedia of American Journalism*, 121.

146. "To Free the Child-Slaves: Why You Should Join the Federation to Liberate the Little Toilers," *Cosmopolitan*, vol. 41, issue 6 (1906), 679–80.

147. Ibid., 680.

148. "Child Labor: The Cosmopolitan's Readers Agree That This Disgrace Must Go," *Cosmopolitan*, vol. 42, issue 1 (1907), 111.

149. Ibid.

150. Proceedings of the Second Annual Meeting, December 8–10, 1905, box 10, NCLC-LOC.

151. Proceedings of the Seventh Annual Meeting of the National Child Labor Committee, March 9–12, 1911, box 10, NCLC-LOC.

152. Proceedings of the Second Annual Meeting, December 8–10, 1905, box 10, NCLC-LOC.

153. John Braeman, "Albert J. Beveridge and the First National Child Labor Bill," *Indiana Magazine of History*, vol. 60, no. 1 (1964), 1–3.

154. Albert J. Beveridge, "The March of the Flag" (1898), in *An American Primer*, ed. Daniel Boorstin (Chicago: University of Chicago Press, 1966), 621–29.

155. Ibid., 625.

156. Ibid., 622, 628.

157. See John Braeman, *Albert J. Beveridge: American Nationalist* (Chicago: University of Chicago Press, 1971), 26–41. Election of United States senators would not be by direct election until passage of the Seventeenth Amendment in 1913. See https://www.law.cornell.edu/constitution/amendmentxvii for text of the Seventeenth Amendment (retrieved September 23, 2019).

158. Braeman, "Albert J. Beveridge and the First National Child Labor Bill," 4–6.

Notes to Chapter 3   185

159. Quoted in ibid., 7.

160. Quoted in ibid., 17.

161. Ibid., 17–18.

162. Ibid., 18–19. For text of the "commerce clause" from Article 1 of the United States Constitution, see http://caselaw.lp.findlaw.com/data/constitution/article01/ (retrieved September 23, 2019).

163. National Child Labor Bill proposed by Senator Albert J. Beveridge of Indiana, November 1906, box 10, NCLC-LOC.

164. Letter from Samuel Lindsay to Edgar Gardner Murphy, November 26, 1906, Murphy Papers–UNC, series 1, part 1, General Papers and Correspondence.

165. Letter from Edgar Gardner Murphy to Felix Adler, May 27, 1907, Murphy Papers–UNC, series 1, part 1, General Papers and Correspondence.

166. Minutes of the Board of Trustees, December 6, 1906, box 10, NCLC-LOC.

167. Letter from Murphy to Francis Caffey, November 30, 1906, Murphy Papers–UNC, series 1, part 1, General Papers and Correspondence.

168. Minutes of the Board of Trustees, December 6, 1906, box 10, NCLC-LOC.

169. Letter from Murphy to Adler, December 18, 1906, box 10, NCLC-LOC.

170. Letter from Lindsay to Murphy, January 10, 1907, Murphy Papers–UNC, series 1, part 1, General Papers and Correspondence.

171. See Luker, *Southern Tradition*, 338–39.

172. Proceedings of the Third Annual Meeting of the NCLC, December 1906, box 10, NCLC-LOC.

173. Proceedings of the Third Annual Meeting of the NCLC, "Child Labor and the Nation," December 13, 1906, box 10, NCLC-LOC.

174. Proceedings of the Third Annual Meeting, December 15, 1906, box 10, NCLC-LOC.

175. Congressional Record, 41, Senate, January 23, 1907, 1552–57.

176. Congressional Record, 41, Senate, January 28, 1907, 1795.

177. Ibid., 1798.

178. See ibid., 1797, 1801, 1807–1808.

179. Ibid., 1805–1806.

180. Ibid., 1821.

181. Ibid.

182. Congressional Record, 41, Senate, January 29, 1907, 1867–83.

183. Letter from Murphy to Teddy Roosevelt, February 4, 1907, Murphy Papers–UNC, series 1, part 1, General Papers and Correspondence.

184. Letter from Teddy Roosevelt to Murphy, November 15, 1907, Murphy Papers–UNC, series 1, part 1, General Papers and Correspondence.

185. Resolution Adopted by the Trustees of the National Child Labor Committee, November 26, 1907, Murphy Papers–UNC, series 1, part 1, General Papers and Correspondence.

186. Edgar Gardner Murphy Memorial Service, New York City, December 7, 1913, Murphy Papers–UNC, series 1, part 1, General Papers and Correspondence.

186   *Notes to Chapter 4*

Chapter 4. Child Labor Abolitionists

1. The New York State Department of Labor reported that of roughly sixty thousand children between the ages of ten and fifteen employed in the state in 1910, thirty-six thousand were boys and twenty-four thousand were girls. Girls worked in tenement houses, factories, clerical occupations, and agriculture. See New York State Bureau of Women in Industry, "The Trend of Child Labor in New York State: 1910–1922" (Albany: State of New York Department of Labor, 1922), 12–13. A new focus on girls in child labor reform became apparent after *Muller v. Oregon* (1908) declared the state's special interest in protecting female workers due to their "maternal function." Additionally, the Triangle Shirtwaist Factory fire of 1911 aroused more public concern and sympathy for girl laborers, as the majority of the 146 garment workers who died were teenage girls. See Leon Stein, *The Triangle Fire* (Ithaca, NY: Cornell University Press, 1962). The NCLC in conjunction with the New York Child Labor Committee also pushed the New York Factory Investigating Commission (FIC) to look into the problem of child labor in tenements with a special concern for girls. See Eileen Boris, *Home to Work: Motherhood and the Politics of Industrial Homework in the United States* (New York: Cambridge University Press, 1994), 97. See also Jeremy P. Felt, *Hostages of Fortune: Child Labor Reform in New York State* (Syracuse, NY: Syracuse University Press, 1965), 6–7.

2. Edwin Markham, Benjamin B. Lindsey, and George Creel, *Children in Bondage: A Complete and Careful Presentation of the Anxious Problem of Child Labor—Its Causes, Its Crimes, and Its Cure* (New York: Hearst's International Library, 1914). For more on Lewis Hine and his work as a photographer for the NCLC, see Russell Freedman, ed., *Kids at Work: Lewis Hine and the Crusade against Child Labor* (New York: Houghton Mifflin, 1998); Verna Posever Curtis and Stanley Mallach, *Photography and Reform: Lewis Hine and the National Child Labor Committee* (Milwaukee: Milwaukee Art Museum, 1984); and Judith Mara Gutman, *Lewis W. Hine and the American Social Conscience* (New York: Walker, 1967).

3. See Pamphlet No. 251, "Do You Know Why the Keating-Owen Bill to Regulate Child Labor Demands Your Support?," December 1915, box 15, NCLC-LOC; Pamphlet No. 240, "Why You Should Support the Palmer-Owen Bill," January 1915, box 15, NCLC-LOC; and other untitled letters, press releases, speeches, and pamphlets related to "Keating-Owen" (and formerly named "Palmer-Owen") in box 15, NCLC-LOC.

4. Walter I. Trattner, *Crusade for the Children: A History of the National Child Labor Committee and Child Labor Reform in America* (Chicago: Quadrangle Books, 1970), 124.

5. Ibid., 125.

6. William A. Link, *The Paradox of Southern Progressivism, 1880–1930* (Chapel Hill: University of North Carolina Press, 1992), 176.

7. For a starting point on Progressive reform, see Richard Hofstadter, *The Age of Reform: From Bryan to FDR* (New York: Vintage Books, 1955); Robert Wiebe, *The Search for Order, 1877–1920* (New York: Hill & Wang, 1966); Daniel Rodgers, *Atlan-*

Notes to Chapter 4   187

tic Crossings: Social Politics in a Progressive Age (Cambridge: Harvard University Press, 1998); Michael Willrich, *City of Courts: Socializing Justice in Progressive-Era Chicago* (Cambridge: Harvard University Press, 2003); and Linda Gordon, *Pitied but Not Entitled: Single Mothers and the History of Welfare, 1890–1935* (Cambridge: Harvard University Press, 1994). Hofstadter's work set the stage for debates about the Progressive era, arguing that reformers were motivated by "status anxiety" in an era of great social and economic change. In contrast, Wiebe argued that reformers created a "bureaucratic worldview" that was capable of dealing with social problems in modern American life.

8. W. Link, *Paradox of Southern Progressivism*, 180.

9. Ibid.

10. In its editorial notes the NCLC published a statement suggesting that Murphy's death had marked the end of one era of child labor reform and the beginning of another: "The death of Edgar Gardner Murphy last summer has brought home to us the fact that the first stage in child labor reform is passed. . . . Mr. Murphy's special work is done." See *Child Labor Bulletin* (November 1913), 9.

11. Press Releases of the National Child Labor Committee, "2,000,000 Children at Work in the United States," June 12, 1912, box 16, NCLC-LOC. This press release was sent to 1,130 newspapers across the country. An NCLC pamphlet from 1913 dramatized the 2,000,000 figure by stating that if "placed in a procession twelve feet apart," the child laborers of America "would reach from San Francisco to Boston and thence to New Orleans." See "Nearly Two Million Child Workers under Sixteen Years Today," *Child Labor Bulletin* (November 1913), 44.

12. "Tenth Anniversary of the National Child Labor Committee," *Child Labor Bulletin* (November 1913), 45.

13. Ibid., 46.

14. Because of their supposed "agricultural character," fruit and vegetable canneries, which employed thousands of child laborers, were excluded from child labor laws. See Pauline Goldmark, "Child Labor in Canneries," *Annals of the American Academy of Political and Social Science* 35 (1910): 152–54.

15. Owen R. Lovejoy, "Seven Years of Child Labor Reform," *Annals of the American Academy of Political and Social Science* 38 (July 1911): 37. On the eve of its ten-year anniversary, the NCLC still maintained a strong emphasis on child labor in Southern textile mills. In 1913 the average amount of time spent by one NCLC investigator per month was highest in textile mills (twenty hours) followed by canneries, street trades, and glass factories. See "Investigation," *Child Labor Bulletin* (November 1913), 18.

16. Ibid., 36–37.

17. "Tenth Anniversary of the National Child Labor Committee," 46.

18. Trattner, *Crusade for the Children*, 122–123. See also Pamphlet No. 240, "Why You Should Support the Palmer-Owen Bill," January 1915, box 15, NCLC-LOC.

19. Pamphlet No. 240, "Why You Should Support the Palmer-Owen Bill," January 1915, box 15, NCLC-LOC.

20. Ibid.

188 *Notes to Chapter 4*

21. Ibid. Florence Kelley argued that a national law was necessary since child labor was not confined to one region but rather was a "national evil." See "Judicial Obstacles to Labor Legislation," box 9, folder 5, Florence Kelley Papers, New York Public Library, Manuscripts and Archives Division.

22. The following year, the Children's Bureau was transferred to the newly created Department of Labor. See Trattner, *Crusade for the Children*, 120.

23. Ibid. As Theda Skocpol has argued, the creation of the US Children's Bureau was a key moment in the rise of a modern bureaucratic state concerned with protecting children and women. See Skocpol, *Protecting Soldiers and Mothers: The Political Origins of Social Policy in the United States* (Cambridge: Harvard University Press, 1995). For more on the rise of the modern bureaucratic state and the logic of political reform in this period, see also Stephen Skowronek, *Building a New American State: The Expansion of National Administrative Capacities, 1877–1920* (New York: Cambridge University Press, 1982).

24. "Federal Children's Bureau," *Child Labor Bulletin* (November 1912), 10.

25. Trattner, *Crusade for the Children*, 120.

26. Paul U. Kellogg, "The Industrial Platform of the New Party," *The Survey*, vol. 28, no. 21 (1912), 668.

27. President Taft disappointed Progressives in many ways. He cozied up to corporate interests by proposing to rescind railroad antitrust laws and acquiesced to the Senate's protectionist demands for higher tariffs. In 1910 President Taft openly campaigned against Progressive members of Congress, which infuriated Teddy Roosevelt and other progressive Republicans. See Steven J. Rosenstone, Roy L. Behr, and Edward H. Lazarus, eds., *Third Parties in America: Citizen Response to Major Party Failure* (Princeton, NJ: Princeton University Press, 1996), 81–84; Lewis L. Gould, *The William Howard Taft Presidency* (Lawrence: University Press of Kansas, 2009); Michael A. Genovese, *Encyclopedia of the American Presidency* (New York: Infobase Publishing, 2010), 463–65.

28. The party was later dubbed the Bull Moose Party, a nickname that stuck when someone in a crowd on the campaign trail yelled out, asking Roosevelt how he felt. "Like a bull moose," he replied. Genovese, *Encyclopedia of the American Presidency*, 54.

29. Sidney M. Milkis, *Theodore Roosevelt, the Progressive Party, and the Transformation of American Democracy* (Lawrence: University Press of Kansas, 2009).

30. Kellogg, "Industrial Platform of the New Party," 668–70.

31. Wilson received 42 percent of the vote, Roosevelt had 27 percent, Taft had 23 percent, and Socialist Party candidate Eugene Debs finished with 6 percent. See James Chace, *1912: Wilson, Roosevelt, Taft, and Debs—The Election That Changed the Country* (New York: Simon & Schuster, 2004).

32. *The Survey*, vol. 29 (February 1913), 639–40.

33. Woodrow Wilson, *Constitutional Government in the United States* (New York: Columbia University Press, 1908), 179.

Notes to Chapter 4

189

34. Senator Ira Copley of Illinois and Representative Miles Poindexter of Washington introduced a bill that was nearly identical to the Beveridge Bill. The commerce power of the federal government would be used to prohibit child-made goods from crossing state lines. Senator William Kenyon introduced a similar measure that would apply only to children fourteen years of age or younger. See Trattner, *Crusade for the Children*, 122; and Stephen B. Wood, *Constitutional Politics in the Progressive Era: Child Labor and the Law* (Chicago: University of Chicago Press, 1968), 28–29. See also "Federal Control over Anti-Social Labor," *The Survey*, vol. 30 (August 16, 1913), 615.

35. Quoted in Trattner, *Crusade for the Children*, 123.

36. Felix Adler, "The Abolition of Child Labor: A National Duty," *Child Labor Bulletin* (May 1914), 20, 23, 24.

37. See chapter 3 of the present text.

38. Trattner, *Crusade for the Children*, 123.

39. The committee also found certain aspects of the pending bills in Congress lacking. For instance, Senator Copley's bill had weak enforcement measures and included the word "knowingly," which disappointed the reformers. And Senator Kenyon's bill established a minimum age of fourteen rather than sixteen, as the NCLC wanted. The bills also focused on punishing the interstate carrier of child-made goods instead of the employer himself, which the NCLC found unacceptable. See Owen R. Lovejoy, "Federal Government and Child Labor," *Child Labor Bulletin* (February 1914), 19–25; Pamphlet No. 240, "Why You Should Support the Palmer-Owen Bill"; Trattner, *Crusade for the Children*, 123; "The Common Welfare: Federal Control over Anti-Social Labor," *The Survey*, vol. 30, no. 20 (1913), 615.

40. Pamphlet No. 240, "Why You Should Support the Palmer-Owen Bill," 19.

41. Trattner, *Crusade for the Children*, 124–25.

42. *The Survey*, vol. 31 (February 7, 1914), 539. See also Arthur S. Link, *Wilson: The New Freedom* (Princeton, NJ: Princeton University Press, 1967), 256.

43. Trattner, *Crusade for the Children*, 124–25. For Supreme Court decisions in the Progressive era that affirmed the federal government's power to regulate interstate commerce, see *Hoke v. United States* (1913), which upheld the Mann Act (1910) prohibiting prostitution. In its original form, the Mann Act prohibited the interstate transportation of females for "immoral purposes." See David J. Langum, *Crossing over the Line: Legislating Morality and the Mann Act* (Chicago: University of Chicago Press, 1994). For another example of such legislation that was upheld by the Supreme Court, see *Champion v. Ames* (1903), which prohibited the buying and selling of lottery tickets across states lines. See Wood, *Constitutional Politics*, 29–30.

44. Trattner, *Crusade for the Children*, 125.

45. The classic work on the theology of the social gospel is Walter Rauschenbusch, *A Theology for the Social Gospel* (New York: Macmillan, 1917). See also Rauschenbusch, *Christianity and the Social Crisis* (New York: Macmillan, 1913); and Robert T. Handy, *The Social Gospel in America, 1870–1920* (New York: Oxford University Press, 1966).

Notes to Chapter 4

46. Quoted in Sandra Opdycke, "Lovejoy, Owen Reed," *American National Biography Online*, February 2000, http://www.anb.org/articles/15/15-00424.html, retrieved September 23, 2019.

47. Markham et al., *Children in Bondage*. See Warren T. Francke, "George Creel," in *Dictionary of Literary Biography: American Newspaper Journalists, 1901–1925*, vol. 25, ed. Perry J. Ashley (Farmington Hills, MI: Gale Publishers, 1985). See Ben Barr Lindsey, *The Problem of the Children and How the State of Colorado Cares for Them* (Denver, CO: Merchants Publishing, 1904). See also Lindsey's autobiography, *The Dangerous Life* (New York: Horace Liveright, 1931). The establishment of Lindsey's juvenile court in Denver followed on the founding of the first juvenile court system in Chicago in 1899. For more on the origins of the juvenile court system in America, see Willrich, *City of Courts*.

48. See George Hamlin Fitch, *Great Spiritual Writers of America* (San Francisco: Paul Elder & Company, 1916), 141–45; Edward B. Payne, "The Hoe-Man on Trial," *The Arena*, vol. 22 (New York: Alliance Publishing, 1988), 19; and Leonard D. Abbot, "Edwin Markham: Laureate of Labor," *Comrade* 1, no. 4 (1902): 74–75. See also Louis Filler, *The Unknown Edwin Markham: His Mystery and Its Significance* (Kent, OH: Kent State University Press, 1966).

49. William R. Nash, "Markham, Edwin," *American National Biography Online*, February 2000, http://www.anb.org/articles/16/16-01058.html, retrieved September 23, 2019; and "Markham, Edwin," *Oxford Companion to American Literature*, 6th ed., ed. James D. Hart (New York: Oxford University Press, 1995), 414. See also Hal Powers's biography, *Edwin Markham: A Muckraker Crusading against Child Labor Abuse* (Carbondale: Southern Illinois University Press, 1981); and Edwin Markham, *The Man with the Hoe and Other Poems* (New York: Doubleday & McClure, 1899).

50. *Good Housekeeping*, vol. 59 (1914), 340.

51. *The Dial: A Monthly Journal of Current Literature* 57 (1914): 337.

52. University of the State of New York Bulletin, New York State Library, Bibliography Bulletin 56, "The Best Books of 1914," no. 594 (Albany, NY, July 1, 1915), 11.

53. *Muller v. Oregon*, 208 U.S. 412 (1908).

54. Stein, *Triangle Fire*, ix.

55. Markham et al., *Children in Bondage*, 130, 131.

56. Ibid., 2.

57. Ibid., 17.

58. Ibid., 57.

59. Ibid., 116.

60. Ibid.

61. Ibid., 15–16.

62. Ibid., 324–28.

63. Ibid., 42.

64. Ibid., 42–43.

65. Ibid., 41–44.

66. Ibid., 47.

67. Ibid., 48–49, 50.

Notes to Chapter 4 191

68. Ibid., 55–56.

69. Ibid., 299–300.

70. Clarke A. Chambers, *Seedtime of Reform: American Social Service and Social Action, 1918–1933* (Minneapolis: University of Minnesota Press, 1963), 48.

71. Markham et al., *Children in Bondage*, 301.

72. Ibid., 19.

73. Sermon Texts, Scripture Readings, Addresses, etc. for Child Labor Day, NCLC Scrapbook—Publicity on Child Labor Day, 1907–1917, box 34, NCLC-LOC. Fanny Crosby composed "Hymn for the Working Children" in 1912 at the request of the NCLC. In a note included with the hymn, Crosby wrote, "I never was asked to write a hymn that I have more cheerfully written than this." See "Hymn for the Working Children," *Child Labor Bulletin* (August 1913), 18.

74. Letter from Lovejoy to American clergymen, NCLC Scrapbook—Publicity on Child Labor Day, box 34, January 3, 1914, NCLC-LOC.

75. Letter from Lovejoy to Various Clergymen, NCLC Scrapbook—Publicity on Child Labor Day, box 34, October 22, 1915, NCLC-LOC.

76. Pamphlet No. 251 Endorsing Keating-Owen Bill, NCLC Scrapbook—Publicity on Child Labor Day, box 34, December 1915, NCLC-LOC. See also Trattner, *Crusade for the Children*, 127.

77. Harry Frederick Ward, *The Social Creed of the Churches* (New York: Abingdon Press, 1914). See also Ronald Cedric White and Charles Howard Hopkins, eds., *The Social Gospel: Religion and Reform in Changing America* (Philadelphia: Temple University Press, 1976), 205–12.

78. Susan Curtis, *A Consuming Faith: The Social Gospel and Modern American Culture* (Columbia: Missouri University Press, 2001), 17.

79. White and Hopkins, *Social Gospel*, 209–10.

80. Ward, *Social Creed of the Churches*, 6. For "magna charta" reference, see Eugene P. Link, *Labor-Religion Prophet: The Times and Life of Harry F. Ward* (Boulder, CO: Westview Press, 1984), 37.

81. Walter Rauschenbusch, *Christianizing the Social Order* (New York: Macmillan, 1912), 124.

82. Henry Warner Bowden, "Adler, Felix," *American National Biography Online*, February 2000, http://www.anb.org/articles/08/08-00013.html, retrieved September 23, 2019. In 1876 Adler founded the New York Society for Ethical Culture, which later became a nationwide "Ethical Culture" movement.

83. Felix Adler, "Annual Address of Chairman," *Child Labor Bulletin* (August 1915), 92, 94, 95, 96.

84. Bishop Edwin H. Hughes, "Social Responsibility for Child Labor," *Child Labor Bulletin* (August 1915), 99–100.

85. "A Little Child Shall Feed Them," *Life*, undated, box 48-A, NCLC-LOC.

86. "The Dawn in a Civilized Country," December 20, 1914, box 48-A, NCLC-LOC.

87. Cartoon Collection of the National Child Labor Committee, "The Money Tree of Child Labor," *New York Journal*, July 16, 1914, box 48-A, NCLC-LOC.

192   Notes to Chapter 4

88. For other examples, see the Cartoon Collection of the National Child Labor Committee, box 48-A and box 48-B, NCLC-LOC. See also Sermon Texts, Scripture Readings, Addresses, etc. for Child Labor Day, NCLC Scrapbook—Publicity on Child Labor Day, 1907–1917, box 34, NCLC-LOC. Quoting scripture was commonplace in propaganda supporting passage of the Keating-Owen Act. "As you do unto the least of these" became a rallying cry for the campaign, appearing in newspapers, pamphlets, and sermons agitating for passage of the act. Matthew 18:1–14 was also a commonly cited passage, in which the disciples asked Jesus, "Who, then, is the greatest in the kingdom of Heaven?" Jesus had answered that it was a child. See Pamphlet No. 254, "Program for Child Labor Day," December 1915, box 15, NCLC-LOC.

89. Cartoon Collection of the National Child Labor Committee, "End This Outrage," *Buffalo Enquirer*, March 5, 1915, box 48-A, NCLC-LOC.

90. "Greatest Child Labor Day of Them All," *The Survey* 35 (January 15, 1916), 454. See also Editorial Notes, *Child Labor Bulletin* (February 1916), 169–70.

91. "Greatest Child Labor Day of Them All," 454.

92. Editorial Notes, *Child Labor Bulletin* (February 1916), 169.

93. Congressional Record, 52, US House of Representatives, February 15, 1915, 3834.

94. Ibid., 3836. The vote was clearly sectional in nature. Thirty-five of the forty-three votes against the bill were from the South Atlantic states, where textile manufacturing and canning were centered. A majority of House votes from North Carolina, South Carolina, Georgia, and Mississippi opposed the bill.

95. Congressional Record, 52, US House, 3835–36.

96. Congressional Record, 53, Part 2, US House of Representatives, February 2, 1916, 2010, 2012, 2014, 2015, 2022, 2026.

97. Ibid., 2028. Drawing on the "widowed mother" argument, Congressman William Joseph Sears of Florida stated, "Do not force those who have been so unfortunate as to lose their father to gain their living and their support by the toil and the sweat of the brow of their poor widowed mother" (2024).

98. Ibid.

99. Ibid., 2032.

100. Ibid., 2034.

101. Ibid.

102. Ibid., 2035.

103. Congressional Record, 54, Part 12, US House of Representatives, August 4, 1916, 12084, 12085, 12087–88.

104. "Working Children and the Senate," *The Survey*, vol. 36, no. 3 (April 8, 1916), 69.

105. Cartoon Collection of the National Child Labor Committee, "A New Emancipation Proclamation," *New York World*, July 29, 1916, box 48-B, NCLC-LOC; "End This Slavery for All Time," January 28, 1916, box 48-B, NCLC-LOC; "The Worst Slavery Still Remains," September 13, 1915, box 48-B, NCLC-LOC.

106. Trattner, *Crusade for the Children*, 130.

Notes to Chapter 4   193

107. Congressional Record, 54, 12313. As in the House, the vote in the Senate was along sectional lines. Ten Southern Democrats along with two Republican senators from Pennsylvania voted against the measure.

108. *New York Times*, September 2, 1916, 4. See also Wood, *Constitutional Politics*, 77.

109. For more on Woodrow Wilson and his evolving stance on the issue of federal child labor legislation, see Arthur S. Link, *Woodrow Wilson and the Progressive Era, 1910–1917* (New York: Harper & Row, 1963), 59–60; Wood, *Constitutional Politics*, 65, 66–68, 77–78, 80, 88–91, 101; Trattner, *Crusade for the Children* 121–22, 124–25, 127–29, 130–32, and 138; and Beth Behn, "A Principled Shift: Woodrow Wilson and the Keating-Owen Child Labor Bill," paper presented at the annual meeting of the MPSA Annual National Conference, Palmer House Hotel, Hilton, Chicago, IL, April 3, 2008, http://www.allacademic.com/meta/p265873_index.html, retrieved September 23, 2019.

110. "The Liberator," *Chicago Journal*, October 22, 1916, box 48-B, NCLC-LOC.

111. Gary Gerstle, *American Crucible: Race and Nation in the Twentieth Century* (Princeton, NJ: Princeton University Press, 2001), 89.

112. Trattner, *Crusade for the Children*, 132.

113. Sent on January 16, 1917, the Zimmermann Telegram (also known as the Zimmermann Note) was a coded telegram from Germany to Mexico that revealed Germany's plan to ally with Mexico and Japan if the US declared war on Germany. The British intercepted and passed on the message to the United States, contributing to the US decision to enter World War I. See Barbara W. Tuchman, *The Zimmermann Telegram* (New York: Ballantine Books, 1985). For general overviews of America's involvement in World War I, see David M. Kennedy, *Over Here: The First World War and American Society* (New York: Oxford University Press, 1982); Robert H. Ferrell, *Woodrow Wilson and World War I, 1917–1921* (New York: HarperCollins, 1986); Thomas Knock, *To End All Wars: Woodrow Wilson and the Quest for a New Moral Order* (New York: Oxford University Press, 1992); Ronald Schaffer, *America in the Great War: The Rise of the War Welfare State* (New York: Oxford University Press, 1994); and Ellis W. Hawley, *The Great War and the Search for Modern Order: A History of the American People and Their Institutions, 1917–1933* (Prospect Heights, IL: Waveland Press, 1997).

114. "Must Exert All Our Power to Bring a Government That Is Running Amuck to Terms," *New York Times*, Tuesday, April 3, 1917, 1.

115. War-time Legislation, *Child Labor Bulletin* (August 1917), 86.

116. For more on the labor situation during World War I, see David Montgomery, *The Fall of the House of Labor: The Workplace, the State, and American Labor Activism, 1865–1925* (New York: Cambridge University Press, 1987), 330–47; Robert D. Cuff, *The War Industries Board: Business-Government Relations during World War I* (Baltimore: Johns Hopkins University Press, 1973); Joseph A. McCartin, *Labor's Great War: The Struggle for Industrial Democracy and the Origins of Modern American*

194   *Notes to Chapter 4*

Labor Relations, 1912–1921 (Chapel Hill: University of North Carolina Press, 1997); Schaffer, *America in the Great War*, 64–95.

117. "America's Entry into War Made Pretext for Grinding the Seed Corn," *Child Labor Bulletin* (August 1917), 80.

118. Press Releases of the National Child Labor Committee, "National Child Labor Committee Urges America Not to Forget Children in Wartime," April 26, 1918, box 23, NCLC-LOC.

119. Press Releases of the National Child Labor Committee, "Children in War," May 5, 1917, box 23, NCLC-LOC.

120. Press Releases of the National Child Labor Committee, Owen Lovejoy, "A Warning from the Experience of England," undated, box 23, NCLC-LOC.

121. Press Releases of the National Child Labor Committee, "Child Labor in War-Time," May 17, 1917, box 23, NCLC-LOC.

122. Ibid.

123. Press Releases of the National Child Labor Committee, "U.S. Child Labor Law Must Not Be Suspended," May 23, 1917, box 23, NCLC-LOC.

124. Press Releases of the National Child Labor Committee, "President Wilson Advocates Maintenance of Child Labor Standards," December 31, 1917, box 24, NCLC-LOC.

125. Ibid.

126. Press Releases of the National Child Labor Committee, "Special to T. C. Robinson, Y.M.C.A., Child Labor Sunday," January 27, 1918, box 23, NCLC-LOC.

127. Press Releases of the National Child Labor Committee, "Child Labor Decision," June 5, 1918, box 23, NCLC-LOC. For the full text of the US Supreme Court's decision in *Hammer v. Dagenhart*, 247 U.S. 251 (1918), see http://caselaw.lp.findlaw.com/scripts/getcase.pl?court=US&vol=247&invol=251, retrieved September 23, 2019. See also Wood, *Constitutional Politics*, 96–106, and Trattner, *Crusade for the Children*, 134–37.

128. "Look Out for the Children—Measures for the Safeguarding of Young America in Wartime," *Red Cross Magazine*, November 1917, box 24, NCLC-LOC.

129. Letter from Owen Lovejoy to "Our Members in Cleveland," October 6, 1917, box 24, NCLC-LOC.

130. "The Children in Wartime," *The Bambino*, February 1918, box 25, NCLC-LOC. See also Anne Cipriano Venzon and Paul L. Miles, eds. *The United States in the First World War: An Encyclopedia* (New York: Garland Publishing, 1995), 141–42; Kriste Lindenmeyer, *A Right to Childhood: The U.S. Children's Bureau and Child Welfare, 1912–1946* (Urbana: University of Illinois Press, 1997); Julia Lathrop, "The Children's Bureau in Wartime," *North American Review* (November 1917): 734–46; and *Four Decades of Action for Children: A Short History of the Children's Bureau* (Washington, DC: US Department of Health, Education, and Welfare, 1956).

131. National Child Labor Committee Scrapbook, October 1918–September 1919, Raymond Fuller, "Uncle Sam's Child-Power Policy: Uncle Sam and the Children," October 22, 1918, box 25, NCLC-LOC. See also Cartoon Collection of the National

Child Labor Committee, "The Health of the Child Is the Power of the Nation," President Wilson, August 18, 1918, box 48-B, NCLC-LOC.

132. Scholarship on the rise of consumer culture is vast. See William Leach, *Land of Desire: Merchants, Power, and the Rise of a New American Culture* (New York: Vintage, 1993); T. J. Jackson Lears, *No Place of Grace: Antimodernism and the Transformation of American Culture, 1880–1920* (Chicago: University of Chicago Press, 1981); Kathy Peiss, *Cheap Amusements: Working Women and Leisure in Turn-of-the-Century New York* (Philadelphia: Temple University Press, 1986); Martin Sklar, *The Corporate Reconstruction of American Capitalism, 1890–1916* (New York: Cambridge University Press, 1988); Richard Wightman Fox and T. J. Jackson Lears, eds., *The Culture of Consumption: Critical Essays in American History, 1880–1980* (New York: Pantheon Books, 1983); Susan J. Matt, *Keeping Up with the Joneses: Envy in American Consumer Society, 1890–1930* (Philadelphia: University of Pennsylvania Press, 2003); Simon J. Bronner, ed, *Consuming Visions: Accumulation and Display of Goods in America, 1880–1920* (New York: W. W. Norton, 1989); John F. Kasson, *Amusing the Million: Coney Island at the Turn of the Century* (New York: Hill and Wang, 1978); Richard Butsch, *For Fun and Profit: The Transformation of Leisure into Consumption* (Philadelphia: Temple University Press, 1990); Curtis, *Consuming Faith*; Michael Denning, *Mechanic Accents: Dime Novels and Working-Class Culture in America* (Brooklyn, NY: Verso Press, 1987); Don Slater, *Consumer Culture and Modernity* (Cambridge, MA: Polity Press, 1999); and Daniel Horowitz, *The Morality of Spending: Attitudes toward the Consumer Society in America, 1875–1940* (Chicago: Ivan R. Dee Publisher, 1985).

133. William Leach, *Land of Desire: Merchants, Power, and the Rise of a New American Culture* (New York: Vintage Books, 1993), 3.

134. In *No Place of Grace*, Lears describes the "marriage of material and spiritual progress" that took place in the modern industrial age when liberal Christianity adapted itself to modern capitalist society and embraced the "optimism of the official culture" (4).

135. Historical scholarship on children's consumer culture is relatively new. See Lisa Jacobson, *Raising Consumers: Children and the American Mass Market in the Early Twentieth Century* (New York: Columbia University Press, 2004); Daniel Cook, *The Commodification of Childhood: The Children's Clothing Industry and the Rise of the Child Consumer* (Durham, NC: Duke University Press, 2004); Miriam Formanek-Brunell, *Made to Play Dolls and the Commercialization of American Girlhood, 1830–1930* (Baltimore: Johns Hopkins University Press, 1998); Gary Cross, *Kids' Stuff: Toys and the Changing World of American Childhood* (Cambridge: Harvard University Press, 1998); Beryl Langer, "Commodified Enchantment: Children and Consumer Capitalism," *Thesis Eleven* 69 (May 2002): 67–81; William Leach, "Child-World in the Promised Land," in *The Mythmaking Frame of Mind*, ed. J. Gillbert et al. (1993): 209–38; and Jo B. Paoletti and Carol L. Kregloh, "The Children's Department," in *Men and Women Dressing the Part*, ed. Claudia Kidwell and Valerie Steele, 22–41 (Washington, DC: Smithsonian Institution Press, 1989).

196   *Notes to Chapter 4*

136. Josephine Eschenbrenner, "What Is a Child Worth?" *Child Labor Bulletin*, vol. 3 (May 1914), 159. See also Viviana A. Zelizer, *Pricing the Priceless Child: The Changing Social Value of Children* (New York: Basic Books, 1985), 57. Zelizer argues that the sentimentalization of children in the early twentieth century led to unique kinds of markets that "priced" children according to their sentimental, rather than economic, value. In effect, children's "pricelessness" determined their economic price. For example, the rise of child insurance policies, for-profit adoption agencies, and cash compensation awards for bereaved parents were unusual types of markets that were regulated by sentimental criteria. Zelizer's discussion of child labor centers on the "moral dispute" over "children's economic and sentimental value" (64). She argues that changing views of the child necessitated that children be "economically worthless, but emotionally priceless." Thus, "if children were useful and produced money, they were not being properly loved" (72). Though I am attentive to similar kinds of historical ironies, my argument in this chapter focuses on how and why the "market" disappeared from national debate about child welfare by the end of World War I, giving way to the ascendancy of child consumerism.

137. Ibid.

138. In the May 1915 issue of leading toy trade journal *Toys and Novelties*, a "Made in America" campaign ad read, "If there ever has been, or will be, a Golden Opportunity for the firm establishment of the American Toy as the absolute leader of the Toy World, it is now. . . . Picture the German manufacturer fairly staggering with his . . . heavy war tax, which will lead to a certain prodigious increase in cost of German production. . . . The day will not be far distant when U.S.A. shall be the Toy Mart of the World, and shall be known North, East, South and West as the home of children's playthings. See *Toys and Novelties* 12, no. 6 (1915): 28, Trade Journal Collection, The Center for Research Libraries, Chicago, IL (hereafter cited as TJ-CRL-Chicago); and "Uncle Sam Is Becoming the Biggest Toy-Maker of the World," *Current Opinion* 62, no. 5 (May 1917), 373. See also A. C. Gilbert, *The Man Who Lives in Paradise: The Autobiography of A. C. Gilbert with Marshall McClintock* (New York: Rinehart & Company, 1954), 126.

139. *Toys and Novelties* 16, no. 12 (1919): 41, TJ-CRL-Chicago.

140. *Toys and Novelties* 12, no. 5 (1915): 31, TJ-CRL-Chicago. See also Gilbert, *Man Who Lives in Paradise*, 139.

141. *Toys and Novelties* 12, no. 5 (1915): 33, TJ-CRL-Chicago.

142. Ibid., 31. "Grown ups, for the most part, made the selection for the child. Gradually, there came a change of heart. The need, the actual need for toys, was felt, and the value of this kind of amusement as a means of child betterment came to be looked upon in a newer light. . . . The child was appealed to from a new angle."

143. Ibid., 32.

144. See Lisa Jacobson's excellent study on the rise of the child consumer in early twentieth-century America, *Raising Consumers*.

145. Gerstle, *American Crucible*, 83–87. For more on anti-German propaganda during the war and on the work of the Committee on Public Information, see also

Notes to Chapter 4   197

Frederick C. Luebke, *Bonds of Loyalty: German-Americans and World War I* (DeKalb: Northern Illinois University Press, 1974); Horace Cornelius Peterson, *Propaganda for War: The War against American Neutrality, 1914–1917* (Norman: University of Oklahoma Press, 1939); George Creel, *How We Advertised America* (New York: Harper & Brothers, 1920); Stephen Vaughn, *Holding Fast the Inner Lines: Democracy, Nationalism, and the Committee on Public Information* (Chapel Hill: University of North Carolina Press, 1980); James R. Mock and Cedric Larson, *Words That Won the War* (Princeton, NJ: Princeton University Press, 1939); and Alan Axelrod, *Selling the Great War: The Making of American Propaganda* (New York: Macmillan, 2009).

146. "Supplant German Toys," *Philadelphia Inquirer*, vol. 177, issue 142, November 19, 1917, 18; "Newspapers Big Boost for American Toys," *Toys and Novelties* 14, no. 1 (1917): 31, TJ-CRL-Chicago; "Germany's Lost Toy Trade," *New York Times*, December 25, 1917, 14; "German Toys Called Menace," *Playthings* 16, no. 8 (October 1918), 40, Playthings Magazine Collection, Brian Sutton-Smith Library and Archives of Play, National Museum of Play, Rochester, NY (hereafter cited as PMC-Rochester); "Americans to Shun All Toys Made in Germany," *Playthings* 16, no. 8 (October 1918), 40, PMC-Rochester; and "Into the Ocean with Hun Toys," *Playthings* 16, no. 8 (October 1918), 40, PMC-Rochester.

147. "Toys and 'The Spirit that Quickens': A Justification for Toys as an Article of Commerce in Times of War," *Toys and Novelties* 14, no. 6 (1917): 49, TJ-CRL-Chicago.

148. Historians have long recognized America's entry into the First World War as a moment marking the Social Gospel's decline. Conrad Cherry has argued that the Social Gospel retreated into Protestant divinity schools and was alive and well there when Martin Luther King Jr. arrived at Boston University to study theology in the 1950s. See Conrad Cherry, *Hurrying toward Zion: Universities, Divinity Schools, and American Protestantism* (Bloomington: Indiana University Press, 1995). For other examples, see White and Hopkins, *Social Gospel*; Handy, *Social Gospel in America*; Gary Scott Smith, *The Search for Social Salvation: Social Christianity and America, 1880–1925* (Lanham, MD: Lexington Books, 2000); William D. Lindsey, *Shailer Mathews' Lives of Jesus: The Search for a Theological Foundation for the Social Gospel* (New York: State University of New York Press, 1997). As Lindsey noted, "World War I was the *kairos* moment for social gospel theology, the moment in which the fatuity of its belief in progress was exposed." See Lindsey, *Shailer Mathews' Lives of Jesus*, 13.

149. "Toys and 'The Spirit That Quickens,'" 49.

150. "Our Country's Call," *Playthings*, June 1917, 31, PMC-Rochester.

151. "American Toys," *Playthings*, January 1915, 30, PMC-Rochester.

152. "Toy Talks," *Toys and Novelties* 14, no. 7 (1917): 81–82, TJ-CRL-Chicago.

153. "All for America!" *Playthings* 15, no. 3, April 1917, 41, PMC-Rochester.

154. For patriotic window displays in toy departments, see Photograph of Christmas Toy Window at Mandel Brothers, Chicago, *Playthings*, December 1917, 21, PMC-Rochester; War-Time Toy Window at Van Ault Store, Atlantic City, NJ, *Playthings*, December 1917, 39, PMC-Rochester; Toy Window Display at W. J. Pettee & Co., Oklahoma City, OK, *Toys and Novelties* 14, no. 5 (1917), TJ-CRL-Chicago. For Liberty Bond

198   *Notes to Chapter 4*

ads, see "Fight or Buy Bonds," *Playthings*, April 1918, PMC-Rochester; and "Worth Fighting For?," Wigwam Co., Syracuse, NY, *Playthings*, April 1918, PMC-Rochester. On conducting patriotic plays in the toy department, see "Give a Patriotic Play in the Toy Department," *Playthings* 69, April 1917, PMC-Rochester.

155. Photograph of Walbridge & Co., Buffalo, NY, toy store, "Baby Week" window display, *Playthings*, October 1916, 64, PMC-Rochester; photograph of toy store "Baby Week" window display, unidentified store, *Playthings*, October 1916, 65, PMC-Rochester; photograph of Breineser Toy & Novelty Co., "Baby Week" window display, *Playthings*, May 1916, 51, PMC-Rochester.

156. Letter from Detroit Exhibit Campaign Committee, NCLC Scrapbooks, Form Letters, March 2, 1917, box 15, NCLC-LOC.

157. Constitution and By-Laws, Toy Manufacturers of the U.S.A., *Playthings*, June 1916, 63, PMC-Rochester.

158. "Flag Raising at Pittsburgh Toy Factory," *Toys and Novelties* 14, no. 5 (1917): 33, TJ-CRL-Chicago. See also "Maiden America—The National Doll," *Playthings*, March 1916, 10, PMC-Rochester; "Liberty Boy," *Playthings*, January 1918, 14, PMC-Rochester; "A Patriotic Sensation!—Uncle Sam's Kids," *Playthings*, April 1917, 1, PMC-Rochester.

159. Gilbert, *Man Who Lives in Paradise*, 57.

160. See "United States Supreme Toy Market: World War Has Resulted in Predominance of America as Source of Supply for Toys of all Description," *Toys and Novelties* 15, no. 2 (February 1918), 169, TJ-CRL-Chicago. See also Cross, *Kids' Stuff*, 29.

161. "The Trinity That Builds Patriotism," *Playthings*, 1918, PMC-Rochester.

162. "King Air Rifles," *Playthings*, January 1915, 27, PMC-Rochester.

163. "Boys Who Used to Play," *Toys and Novelties* 14, no. 9 (1917): 37, TJ-CRL-Chicago.

164. "Wolverine Automatics," *Toy and Novelties* 14, no. 7 (1917): 30, TJ-CRL-Chicago.

165. "Structo," *Playthings*, PMC-Rochester (undated).

166. "She Knows All about American-Made Toys," *Playthings*, 1918, PMC-Rochester.

167. Ibid.

168. "Little Mother Drowns German Dolls," *Playthings*, July 1918, 34, PMC-Rochester.

169. "The German Doll Is Now Made in America," *Playthings*, January 1915, 60, PMC-Rochester; "The Great American Doll," *Playthings*, November 1915, 12, PMC-Rochester.

170. "The Eugenic Baby," *Playthings*, April 1914, 79, PMC-Rochester. For more on the twentieth-century eugenics movement in America, see Nancy Ordover, *American Eugenics: Race, Queer Anatomy, and the Science of Nationalism* (Minneapolis: University of Minnesota Press, 2003). Ordover links the anti-immigration sentiment of the early twentieth century to the eugenics movement to eliminate the "unfit" from society. See also Stefan Kuhl, *The Nazi Connection: Eugenics, American Racism, and German National Socialism* (New York: Oxford University Press, 2004); and Marouf

Hasian, *The Rhetoric of Eugenics in Anglo-American Thought* (Athens: University of Georgia Press, 1966).

171. See "Uncle Sam's Kids," *Playthings*, April 1917, PMC-Rochester. As Lisa Jacobson put it, "Not surprisingly, the distinctive children's consumer culture that emerged during the interwar years replicated many of the class, racial, and gender stratifications of the wider society. National advertisers recognized white, urban, middle-class children as the most fully enfranchised child consumers, with boys leading the way." See L. Jacobson, *Raising Consumers*, 7.

172. Scrapbooks and Press Releases of the National Child Labor Committee, "Child Care and Conservation—National Child Labor Committee's Work Assumes New Significance in Attempts to Give Greater Measure of Protection," January 1919, box 25, NCLC-LOC.

173. Scrapbooks and Press Releases of the National Child Labor Committee, Owen Lovejoy, "Potential Man Power," May 1919, box 25, NCLC-LOC.

174. "Editorial and News Notes," *American Child* 1, no. 1, May 1919, 6.

Chapter 5. Cultural Warriors

1. As T. J. Jackson Lears noted in *No Place of Grace*, "At bottom the official doctrines were progressive. Faith in the beneficence of material progress has always been a central tenet of modern culture in America" (7). Around the turn of the century, "enthusiasm for material progress is difficult to chart because it was omnipresent and often implicit in the emergent modern culture" (8). Lears, *No Place of Grace: Antimodernism and the Transformation of American Culture, 1880–1920* (Chicago: University of Chicago Press, 1981).

2. For a nuanced discussion of the triumph of the bureaucratic worldview in the modern industrial age, see Lears, *No Place of Grace*, 302–3. Reformers' faith in bureaucracy was increasingly secularized and shaped by the modern child welfare movement, which embraced material progress and consumerist values.

3. Walter I. Trattner, *Crusade for the Children: A History of the National Child Labor Committee and Child Labor Reform in America* (Chicago: Quadrangle Books, 1970), 158.

4. Gertrude H. Folks, "Child Labor in Agriculture," *American Child* 3, no. 3 (1921), 267–73. See also "Children in War Industry," *The Survey* 41, no. 2 (1918), 49–50.

5. Trattner, *Crusade for the Children*, 153.

6. "A Plan to Safeguard Children in Farm Work," *The Survey* 38, no. 4 (1917), 86.

7. Owen R. Lovejoy, "Beginning Where We Don't Leave Off," *American Child* 3, no. 3 (1921), 101–2.

8. Ibid. In addition to being President Wilson's former secretary of agriculture, Houston had a well-known public career. He had been president of the Agricultural and Mechanical College of Texas, dean and president of the University of Texas, chancellor of Washington University, chairman of the Federal Board for Vocational Education, and chairman of the Farm Loan Board. See ibid., 102.

200   *Notes to Chapter 5*

9. Felix Adler, "The Next Step to Be Taken by the National Child Labor Committee," *American Child* 2, no. 2 (1920), 153.

10. Lovejoy, "Beginning Where We Don't Leave Off," 101.

11. "Rural Child Labor: A Symposium," *American Child* 3, no. 1 (1921), 33–50.

12. "Sixteenth National Conference on Child Labor," *American Child* 3, no. 1 (1921), 6.

13. "National Conference on Child Labor," *American Child* 3, no. 2 (1921), 161.

14. Trattner, *Crusade for the Children*, 149.

15. Grace Abbott, *Child and the State*, vol. 1: *Legal Status in the Family, Apprenticeship, and Child Labor* (Chicago: University of Chicago Press, 1938), 564.

16. "National Conference on Child Labor," 161, 162.

17. Charles E. Gibbons, "What Is Rural Child Labor?" *American Child* 3, no. 2 (1921), 175.

18. Ibid., 172.

19. Ibid. See also E. C. Lindeman, "Feeding the Spirit of Childhood," *American Child* 3, no. 2 (1921), 164–70.

20. Sara A. Brown, "Neglected Children of Appalachia," *American Child* 3, no. 2 (1921), 178.

21. See Louis Bernard Schmidt and Earle Dudley Ross, *Readings in the Economic History of American Agriculture* (Ithaca, NY: Cornell University Press, 1925), especially pp. 497–556, 573–82.

22. "National Conference on Child Labor," 162.

23. Beatrice McConnell, "Children in Agriculture," *Annals of the American Academy of Political and Social Science* 236 (1944), 92–100; "Chief of the United States Children's Bureau on Children in Agriculture," in Abbott, *Child and the State*, vol. 1, 570–75; "Children on the Beet Farms of Colorado in 1926," in Abbott, *Child and the State*, vol. 1, 575–78; "Agricultural Child Workers in California," in Abbott, *Child and the State*, vol. 1, 579–84; "Ohio Regulates Farm Work as Irregular Employment in 1921," in Abbott, *Child and the State*, vol. 1, 584–86. See also Trattner, *Crusade for the Children* 150–52.

24. Seventeenth Annual Report of the National Child Labor Committee, *American Child* 3, no. 3 (1921), 227–30.

25. Ibid., 231.

26. *Fifteenth Annual Report*, National Child Labor Committee, *American Child* 1, no. 3 (1919), 159.

27. Owen Lovejoy, prefatory note, in *Rural Child Welfare: An Inquiry by the National Child Labor Committee, Based upon Conditions in West Virginia* by Edward N. Clopper (New York: Macmillan, 1922), x.

28. Ruth Metzger, review of *Rural Child Welfare, The Survey* 48, no. 3 (1922), 83–84.

29. Mabel Carney, review of "Rural Child Welfare," *American Child* 4, no. 1 (May 1922), 19. Rural education professor Mabel Carney made the book required reading in her classes at Columbia University Teachers College as did sociology professor Frank H. Hankins of Clark University, sociology professor E. C. Branson at the

Notes to Chapter 5 201

University of North Carolina, and agriculture professor Kenyon L. Butterfield of Massachusetts Agricultural College. Nat T. Frame, director of agricultural extension at West Virginian University, recommended that a copy of *Rural Child Welfare* "be read carefully by every extension worker, school teacher, Farm Bureau member, and other country life leaders in West Virginia."

30. Ibid., 19–20.

31. Edward N. Clopper, introductory chapter, *Rural Child Welfare*, 1–4.

32. *Seventeenth Annual Report*, National Child Labor Committee, *American Child* 3, no. 3 (1921), 225.

33. Jacob A. Riis, *How the Other Half Lives: Studies among the Tenements of New York* (New York: Charles Scribner's Sons, 1890).

34. John F. Smith, "How the Other Half Lives in the Open Country," *Rural Manhood: Devoted to the Country Work of Young Men's Christian Associations in Village, Town, and Country* 10 (October 1919): 367. See also John F. Smith, "Religious Conditions among the Poor: How the Other Half Lives in the Open Country," in the same volume (3–6).

35. Reformers were quick to point out that the census of 1920 had grossly underestimated the actual numbers of child laborers. The 1910 census had reported 1,990,225 gainfully employed children, whereas the 1920 census reported only 1,060,858, which would have meant a staggering 46.7 percent decrease in child labor over the previous decade. Several factors had contributed to the 1920 deflation of the numbers, the most important of which was the underestimation of agricultural child labor. These numbers were artificially deflated by changing the census date from mid-April in 1910 (during harvest season) to mid-January in 1920, when agriculture was practically at a standstill. Other causes were the seasonality of certain types of agricultural labor and that children working on home farms were not considered "gainfully employed" unless they added to the family income. Moreover, the census did not include children under age ten, even though reformers had plenty of evidence that children under that age worked in the beet, cotton, tobacco, and onion fields as well as in tenement houses, street trades, and domestic service. See "Census Figures and Child Labor," *American Child* 4, no. 3 (1922), 1.

36. *United States Bureau of the Census, Fourteenth Census of the United States*, vol. 4: *Population 1920—Occupations* (Washington, DC: US Government Printing Office, 1923), 479. See Table 6, "Number and Percent Distribution, by General Divisions of Occupations, of the Gainfully Occupied Children of Each Sex 10 to 15 years of Age, in Each Principal Class of the Population, for the United States: 1920 and 1910."

37. "Tenth Annual Report of the Children Bureau, 1922," in Abbott, *Child and the State*, vol. 1, 572–74.

38. Charles E. Gibbons and Clara B. Armentrout, *Child Labor among Cotton Growers of Texas: A Study of Children Living in Rural Communities in Six Counties in Texas* (New York: National Child Labor Committee, 1925), 5, 6, 9.

39. See Mabel Carney, "The Status of Rural Education in the United States: A Memorandum," Seventeenth Annual Report of the National Child Labor Committee,

202 *Notes to Chapter 5*

American Child 3, no. 3 (1921), 274–81. Child labor reformers and "rural education" experts did not explicitly call for an end to racially segregated public schools. Instead, their concern was the inferiority of the rural lifestyle and rural education for what they deemed "country children," who were both black and white. As I show later in this chapter, African American commentators and reformers seized on this rural child welfare discourse to underscore the backwardness of the white South and to push for their own reform efforts, such as a federal antilynching law.

40. Clopper, *Rural Child Welfare*, 60–61.

41. Walter W. Armentrout, "Child Labor on Farms," in Clopper, *Rural Child Welfare*, 62–74.

42. The nine-month schooling standard was relatively new and had been endorsed by the International Child Welfare Conference called by the Children's Bureau in 1919. Many cities and towns in the United States had adopted that standard well before 1919, but rural communities rarely met it. On average, country children were in school two months fewer out of the year than city children. See Gertrude H. Folks, "Rural School Attendance," in Clopper, *Rural Child Welfare*, 94–139.

43. National Conference on Child Labor, *American Child* 3, no. 2 (1921), 161.

44. Clopper, *Rural Child Welfare*, 62.

45. Charles E. Gibbons, "The Rural Home," in Clopper, *Rural Child Welfare*, 12.

46. Clopper, "Administration," in Clopper, *Rural Child Welfare*, 286.

47. See "More Child Labor in Country," *Duluth News Tribune*, March 23, 1921, 12; "Child Labor Is Prevalent in Rural America—Work by Children in Farming Sections Responsible for Poor School Attendance," *Idaho Daily Statesman*, April 10, 1921, 5; "Report Will Show Child Labor Interferes with Schooling," *Daily Herald*, June 9, 1921, 1; "Build Up Rural Schools," *Morning Olympian* (Olympia, WA), June 2, 1921, 2; "Country Children Must Have Chance," *Idaho Daily Statesman*, June 12, 1921, 3; "Country Children," *Anaconda [MT] Standard*, June 23, 1921, 4; "Child Labor in Rural Districts," *Salt Lake Telegram*, June 27, 1921, 2; "Play on Farm Held Need," *Morning Oregonian*, July 16, 1921, 2; "Children of City Get Better Start," *Trenton [NJ] Evening Times*, August 1, 1921, 8; "Fair Deal for Country Child Held Crying Need," *Bellingham [WA] Herald*, December 5, 1921, 1; "Aid for Country Child Needed on Education Lines," *Columbia Ledger*, December 5, 1921, 8; "The Rural Child Neglected," *Lexington [KY] Herald*, December 6, 1921, 5; "Square Deal for Country Child," *Macon [GA] Daily Telegraph*, December 6, 1921, 5; "For Rural Child, Aid Too," *Kansas City Star*, January 10, 1922, 1; "Children of Gotham's Slums Better Off Than Many Rural Kiddies, Says Owen Lovejoy," *Kalamazoo Gazette*, March 21, 1922, 2; "Need of More Country Schools is Shown," *Perry [OK] Republican*, November 30, 1922, 1.

48. There is a rich literature on the intellectual and political foundations of the "freedom of contract" ideology that dominated the Lochner era of the Supreme Court (1897–1937), when the Court struck down economic and labor protections. See Eric Foner, *The Story of American Freedom* (New York: W. W. Norton,1998), 115–37; David Montgomery, *Beyond Equality: Labor and the Radical Republicans, 1862–1872* (Urbana: University of Illinois Press, 1981), 230–49; Heather Cox Richardson, *The Death of Reconstruction: Race, Labor, and Politics in the Post–Civil War North, 1865–1901*

Notes to Chapter 5 203

(Cambridge: Harvard University Press, 2004), 6–40; Amy Dru Stanley, *From Bondage to Contract: Wage Labor, Marriage, and the Market in the Age of Slave Emancipation* (New York: Cambridge University Press, 1998).

49. In *Hammer v. Dagenhart* (June 1918), the Supreme Court declared Keating-Owen unconstitutional in a 5 to 4 decision on the grounds that the bill was an inappropriate use of the commerce power, as it did not regulate interstate commerce but instead local labor conditions. Thus, it was ruled to be a violation of states' rights. See https://www .law.cornell.edu/supremecourt/text/247/251, retrieved September 23, 2019.

50. "Taxes to Drive Out Child Labor," *The Survey* 41, no. 8 (1918), 221.

51. "The New Federal Child Labor Law," *American Child* 1, no. 1 (1919), 8.

52. Ibid., 8–9.

53. For the full-text of the Court's opinion in the case *Bailey v. Drexel Furniture Company*, 259 U.S. 20 (1922), see http://caselaw.lp.findlaw.com/scripts/getcase.pl?navby =case&court=us&vol=259&invol=20, retrieved September 23, 2019. See also "The Second Federal Child Law Held Unconstitutional in the Child Labor Tax Case," in Abbott, *Child and the State*, 1:520–25. For a sample of contemporaneous responses to the Court's decision, see "Child Labor Law Declared Invalid—Supreme Court Holds 1919 Act Unconstitutional in That It Usurps State Functions," *New York Times*, May 16, 1922, 1; "Invalid," *The Survey* 43, no. 8 (1922), 266–67; "Child Labor Law Is Unconstitutional and Invalid," *Columbus [OH] Ledger*, May 15, 1922, 1; "A Dead Law," *Charlotte Observer*, May 16, 1922, 6; "Child Labor Act Hit—Supreme Court Declares Unconstitutional," *Kansas City Star*, May 15, 1922, 1; "Child Labor Law Invalid," *Evening News* (Harrisburg, PA), May 15, 1922, 1; "Child Labor Law Is Invalid—Act Held Invasion of State Power," *Fort Worth Star-Telegram*, May 15, 1922, 1; "Child Labor Law Declared Invalid," *Baltimore-American*, May 16, 1922, 3.

54. Trattner, *Crusade for the Children*, 163.

55. See "Editorial Comment on Child Labor Decision," *American Child* 4, no. 1 (1922), 91.

56. Ibid., 91–92.

57. For scholarship on Prohibition, see Norman H. Clark, *Deliver Us from Evil: An Interpretation of American Prohibition* (New York: W. W. Norton, 1976); Michael A. Lerner, *Dry Manhattan: Prohibition in New York City* (Cambridge: Harvard University Press, 2007); and Daniel Okrent, *Last Call: The Rise and Fall of Prohibition* (New York: Scribner, 2010). On women's suffrage, see Aileen S. Kraditor, *The Ideas of the Woman Suffrage Movement, 1890–1920* (New York: W. W. Norton, 1981); Ellen Dubois, *Woman Suffrage and Women's Rights* (New York: New York University Press, 1998); Jean H. Baker, *Votes for Women: The Struggle for Suffrage Revisited* (New York: Oxford University Press, 2002).

58. "Editorial Comment," *American Child* (May 1922), 93.

59. "Working Children," *The Survey* 48, no. 10 (1922), 381.

60. "Will Fight to Save Children from Toil—Federation of Labor Plans an Active Campaign for a Constitutional Amendment—National Meeting Called—Leaders Will Discuss Means to Overcome Supreme Court Rulings against Child Labor Laws," *New York Times*, May 26, 1922, 19.

Notes to Chapter 5

61. "Organizes for Law to End Child Labor—Gompers Heads New Body Seeking Amendment to the Constitution," *New York Times*, June 2, 1922, 15.

62. "Will Fight to Save Children from Toil," *New York Times*, 19.

63. Ibid. When Gompers spoke to the press, he often framed the issue in terms of childhood emancipation.

64. "Organizes for Law to End Child Labor," *New York Times*, 15. See also "Draft Amendment to End Child Labor—Twenty-five Organizations Decide to Submit Measure to Congress This Winter," *New York Times*, November 21, 1922, 21.

65. "Organizes for Law to End Child Labor," *New York Times*, 15.

66. For more on the antilynching crusade, see Paula Giddings, *Ida: A Sword among Lions: Ida B. Wells and the Campaign against Lynching* (New York: HarperCollins, 2008). For a starting point on African American Progressive reform, see Nora Lee Frankel and Nancy S. Dye, eds., *Gender, Class, Race, and Reform in the Progressive Era* (Lexington: University Press of Kentucky, 1991).

67. "Indiana Women Condemn Lynching, Child Labor," *Chicago Defender*, June 17, 1922, 3.

68. Ibid.

69. "An Object Lesson," *Chicago Defender*, July 29, 1922, 12.

70. "Child Labor Amendment," *Chicago Defender*, October 27, 1924, 12.

71. "Prominent Social Workers Discuss American Problem," *Chicago Defender*, December 13, 1924, 4.

72. "Zion Bishops Give Message on Problems," *Chicago Defender*, February 7, 1925, A1.

73. Press Release of the National Child Labor Committee, untitled, September 1, 1922, box 30, Records of the National Child Labor Committee, U.S., Manuscript Division, Library of Congress, Washington, DC (hereafter cited as NCLC-LOC).

74. "Seventeenth National Conference on Child Labor," *American Child* 4, no. 2 (1922), 70, 71.

75. Wilson tried to garner support for the Treaty of Versailles, but the Senate rejected it after acrimonious debate primarily over the League of Nations. See David J. Goldberg, *Discontented America: The United States in the 1920s* (Baltimore: Johns Hopkins University Press, 1999), 20–26. See also Robert K. Murray, *Red Scare: A Study in National Hysteria, 1919–1920* (Minneapolis: University of Minnesota Press, 1955), 3–9.

76. Ibid., 25.

77. Ibid., 10.

78. For instance, Socialist Party leader Eugene V. Debs was convicted under the Espionage Act and imprisoned for expressing antiwar views and for interfering with military recruitment. For more on wartime repression of dissent, see H. C. Peterson and Gilbert C. Fite, *Opponents of War, 1917–1918* (Madison: University of Wisconsin Press, 1957); William Preston Jr., *Aliens and Dissenters: Federal Suppression of Radicals, 1903–1933* (Urbana: University of Illinois Press, 1994); and Harry N. Scheiber, *The Wilson Administration and Civil Liberties, 1917–1921* (Ithaca, NY: Cornell University Press, 1960).

79. See Murray, *Red Scare*, 15.

Notes to Chapter 5

80. Quoted in ibid., 17.

81. Goldberg, *Discontented America*, 42.

82. Ibid., 48.

83. See Wesley M. Bagby, *The Road to Normalcy: The Presidential Campaign and Election of 1920* (Baltimore: Johns Hopkins University Press, 1962); and Donald R. McCoy, "The Election of 1920," in *History of American Presidential Elections*, ed. Arthur M. Schlesinger Jr. and Fred L. Israel (New York: Chelsea House, 1971).

84. Linda Gordon's *The Second Coming of the KKK: The Second Ku Klux Klan of the 1920s and the American Political Tradition* (New York: W. W. Norton, 2017) argues that the Klan of this decade was surprisingly widespread and ordinary, infiltrating national politics at the highest levels and focused in the North.

85. See James Grossman, *Land of Hope: Chicago, Black Southerners, and the Great Migration* (Chicago: University of Chicago Press, 1989).

86. Ronald Allen Goldberg, *America in the Twenties* (Syracuse, NY: Syracuse University Press, 2003), 18.

87. See Kim E. Nielsen, *Un-American Womanhood: Antiradicalism, Antifeminism, and the First Red Scare* (Columbus: Ohio State University Press, 2001), especially 104–5.

88. Goldberg, *Discontented America*, 66–88.

89. Henry F. May, *Protestant Churches and Industrial America* (New York: Harper and Brothers, 1949), 231.

90. See George M. Marsden, *Fundamentalism and American Culture: The Shaping of Twentieth-Century Evangelicalism, 1870–1925* (New York: Oxford University Press, 1980), 141–53.

91. Ibid., 146. As Marsden argues, "World War I was a tremendous challenge to faith in the progress of both culture and kingdom. European culture, for all its faults, had generally been viewed—together with its American offspring—as the best hope for the world. Now it seemed bent on destroying on itself."

92. Ibid., 148–49. Walter Rauschenbusch, the best-known articulator of Social Gospel theology, was deeply influenced by German higher criticism.

93. Ibid.

94. Ibid., 159.

95. Famously, the controversy between fundamentalists who favored the teaching of creationism and modernists who favored the teaching of evolution came to a head in the summer of 1925 at the Scopes Trial in Dayton, Tennessee, when a teacher was put on trial for teaching evolution in the classroom. See Edward John Larson, *Summer for the Gods: The Scopes Trial and America's Continuing Debate over Science and Religion* (New York: Basic Books, 1997).

96. Marsden, *Fundamentalism and American Culture*, 164.

97. Lawrence W. Levine, "Progress and Nostalgia: The Self Image of the Nineteen Twenties," in *The Unpredictable Past: Explorations in American Cultural History* (New York: Oxford University Press, 1993), 197. See also Robert Moats Miller, "A Note on the Relationship between the Protestant Churches and the Revived Ku Klux Klan," *Journal of Southern History* 22 (August 1956): 368.

206   *Notes to Chapter 5*

98. Text of Proposed Constitutional Amendment, *American Child* 4, no. 2 (1922), 72–73.

99. Ibid., 70. See also Trattner, *Crusade for the Children*, 167–68.

100. "Explain Child Labor Stand—Proposed Amendment Different from a Law, Says Committee," *New York Times*, October 1, 1922, 34.

101. Ibid.

102. Richard B. Sherman, "The Rejection of the Child Labor Amendment," *Mid-America*, January 1963, 6. See also Trattner, *Crusade for the Children*, 165.

103. "For Child Labor Control—Senate Committee Approves Bill for Constitutional Amendment," *New York Times*, February 20, 1923, 16.

104. "The Children Who Picked Your Cranberries," *American Child* 4, no. 3 (1922), 4.

105. "What Thanksgiving Day Cost," *American Child* 4, no. 3 (1922), 4.

106. "Child Labor Day Where You Live," *American Child* 4, no. 4 (1922), 4.

107. Statement of Mr. Owen R. Lovejoy, Executive Secretary, National Child Labor Committee, *Proposed Child Labor Amendments to the Constitution of the United States—Hearings before the Committee on the Judiciary House of Representatives—Sixty-Eighth Congress, First Session—February 7, 15, 16, 27, 28, and 29, 1924, and March 1, 6, 7, and 8, 1924—Serial 16* (Washington, DC: US Government Printing Office, 1924), 76.

108. Ibid., 76–77.

109. Statement of Hon. Frederick W. Dallinger, a Representative in Congress from Massachusetts, in ibid., 7.

110. Statement of Miss Grace Abbott, Chief of the Children's Bureau, United States Department of Labor, in ibid., 35–36.

111. Ibid., 37.

112. See Molly Ladd-Taylor, "Federal Help for Mothers: The Rise and Fall of the Sheppard-Towner Act in the 1920s," in *Gendered Domains: Rethinking Public and Private in Women's History,* ed. Dorothy O. Helly and Susan M. Reverby, 217–27 (Ithaca, NY: Cornell University Press, 1992); and Jan Doolittle Wilson, "The Lobby for the Sheppard-Towner Bill, 1921," in *The Women's Joint Congressional Committee and the Politics of Maternalism, 1920–1930* (Urbana: University of Illinois Press, 2007), 27–49.

113. Statement of Mrs. Ruben Ross Holloway, of Baltimore, Maryland, Representing the Women's Constitutional League of Maryland, in *Proposed Child Labor Amendments*, 107.

114. Ibid.

115. Ibid.

116. Statement of Mr. Willis R. Jones, Attorney at Law, Baltimore, Maryland, in *Proposed Child Labor Amendments*, 99, 105, 106.

117. Sentinels of the Republic to Alice Robertson, March 3, 1923, Alice M. Robertson Collection, McFarlin Library, University of Tulsa, Series 2: Correspondence, box 20, folder 1.

118. Ibid.

Notes to Chapter 5   207

119. Statement of Mr. Louis A. Coolidge, Boston, Massachusetts, Chairman of the Sentinels of the Republic, in *Proposed Child Labor Amendments*, 216.

120. Ibid., 218–19. The Sentinels opposed federal aid to education and federal funding of maternity and infancy care for women for similar reasons. The group's motto was "Every citizen a Sentinel! Every home a sentry box." See Sentinels of the Republic to Alice Robertson, March 3, 1923, Alice M. Robertson Collection, McFarlin Library, University of Tulsa, series 2: Correspondence, box 20, folder 1.

121. Kathryn Kish Sklar and Beverly Wilson Palmer, eds., *The Selected Letters of Florence Kelley, 1869–1931* (Urbana: University of Illinois Press, 2009), 288.

122. Statement of Miss Mary G. Kilbreth, President of the Woman Patriotic Publishing Company, in *Proposed Child Labor Amendments*, 159–60, 178.

123. "Foes of the Amendment," *American Child* 4, no. 3 (1924), 2.

124. Statement of Mr. James A. Emery, General Counsel of the National Association of Manufacturers of the United States, in *Proposed Child Labor Amendments*, 204, 212–13.

125. Ibid., 213.

126. Congressional Record—Proceedings and Debates of the First Session of the Sixty-Eighth Congress of the United States of America, 65, Part 7, April 26, 1924, 7300.

127. Ibid.

128. Ibid., 7305.

129. Ibid., April 25, 1924, 7198. In Roman mythology, "Lares and Penates" were gods who served as guardians of the household. See https://www.merriam-webster .com/dictionary/lares and penates, retrieved January 9, 2020.

130. Ibid., 7199.

131. Ibid., April 26, 1924, 7312.

132. Ibid., 7308.

133. Ibid., 7305.

134. Ibid., 7298.

135. Ibid., 7313. To make his point, Representative Weaver all but gave the congressmen a history lesson:

> At the time the Constitution was adopted, the 13 original states were sparsely settled. There were no manufacturing plants worth mentioning. Industry had not spread itself over the Nation as it has today. There were no great congested centers of population. We were a pioneer people. There were no telegraphs. There were no telephones. There were no railroads. The steamboats had not been invented, and the methods of communication were slow and uncertain. It is but natural that under those conditions the States should have been jealous of their reserved powers. . . . A central Government in Washington remote from the States themselves was a matter of concern to all of the 13 original Commonwealths.

136. Ibid., 7317, 7318.

208 *Notes to Chapter 5*

137. Ibid., June 2, 1924, 10122.

138. Ibid., 7295. See also Elizabeth H. Davidson, *Child Labor Legislation in the Southern Textile States* (Chapel Hill: University of North Carolina Press, 1939), 270; "Senate and House Committees Report Favorably on Child Labor Amendment," *American Child* 6, no. 4 (1924), 1; "The First Victory," *American Child* 6, no. 5 (1924), 1–7; Geddes Smith, "Ghosts v. Children," *The Survey* 51 (March 15, 1924), 673–76; "Child Labor Ban Approved by House: Vote Is 297 to 69 for Proposal to Amend the Constitution to Permit Action—Uniform Law Is Sought—Advocates in Debate Stress Need of States—Opponents Fear Federal Dominance," *New York Times*, April 27, 1924, 1.

139. Congressional Record—Proceedings and Debates of the First Session of the Sixty-Eighth Congress of the United States of America, 65, Part 10, June 2, 1924, 10142. See also "Back to the People," *American Child* 6, no. 7 (1924), 1, 6; and "100 Plans Now Afoot to Amend Constitution: Child Labor Amendment Recently Passed—Proposal to Install New Administration Soon after Election—Only 19 Changes in Century," *New York Times*, June 15, 1924, 8.

140. See *American Child* 6, no. 7 (1924), 2.

141. "Arkansas First State to Ratify Amendment—1 Up, 35 to Go," *American Child* 6, no. 7 (1924), 1; "First State Ratifies: Arkansas Senate Votes for the Child Labor Amendment," *New York Times*, June 29, 1924, 2; "Arkansas Makes a Record: First to Complete Ratification of Child Labor Amendment," *New York Times*, June 30, 1924, 16.

142. "Campaign for Ratification of the Amendment," in *History of Labor in the United States, 1896–1932*, vols. 3 and 4, ed. John R. Commons, Don D. Lescohier, and Elizabeth Brandeis (New York: Macmillan, 1935), 446.

143. Albion Guilford Taylor, "Labor Policies of the National Association of Manufacturers," *University of Illinois Studies in the Social Sciences*, 15, no. 1 (1927): 130–31.

144. "Who Are against the Amendment?," July 1924, box 40, Edith and Grace Abbott Papers, University of Chicago, Special Collections Regenstein Library, Chicago, IL (hereafter cited as EGAP-SC-Chicago).

145. Taylor, "Labor Policies," 131.

146. Farmers States Rights League, Grace Abbott's Notes on the Opposition, June 1924, box 95, folder 4, EGAP-SC-Chicago.

147. Ibid. See also Commons et al., *History of Labor*, 448; and Katharine DuPre Lumpkin and Dorothy Wolff Douglas, *Child Workers in America* (New York: Robert M. McBride, 1937), 208–9.

148. Taylor, "Labor Policies," 132–33.

149. For instance, the NCLC hired preeminent legal scholars in the country, like Professor Roscoe Pound of Harvard Law School, to write pamphlets rebutting the false charges of the amendment's opponents. See "Dean Roscoe Pound of Harvard Law School on the Child Labor Amendment," pamphlet, October 1924, box 1, folder 8, National Consumers League Records, Kheel Center, Cornell University, Ithaca, NY (hereafter cited as NCL-KC-Cornell). See also "Let the Facts Be Known," February 1925, box 1, folder 8, NCL-KC-Cornell.

Notes to Chapter 5   209

150. NCLC pamphlet, "Brass Tacks on the Pending Child Labor Amendment to the Federal Constitution," undated, box 40, EGAP-SC-Chicago. See also "The Pending Child Labor Amendment: Questions and Answers," undated pamphlet, box 1, folder 5, NCL-KC-Cornell.

151. E. C. Lindeman, "Child Labor Amendment and the Farmers," *American Review of Reviews: An International Magazine* 70 (July 1924), 62–65.

152. Sherman, "Rejection of the Child Labor Amendment," 7.

153. Quoted in *The Nation* 119 (November 12, 1924), 509.

154. Sherman, "Rejection of the Child Labor Amendment," 13. See also Trattner, *Crusade for the Children*, 175.

155. "Lost Children's Amendment," January 1925, box 93, folder 1, EGAP-SC-Chicago.

156. Leaflet issued by the Citizens' Committee to Protect our Homes and Children, in Commons et al., *History of Labor*, 447. See also "Catholics and Child Labor," *The Nation* 120, no. 3107 (1925), 59.

157. Sherman, "Rejection of the Child Labor Amendment," 13.

158. Ibid.

159. "The Pilot," October 4, 1924, box 40, EGAP-SC-Chicago.

160. Commons et al., *History of Labor*, 448–49; and Sherman, "Rejection of the Child Labor Amendment," 12–13.

161. Pamphlet to Catholics, Father John A. Ryan, "The Proposed Child Labor Amendment," October 1924, box 95, folder 6, EGAP-SC-Chicago.

162. Walter F. Dodd, "Advisory Referendum in Massachusetts on the Child Labor Amendment," *American Political Science Review* 19, no. 1 (1925): 69–73; "Senator Walsh Scores Propaganda against Child Labor Amendment," *American Labor Legislation Review* 15, rev. 119 (1925): 123–24. See also "The Struggle for the Child Labor Amendment—As Revealed by the Massachusetts Referendum," pamphlet, January 1925, box 40, EGAP-SC-Chicago.

163. Sherman, "Rejection of the Child Labor Amendment," 13l. See also "Catholics and Child Labor," *The Nation*, 59.

164. Trattner, *Crusade for the Children*, 176; Commons et al., *History of Labor*, 449; and "Misinformed Massachusetts," *The Survey* 53, no. 4 (1924), 177–78.

165. "Status of Amendment Action by States," *American Child* 7, no. 3 (1925), 8.

166. Quoted in Trattner, *Crusade for the Children*, 178.

167. "Massachusetts Spent $15,522 to Defeat Child Labor Amendment," *American Child* 7, no. 1 (1925), 5.

168. Lumpkin and Douglas, *Child Workers in America*, 210.

169. Mr. J. H. Walker, President, The Illinois Federation of Labor, in a Radio Talk over W.O.C. (Davenport, IL), March 13, 1925, box 40, EGAP-SC-Chicago.

170. "Exposing Cotton Mills Fake 'Farmers' League,'—A Fake and a Fraud," January 1925, box 40, EGAP-SC-Chicago. See also "Farmers' States Rights League Is Ferreted Out—Leading Opponent of Amendment Not a Farmers' Organization," *American Child* 7, no. 3 (1925), 1; "Southern Textile Interests Organize a Farmers' States Rights

210   *Notes to Chapter 5 and Conclusion*

League to Oppose the Amendment," in Grace Abbott, *Child and the State*, 537–42; and Commons et al., *History of Labor*, 448.

171. William L. Chenery, "Child Labor—The New Alignment," *The Survey* 53, no. 7 (1925), 379–82; 425–26.

172. S. G. McLendon, Secretary of the State of Georgia, "The Right to Make Labor a Crime—A Startling Proposition," *Manufacturers' Record* 86, no. 14 (1924), 91, in Anne Kruesi Brown, "Opposition to the Child Labor Amendment Found in Trade Journals, Industrial Bulletins, and Other Publications for and by Business Men," unpublished dissertation, University of Chicago (March 1937), 46.

173. *Manufacturers' News* 26 (August 30, 1924), 45, in Brown, "Opposition to the Child Labor Amendment," 46.

174. Ibid.

175. Hubert C. Herring, "The Shame of Massachusetts," *The Christian Century: An Undenominational Journal of Religion* 41, no. 50 (1924): 1594–95.

176. A. Maude Royden, "Christianity and Politics," *Federal Council Bulletin: A Journal of Religious Cooperation and Inter-Church Activities* 8, no. 3 (1925): 25.

177. Ibid. For more on the continued involvement of the Social Gospel FCCC with the child labor movement, including the battle for the Child Labor Amendment, see Rev. Worth M. Tippy, "The Interest of the Churches in Child Labor," *Federal Council Bulletin* 8, no. 1 (1925): 12.

178. By November 1925 a staggering twenty-two states had voted to reject ratification of the Child Labor Amendment while only four had ratified. See "Constitutional Amendment," *American Child* 9, no. 11 (1925), 1.

179. "Child Labor, the Home, and Liberty," *New Republic*, December 3, 1924.

180. Ibid.

Conclusion

1. "Twentieth-Fifth Anniversary Conference," *American Child* 11, no. 10 (1929), 6–7.

2. Honorable Franklin D. Roosevelt, Governor of the State of New York, "The Function of Government in Child Protection," *American Child* 12, no. 1 (1930), 1.

3. "Child Labor Curbs to Be Celebrated—Progress of Quarter Century to Be Discussed Here at White House Conference—Committee Declares Much Remains to Be Accomplished before Protection Is Complete," *New York Times*, December 15, 1929, N20.

4. Ibid.

5. Roosevelt, "Function of Government," 3–4.

6. Walter I. Trattner, *Crusade for the Children: A History of the National Child Labor Committee and Child Labor Reform in America* (Chicago: Quadrangle Books, 1970), 184–85.

7. "Time to Ratify," *Collier's*, April 10, 1937, box 35, folder 10, Edith and Grace Abbott Papers, University of Chicago, Special Collections Regenstein Library, Chicago, IL (hereafter cited as EGAP-SC-Chicago).

Notes to Conclusion 211

8. *American Child* 16 (January 1934), 1.

9. "The National Recovery Act," May 1937, box 35, folder 10, EGAP-SC-Chicago.

10. Ibid.

11. *American Child* 16 (January 1934), 1.

12. "Handbook on the Federal Child Labor Amendment," 1937, box 1, National Child Labor Committee Records, Kheel Center, Cornell University, Ithaca, NY (hereafter cited as NCLC-KC-Cornell).

13. Ibid. See also Trattner, *Crusade for the Children*, 198–99.

14. "Handbook on the Federal Child Labor Amendment," 1937, box 1, NCLC-KC-Cornell.

15. See Leonard Baker, *Back to Back: The Duel between FDR and the Supreme Court* (New York: Macmillan, 1967); and Marian C. McKenna, *Franklin Roosevelt and the Great Constitutional War: The Court-Packing Crisis of 1937* (New York: Fordham University Press, 2002).

16. "The Fair Labor Standards Act of 1938," July 1938, box 35, folder 9, EGAP-SC-Chicago.

17. Ibid.

18. Ibid.

19. "President's Curbs on Child Labor," May 27, 1937, box 35, folder 7, EGAP-SC-Chicago.

20. "Time to Ratify."

21. Trattner, *Crusade for the Children*, 206.

22. "Time to Ratify."

23. "President's Curbs on Child Labor."

24. "Old Evils of Child Labor Curbed by Wage-Hour Law—With Cooperation of the States and Backing of the Public, a Long Crusade Is Believed to Be Approaching a Successful Ending," *New York Times*, January 8, 1939, 51.

25. Quoted in Trattner, *Crusade for the Children*, 204.

Bibliography

Manuscript Collections

The Brian Sutton-Smith Library and Archives of Play (The National Museum of Play)
    Playthings Magazine Collection
The Center for Research Libraries
    Trade Journals Collection
The Kheel Center for Labor-Management Documentation and Archives, Cornell University, Ithaca, NY
    American Association for Labor Legislation Records
    Consumers' League of New York City Records
    National Child Labor Committee Records
    National Consumers' League Records
The Library of Congress
    Records of the National Child Labor Committee, US
The New York Public Library, Manuscripts and Archives Division
    Florence Kelley Papers
The University of Chicago Special Collections Research Center
    Edith and Grace Abbott Papers
The University of North Carolina Louis Round Wilson Library, Southern Historical Collection
    Edgar Gardner Murphy Papers
The University of Tulsa McFarlin Library
    Alice M. Robertson Collection

Newspapers

Anaconda Standard
Baltimore American
Baltimore Sun

214   *Bibliography*

Bellingham Herald
Boston Daily Globe
Boston Post
Charlotte Observer
Chicago Daily Tribune
Chicago Defender
Cleveland Plain Dealer
Columbus Ledger
Daily Herald
Dallas Morning News
Duluth News Tribune
Evening News
Flake's Bulletin
Fort Wayne News and Sentinel
Fort Worth Star-Telegram
Grand Forks Herald
Idaho Daily Statesman
Kalamazoo Gazette
Kansas City Star
Lexington Herald
Macon Daily Telegraph
Memphis Daily Avalanche
Morning Olympian
Morning Oregonian
New York Mail
New York Times
The Patriot
Perry Republican
Philadelphia Inquirer
Salt Lake Telegram
San Francisco Bulletin
San Francisco Journal
The State
Times-Picayune
Trenton Evening Times
Trenton State Gazette
Tucson Daily Citizen
Tulsa Daily World
Wilkes-Barre Times

Periodicals

The American Child
The American Review of Reviews
Annual Reports of the Children's Aid Society

The Arena
Charities Review
Child Labor Bulletin
Christian Century
Cosmopolitan: A Monthly Illustrated Magazine
Current Opinion
The Dial
Federal Council Bulletin
Good Housekeeping
Harper's Weekly
Life
Massachusetts Report of the Bureau of Statistics of Labor
The Nation
The New Republic
The Outlook
Rural Manhood
Scribner's Monthly
The Social Welfare Forum
Survey Magazine
The World's Work

Journals

American Journal of Sociology
American Labor Legislation Review
American Law Times: U.S. Court Reports
American Political Science Review
Annals of the American Academy of Political and Social Science
Harvard Educational Review
Indiana Magazine of History
Journal of Negro Education
Journal of Social History
Journal of Southern History
Manufacturers' Record
Mid-America: An Historical Review
North American Review
North Carolina Historical Review
Playthings
Toys and Novelties
University of Illinois Studies in the Social Sciences

Court Cases

Ancarola v. United States (1880)
Bailey v. Drexel Furniture Company (1922)

216   *Bibliography*

Champion v. Ames (1903)
Dred Scott v. Sandford (1857)
Hammer v. Dagenhart (1918)
Hoke v. United States (1913)
Muller v. Oregon (1908)
Plessy v. Ferguson (1896)
West Coast Hotel Co. v. Parrish (1937)

Government Publications

Census Records of the United States Bureau of the Census
The Congressional Record: Proceedings and Debates of the U.S. Congress
Journal of the Senate of the State of New York
Proposed Child Labor Amendments to the Constitution of the United States—Hearings before the Committee on the Judiciary House of Representatives—Sixty-Eighth Congress

Books and Articles (Primary and Secondary)

Abbot, Edith. "A Study of the Early History of Child Labor in America." *American Journal of Sociology* 14, no. 1 (1908): 15–37.

Abbot, Leonard D. "Edwin Markham: Laureate of Labor," *Comrade* 1, no. 4 (1902): 74–75.

Abbott, Grace. *The Child and the State: Legal Status in the Family, Apprenticeship, and Child Labor.* 2 vols. Chicago: University of Chicago Press, 1938.

Abzug, Robert H. *Cosmos Crumbling: American Reform and the Religious Imagination.* New York: Oxford University Press, 1994.

Alger, Horatio, Jr. *Phil, the Fiddler; or, the Story of a Young Street Musician.* Philadelphia: Porter and Coates, 1872.

Alphonso, Gwendolyn. "Of Families or Individuals? Southern Child Workers and the Progressive Crusade for Child Labor Regulation, 1899–1920." In *Child and Youth during the Gilded Age and Progressive Era*, ed. James Marten, 59–80. New York: New York University Press, 2014.

Anbinder, Tyler. *Nativism and Slavery: The Northern Know Nothings and the Politics of the 1850s.* New York: Oxford University Press, 1992.

Ariès, Phillipe. *Centuries of Childhood.* New York: Vintage Books, 1962.

Armentrout, Walter W. "Child Labor on Farms." In Clopper, *Rural Child Welfare,* 62–74.

Arnold, Fred, et al. *The Value of Children.* Honolulu: East-West Population Institute, 1975.

Ashby, Irene M. "Child Labor in Southern Cotton Mills: A Personal Investigation of Its Extent and Abuses—The South Going through the Barbarous Experience of England and New England—Abuses That Cry to Heaven for Correction," *World's Work*, vol. 2 (May 1901–October 1901): 1290–95.

Bibliography

Ashworth, John. "Free Labor, Wage Labor, and the Slave Power: Republicanism and the Republican Party in the 1850s." In *The Market Revolution in America: Social, Political, and Religious Expressions, 1800–1860,* edited by Melvyn Stokes and Stephen Conway, 28–46. Charlottesville: University Press of Virginia, 1996.

———. *Slavery, Capitalism, and Politics in the Antebellum Republic.* Vol. 2, *The Coming of the Civil War, 1850–1861.* New York: Cambridge University Press, 1995.

Axelrod, Alan. *Selling the Great War: The Making of American Propaganda.* New York: Macmillan, 2009.

Ayers, Edward L. *Promise of the New South: Life after Reconstruction.* New York: Oxford University Press, 1992.

Bagby, Wesley M. *The Road to Normalcy: The Presidential Campaign and Election of 1920.* Baltimore: Johns Hopkins University Press, 1962.

Bailey, Hugh C. *Edgar Gardner Murphy: Gentle Progressive.* Coral Gables, FL: University of Miami Press, 1968.

Bailyn, Bernard. *The Ideological Origins of the American Revolution.* Cambridge: Harvard University Press, 1967.

Baker, Jean H. *Votes for Women: The Struggle for Suffrage Revisited.* New York: Oxford University Press, 2002.

Baker, Leonard. *Back to Back: The Duel between FDR and the Supreme Court.* New York: Macmillan, 1967.

Baldwin, B. J. "History of Child Labor Reform in Alabama." *Annals of the American Academy of Political and Social Science* 38 (July 1911): 111–13.

Bannister, Richard. *Social Darwinism: Science and Myth in Anglo-American Social Thought.* Philadelphia: Temple University Press, 1979.

Barnes, Gilbert H. *The Anti-Slavery Impulse, 1830–1844.* New York: Harcourt Brace, 1964.

Becker, Gary S. *A Treatise on the Family.* Cambridge: Harvard University Press, 1981.

Beckert, Sven. *The Monied Metropolis: New York City and the Consolidation of the American Bourgeoisie, 1850–1896.* New York: Cambridge University Press, 2003.

Bederman, Gail. *Manliness and Civilization: A Cultural History of Gender and Race in the United States, 1880–1917.* Chicago: University of Chicago Press, 1995.

Bender, Thomas, ed. *The Antislavery Debate: Capitalism and Abolitionism as a Problem in Historical Interpretation.* Berkeley: University of California Press, 1992.

Bendroth, Margaret. "Horace Bushnell's *Christian Nurture.*" In *The Child in Christian Thought,* edited by Marcia JoAnn Bunge, 350–64. Grand Rapids, MI: William B. Eerdmans Publishers, 2001.

Berlin, Ira. *Many Thousands Gone: The First Two Centuries of Slavery in North America.* Cambridge: Harvard University Press, 1998.

Berry, Mary Frances. "Repression of Blacks in the South, 1890–1945: Enforcing the System of Segregation." In *The Age of Segregation: Race Relations in the South, 1890–1945,* edited by Robert Haws, 29–44. Oxford: University of Mississippi Press, 2008.

Beveridge, Albert J. "The March of the Flag" (1898). In *An American Primer,* edited by Daniel Boorstin, 621–29. Chicago: University of Chicago Press, 1966.

Blassingame, John. *Black New Orleans, 1860–1880*. Chicago: University of Chicago Press, 1973.

———. *The Slave Community: Plantation Life in the Antebellum South*. New York: Oxford University Press, 1972.

Blight, David W. *Race and Reunion: The Civil War in American Memory*. Cambridge: Harvard University Press, 2002.

Blum, Edward J. *Reforging the White Republic: Race, Religion, and American Nationalism, 1865–1898*. Baton Rouge: Louisiana State University Press, 2007.

Boorstin, Daniel, ed. *An American Primer*. Chicago: University of Chicago Press, 1966.

Boris, Eileen. *Home to Work: Motherhood and the Politics of Industrial Homework in the United States*. New York: Cambridge University Press, 1994.

Boydston, Jeanne. *Home and Work: Housework, Wages, and the Ideology of Labor in the Early Republic*. New York: Oxford University Press, 1994.

Boyer, Paul. *Urban Masses and Moral Order in America, 1820–1920*. Cambridge: Harvard University Press, 1978.

Brace, Charles Loring. *The Dangerous Classes of New York and Twenty Years' Work among Them*. New York: Wynkoop and Hallenbeck, 1872.

———. *Home-Life in Germany*. New York: Charles Scribner, 1853.

Brace, Charles Loring, and Emma Brace. *The Life of Charles Loring Brace, Chiefly Told in His Own Letters*. New York: Charles Scribner's Sons, 1894.

Braeman, John. *Albert J. Beveridge: American Nationalist*. Chicago: University of Chicago Press, 1971.

Brekus, Catherine A. "Children of Wrath, Children of Grace: Jonathan Edwards and the Puritan Culture of Child Rearing." In Bunge, *Child in Christian Thought*, 300–328.

Bronner, Simon J., ed. *Consuming Visions: Accumulation and Display of Goods in America, 1880–1920*. New York: W. W. Norton, 1989.

Brown, Anne Kruesi. "Opposition to the Child Labor Amendment Found in Trade Journals, Industrial Bulletins, and Other Publications for and by Business Men." Unpublished dissertation. Chicago: University of Chicago, March 1937.

Brundage, W. Fitzhugh. *Lynching in the New South: Georgia and Virginia, 1880–1930*. Urbana: University of Illinois Press, 1993.

Buenger, Walter Louis. *The Path to a Modern South: Northeast Texas between Reconstruction and the Great Depression*. Austin: University of Texas Press, 2003.

Bunge, Marcia JoAnn. *The Child in Christian Thought*. Grand Rapids, MI: William B. Eerdmans Publishers, 2001.

Burgess, Charles, and Merle L. Borrowman. *"What Doctrines to Embrace": Studies in the History of American Education*. Glenview, IL: Scott, Foresman, 1969.

Bushnell, Horace. *The Northern Iron: A Discourse Delivered in the North Church, Hartford, on the Annual State Fast, April 14, 1854*. Hartford, CT: L. E. Hunt, 1854.

———. *Views of Christian Nurture, and of subjects adjacent thereto*. Hartford, CT: L. E. Hunt, 1847.

Bibliography 219

Butler, John. *Awash in a Sea of Faith: Christianizing the American People*. Cambridge: Harvard University Press, 1990.

Butsch, Richard. *For Fun and Profit: The Transformation of Leisure into Consumption*. Philadelphia: Temple University Press, 1990.

Chace, James. *1912: Wilson, Roosevelt, Taft, and Debs—The Election That Changed the Country*. New York: Simon and Schuster, 2004.

Chambers, Clarke A. *Seedtime of Reform: American Social Service and Social Action, 1918–1933*. Minneapolis: University of Minnesota Press, 1963.

Chenery, William L. "Child Labor—The New Alignment." *The Survey* 53, no. 7 (1925), 379–82, 425–26.

Cherry, Conrad. *Hurrying toward Zion: Universities, Divinity Schools, and American Protestantism*. Bloomington: Indiana University Press, 1995.

"Child Labor in Factories." *Harper's Weekly* 46, part 2 (1902), 1280.

"Children in War Industry." *The Survey* 41, no. 2 (1918), 49–50.

Children's Aid Society. *First Annual Report of the Children's Aid Society, February 1854*. New York: C. W. Benedict, 1854.

———. *Second Annual Report of the Children's Aid Society, February 1855*. New York: M. B. Wynkoop, Book, and Job, 1855.

———. *Third Annual Report of the Children's Aid Society, February 1856*. New York: M. B. Wynkoop, Book, and Job, 1856.

———. *Fourth Annual Report of the Children's Aid Society, February 1857*. New York: John P. Prall, 1857.

———. *Fifth Annual Report of the Children's Aid Society, February 1858*. New York: Wynkoop, Hallenbeck, and Thomas, 1858.

———. *Sixth Annual Report of the Children's Aid Society, February 1859*. New York: Wynkoop, Hallenbeck, and Thomas, 1859.

———. *Seventh Annual Report of the Children's Aid Society, February 1860*. New York: Wynkoop, Hallenbeck, and Thomas, 1860.

———. *Eighth Annual Report of the Children's Aid Society, February 1861*. New York: Wynkoop, Hallenbeck, and Thomas, 1861.

———. *Ninth Annual Report of the Children's Aid Society, February 1862*. New York: Wynkoop, Hallenbeck, and Thomas, 1862.

———. *Tenth Annual Report of the Children's Aid Society, February 1863*. New York: Press of Wynkoop, Hallenbeck, and Thomas, 1863.

———. *Eleventh Annual Report of the Children's Aid Society, February 1864*. New York: Press of Wynkoop, Hallenbeck, and Thomas, 1864.

———. *Twelfth Annual Report of the Children's Aid Society, February 1865*. New York: Press of Wynkoop and Hallenbeck, 1865.

———. *Sixteenth Annual Report of the Children's Aid Society, February 1869*. New York: Press of Wynkoop and Hallenbeck, 1869.

———. *Nineteenth Annual Report of the Children's Aid Society, November 1871*. New York: Press of Wynkoop and Hallenbeck, 1871.

Bibliography

———. *Twentieth Annual Report of the Children's Aid Society, November 1872*. New York: Press of Wynkoop and Hallenbeck, 1872.

———. *Twenty-First Annual Report of the Children's Aid Society, November 1873*. New York: Wynkoop and Hallenbeck, 1873.

———. *Twenty-Second Annual Report of the Children's Aid Society*. New York: Wynkoop and Hallenbeck, 1874.

Clark, Norman H. *Deliver Us from Evil: An Interpretation of American Prohibition*. New York: W. W. Norton, 1976.

Clopper, Edward N. *Rural Child Welfare: An Inquiry by the National Child Labor Committee, Based upon Conditions in West Virginia*. New York: Macmillan, 1922.

Commons, John R., Don D. Lescohier, and Elizabeth Brandeis. *History of Labor in the United States, 1896–1932*. Vols. 3 and 4. New York: Macmillan, 1935.

Cook, Daniel. *The Commodification of Childhood: The Children's Clothing Industry and the Rise of the Child Consumer*. Durham, NC: Duke University Press, 2004.

Copeland, Melvin Thomas. *The Cotton Manufacturing Industry of the United States*. Cambridge: Harvard University Press, 1912.

Cott, Nancy. *The Bonds of Womanhood: "Woman's Sphere" in New England, 1780–1835*. New Haven, CT: Yale University Press, 1977.

Creel, George. *How We Advertised America*. New York: Harper and Brothers, 1920.

Cremin, Lawrence A. *American Education: The National Experience, 1783–1876*. New York: Harper and Row, 1982.

Cross, Gary. *Kids' Stuff: Toys and the Changing World of American Childhood*. Cambridge: Harvard University Press, 1997.

Cross, Whitney R. *The Burned-Over District: The Social and Intellectual History of Enthusiastic Religion in Western New York, 1800–1850*. Ithaca, NY: Cornell University Press, 2006.

Cuff, Robert D. *The War Industries Board: Business-Government Relations during World War I*. Baltimore: Johns Hopkins University Press, 1973.

Curtis, Susan. *A Consuming Faith: The Social Gospel and Modern American Culture*. Columbia: Missouri University Press, 2001.

Curtis, Verna Posever, and Stanley Mallach. *Photography and Reform: Lewis Hine and the National Child Labor Committee*. Milwaukee: Milwaukee Art Museum, 1984.

Daniels, Roger. *Coming to America: A History of Immigration and Ethnicity in American Life*. New York: Harper Perennial, 1991.

Davidson, Elizabeth H. *Child Labor Legislation in the Southern Textile States*. Chapel Hill: University of North Carolina Press, 1939.

———. "Early Development of Public Opinion against Southern Child Labor," *North Carolina Historical Review* 14, no. 3 (1937): 230–50.

Davis, David Brion. *The Problem of Slavery in the Age of Revolution, 1770–1823*. Ithaca, NY: Cornell University Press, 1975.

———. *The Problem of Slavery in Western Culture*. Ithaca, NY: Cornell University Press, 1966.

Bibliography

DeForest, Robert W. "President's Address." Official Proceedings of the Annual Meeting of the National Conference on Charities and Corrections at the Thirtieth Annual Session held in the city of Atlanta, May 6–12, 1903, 1–12.

Degler, Carl. *At Odds: Women and the Family in America from the Revolution to the Present*. New York: Oxford University Press, 1980.

———. *In Search of Human Nature: The Decline and Revival of Darwinism in American Social Thought*. New York: Oxford University Press, 1992.

Denning, Michael. *Mechanic Accents: Dime Novels and Working-Class Culture in America*. Brooklyn, NY: Verso Press, 1987.

Dennis, Michael. "Schooling Along the Color Line: Progressives and the Education of Blacks in the New South." *Journal of Negro Education* 67, no. 2 (1998): 142–56.

Dublin, Thomas, ed. *Immigrant Voices: New Lives in America, 1773–1986*. Urbana: University of Illinois Press, 1993.

Dubois, Ellen. *Woman Suffrage and Women's Rights*. New York: New York University Press, 1998.

Du Bois, W.E.B. *Black Reconstruction in America, 1860–1880*. New York: Harcourt and Brace, 1935.

Edwards, Laura F. *Gendered Strife and Confusion: The Political Culture of Reconstruction*. Urbana: University of Illinois Press, 1997.

Edwards, Rebecca. *New Spirits: Americans in the Gilded Age, 1865–1905*. New York: Oxford University Press, 2006.

Etcheson, Nicole. *Bleeding Kansas: Contested Liberty in the Civil War Era*. Lawrence: University Press of Kansas, 2004.

Faust, Drew Gilpin. "A Southern Stewardship: The Intellectual and the Proslavery Argument." *American Quarterly* 31, no. 1 (1979): 63–80.

Fehrenbacher, Don E. *The Dred Scott Case: Its Significance in American Law and Politics*. New York: Oxford University Press, 1978.

Felt, Jeremy P. *Hostages of Fortune: Child Labor Reform in New York State*. Syracuse, NY: Syracuse University Press, 1965.

Ferrell, Robert H. *Woodrow Wilson and World War I, 1917–1921*. New York: Harper Collins, 1986.

Fields, Barbara Jeanne. *Slavery and Freedom on the Middle Ground: Maryland during the Nineteenth Century*. New Haven, CT: Yale University Press, 1987.

Filler, Louis. *Crusade against Slavery: Friends, Foes, and Reforms, 1820–1860*. New York: Harper, 1960.

———. *The Unknown Edwin Markham: His Mystery and Its Significance*. Kent, OH: Kent State University Press, 1966.

Finkelman, Paul. *Defending Slavery: Proslavery Thought in the Old South*. Boston: Bedford Press, 2003.

Fitch, George Hamlin. *Great Spiritual Writers of America*. San Francisco: Paul Elder, 1916.

Fitzhugh, George. *Cannibals All! Or Slaves without Masters*. Richmond, VA: A. Morris, 1857.

222 *Bibliography*

Fliter, John A. *Child Labor in America: The Epic Legal Struggle to Protect Children.* Lawrence: University Press of Kansas, 2018.

Folks, Gertrude H. "Child Labor in Agriculture." *American Child* 3, no. 3 (1921), 267–73.

Foner, Eric. *Free Soil, Free Labor, Free Men: The Ideology of the Republican Party before the Civil War.* New York: Oxford University Press, 1970.

———. *Nothing but Freedom: Emancipation and Its Legacy.* Baton Rouge: Louisiana State University Press, 1983.

———. *Reconstruction: America's Unfinished Revolution, 1863–1877.* New York: Harper and Row, 1988.

———. *The Story of American Freedom.* New York: W. W. Norton, 1998.

Forbes, Robert Pierce. *The Missouri Compromise and Its Aftermath: Slavery and the Meaning of America.* Chapel Hill: University of North Carolina Press, 2007.

Formanek-Brunell, Miriam. *Made to Play Dolls and the Commercialization of American Girlhood, 1830–1930.* Baltimore: Johns Hopkins University Press, 1998.

Foster, Gaines M. *Moral Reconstruction: Christian Lobbyists and the Federal Legislation of Morality, 1865–1920.* Chapel Hill: University of North Carolina Press, 2007.

Fox, Richard Wightman, and T. J. Jackson Lears, eds. *The Culture of Consumption: Critical Essays in American History, 1880–1980.* New York: Pantheon Books, 1983.

Francke, Warren T. "George Creel." In *Dictionary of Literary Biography: American Newspaper Journalists, 1901–1925.* Vol. 25. Ed. Perry J. Ashley. Farmington Hills, MI: Gale Publishers, 1985.

Frankel, Nora Lee, and Nancy S. Dye, eds. *Gender, Class, Race, and Reform in the Progressive Era.* Lexington: University Press of Kentucky, 1991.

Freedman, Russell. *Kids at Work: Lewis Hine and the Crusade against Child Labor.* New York: Houghton Mifflin, 1998.

Gasman, Marybeth, and Katherine Sedgwick, eds. *Uplifting a People: African American Philanthropy and Education.* New York: Peter Lang Publishers, 2005.

Gaston, Paul M. *The New South Creed: A Study in Southern Mythmaking.* New York: Alfred A. Knopf, 1970.

Gatewood, Willard B., Jr. *Black Americans and the White Man's Burden, 1898–1903.* Urbana: University of Illinois Press, 1975.

Genovese, Michael A. *Encyclopedia of the American Presidency.* New York: Infobase Publishing, 2010.

Gerstle, Gary. *American Crucible: Race and Nation in the Twentieth Century.* Princeton, NJ: Princeton University Press, 2001.

Gewen, Barry. "The Intellectual Foundations of the Child Labor Reform Movement." PhD diss. Harvard University, Boston, 1972.

Gibbons, Charles E., and Clara B. Armentrout. *Child Labor among Cotton Growers of Texas: A Study of Children Living in Rural Communities in Six Counties in Texas.* New York: National Child Labor Committee, 1925.

Giddings, Paula. *Ida: A Sword among Lions: Ida B. Wells and the Campaign against Lynching.* New York: HarperCollins, 2008.

Bibliography 223

Gilbert, A. C. *The Man Who Lives in Paradise: The Autobiography of A. C. Gilbert with Marshall McClintock*. New York: Rinehart and Company, 1954.

Gilfoyle, Timothy J. "Street Rats and Gutter-Snipes: Pickpockets and Street Culture in New York City, 1850–1900." *Journal of Social History* 37, no. 4 (2004): 853–62.

Gilmore, Glenda Elizabeth. *Gender and Jim Crow: Women and the Politics of White Supremacy in North Carolina, 1896–1920*. Chapel Hill: University of North Carolina Press, 1996.

Gilmore, Michael T. *American Romanticism and the Marketplace*. Chicago: University of Chicago Press, 1985.

Ginzberg, Lori. *Women and the Work of Benevolence: Morality, Politics, and Class in the Nineteenth-Century United States*. New Haven, CT: Yale University Press, 1992.

Gjerde, Jon, ed. *Major Problems in Immigration and Ethnic History*. New York: Houghton Mifflin, 1998.

Glickstein, Jonathan A. *Concepts of Free Labor in Antebellum America*. New Haven, CT: Yale University Press, 1991.

Goldberg, David J. *Discontented America: The United States in the 1920s*. Baltimore: Johns Hopkins University Press, 1999.

Goldberg, Ronald Allen. *America in the Twenties*. Syracuse, NY: Syracuse University Press, 2003.

Goodier, Susan. *No Votes for Women: The New York State Anti-Suffrage Movement*. Urbana: University of Illinois Press, 2013.

Goodrich, Thomas. *War to the Knife: Bleeding Kansas, 1854–1861*. Lincoln, NE: Bison Books, 1998.

Gordon, Linda. *Pitied but Not Entitled: Single Mothers and the History of Welfare, 1890–1935*. Cambridge: Harvard University Press, 1994.

———. *The Second Coming of the KKK: The Second Ku Klux Klan of the 1920s and the American Political Tradition*. New York: W. W. Norton, 2017.

Gould, Lewis L. *The William Howard Taft Presidency*. Lawrence: University Press of Kansas, 2009.

Gould, Stephen Jay. *The Mismeasure of Man*. New York: W. W. Norton, 1981.

Grady, Henry W. *The New South*. New York: Robert Bonner's Sons, 1890.

Graff, Harvey J. *The Literacy Myth: Cultural Integration and Social Structure in the Nineteenth Century*. New York: Academic Press, 1977.

Grantham, Dewey W. *Southern Progressivism: The Reconciliation of Progress and Tradition*. Knoxville: University of Tennessee Press, 1983.

Greven, Philip. *The Protestant Temperament*. New York: Signet, 1977.

Gross, Laurence F. *The Course of Industrial Decline: The Boott Cotton Mills of Lowell, Massachusetts, 1835–1955*. Baltimore: Johns Hopkins University Press, 1993.

Grossman, James. *Land of Hope: Chicago, Black Southerners, and the Great Migration*. Chicago: University of Chicago Press, 1989.

Gutman, Herbert G. *The Black Family in Slavery and Freedom, 1750–1925*. New York: Pantheon Books, 1976.

Gutman, Judith Mara. *Lewis W. Hine and the American Social Conscience*. New York: Walker, 1967.

Hacsi, Timothy A. *Second Home: Orphan Asylums and Poor Families in America*. Cambridge: Harvard University Press, 1998.

Hahn, Steven. *Nation under Our Feet: Black Political Struggles in the Rural South from Slavery to the Great Migration*. Cambridge: Harvard University Press, 2003.

———. *The Roots of Southern Populism: Yeoman Farmers and the Transformation of the Georgia Upcountry, 1850–1890*. New York: Oxford University Press, 1983.

Hahn, Steven, et al., eds. *Freedom: A Documentary History of Emancipation, 1861–1867*, Ser. 3, Vol. 1, *Land and Labor, 1865*. Chapel Hill: University of North Carolina Press, 2008.

Hall, Jacquelyn Dowd, et al. *Like a Family: The Making of a Southern Cotton Mill World*. New York: W. W. Norton, 1987.

Handy, Robert T. *The Social Gospel in America, 1870–1920*. New York: Oxford University Press, 1966.

Harlan, Louis R. "The Southern Education Board and the Race Issue in Public Education." *Journal of Southern History* 23, no. 2 (1957): 189–202.

Hart, James D., ed. *Oxford Companion to American Literature*, 6th ed. New York: Oxford University Press, 1995.

Harvey, Rowland Hill. *Samuel Gompers: Champion of the Toiling Masses*. Palo Alto, CA: Stanford University Press, 1935.

Hasian, Marouf. *The Rhetoric of Eugenics in Anglo-American Thought*. Athens: University of Georgia Press, 1966.

Hatch, Nathan O. *Democratization of American Christianity*. New Haven, CT: Yale University Press, 1991.

Hawes, Joseph M. *Children in Urban Society: Juvenile Delinquency in Nineteenth-Century America*. New York: Oxford University Press, 1971.

Hawley, Ellis W. *The Great War and the Search for Modern Order: A History of the American People and Their Institutions, 1917–1933*. Prospect Heights, IL: Waveland Press, 1997.

Herndon, Ruth Wallis, and John E. Murray, eds., *Children Bound to Labor: The Pauper Apprentice System in Early America*. Ithaca, NY: Cornell University Press, 2009.

Hindman, Hugh D. *Child Labor: An American History*. Armonk, NY: M. E. Sharpe, 2002.

Hine, Robert V., and John Mack Faragher. *The American West: A New Interpretive History*. New Haven, CT: Yale University Press, 2000.

Hofstadter, Richard. *The Age of Reform: From Bryan to FDR*. New York: Vintage Books, 1955.

———. "Cuba, the Philippines, and Manifest Destiny." In *The Paranoid Style in American Politics*. New York: Alfred A. Knopf, 1965. 145–87.

———. *Social Darwinism in American Thought*. Philadelphia: University of Pennsylvania Press, 1944.

Bibliography

Hoganson, Kristin L. *Fighting for American Manhood: How Gender Politics Provoked the Spanish-American and Philippine-American Wars*. New Haven, CT: Yale University Press, 2000.

Holmes, Julia A. "Children Who Work." *Scribner's Monthly* 1, no. 6 (1871): 607–8.

Holt, Thomas C. *Black over White: Negro Political Leadership in South Carolina during Reconstruction*. Urbana: University of Illinois Press, 1979.

———. *The Problem of Freedom: Race, Labor, and Politics in Jamaica and Britain, 1832–1938*. Baltimore: Johns Hopkins University Press, 1992.

Holzer, Harold, and Sara Vaughn Gabbard, eds. *Lincoln and Freedom: Slavery, Emancipation, and the Thirteenth Amendment*. Carbondale: Southern Illinois University Press, 2007.

Horowitz, Daniel. *The Morality of Spending: Attitudes toward the Consumer Society in America, 1875–1940*. Chicago: Ivan R. Dee Publisher, 1985.

Howe, Daniel Walker. *What God Hath Wrought: The Transformation of America, 1815–1848*. New York: Oxford University Press, 2007.

Iorizzo, Luciano J., and Francesco Cardasco. *Italian Immigration and the Impact of the Padrone System*. New York: Arno Press, 1980.

"The Italian Boys." *Harper's Weekly* (September 13, 1873), 802.

"The Italian Boys in New York—Tortures of the Training Room." *Harper's Weekly* (September 13, 1873), 801.

Jacobson, Lisa. *Raising Consumers: Children and the American Mass Market in the Early Twentieth Century*. New York: Columbia University Press, 2004.

Jacobson, Matthew Frye. *Whiteness of a Different Color: European Immigrants and the Alchemy of Race*. Cambridge: Harvard University Press, 1998.

Jenkins, William. *Proslavery Thought in the Old South*. Chapel Hill: University of North Carolina Press, 1935.

Johnson, Paul E. *A Shopkeeper's Millennium: Society and Revivals in Rochester, New York, 1815–1837*. New York: Hill and Wang, 1978.

Jones, Catherine A. *Intimate Reconstructions: Children in Postemancipation Virginia*. Charlottesville: University of Virginia Press, 2015.

Kaestle, Carl F., Helen Damon-Moore, and Katherine Tinsley. *Literacy in the United States: Readers and Reading since 1880*. New Haven, CT: Yale University Press, 1993.

Kasson, John F. *Amusing the Million: Coney Island at the Turn of the Century*. New York: Hill and Wang, 1978.

Katz, Michael B. *In the Shadow of the Poorhouse: A Social History of Welfare in America*. New York: Basic Books, 1986.

Katz, Michael S. *A History of Compulsory Education Laws*. Bloomington: Phi Delta Kappa Educational Foundation, 1976.

Kelley, Catherine E. *In the New England Fashion: Reshaping Women's Lives in the Nineteenth Century*. Ithaca, NY: Cornell University Press, 1999.

Kelley, Florence. *Some Ethical Gains through Legislation*. New York: Macmillan, 1905.

Kennedy, David M. *Over Here: The First World War and American Society*. New York: Oxford University Press, 1982.

226   *Bibliography*

Kirby, Jack T. *Darkness at the Dawning: Race and Reform in the Progressive South*. Philadelphia: J. B. Lippincott, 1972.

Knock, Thomas. *To End All Wars: Woodrow Wilson and the Quest for a New Moral Order*. New York: Oxford University Press, 1992.

Kraditor, Aileen S. *The Ideas of the Woman Suffrage Movement, 1890–1920*. New York: W. W. Norton, 1981.

Kuhl, Stefan. *The Nazi Connection: Eugenics, American Racism, and German National Socialism*. New York: Oxford University Press, 2004.

Ladd-Taylor, Molly. "Federal Help for Mothers: The Rise and Fall of the Sheppard-Towner Act in the 1920s." In *Gendered Domains: Rethinking Public and Private in Women's History*, edited by Dorothy O. Helly and Susan M. Reverby, 217–27. Ithaca, NY: Cornell University Press, 1992.

Langer, Beryl. "Commodified Enchantment: Children and Consumer Capitalism." *Thesis Eleven* 69 (May 2002): 67–81.

Langum, David J. *Crossing over the Line: Legislating Morality and the Mann Act*. Chicago: University of Chicago Press, 1994.

Larson, Edward John. *Summer for the Gods: The Scopes Trial and America's Continuing Debate over Science and Religion*. New York: Basic Books, 1997.

Lasch, Christopher. *Haven in a Heartless World*. New York: Basic Books, 1979.

Lathrop, Julia. *Four Decades of Action for Children: A Short History of the Children's Bureau*. Washington, DC: US Department of Health, Education, and Welfare, 1956.

Leach, William. "Child-World in the Promised Land." In *The Mythmaking Frame of Mind: Social Imagination and American Culture*, edited by J. Gilbert, et al., 209–38. Belmont, CA: Wadsworth Publishing, 1993.

———. *Land of Desire: Merchants, Power, and the Rise of a New American Culture*. New York: Vintage Books, 1993.

Lears, T. J. Jackson. *No Place of Grace: Antimodernism and the Transformation of American Culture, 1880–1920*. Chicago: University of Chicago Press, 1981.

LeFeber, William. *The New Empire: An Interpretation of American Expansion, 1860–1898*. Ithaca, NY: Cornell University Press, 1963.

Lerner, Michael A. *Dry Manhattan: Prohibition in New York City*. Cambridge: Harvard University Press, 2007.

Levine, Lawrence W. "Progress and Nostalgia: The Self Image of the Nineteen Twenties." In *The Unpredictable Past: Explorations in American Cultural History*. New York: Oxford University Press, 1993. 189–205.

Lincoln, Abraham. *Abraham Lincoln: Complete Works, Comprising His Speeches, Letters, State Papers, and Miscellaneous Writings*. Vol. 1. Ed. John George Nicolay and John Jay. New York: Century Co., 1907.

Lindenmeyer, Kriste. *A Right to Childhood: The U.S. Children's Bureau and Child Welfare, 1912–1946*. Urbana: University of Illinois Press, 1997.

Lindsey, Ben Barr, with Rube Burrough. *The Dangerous Life*. New York: Horace Liveright, 1931.

Bibliography 227

————. *The Problem of the Children and How the State of Colorado Cares for Them.* Denver, CO: Merchants Publishing, 1904.

Lindsey, William D. *Shailer Mathews' Lives of Jesus: The Search for a Theological Foundation for the Social Gospel.* New York: State University of New York Press, 1997.

Link, Arthur S. *Wilson: The New Freedom.* Princeton, NJ: Princeton University Press, 1967.

Link, Eugene P. *Labor-Religion Prophet: The Times and Life of Harry F. Ward.* Boulder, CO: Westview Press, 1984.

————. *Woodrow Wilson and the Progressive Era, 1910–1917.* New York: Harper and Row, 1963.

Link, William A. *The Paradox of Southern Progressivism, 1880–1930.* Chapel Hill: University of North Carolina Press, 1992.

Litwack, Leon F. *Been in the Storm So Long: The Aftermath of Slavery.* New York: Alfred A. Knopf, 1979.

Lomotey, Kofi, ed. *Encyclopedia of African American Education.* Thousand Oaks, CA: Sage Publications, 2010.

Lovejoy, Owen R. "Seven Years of Child Labor Reform." *Annals of the American Academy of Political and Social Science* 38 (July 1911): 31–38.

Lowance, Mason, ed., *Against Slavery: An Abolitionist Reader.* New York: Penguin Books, 2000.

Luebke, Frederick C. *Bonds of Loyalty: German-Americans and World War I.* DeKalb: Northern Illinois University Press, 1974.

Luker, Ralph. *A Southern Tradition in Theology and Social Criticism, 1830–1930: The Religious Liberalism and Social Conservatism of James Miles, William Porcher Dubose, and Edgar Gardner Murphy.* New York: Edwin Mellen Press, 1984.

Lumpkin, Katharine DuPre, and Dorothy Wolff Douglas. *Child Workers in America.* New York: Robert M. McBride, 1937.

Markham, Edwin. "The Child at the Loom." *The Cosmopolitan: A Monthly Illustrated Magazine,* vol. 41, issue 5 (1906), 480–87.

————. *The Man with the Hoe and Other Poems.* New York: Doubleday & McClure, 1899.

Markham, Edwin, Benjamin B. Lindsey, and George Creel. *Children in Bondage: A Complete and Careful Presentation of the Anxious Problem of Child Labor—Its Causes, Its Crimes, and Its Cure.* New York: Hearst's International Library, 1914.

Marsden, George M. *Fundamentalism and American Culture: The Shaping of Twentieth-Century Evangelicalism, 1870–1925.* New York: Oxford University Press, 1980.

Martin, Scott C., ed. *Cultural Change and the Market Revolution, 1790–1860.* New York: Rowman and Littlefield, 2004.

Matt, Susan J. *Keeping Up with the Joneses: Envy in American Consumer Society, 1890–1930.* Philadelphia: University of Pennsylvania Press, 2003.

May, Ernest R. *Imperial Democracy: The Emergence of America as a Great Power.* New York: Harcourt, Brace, and World, 1961.

228   Bibliography

May, Henry F. *The Enlightenment in America*. New York: Oxford University Press, 1976.

———. *Protestant Churches and Industrial America*. New York: Harper and Brothers, 1949.

Mayer, Henry. *All on Fire: Henry Lloyd Garrison and the Abolition of Slavery*. New York: W. W. Norton, 1998.

McCartin, Joseph A. *Labor's Great War: The Struggle for Industrial Democracy and the Origins of Modern American Labor Relations, 1912–1921*. Chapel Hill: University of North Carolina Press, 1997.

McCoy, Donald R. "The Election of 1920." In *History of American Presidential Elections*, edited by Arthur M. Schlesinger Jr. and Fred L. Israel. New York: Chelsea House, 1971.

McCurry, Stephanie. *Masters of Small Worlds: Yeoman Households, Gender Relations, and the Political Culture of the Antebellum South Carolina Low Country*. New York: Oxford University Press, 1995.

McFeely, William S. *Yankee Stepfather: General O. O. Howard and the Freedmen*. New Haven, CT: Yale University Press, 1968.

McKenna, Marian C. *Franklin Roosevelt and the Great Constitutional War: The Court-Packing Crisis of 1937*. New York: Fordham University Press, 2002.

McPherson, James M. *Battle Cry of Freedom: The Civil War Era*. New York: Oxford University Press, 1998.

Mennel, Robert M. *Thorns and Thistles: Juvenile Delinquents in the United States, 1825–1940*. Hanover, CT: University Press of New England, 1973.

Milkis, Sidney M. *Theodore Roosevelt, the Progressive Party, and the Transformation of American Democracy*. Lawrence: University Press of Kansas, 2009.

Miller, Robert Moats. "A Note on the Relationship between the Protestant Churches and the Revived Ku Klux Klan." *Journal of Southern History* 22 (August 1956): 355–68.

Mitchell, Mary Niall. *Raising Freedom's Child: Black Children and Visions of the Future after Slavery*. New York: New York University Press, 2008.

Mock, James R., and Cedric Larson. *Words That Won the War*. Princeton, NJ: Princeton University Press, 1939.

Montgomery, David. *Beyond Equality: Labor and the Radical Republicans, 1862–1872*. Urbana: University of Illinois Press, 1981.

———. *The Fall of the House of Labor: The Workplace, the State, and American Labor Activism, 1865–1925*. New York: Cambridge University Press, 1987.

Morgan, Edmund S. *American Slavery, American Freedom*. New York: W. W. Norton, 1975.

Morris, Thomas D. *Free Men All: The Personal Liberty Laws of the North, 1780–1861*. Baltimore: Johns Hopkins University Press, 1974.

Murphy, Edgar Gardner. *The Basis of Ascendancy: A Discussion of Certain Principles of Public Policy Involved in the Development of the Southern States*. New York: Longmans, Green, 1909.

Bibliography

229

————. *The Larger Life: Sermons and an Essay*. New York: Longmans, Green, 1897.

————. *Problems of the Present South: A Discussion of Certain of the Educational, Industrial, and Political Issues in the Southern States*. New York: Macmillan, 1904.

Murphy, Maud King. *Edgar Gardner Murphy: From Records and Memories*. New York, 1943.

Murray, Robert K. *Red Scare: A Study in National Hysteria, 1919–1920*. Minneapolis: University of Minnesota Press, 1955.

Nardinelli, Clark. *Child Labor and the Industrial Revolution*. Bloomington: Indiana University Press, 1990.

Nevels, Cynthia Skove. *Lynching to Belong: Claiming Whiteness through Racial Violence*. College Station: Texas A&M University Press, 2007.

Ngozi-Brown, Scot. "African-American Soldiers and Filipinos: Racial Imperialism, Jim Crow, and Social Relations." *Journal of Negro History* 82, no. 1 (1997): 42–53.

Nielsen, Kim E. *Un-American Womanhood: Antiradicalism, Antifeminism, and the First Red Scare*. Columbus: Ohio State University Press, 2001.

Nixon, Raymond. *Henry W. Grady: Spokesman of the New South*. New York: Alfred A. Knopf, 1943.

Noll, Mark A. *America's God: From Jonathan Edwards to Abraham Lincoln*. New York: Oxford University Press, 2002.

Noll, Mark A., ed. *God and Mammon: Protestants, Money, and the Market, 1790–1860*. New York: Oxford University Press, 2001.

Oates, Stephen B. *To Purge This Land with Blood: A Biography of John Brown*. Amherst: University of Massachusetts Press, 1984.

O'Connor, Stephen. *Orphan Trains: The Story of Charles Loring Brace and the Children He Saved and Failed*. Boston: Houghton Mifflin, 2001.

Okrent, Daniel. *Last Call: The Rise and Fall of Prohibition*. New York: Scribner, 2010.

Ordover, Nancy. *American Eugenics: Race, Queer Anatomy, and the Science of Nationalism*. Minneapolis: University of Minnesota Press, 2003.

Paoletti, Jo B., and Carol L. Kregloh. "The Children's Department." In *Men and Women Dressing the Part*, edited by Claudia Kidwell and Valerie Steele, 22–41. Washington, DC: Smithsonian Institution Press, 1989.

Peck, Gunther. *Reinventing Free Labor: Padrones and Immigrant Workers in the North American West, 1880–1930*. New York: Cambridge University Press, 2000.

Peiss, Kathy. *Cheap Amusements: Working Women and Leisure in Turn-of-the-Century New York*. Philadelphia: Temple University Press, 1986.

Perry, Lewis. *Antislavery Reconsidered: New Perspectives on the Abolitionists*. Baton Rouge: Louisiana State University Press, 1979.

Peterson, Horace Cornelius. *Propaganda for War: The War against American Neutrality, 1914–1917*. Norman: University of Oklahoma Press, 1939.

Powers, Hal. *Edwin Markham: A Muckraker Crusading against Child Labor Abuse*. Carbondale: Southern Illinois University Press, 1981.

Preston, William, Jr. *Aliens and Dissenters: Federal Suppression of Radicals, 1903–1933*. Urbana: University of Illinois Press, 1994.

230   *Bibliography*

Proctor, Ben H. *William Randolph Hearst: The Early Years, 1863–1910*. New York: Oxford University Press, 1998.

Rauschenbusch, Walter. *Christianity and the Social Crisis*. New York: Macmillan, 1913.

———. *Christianizing the Social Order*. New York: Macmillan, 1912.

———. *A Theology for the Social Gospel*. New York: Macmillan, 1917.

Rawley, James A. *Race and Politics: "Bleeding Kansas" and the Coming of the Civil War*. Lincoln: University of Nebraska Press, 1980.

Richardson, Heather Cox. *The Death of Reconstruction: Race, Labor, and Politics in the Post–Civil War North, 1865–1901*. Cambridge: Harvard University Press, 2001.

Riis, Jacob A. *How the Other Half Lives: Studies among the Tenements of New York*. New York: Charles Scribner's Sons, 1890.

Rodgers, Daniel T. *Atlantic Crossings: Social Politics in a Progressive Age*. Cambridge: Harvard University Press, 1998.

———. *The Work Ethic in Industrial America, 1850–1920*. Chicago: University of Chicago Press, 1979.

Rosenstone, Steven J., Roy L. Behr, and Edward H. Lazarus, eds. *Third Parties in America: Citizen Response to Major Party Failure*. Princeton, NJ: Princeton University Press, 1996.

Rothman, David J. *The Discovery of the Asylum: Social Order and Disorder in the New Republic*. Boston: Little, Brown, 1990.

Sallee, Shelley. *The Whiteness of Child Labor Reform in the New South*. Athens: University of Georgia Press, 2004.

Salvatore, Nick, ed. *Seventy Years of Life and Labor: An Autobiography of Samuel Gompers*. Ithaca, NY: ILR Press, 1984.

Saville, Julie. *The Work of Reconstruction: From Slave to Wage Labor in South Carolina, 1860–1870*. New York: Cambridge University Press, 1994.

Sawhill, Isabel. "Economic Perspectives on the Family." *Daedalus* 106 (Spring 1977): 116–25.

Schaffer, Ronald. *America in the Great War: The Rise of the War Welfare State*. New York: Oxford University Press, 1994.

Scheiber, Harry N. *The Wilson Administration and Civil Liberties, 1917–1921*. Ithaca, NY: Cornell University Press, 1960.

Schmidt, James. *Industrial Violence and the Legal Origins of Child Labor*. New York: Cambridge University Press, 2010.

Schmidt, Louis Bernard, and Earle Dudley Ross. *Readings in the Economic History of American Agriculture*. Ithaca, NY: Cornell University Press, 1925.

Schultz, Theodore W. "The Value of Children: An Economic Perspective." *Journal of Political Economy* 81 (March–April 1973): 2–13.

Scott, Rebecca J. "The Battle over the Child: Child Apprenticeship and the Freedmen's Bureau in North Carolina." *Prologue* 10 (1978): 101–13.

———. *Degrees of Freedom: Louisiana and Cuba after Slavery*. Cambridge: Harvard University Press, 2005.

Bibliography 231

Sellers, Charles. *The Market Revolution: Jacksonian America, 1815–1846.* New York: Oxford University Press, 1991.

Seward, William H. "Speech of the Honorable William H. Seward, In the Senate, Feb. 17, 1854, 'Freedom and Public Faith.'" In *The Nebraska Question: Comprising Speeches in the United States Senate by Mr. Douglas, Mr. Chase, Mr. Smith, Mr. Everett, Mr. Wade, Mr. Badger, Mr. Seward and Mr. Sumner, Together with The History of the Missouri Compromise, Daniel Webster's Memorial in Regard to It— History of the Annexation of Texas—The Organization of Oregon Territory—and The Compromise of 1850.* New York: Redfield, 1854. 95–105.

Sherman, Richard B. "The Rejection of the Child Labor Amendment." *Mid-America* (January 1963): 3–17.

Silber, Nina. *The Romance of Reunion: Northerners and the South, 1865–1900.* Chapel Hill: University of North Carolina Press, 1997.

Sklar, Kathryn Kish, and Beverly Wilson Palmer, eds. *The Selected Letters of Florence Kelley, 1869–1931.* Urbana: University of Illinois Press, 2009.

Sklar, Martin. *The Corporate Reconstruction of American Capitalism, 1890–1916: The Market, the Law, and Politics.* New York: Cambridge University Press, 1988.

Skocpol, Theda. *Protecting Soldiers and Mothers: The Political Origins of Social Policy in the United States.* Cambridge: Harvard University Press, 1995.

Skowronek, Stephen. *Building a New American State: The Expansion of National Administrative Capacities, 1877–1920.* New York: Cambridge University Press, 1982.

Slater, Don. *Consumer Culture and Modernity.* Cambridge, MA: Polity Press, 1999.

Smedley, Audrey. *Race in North America: Origin and Evolution of a Worldview.* Boulder, CO: Westview Press, 2007.

Smith, Gary Scott. *The Search for Social Salvation: Social Christianity and America, 1880–1925.* Lanham, MD: Lexington Books, 2000.

Smith, Joseph. *The Spanish-American War: Conflict in the Caribbean and the Pacific, 1895–1902.* New York: Longman Publishers, 1994.

Southern, David W. *The Progressive Era and Race: Reaction and Reform, 1900–1917.* Wheeling, IL: Harlan Davidson, 2005.

Spargo, John. *Bitter Cry of the Children.* New York: Macmillan, 1906.

Stanley, Amy Dru. *From Bondage to Contract: Wage Labor, Marriage, and the Market in the Age of Slave Emancipation.* New York: Cambridge University Press, 1998.

———. "Home Life and the Morality of the Marketplace." In Stokes and Conway, *Market Revolution,* 74–96.

Stansell, Christine. *City of Women: Sex and Class in New York, 1789–1860.* Urbana: University of Illinois Press, 1987.

Stein, Leon. *The Triangle Fire.* Ithaca, NY: Cornell University Press, 1962.

Steinfeld, Robert J. *The Invention of Free Labor: The Employment Relation in English and American Law and Culture.* Chapel Hill: University of North Carolina Press, 2002.

Stewart, James Brewer. *Holy Warriors: The Abolitionists and American Slavery.* New York: Hill and Wang, 1976.

232   *Bibliography*

Stokes, Melvyn, and Stephen Conway, eds. *The Market Revolution in America: Social, Political, and Religious Expressions, 1800–1860.* Charlottesville: University Press of Virginia, 1996.

Sutherland, Jonathan D. *African Americans at War: An Encyclopedia.* Vol. 1. Santa Barbara: ABC-CLIO, 2004.

Sweet, John Wood. *Bodies Politic: Negotiating Race in the American North, 1730–1830.* Baltimore: Johns Hopkins University Press, 2003.

Syrett, John. *The Civil War Confiscation Acts: Failing to Reconstruct the South.* New York: Fordham University Press, 2005.

Sznaider, Natan. *The Compassionate Temperament: Care and Cruelty in Modern Society.* New York: Rowman and Littlefield, 2000.

Taylor, Robert M., ed. *The Northwest Ordinance, 1787: A Bicentennial Handbook.* Ann Arbor: University of Michigan Press, 1987.

Thomas, Brook, ed. *Plessy v. Ferguson: A Brief History with Documents.* New York: Bedford/St. Martin's Press, 1997.

Tocqueville, Alexis de. *Democracy in America.* Vol. 2. Trans. Henry Reeves. New York: D. Appleton, 1904.

Tomlin, Christopher L. *Law, Labor, and Ideology in the Early American Republic.* New York: Cambridge University Press, 1993.

Trachtenberg, Alan. *The Incorporation of America: Culture and Society in the Gilded Age.* New York: Hill and Wang, 1982.

Trattner, Walter I. *Crusade for the Children: A History of the National Child Labor Committee and Child Labor Reform in America.* Chicago: Quadrangle Books, 1970.

———. *From Poor Law to Welfare State: A History of Social Welfare in America.* New York: Free Press, 1974.

Tsesis, Alexander. *The Thirteenth Amendment and American Freedom: A Legal History.* New York: New York University Press, 2004.

Tuchman, Barbara W. *The Zimmermann Telegram.* New York: Ballantine Books, 1985.

Tyack, David B. "Ways of Seeing: An Essay on the History of Compulsory Schooling." *Harvard Educational Review* 46, no. 3 (1976): 355–89.

Uhlenberg, Peter. "Death and the Family." In *The American Family*, edited by Michael Gordon, 157–65. New York: St. Martin's Press, 1978.

Van Vorst, Mary. *The Cry of the Children: A Study of Child Labor.* New York: Moffat, Yard, and Co., 1908.

Vaughn, Stephen L., ed. *The Encyclopedia of American Journalism.* New York: Routledge Press, 2008.

———. *Holding Fast the Inner Lines: Democracy, Nationalism, and the Committee on Public Information.* Chapel Hill: University of North Carolina Press, 1980.

Venzon, Anne Cipriano, and Paul L. Miles, eds. *The United States in the First World War: An Encyclopedia.* New York: Garland Publishing, 1995.

Vey, Shauna. "Good Intentions and Fearsome Prejudice: New York's 1876 Act to Prevent and Punish Wrongs to Children." *Theatre Survey* 42, no. 1 (2001): 53–68.

Bibliography

Vorenberg, Michael. *Final Freedom: The Civil War, the Abolition of Slavery, and the Thirteenth Amendment*. New York: Cambridge University Press, 2001.

Wagner, David. *The Poorhouse: America's Forgotten Institution*. Lanham, MD: Rowman and Littlefield, 2005.

Walters, Ronald G. *American Reformers, 1815–1860*. New York: HarperCollins, 1978.

———. *The Antislavery Appeal: American Abolitionism after 1830*. New York: W. W. Norton, 1984.

Ward, Harry Frederick. *The Social Creed of the Churches*. New York: Abingdon Press, 1914.

Welch, Richard E. *Response to Imperialism: The United States and the Philippine-American War, 1899–1902*. Chapel Hill: University of North Carolina Press, 1979.

Weston, Rubin Francis. *Racism in U.S. Imperialism: The Influence of Racial Assumptions on American Foreign Policy, 1893–1946*. Columbia: University of South Carolina Press, 1972.

White, Ronald Cedric, and Charles Howard Hopkins, eds. *The Social Gospel: Religion and Reform in Changing America*. Philadelphia: Temple University Press, 1976.

Wiebe, Robert. *The Search for Order, 1877–1920*. New York: Hill and Wang, 1966.

Williams, Robert Chadwell. *Horace Greeley: Champion of American Freedom*. New York: NYU Press, 2006.

Willrich, Michael. *City of Courts: Socializing Justice in Progressive Era Chicago*. New York: Cambridge University Press, 2003.

Wilson, Jan Doolittle. "The Lobby for the Sheppard-Towner Bill, 1921." In *The Women's Joint Congressional Committee and the Politics of Maternalism, 1920–1930*. Urbana: University of Illinois Press, 2007. 27–49.

Wilson, Theodore Brantner. *The Black Codes of the South*. Tuscaloosa: University of Alabama, 1965.

Wilson, Woodrow. *Constitutional Government in the United States*. New York: Columbia University Press, 1908.

Wood, Amy Louise. *Lynching and Spectacle: Witnessing Racial Violence in America, 1890–1940*. Chapel Hill: University of North Carolina Press, 2009.

Wood, Stephen B. *Constitutional Politics in the Progressive Era: Child Labor and the Law*. Chicago: University of Chicago Press, 1968.

Woodward, C. Vann. *Origins of the New South, 1877–1913*. Baton Rouge: Louisiana State University Press, 1951.

———. *The Strange Career of Jim Crow*. New York: Oxford University Press, 1955.

Zelizer, Viviana A. *Pricing the Priceless Child: The Changing Social Value of Children*. New York: Basic Books, 1985.

Zipf, Karin L. *Labor of Innocents: Forced Apprenticeship in North Carolina, 1715–1919*. Baton Rouge: Louisiana State University Press, 2005.

Zucchi, John E. *The Little Slaves of the Harp: Italian Child Street Musicians in Nineteenth-Century Paris, London, and New York*. Montreal: McGill-Queen's University Press, 1992.

Index

Abbott, Grace, 132, 133, 151
abolitionism, 12, 40, 53, 85, 87, 98, 139. *See also* antislavery thought
Addams, Jane, 71
Adler, Felix, 71–72, 75, 77, 80, 90–91, 97, 116
African Americans: enslaved children, 1, 3–4, 7, 25–26; freed children, 26–27, 29, 31, 33, 36; freed parents, 28, 32–33; reformers, 125–26; support for child labor reform, 115, 125–26; wage labor, 3. *See also* emancipation, meaning of; freed people; Reconstruction; slave emancipation; slavery
African Methodist Episcopal Zion Church, 126
agricultural labor, 8, 16, 18, 20–22, 24, 116–18, 120, 131–33, 135–38, 141–42. *See also* free labor
Alabama: and capitalists, 66–67; and child labor, 51–52, 54, 56; and cotton manufacturers opposed to child labor reform, 60; opposition to Keating-Owen Act, 100; and Southern Progressivism, 57–58, 61, 65–67, 71, 74; and state child labor legislation, 59–60, 66. *See also* Alabama Child Labor Bill; Alabama Child Labor Committee; anti-child labor reform; Southern Progressivism
Alabama Child Labor Bill, 59–60, 66
Alabama Child Labor Committee (ACLC), 56–57, 61, 65–67, 71, 74
Alabama City mill, 60
Alger, Horatio, 41

almsgiving, 11–12
American Country Life Association, 118
American empire, 61, 70, 74–76, 78–79, 88, 104, 110, 115, 152. *See also* imperialism
American Federation of Labor (AFL), 58–59, 86, 125, 132
American Medical Association, 86
American toy industry, 87–88, 107, 112; and boys' leisure, 88, 110; contribution to campaign against child labor, 109–10; and girls' leisure, 111; and modern child welfare movement, 88, 107–8; profits of during First World War, 110. *See also* consumerism
Ancarola, Antonio Giovanni, 41
Anderson, Clifton, 143
Anderson, Neal, 71
Anne Arundel County, 31
anti-child labor reform, 2, 5–6, 53, 60, 87, 95, 99–105, 114–15, 127–29, 133–37, 140–52. *See also* antimodernism; Child Labor Amendment; Farmers' States Rights League; *Hammer v. Dagenhart*; National Association of Manufacturers (NAM); National Committee for the Protection of Child, Family, School, and Church; National Committee for the Rejection of the 20th Amendment
antilynching, 125–26
antimodernism, 3, 5–6, 112, 114–15, 134–38
anti-Red, 128, 152
antiregulation. *See* anti-child labor reform

236   *Index*

antislavery thought, 1–2; and free labor ideology, 1, 8, 24; influence on Children's Aid Society, 8–12, 18–20, 21–22, 24; and politics of the 1850s, 14–16, 24; in rhetoric of child labor reformers, 48, 53, 71, 85, 87, 94, 98, 139, 146; in rhetoric of campaign to abolish padrone system, 35, 40, 37–38, 40. *See also* abolitionism; free labor

anti-suffrage, 3, 125, 135

Anti-Suffrage Association, 135

Arkansas: and child labor, 118; only Southern state to ratify Child Labor Amendment, 140

Ashby, Irene, 59–60, 65

Associated Industries of Massachusetts (AIM), 143

asylum system, 8, 22, 24–25; and reformers' comparisons to Southern slavery, 11–12, 19, 24. *See also* almsgiving

Atherton Mills, 124

Bacon, Augustus Octavius, 81

Baker, Newton D., 105, 126

Baldwin, William H., 71–72

Barnhart, Henry, 100

"best men" of the South, 52, 56, 61–63. *See also* New South

Beveridge, Albert, 78–82

Beveridge Bill, 79, 80–82, 86, 90–91

Black Codes, 32

Bleeding Kansas, 24

Boer War, 82

Bolshevik Revolution, 128, 152

Bonaparte, Charles Joseph, 78

Borah, William, 101

Bowery, 14

Boyd, James E., 106,124

boys: in antebellum child rescue, 8, 10–14, 16, 19–20, 24; in arguments about child labor during the First World War, 103–4, 112; in arguments about gender-specific skills learned through toys, 88, 107, 109–10, 115, 117; in arguments of opponents of reform, especially regarding farm labor as healthy for boys, 4–6, 87, 105–6, 114, 135, 137–38, 141–42; and the padrone system of child labor, 36–39, 47–49; in Southern textile mills, 52, 60; in Union Army, 21–24. *See also* anti-child labor reform

boys' lodging houses, 11,13–14, 20–21

Brace, Charles Loring, 10–14, 16, 21–24, 34, 43, 45–47, 49. *See also* Children's Aid Society

Brace, Letitia Neill, 12

Brand, Charles, 137

Britt, Danny Earl, 99

Brown, Sara A., 118

Bull Moose Party. *See* Progressive Party

bureaucratic state, 3, 5, 87; opponents of bureaucratic state, 114, 127, 133, 135–37, 140–41, 143, 145–47, 152; and protection of women and girls in the Progressive era, 87. *See also* Progressive Era

Bureau of Labor Statistics, 44

Bushnell, Horace, 12

Byrnes, James F., 99

California: and child labor, 118; support for the Child Labor Amendment, 124, 144; support for Keating-Owen Act, 100

capitalism: antislavery defense of, 8–10; capitalist authority, 27, 32, 35, 41; corporate reconstruction of, 107; disappearance of "greedy capitalist" from campaign against child labor, 105, 108, 111,112, 119, 123, 127; "enlightened" capitalist arguments, 25, 44–49, 52; girls as "worst victims" of, 5, 85, 87, 92–93, 105; moral boundaries of, 1–2, 6, 86, 107, 113, 115–16; moral regulation of, 101, 105, 127, 147; Social Gospel critique of, 85–86, 91–92, 94, 97–98, 127; Southern capitalists, 3, 5, 52–53, 64–65, 85–87, 114, 123, 145–46; Southern support for, 68–69, 70, 114, 147. *See also* class; consumerism; freedom; free labor; industrialization; market; progress

Carcone, Michele, 38–39

Careli, Luigi, 37

Carmack, Edward W., 81

Catholicism: opposition to Child Labor Amendment, 114, 127, 143–46; support for child labor reform, 125, 132, 143–46

Cerqua, A. E., 26

Chamberlain, Joseph, 126

Charity Organizations Society, 72

Chase, Daniel, 28

Chenery, William L., 145–46

childhood, 2; changing views of in antebellum America, 19–20; and Christian duty to protect, 75, 85, 96–97, 100; and leisure as essence of, 108, 113, 115, 117–19, 121–22; as sacred and off-limits to capitalism, 72, 92, 107, 127. *See also* American toy industry; boys; child labor; consumerism; girls

child labor: agricultural child labor, 8, 16, 20–22, 24, 116–18, 120, 131–33, 135–38,

Index

141–42; in antebellum New York City, 13–14, 16–17; and arguments about farm labor as healthy for boys, 4–6, 87, 105–6, 114, 135, 137–38, 141–42; and canneries, 91, 124, 149; and distinctiveness in broader landscape of Progressive reform, 3; in early America, 2; factory child labor in the North, 26–27, 41–45; factory child labor in the South, 51–52, 54, 58–60, 68, 72; on farms in the antebellum West, 18–19; in the First World War, 103–4, 112; former slave child apprentices, 26–27, 31–33, 35, 41, 43; gender and race in debates about, 3–4; and movies, 149; and New Deal, 5, 151–52; newsboys, 13–14, 20–21, 150; opposing North-South views in debates about, 1–3, 5–6, 9–10, 15–16, 18, 20, 24, 42, 52–53, 60, 64, 73, 85–87, 95; padrone children, 27, 33–34, 36–39; rise of child labor as a "national problem," 66, 68, 70–71, 83; and street trades, 35, 39, 43, 88, 126, 149; and tenement houses, 43, 85, 88, 90, 126, 131, 149. *See also* free labor

Child Labor Amendment, 3, 5, 123; African American support for, 125–26; coalition in support of, 124–25, 130, 132; Congressional debates about, 136–40; defeat of, 144–45; journalistic reporting of, 131; and Massachusetts Catholics, 143–44; opponents of, 127, 132–35, 141–42; second attempt at passage, 150–51; second defeat of, 152

Child Labor Bill. *See* Keating-Owen Act

Child Labor Day, 96, 98, 132

Child Labor Tax Law, 123–24

Children in Bondage, 85, 92–95

Children's Aid Society: and boys, 8, 10–11, 13–14, 16, 18, 21–23; and Civil War, 21–23; and dependency, 9, 11–13, 24; and free labor ideals, 7–10; and girls, 13–14, 18; and influence of antislavery movement on, 8, 12, 14–15, 24;

Children's Bureau, 86, 89, 90–91, 106, 109, 118, 122, 125, 132, 135, 151

child rescue, 8–9, 11–12; of boys in antebellum North, 8, 10–14, 16, 19–20, 24; of girls in antebellum North, 13–14, 16, 18

Child Welfare Commissions, 118

Christianity, 5, 22, 60; alliance of fundamentalists and Catholics, 145; Biblical arguments in favor of child labor reform, 75–76, 91, 93–94, 96–99; Biblical arguments opposed to child labor reform, 100, 137–38, 145–46; Christian split over Child Labor Amendment, 146; decline of Social Gospel, 129–30; and imperialism, 76–77, 79; rise of fundamentalist Christianity, 130. *See also* Catholicism; fundamentalism; Social Gospel

Citizens' Committee to Protect Our Homes and Children, 143

Civil Rights Act of 1866, 39

Civil War, 4, 7, 9, 10, 14, 18; black orphanages established during, 25; service of former Children's Aid Society boys in Union Army, 21–24. *See also* sectional crisis; slavery

Clark, David, 105–6, 123–24, 133, 136, 141, 145. *See also* Southern Textile Association

class, 1, 9, 11–12; capitalist class, 48–49; and "dishonest" forms of labor, 12–13, 16; English working class, 74; former slaveholding class, 52, 57; middle-class white children, 111–12; and poor whites in the South, 3–4, 54, 56–58, 60, 63–64, 67; working-class Catholics, 127, 143. *See also* capitalism; consumerism; freedom; free labor; industrialization; market; progress

Clay, Cassius, 9, 12

Clay, Henry, 15

Clopper, Edward N., 119

Colored National League of Boston, 62

Commissioners of Public Charities and Corrections, 40

Committee on Public Information (CPI), 108–9, 128

Committees on Manufacture, 47

Compromise of 1850, 15

Compromise of 1877, 54

consumerism, 2, 4–6, 87, 107; and influence on the child labor reform movement, 110, 112, 114, 127, 152; and the rise of children's consumer culture, 107–8. *See also* American toy industry

Coolidge, Calvin, 128–29, 140

Coolidge, Louis A., 134

Cotton Textile Institute, 152

Cox, James M., 128

Croly, Herbert, 144

Crosby, Fanny, 96

Curley, James M., 144

Curry, George W., 30–31

Dagenhart, Roland, 106, 123. See also *Hammer v. Dagenhart*

Davis, W. John, 140

238   Index

DeForest, Robert W., 68, 72, 80,
Delaware: and child labor, 7, 9, 19; child la-
  bor laws in, 74; opposition to Child Labor
  Amendment, 144
Department of Commerce and Labor, 89
dependency: and lodging houses, 13; as op-
  posite of free labor, 9, 11–12, 24
Devanter, Willis Van, 151
Devine, Edward T., 75
Douglass, Frederick, 12
Dred Scott decision, 15, 24
Dubose, William Porcher, 56
Dyer antilynching bill, 125

emancipation, meaning of, 2, 4, 24; and
  ambiguities of factory child labor, 48–49;
  application of emancipation laws to
  padrone children, 33, 37–40; competing
  definitions among Freedmen's Bureau
  agents and freed people, 27–28, 31–32;
  competing definitions in the movement
  to abolish child labor, 52; and industrial
  child labor in the Progressive era, 98, 102;
  and Southern white child labor, 58, 70.
  See also antislavery thought; free labor;
  slave emancipation
embargoes, 110
Emery, James A., 133, 136. See also National
  Association of Manufacturers
emigration plan, 16–20, 24
Espionage and Sedition Acts, 128
ex-slaves. See freed people

factories: during the First World War, 104–5,
  109; in the North, 26–27, 41–45; in the
  South, 51–52, 54, 58–60, 68, 72
Fair Labor Standards Act (FLSA), 5, 151–52
Fall River, 41–42
Farmers' States Rights League, 141–42, 145
farm families, 3; opposition to child labor
  reform, 127, 132, 136–38, 141–42, 144–47;
  reformers' views about, 117–19, 131–32; in
  the South, 32, 113, 115, 127, 135, 144; in the
  West, 8, 18, 22, 24. See also rural America
farm labor. See agricultural labor
Feagin, N. B., 71
Federal Council of Churches of Christ in
  America (FCCC), 96, 146
Federalist Papers, 136
First Confiscation Act of 1861, 168
First World War, 5, 87, 89, 102; impact on
  child labor reform movement, 105, 112,
  122–23; impact on Social Gospel, 129–30;

wartime rise of American toy industry,
  108–10
Fitzgerald, Roy G., 124
Fitzhugh, George, 9–10
Florida: opposition to Keating-Owen Act,
  100. See also anti-child labor reform
forced apprenticeships, 27–30; challenges to
  based on free labor principles, 29, 32–33
formerly enslaved children, 26–27, 29, 31, 33,
  36. See also freed people
Fort Sumter, 21
founding fathers, 134, 137
4-H clubs, 122
Fourteenth Amendment, 32
Freedmen's Bureau, 25, 27; and complaints of
  freed persons regarding the apprenticing
  of their children, 27–32; and views about
  free labor, 29–33. See also emancipation
freedom, 1–2, 4–6; and campaign to emancipate padrone children, 26–27, 33, 35, 39,
  41, 43–44; factory child labor as "unfree,"
  52–53, 58, 70; and Freedmen's Bureau's
  views of, 29, 32–33; and freed persons'
  views of, 27–28, 31–32; labor as essence of,
  8–9, 12, 15, 24, 87, 105–6, 114, 135, 137–38,
  141–42, 147; overview of varying definitions of, 152; proslavery critique of labor
  as essence of, 9–10; and restraining sinful
  capitalism, 85–86, 95–98, 102; self-fulfillment and personal growth as essence of,
  107–8, 110, 112, 114, 117–18, 122–23, 127. See
  also abolition; antislavery thought; emancipation; free labor; slave emancipation
freed people, 4, 25; freed children, 26–27, 29,
  31, 33, 36; freed parents, 28, 32–33
free labor, 1–3; in antislavery Republicanism, 8–9, 12, 15, 24; in arguments against
  the padrone trade in Italian children,
  26–27, 33, 35, 39, 41, 43–44; in arguments
  of opponents of child labor reform, 4–6,
  87, 105–6, 114, 135, 137–38, 141–42; and
  decline of free labor ideology in reformers' arguments, 52; in Freedmen's Bureau
  arguments against forced apprenticeships, 29, 32–33; in rhetoric of Children's
  Aid Society, 8–12, 18–20, 21–22, 24
Freund, Ernest, 126
Fugitive Slave Act, 15
Fullerton, James S., 25–26
Fulmer, Hampton Pitts, 137
fundamentalism, 130, 133–34, 139, 145–46

Gallicano, Giuseppe, 38–39

Index

Gant, Virgil, 28
Garland, Mahlon M., 100
Garrison, William Lloyd, 12
Gaston, Judge J. B., 71
gender, 3–4; gender difference arguments
for state protection of child laborers,
87–88; gender difference arguments in
child leisure, 88, 110–11; gender difference
arguments in free labor ideology, 13–14,
16, 18; shifting gender dynamics of child
labor debate, 141–42. *See also* boys; girls
Georgia: and child labor, 51, 54–55; and
Freedmen's Bureau, 29; opposition to
Beveridge Bill, 81, opposition to Child Labor Amendment, 142, 144–45; and Southern Progressivism, 71. *See also* anti-child
labor reform; Southern Progressivism
Gibbon, Charles, 117
Gill, Nelson G., 32
girls: in antebellum child rescue, 13–14, 16,
18; in arguments about gender-specific
skills learned through toys, 88, 110–11,
141; in arguments of opponents of reform,
regarding the value of housework for
girls, 135; in post-Civil War factory labor
in North, 41–42; in reformers' arguments
for child labor regulation, 5, 85, 87, 92–93,
105; in Southern textile mills, 52, 60. *See
also* bureaucratic state, protection of
women and girls
Glione, Giovanni, 38
Golone, Joseph, 37
Gompers, Samuel, 58–59, 125
Graham, George S., 132
Granite Mill, 41–44
Grayson, Frederick, 28
Great Fire of 1871, 42
Great Western Railroad Company, 17
Greeley, Horace, 9, 12, 15, 24

Hammer, W. C., 106. See also *Hammer v.
Dagenhart*
Hammer v. Dagenhart: overturning of, 151;
ruling of, 106, 123
Harding, Warren G., 128–30, 133
Healy, Margaret, 41, 43–44
Hearst, William Randolph, 77, 79, 92
Hepburn Railroad Rate Act, 79
Holloway, Ruben Ross, 133–34
Holmes, Carter, 29
House Judiciary Committee, 132, 135
House of Refuge, 7
Houston, David F., 116

Howard, O. O., 30
Howell, Clark, 71
Hubbard, Elbert, 65
Hughes, Edwin H., 97
Hull House, 89
Hunter, Robert, 71

Illinois: and Children's Aid Society, 16–17;
and lynching, 126; support for Child
Labor Amendment, 130, 150. *See also*
emigration plan
immigration, 10, 21,35, 41, 46, 69, 76, 81, 111,
120, 128–29. *See also* nativism
Immigration Act of 1924, 129
imperialism: in the Spanish-American War,
52–53, 61, 63–64
Indiana: and Children's Aid Society, 16; and
Dyer antilynching bill, 125–26; and support for Beveridge Bill, 78–79; and support for Keating-Owen Act, 100. *See also*
Beveridge, Albert; emigration plan
Indiana Federation of Colored Women, 125
industrialization, 4–6, 24, 26, 52, 54–55, 58,
68, 72, 74, 86–87, 111, 113, 116, 119, 136, 147
International Child Welfare League, 86

J. L. Hudson Company, 109
Johnson, Hiram, 124
Johnston, Eugene W., 124
Jones, Willis R., 134
Judicial Procedures Reform Plan, 151

Kamper, Jane, 28
Kansas-Nebraska Act, 14–15
Kansas Territory, 14
Keating, Edward, 99. *See also* Keating-Owen
Act
Keating-Owen Act, campaign for, 86, 98,
101–3, 111, 117, 127; legal challenge to, 105–
6, 123–24; Supreme Court overturning of,
106; Wilson signing into law of, 102. See
also *Hammer v. Dagenhart*
Kelley, Florence, 70–71, 75, 80, 125
Kent, William, 100
Kilbreth, Mary G., 135
Kirkland, James, 71
Ku Klux Klan, 129–30

labor unions: American Federation of Labor
(AFL), 58, 86, 125, 132; attack on unions
during Red Scare, 128; interest in child
labor issue, 58–59, 125, 146; National
Women's Trade Union, 125

240 *Index*

LaFollette, Robert M., 140
LaGuardia, Fiorello, 139
Langdale (AL) mill settlement, 67
Lanham, Fritz G., 137–38
Lathrop, Julia C., 89
law: and apprenticeship, 30–32, 35; and attempts at federal child labor law, 80–82, 86, 90–92, 94, 96–97, 99, 102, 124; and child labor in North, 43, 47–48, 70, 74, 88–89; and child labor in South, 51, 58–59, 70, 85, 88–89; and defeat of Child Labor Amendment, 144–45; and federal progressive reforms, 79; and mixed legacy of child labor provisions in Fair Labor Standards Act, 151–52; and prohibition of padrone trade in children, 40; and protection of emancipated persons, 27, 37–39; and second attempt at passage of Child Labor Amendment, 150–52; and Supreme Court overturning of federal child labor laws, 106, 124; and suspension of child labor laws and compulsory education laws during First World War, 103–5. *See also* Beveridge Bill; Child Labor Amendment; Child Labor Tax Law; *Hammer v. Dagenhart*; Keating-Owen Act; Lochner era
Lenroot, Irvine Luther, 99
Lindeman, E. C., 142
Lindsay, Matilda, 125
Lindsay, Samuel McCune, 73–75, 78, 80–81
Lindsey, Benjamin, 92–93
Link, William A., 3, 86–87
Lochner era, 123, 151
Lockwood, Henry, 30–32
lodging houses, 11, 13–14, 20–21
Lottery Act, 91, 101
Louisiana: and Freedmen's Bureau, 25, 28; opposition to Child Labor Amendment, 142. *See also* anti-child labor reform
Louisiana Purchase, 15
Lovejoy, Owen, 86, 89–96, 98, 104, 106, 111, 116–18, 122, 125–26, 132, 135
Lowell, A. Lawrence, 144
Lumpkin, Katharine, 144
Lusitania, 102
lynching, 56, 62, 70, 115, 129

Manifest Destiny, 78
Mann Act, 101
market: child labor reformers' critique of, 70, 74, 86, 97, 127; child labor reformers' embrace of consumer market hegemony, 109, 112; crash of the stock market, 149–

50; expansion of market after the Civil War, 24, 26–27, 35, 45, 48–49, 52; proslavery critique of, 1, 9–10; rejection of consumer market hegemony by opponents of reform, 114, 146–47; rise of consumer market in early twentieth century, 3–4, 6, 107–8. *See also* consumerism; free labor
Markham, Edwin, 76–78, 92–93
Maryland: and child labor, 118, 120; and Freedmen's Bureau, 28–29; and opposition to Child Labor Amendment, 133, 138–39; and orphans court of Anne Arundel County, 30–31. *See also* anti-child labor reform
Mason-Dixon Line, 1, 5, 147, 152
Massachusetts: and capitalists, 44, 66–67; and child labor, 41–43; and labor unions, 59; and opposition to Child Labor Amendment among urban Catholics, 143–46
McCambridge, C. P., 78
McCormick, Medill, 130–31
McCormick-Foster measure, 131
McKellar, Kenneth, 99
McKelway, Alexander, 74–75, 80, 90–91
McKinley, William, 61–62
McLendon, S. G., 145–46
McSwain, John J., 138
McVickar, William N., 75–76
Meat Inspection Act, 79
Methodist Episcopal Church, 97
Mexican-American War, 15
Michigan Central Railroad, 17
mill families, 53–54, 67, 106. *See also* Southern textile industry
Ministers' Union, 57
Missionary Society, 72
Mississippi: and Freedmen's Bureau, 32; opposition to Child Labor Amendment, 132. *See also* anti-child labor reform
Missouri Compromise, 14–15
Moderation League, 133
modern child welfare, 5, 87–88, 91, 106–9, 111–12, 115, 117, 147. *See also* First World War
Montague, Andrew J., 133
Montgomery (AL), 51, 57–59, 61, 63
Moreno, Celso Caesar, 40
Muller v. Oregon, 87, 92. *See also* bureaucratic state
Murphy, Edgar Gardner: and Alabama Child Labor Bill, 59–60; and Alabama Child Labor Committee, 61; death of, 83; and founding of National Child Labor

Index

Committee (NCLC), 71; and investigations of child labor in South, 51–52; and Jim Crow, 73; and lynching, 56; and "nationalizing" of child labor problem, 68–70; and opposition to Beveridge Bill, 80–82; and resignation from NCLC, 80; and Southern progressivism, 57–58, 63; Spanish-American War, 61–62; and white supremacy arguments, 52, 56–58, 60, 63–64. *See also* Southern Progressivism

National Association of Manufacturers, 133, 135, 141, 152. *See also* Emery, James A.
National Baby Week, 106, 109
National Catholic Welfare Council, 125
National Child Labor Committee (NCLC): and the battle over the Child Labor Amendment, 123–25, 130, 132, 144–45, 150–51; campaign for Keating-Owen, 86, 88–89, 91–92, 96–97, 102; coordination with churches, 76, 81, 96–97; and First World War, 103–6, 111; focus on agricultural child labor, 116–17; founding of, 71–72, 77–78; influence of Social Gospel on, 92, 94, 96–97; and Lewis Hine, 85; support for Beveridge Bill, 80–82
National Commissioners of Education, 46
National Committee for the Protection of Child, Family, School, and Church, 143, 150
National Committee for the Rejection of the 20th Amendment, 141–43
National Conference of Charities and Corrections, 89
National Conference of Social Work, 118
National Conference on Child Labor, 116
National Consumers' League, 86
National Council of Catholic Women, 132, 143
National Council of Defense, 107
National Council of Rural Agencies, 118
National Education Association, 118
National League of Women Voters, 125, 140
National Progressive Party Convention, 89
National Recovery Administration (NRA), 150–51
National Security League, 128
National Women's Trade Union League, 125
nativism, 35, 46, 69, 77, 81, 94, 128–29. *See also* immigration
New Deal, 151–52
New Jersey: and child labor, 118, 120, 132; support for Child Labor Amendment, 150

Newsboys' Lodging House, 21
New South: and "best men" of the South, 56; and education of poor whites, 57; and industrialization, 54–55; and Jim Crow racial segregation, 73; racial order, 52, 60, 62–63; and romanticizing of Old South, 58
New York: and child labor, 13–14, 17, 20, 26, 33–36, 44, 46; child labor laws in, 40–41, 48, 105; reform work in, 70–72, 80, 91–92, 149; support for Child Labor Amendment, 139. *See also* New York City
New York Central Railroad Company, 17
New York Child Labor Committee, 71
New York City, 7, 12, 33, 37–38, 46, 70, 76, 80, 82, 92, 119, 149
Nichols, Howard, 66–67, 74
North Carolina: and child labor, 51, 54, 89; and Freedmen's Bureau, 30; opposition to Beveridge bill, 81; opposition to Child Labor Amendment, 139, 141–42, 144–45; opposition to child labor reform in general, 87; opposition to Child Labor Tax Law, 124; opposition to Keating-Owen Act, 99, 105–6; and Southern Progressivism, 74. *See also* anti-child labor reform; Southern Progressivism
Northwest Ordinance, 15

O'Connell, William Cardinal, 143
Ohio: and antislavery Republicanism, 15; child labor laws in, 89; and Children's Aid Society, 16; support for Child Labor Amendment, 124, 150. *See also* emigration plan
Old South, 53, 57–58, 87
Olmsted, Frederick Law, 12, 24
orphans court, 28, 31
Overman, Lee Slater, 81
Owen, Robert, 91, 99. *See also* Keating-Owen Act

Padrone Act, 40–41
padrone system, 26–27, 33–41, 43–45, 47, 49
Palmer, Mitchell, 91, 98
Palmer-Owen Bill. *See* Keating-Owen Act
Parsons, Henry, 79
paternalism, 56
Pennsylvania: and child labor, 68, 92; child labor laws in, 40, 105; support for Child Labor Amendment, 150; support for Keating-Owen Act, 9, 100;
Permanent Conference for the Abolition of Child Labor, 125, 130–31, 140

242   *Index*

Personal Liberty Bill of 1854, 38
Phil, the Fiddler, 41
pick-pocketing, 13
Pollock, William, 77
poorhouses, 11
Poor Law of England, 2
post-emancipation, 2, 26, 41
postmillennialism, 129
Pottawatomie Creek, 161
Pound, Roscoe, 126
premillennialism, 129
progress: and consumer values, 107, 112–13; and industry, 26, 68–69, 74, 77; in New South creed, 55, 57–58, 61, 66; as opposite of the rural way of life, 114, 119–20, 122, 127, 147, 152. *See also* capitalism; consumerism; freedom; free labor; industrialization; market
Progressive amendments, 3
Progressive Era, 3, 85; decline in the 1920s, 128–29; protection of women and children, 87, 92; in the South, 57, 63, 86. *See also* Progressive reform
Progressive reform, 3, 57, 79, 86, 128–29
Prohibition, 3, 87, 124–25, 129–30
Prohibition Amendment, 129
proslavery, 1, 9–10, 15–16, 71, 146
Protestant Episcopal Church, 72
Protestantism
Pure Food and Drug Act, 79

race, 3–4; in arguments against child labor legislation, 138–39; and Children's Aid Society in the 1850s, 18; and compulsory education, 46; and nationalizing of the child labor problem, 52–53, 56–58, 60–64, 69, 73, 81–82; race-specific arguments for child labor protections, 94–95. *See also* African Americans; immigration; imperialism; lynching; Murphy, Edgar Gardner; nativism; New South; paternalism; sectional reconciliation; Southern Progressivism; white supremacy
Rauschenbusch, Walter, 97
Reavis, Charles Frank, 99
Reconstruction, 24, 52, 53, 54–57, 62, 73, 115
Reconstruction amendments, 24
Redeemers, 54
Red Scare, 128–29
Regan, Agnes, 132
Reilly-Morrow Bill, 59
Republican National Committee, 128
Riis, Jacob, 119

Roberts, Owen J., 151
Roosevelt, Franklin Delano, 129, 149–51
Roosevelt, Theodore, 74, 78–82, 89–90, 102
rural America, 3, 5; child welfare reformers' investigations of, 116, 117–23; opposition to child labor reform in, 127, 132, 136–38, 141–42, 144–47; post-Reconstruction South, 53, 56; post-World War I rural South, 112–15; Western farms, 8, 17, 19, 22. *See also* farm families
Ryan, John A., 125, 143–44

Saraceno, Vito Nicola, 38
Savings Bank, 13, 21
Sears, Horace, 67, 74
sectional crisis, 1–2, 4, 8, 10, 15–16, 18, 20, 24. *See also* sectionalism
sectionalism, 1–4, 8, 10, 15–16, 18, 20, 24; in arguments of opponents of child labor reform, 42, 52, 60, 64, 73; in child labor reform movement, 52–53, 64, 85–87, 95
sectional reconciliation, 61, 64, 73
Senate Judiciary Committee, 131
Sentinels of the Republic, 133–34, 143
Seward, William H., 14–15
Shank, T. W., 77
Sheppard-Towner Act, 129, 133, 135
slave emancipation, 2, 4, 24, 27, 32. *See also* emancipation, meaning of
Slave Power conspiracy, 12, 14–15, 24
slavery, 1–2; in arguments against the apprenticing of freed children, 28, 30, 32; as a metaphor for the asylum system and poorhouses, 11–12, 19, 24; as a metaphor for industrial child labor, 48–49, 52–53, 64–65, 67, 85–86, 94–95, 98–99, 102, 114, 139, 146; as a metaphor for the padrone system, 26, 33–34, 37–38, 40, 43–44; as the opposite of "free labor," 810, 14,16, 20, 24. *See also* sectional crisis; Slave Power conspiracy
Smith, Henry, 56
Smith, Hoke, 71
Smith, John F., 119–20
Smothers, Derinda, 28
Social Creed, 96–97
social Darwinism, 56–57
Social Gospel, 5, 85–87; decline of the Social Gospel's influence, 105–8,112, 129–30; influence on the campaign for a federal child labor law, 91–93, 95–98, 100–102, 127; support for the Child Labor Amendment, 125, 146
socialism, 134–35

Society for the Prevention of Cruelty to Children (SPCC), 40–41
Sociological Club, 91
South Carolina: and child labor, 51, 54, 65; and opposition to the Beveridge Bill, 82; and opposition to the Child Labor Amendment, 137–38, 144; and opposition to the Keating-Owen Act, 99; and Southern Progressivism, 71. *See also* anti-child labor reform; Southern Progressivism
Southern Education Board (SEB), 57, 63, 71–72
Southern Progressivism, 57, 63, 86
Southern Society, 57
Southern Textile Association, 105, 133, 135, 141. *See also* Clark, David
Southern textile industry, 55, 94, 115, 120, 133, 142
Spanish-American War, 52, 61–62, 64, 73
Stafford, Andrew, 30
Stephens, Hubert, 139
Storey, Moorfield, 144
Stowe, Harriet Beecher, 64
Sumner, Charles, 40–41
Sumners, Hatton W., 132–33, 136

Taft, William Howard, 89
Tennessee: and Congressional argument in favor of Keating-Owen Act, 99; and Freedmen's Bureau, 28; opposition to Beveridge Bill, 81; opposition to Child Labor Amendment, 144. *See also* anti-child labor reform; Southern Progressivism
Texas: and child labor, 118, 121; and lynching, 56; and opposition to Child Labor Amendment, 132, 136–37, 144. *See also* anti-child labor reform
Thirteenth Amendment, 27
Tillman, Benjamin, 71, 82
Tillson, Davis, 29–30
Tomlinson Hall, 78
Townsend, William, 28
toy industry. *See* American toy industry
Toy Manufacturers of the USA, 109
Tracy, C. C., 13
Treaty of Paris, 61
Triangle Shirtwaist Factory fire, 92–93
Tucker, Henry St. George, 138
Tydings, Millard, 138

Uncle Tom's Cabin, 65, 94
Union Army, 21–23
Union Theological Seminary, 12

University of the South–Sewanee, 56
Upper South, 55
Urban League, 126
US Children's Bureau, 86, 89, 90–91, 106, 109, 118, 122, 125, 132, 135, 151
US Constitution, 5, 123, 132, 137

vagrancy: of children in New York City, 8, 13, 18, 21–22, 34; of formerly enslaved parents, 31
Virginia: and child labor, 118, 120; opposition to Child Labor Amendment, 133, 138; proslavery, 9. *See also* anti-child labor reform

Wald, Lillian, 70, 72
Wallace, Edgar, 132
war pamphlets, 103
Washington, DC, 28, 30, 78, 125, 140
Watson, E. O., 125, 132
Weaver, Zebulon, 139
Webb, Edwin Yates, 99–100
Wefald, Knud, 139
Westfield College, 59
West Point Manufacturing Company, 67
West/Western territories, 8, 12, 14–18, 20–22, 24, 89
Whitehead, Charles E., 46–47
white supremacy, 52, 56–58, 60–64, 69, 73, 81–82, 94, 115, 125, 138, 152. *See also* African Americans; imperialism; lynching; Murphy, Edgar Gardner; nativism; New South; paternalism; sectional reconciliation; Southern Progressivism
Whittlesey, Eliphalet, 30
Williams, John E., 23
Wilson, Woodrow, 90–91, 102–3, 105–6, 108–9, 116, 128
Wisconsin: and child labor, 118; reform activity in, 116; support for Child Labor Amendment, 144; support for Keating-Owen Act, 99
Woman's Patriotic Publishing Company, 133, 135
Women's Constitutional League of Maryland, 133–34
Wood, John W., 72
Works, John D., 101
World War I. *See* First World War

Young, Ira, 28

Zimmermann Telegram, 102

BETSY WOOD is a professor of history at Hudson County Community College.

The Working Class in American History

Worker City, Company Town: Iron and Cotton-Worker Protest in Troy and
Cohoes, New York, 1855–84   *Daniel J. Walkowitz*

Life, Work, and Rebellion in the Coal Fields: The Southern West Virginia Miners,
1880–1922   *David Alan Corbin*

Women and American Socialism, 1870–1920   *Mari Jo Buhle*

Lives of Their Own: Blacks, Italians, and Poles in Pittsburgh, 1900–1960
John Bodnar, Roger Simon, and Michael P. Weber

Working-Class America: Essays on Labor, Community, and American
Society   *Edited by Michael H. Frisch and Daniel J. Walkowitz*

Eugene V. Debs: Citizen and Socialist   *Nick Salvatore*

American Labor and Immigration History, 1877–1920s: Recent European
Research   *Edited by Dirk Hoerder*

Workingmen's Democracy: The Knights of Labor and American Politics
Leon Fink

The Electrical Workers: A History of Labor at General Electric and
Westinghouse, 1923–60   *Ronald W. Schatz*

The Mechanics of Baltimore: Workers and Politics in the Age of Revolution,
1763–1812   *Charles G. Steffen*

The Practice of Solidarity: American Hat Finishers in the Nineteenth
Century   *David Bensman*

The Labor History Reader   *Edited by Daniel J. Leab*

Solidarity and Fragmentation: Working People and Class Consciousness
in Detroit, 1875–1900   *Richard Oestreicher*

Counter Cultures: Saleswomen, Managers, and Customers in American
Department Stores, 1890–1940   *Susan Porter Benson*

The New England Working Class and the New Labor History
Edited by Herbert G. Gutman and Donald H. Bell

Labor Leaders in America   *Edited by Melvyn Dubofsky and Warren Van Tine*

Barons of Labor: The San Francisco Building Trades and Union Power in the
Progressive Era   *Michael Kazin*

Gender at Work: The Dynamics of Job Segregation by Sex during
World War II   *Ruth Milkman*

Once a Cigar Maker: Men, Women, and Work Culture in American Cigar
Factories, 1900–1919   *Patricia A. Cooper*

A Generation of Boomers: The Pattern of Railroad Labor Conflict in
Nineteenth-Century America   *Shelton Stromquist*

Work and Community in the Jungle: Chicago's Packinghouse Workers, 1894–1922
James R. Barrett

Workers, Managers, and Welfare Capitalism: The Shoeworkers and Tanners
of Endicott Johnson, 1890–1950   *Gerald Zahavi*

Men, Women, and Work: Class, Gender, and Protest in the New England Shoe
Industry, 1780–1910   *Mary Blewett*

Workers on the Waterfront: Seamen, Longshoremen, and Unionism in the
1930s   *Bruce Nelson*

German Workers in Chicago: A Documentary History of Working-Class Culture
from 1850 to World War I   *Edited by Hartmut Keil and John B. Jentz*

On the Line: Essays in the History of Auto Work   *Edited by Nelson Lichtenstein
and Stephen Meyer III*

Labor's Flaming Youth: Telephone Operators and Worker Militancy, 1878–1923
Stephen H. Norwood

Another Civil War: Labor, Capital, and the State in the Anthracite Regions
of Pennsylvania, 1840-68   *Grace Palladino*

Coal, Class, and Color: Blacks in Southern West Virginia, 1915–32
Joe William Trotter Jr.

For Democracy, Workers, and God: Labor Song-Poems and Labor Protest, 1865–95
Clark D. Halker

Dishing It Out: Waitresses and Their Unions in the Twentieth Century
Dorothy Sue Cobble

The Spirit of 1848: German Immigrants, Labor Conflict, and the Coming of
the Civil War   *Bruce Levine*

Working Women of Collar City: Gender, Class, and Community in Troy,
New York, 1864–86   *Carole Turbin*

Southern Labor and Black Civil Rights: Organizing Memphis Workers
Michael K. Honey

Radicals of the Worst Sort: Laboring Women in Lawrence, Massachusetts,
1860–1912   *Ardis Cameron*

Producers, Proletarians, and Politicians: Workers and Party Politics in Evansville
and New Albany, Indiana, 1850–87   *Lawrence M. Lipin*

The New Left and Labor in the 1960s   *Peter B. Levy*

The Making of Western Labor Radicalism: Denver's Organized Workers, 1878–1905
David Brundage

In Search of the Working Class: Essays in American Labor History and Political
Culture   *Leon Fink*

Lawyers against Labor: From Individual Rights to Corporate Liberalism
Daniel R. Ernst

"We Are All Leaders": The Alternative Unionism of the Early 1930s
Edited by Staughton Lynd

The Female Economy: The Millinery and Dressmaking Trades, 1860–1930
Wendy Gamber

"Negro and White, Unite and Fight!": A Social History of Industrial Unionism
in Meatpacking, 1930–90   *Roger Horowitz*

Power at Odds: The 1922 National Railroad Shopmen's Strike   *Colin J. Davis*

The Common Ground of Womanhood: Class, Gender, and Working Girls' Clubs, 1884–1928   *Priscilla Murolo*

Marching Together: Women of the Brotherhood of Sleeping Car Porters   *Melinda Chateauvert*

Down on the Killing Floor: Black and White Workers in Chicago's Packinghouses, 1904–54   *Rick Halpern*

Labor and Urban Politics: Class Conflict and the Origins of Modern Liberalism in Chicago, 1864–97   *Richard Schneirov*

All That Glitters: Class, Conflict, and Community in Cripple Creek   *Elizabeth Jameson*

Waterfront Workers: New Perspectives on Race and Class   *Edited by Calvin Winslow*

Labor Histories: Class, Politics, and the Working-Class Experience   *Edited by Eric Arnesen, Julie Greene, and Bruce Laurie*

The Pullman Strike and the Crisis of the 1890s: Essays on Labor and Politics   *Edited by Richard Schneirov, Shelton Stromquist, and Nick Salvatore*

AlabamaNorth: African-American Migrants, Community, and Working-Class Activism in Cleveland, 1914–45   *Kimberley L. Phillips*

Imagining Internationalism in American and British Labor, 1939–49   *Victor Silverman*

William Z. Foster and the Tragedy of American Radicalism   *James R. Barrett*

Colliers across the Sea: A Comparative Study of Class Formation in Scotland and the American Midwest, 1830–1924   *John H. M. Laslett*

"Rights, Not Roses": Unions and the Rise of Working-Class Feminism, 1945–80   *Dennis A. Deslippe*

Testing the New Deal: The General Textile Strike of 1934 in the American South   *Janet Irons*

Hard Work: The Making of Labor History   *Melvyn Dubofsky*

Southern Workers and the Search for Community: Spartanburg County, South Carolina   *G. C. Waldrep III*

We Shall Be All: A History of the Industrial Workers of the World (abridged edition)   *Melvyn Dubofsky, ed. Joseph A. McCartin*

Race, Class, and Power in the Alabama Coalfields, 1908–21   *Brian Kelly*

Duquesne and the Rise of Steel Unionism   *James D. Rose*

Anaconda: Labor, Community, and Culture in Montana's Smelter City   *Laurie Mercier*

Bridgeport's Socialist New Deal, 1915–36   *Cecelia Bucki*

Indispensable Outcasts: Hobo Workers and Community in the American Midwest, 1880–1930   *Frank Tobias Higbie*

After the Strike: A Century of Labor Struggle at Pullman   *Susan Eleanor Hirsch*

Corruption and Reform in the Teamsters Union   *David Witwer*

Waterfront Revolts: New York and London Dockworkers, 1946–61   *Colin J. Davis*

Black Workers' Struggle for Equality in Birmingham   *Horace Huntley and David Montgomery*

The Tribe of Black Ulysses: African American Men in the Industrial South   *William P. Jones*

City of Clerks: Office and Sales Workers in Philadelphia, 1870–1920   *Jerome P. Bjelopera*

Reinventing "The People": The Progressive Movement, the Class Problem, and the Origins of Modern Liberalism   *Shelton Stromquist*

Radical Unionism in the Midwest, 1900–1950   *Rosemary Feurer*

Gendering Labor History   *Alice Kessler-Harris*

James P. Cannon and the Origins of the American Revolutionary Left, 1890–1928   *Bryan D. Palmer*

Glass Towns: Industry, Labor, and Political Economy in Appalachia, 1890–1930s   *Ken Fones-Wolf*

Workers and the Wild: Conservation, Consumerism, and Labor in Oregon, 1910–30   *Lawrence M. Lipin*

Wobblies on the Waterfront: Interracial Unionism in Progressive-Era Philadelphia   *Peter Cole*

Red Chicago: American Communism at Its Grassroots, 1928–35   *Randi Storch*

Labor's Cold War: Local Politics in a Global Context   *Edited by Shelton Stromquist*

Bessie Abramowitz Hillman and the Making of the Amalgamated Clothing Workers of America   *Karen Pastorello*

The Great Strikes of 1877   *Edited by David O. Stowell*

Union-Free America: Workers and Antiunion Culture   *Lawrence Richards*

Race against Liberalism: Black Workers and the UAW in Detroit   *David M. Lewis-Colman*

Teachers and Reform: Chicago Public Education, 1929–70   *John F. Lyons*

Upheaval in the Quiet Zone: 1199/SEIU and the Politics of Healthcare Unionism   *Leon Fink and Brian Greenberg*

Shadow of the Racketeer: Scandal in Organized Labor   *David Witwer*

Sweet Tyranny: Migrant Labor, Industrial Agriculture, and Imperial Politics   *Kathleen Mapes*

Staley: The Fight for a New American Labor Movement   *Steven K. Ashby and C. J. Hawking*

On the Ground: Labor Struggles in the American Airline Industry   *Liesl Miller Orenic*

NAFTA and Labor in North America   *Norman Caulfield*

Making Capitalism Safe: Work Safety and Health Regulation in America, 1880–1940   *Donald W. Rogers*

Good, Reliable, White Men: Railroad Brotherhoods, 1877–1917   *Paul Michel Taillon*

Spirit of Rebellion: Labor and Religion in the New Cotton South   *Jarod Roll*
The Labor Question in America: Economic Democracy in the
   Gilded Age   *Rosanne Currarino*
Banded Together: Economic Democratization in the Brass Valley
   Jeremy Brecher
The Gospel of the Working Class: Labor's Southern Prophets in New Deal
   America   *Erik Gellman and Jarod Roll*
Guest Workers and Resistance to U.S. Corporate Despotism   *Immanuel Ness*
Gleanings of Freedom: Free and Slave Labor along the Mason-Dixon Line,
   1790–1860   *Max Grivno*
Chicago in the Age of Capital: Class, Politics, and Democracy during the
   Civil War and Reconstruction   *John B. Jentz and Richard Schneirov*
Child Care in Black and White: Working Parents and the History of
   Orphanages   *Jessie B. Ramey*
The Haymarket Conspiracy: Transatlantic Anarchist Networks
   Timothy Messer-Kruse
Detroit's Cold War: The Origins of Postwar Conservatism   *Colleen Doody*
A Renegade Union: Interracial Organizing and Labor Radicalism   *Lisa Phillips*
Palomino: Clinton Jencks and Mexican-American Unionism in the
   American Southwest   *James J. Lorence*
Latin American Migrations to the U.S. Heartland: Changing Cultural Landscapes
   in Middle America   *Edited by Linda Allegro and Andrew Grant Wood*
Man of Fire: Selected Writings   *Ernesto Galarza, ed. Armando Ibarra and Rodolfo
   D. Torres*
A Contest of Ideas: Capital, Politics, and Labor   *Nelson Lichtenstein*
Making the World Safe for Workers: Labor, the Left, and Wilsonian
   Internationalism   *Elizabeth McKillen*
The Rise of the Chicago Police Department: Class and Conflict, 1850–1894
   Sam Mitrani
Workers in Hard Times: A Long View of Economic Crises   *Edited by Leon Fink,
   Joseph A. McCartin, and Joan Sangster*
Redeeming Time: Protestantism and Chicago's Eight-Hour Movement, 1866–1912
   William A. Mirola
Struggle for the Soul of the Postwar South: White Evangelical Protestants and
   Operation Dixie   *Elizabeth Fones-Wolf and Ken Fones-Wolf*
Free Labor: The Civil War and the Making of an American Working Class
   Mark A. Lause
Death and Dying in the Working Class, 1865–1920   *Michael K. Rosenow*
Immigrants against the State: Yiddish and Italian Anarchism in America
   Kenyon Zimmer
Fighting for Total Person Unionism: Harold Gibbons, Ernest Calloway,
   and Working-Class Citizenship   *Robert Bussel*
Smokestacks in the Hills: Rural-Industrial Workers in West Virginia   *Louis Martin*

Disaster Citizenship: Survivors, Solidarity, and Power in the Progressive
Era   *Jacob A. C. Remes*

The Pew and the Picket Line: Christianity and the American Working
Class   *Edited by Christopher D. Cantwell, Heath W. Carter, and Janine
Giordano Drake*

Conservative Counterrevolution: Challenging Liberalism in 1950s
Milwaukee   *Tula A. Connell*

Manhood on the Line: Working-Class Masculinities in the American
Heartland   *Steve Meyer*

On Gender, Labor, and Inequality   *Ruth Milkman*

The Making of Working-Class Religion   *Matthew Pehl*

Civic Labors: Scholar Activism and Working-Class Studies
Edited by Dennis Deslippe, Eric Fure-Slocum, and John W. McKerley

Victor Arnautoff and the Politics of Art   *Robert W. Cherny*

Against Labor: How U.S. Employers Organized to Defeat Union Activism
Edited by Rosemary Feurer and Chad Pearson

Teacher Strike! Public Education and the Making of a New American Political
Order   *Jon Shelton*

Hillbilly Hellraisers: Federal Power and Populist Defiance in the Ozarks
J. Blake Perkins

Sewing the Fabric of Statehood: Garment Unions, American Labor, and the
Establishment of the State of Israel   *Adam Howard*

Labor and Justice across the America   *Edited by Leon Fink
and Juan Manuel Palacio*

Frontiers of Labor: Comparative Histories of the United States and
Australia   *Edited by Greg Patmore and Shelton Stromquist*

Women Have Always Worked: A Concise History, Second Edition
Alice Kessler-Harris

Remembering Lattimer: Labor, Migration, and Race in Pennsylvania Anthracite
Country   *Paul A. Shackel*

Disruption in Detroit: Autoworkers and the Elusive Postwar Boom
Daniel J. Clark

To Live Here, You Have to Fight: How Women Led Appalachian Movements
for Social Justice   *Jessica Wilkerson*

Dockworker Power: Race and Activism in Durban and the San Francisco Bay
Area   *Peter Cole*

Labor's Mind: A History of Working-Class Intellectual Life   *Tobias Higbie*

The World in a City: Multiethnic Radicalism in Early Twentieth-Century
Los Angeles   *David M. Struthers*

Death to Fascism: Louis Adamic's Fight for Democracy   *John P. Enyeart*

Upon the Altar of Work: Child Labor and the Rise of a New American
Sectionalism   *Betsy Wood*

The University of Illinois Press
is a founding member of the
Association of University Presses.

University of Illinois Press
1325 South Oak Street
Champaign, IL 61820-6903
www.press.uillinois.edu

Printed by Printforce, United Kingdom